The Edinburgh Comp.
Scottish Romanticism

Edinburgh Companions to Scottish Literature

Series Editors: Ian Brown and Thomas Owen Clancy

Titles in the series include:

Visit the Edinburgh Companions to Scottish Literature website at
www.euppublishing.com/series/ecsl

The Edinburgh Companion to
Scottish Romanticism

Edited by Murray Pittock

Edinburgh University Press

© in this edition Edinburgh University Press, 2011
© in the individual contributions is retained by the authors

Edinburgh University Press Ltd
22 George Square, Edinburgh

www.euppublishing.com

Typeset in 10.5/12.5 Adobe Goudy
by Servis Filmsetting Ltd, Stockport, Cheshire, and
printed and bound in Great Britain by
CPI Antony Rowe, Chippenham and Eastbourne

A CIP record for this book is available from the British Library

ISBN 978 0 7486 3845 1 (hardback)
ISBN 978 0 7486 3846 8 (paperback)

Contents

       Caroline McCracken-Flesher
12 Byron   150
       Brean Hammond
13 John Galt's Fictional and Performative Worlds   166
       Angela Esterhammer
14 *The Private Memoirs and Confessions of a Justified Sinner*   178
       Peter Garside
15 The Function of Linguistic Variety in Walter Scott's *The Heart
    of Mid-Lothian*   190
       Fernando Toda

    Endnotes   202
    Further Reading   238
    Notes on Contributors   243
    Index   246

To Anne

Series Editors' Preface

The third tranche of this series has as a common theme, one that underlies the whole series, the re-evaluation of the nature of Scottish literature. The volume on Hugh MacDiarmid places him not simply within the traditional setting of the so-called Scottish Literary Renaissance, but in the far wider and more internationally significant Modernist movement. Seen in that light, it is clear why MacDiarmid's work retains an international importance often elided when it is assessed only within a Scottish context. The volume on Scottish Romanticism likewise sheds a distinctive Scottish light on an internationally significant literary movement. It reveals a number of key perspectives including the relationship of the literature of the period to other art forms and the significance of Romanticism in relation to Scottish literature in Gaelic. It also argues clearly and persuasively for recognition of the relationship of Scottish Romanticism to the Enlightenment in a fresh and innovative way. The volume on Drama takes on squarely the canard that somehow Scottish drama was suppressed for long periods. The evidence it provides is conclusive in showing that so far from drama being generally suppressed in Scotland it showed variety, vitality, vibrancy – and resilience against attempts at suppression when they existed. It appears in the earliest records and asserts itself through many forms including folk drama, drama in schools and professional theatre and in all Scotland's languages, including the Latin of George Buchanan's internationally highly influential renaissance drama.

The Edinburgh Companions continue to challenge restrictive perceptions of the richness of Scottish literature. They also open up to scholars and students fresh ideas that will change readers' understanding of the range and depth of the topics under discussion.

Ian Brown
Thomas Owen Clancy

What is Scottish Romanticism?

Murray Pittock

This Companion sets out to do three things: to provide a guided analysis to the main authors and movements of the Scottish Romantic era; to offer some contemporary theoretical and historicist approaches to support better understanding of Scotland's writers from a variety of perspectives; and last, but far from least, to demonstrate the basis for its title by theorising Scotland's claim to the possession of a national Romanticism. This third and last objective is the subject of this Introduction.

In recent years, Scotland has once again been increasingly seen as having a central role in the Romantic era, a position from which it had largely been excluded in accounts of the last sixty years. Katie Trumpener's *Bardic Nationalism* (1997) invigorated the idea of a powerful and dynamic Scottish Romanticism, one which was not simply a cheat and a fraud perpetrated on Scottish history by the purveyors of 'Scotch Myths ' criticised in studies such as Peter Womack's *Improvement and Romance* (1989) and Hugh Trevor-Roper's *The Invention of Scotland* (2008), which simplified some of the complex arguments made in my 1991 book of the same name. The idea that James Macpherson was a simple attention-seeking fraud, that Scott deceived a nation into inventing itself as the home of tartan kitsch, and the confusion of Burns with his cult all served to undermine the status of Scottish Romanticism as an assemblage of the 'sham bards of a sham nation' (Edwin Muir's phrase) at home. Furth of Scotland, the conflation of literary Scots with regional dialect, the critical turn from a social and engaged Romantic era to the valorisation of an aesthetic, and the diminishing understanding of Great Britain as a multinational polity all contributed further to a deep recession in the reputations of writers such as Burns and Scott who had previously been regarded as colossal.

The launch of major textual editions of Walter Scott (1985) and James Hogg (1991) began to reverse this situation, but the critical apparatus needed to sustain these editorial developments did not really begin to appear until Trumpener's work, and it is a matter of regret that for personal reasons she has had to withdraw from contributing to this volume. That there are so many outstanding scholars who have contributed to it is testament to how many critics quickly followed her lead, and how effectively the notion of a Scottish national Romanticism is *en route* to being recaptured.

Janet Sorensen's *The Grammar of Empire* (2000) began to address the language issue in Scottish Romanticism in detail, while Gerard Carruthers and Alan Rawes' groundbreaking collection on *English Romanticism and the Celtic World* (2003) was accompanied by two other collections: Leith Davis, Ian Duncan and Janet Sorensen's *Scotland and the Borders of Romanticism* (2004) and David Duff and Catherine Jones's *Scotland, Ireland and the Romantic Aesthetic* (2007). In the midst of this, a major conference on 'Scottish Romanticism in World Literatures' was held at University of California Berkeley in 2006, jointly organised by Ian Duncan and the present author, whose studies of *Scott's Shadow* (Duncan, 2007) and *Scottish and Irish Romanticism* (Pittock, 2008) followed shortly afterwards. These works in their turn are supported by a range of new author-focused studies, such as Robert Crawford's *The Bard* (2009) and Andrew Lincoln's *Walter Scott and Modernity* (2007), together with the major textual editions which now dominate the landscape of Scottish Romantic scholarship: the Edinburgh Edition of the Waverley Novels, the Stirling–South Carolina Research Edition of the Works of James Hogg, the Oxford Collected Burns and the Yale Edition of the Private Papers of James Boswell.

Two major conceptual questions arose and were addressed in the course of this research. The first was 'What are the qualities which render Scottish Romantic writing national – what is a national Romanticism?' The second was 'What is the relationship between the Scottish Enlightenment and Scottish Romanticism?' This latter appears to be a much more specific question, but in reality the answer to it carries a freight of implication respecting the thinking of Scottish Romantic writers, their attitude towards the imagination (a topic which began to be addressed by Cairns Craig in *Associationism and the Literary Imagination* (2007)) and above all, perhaps, the periodicity of Romanticism implied by the relationship. Is Scottish Romanticism a creature of the 1760s, and Macpherson's reaction to theories of moral sentiment? Is it to be found even earlier, in the song-collecting and linguistic code-switching of Allan Ramsay in the 1720s? The relationship of Scottish Romanticism to the Scottish Enlightenment is key to what it is, and where it begins and ends. We will return to this question at the end of this Introduction.

The first issue – what is a national Romanticism? – is in significant part the subject of my 2008 study, cited above. There are perhaps at least five different criteria of definition, which apply to any aspect of what makes a culture national, and not just to Romantic art and letters. These can be found discussed at greater length in *Scottish and Irish Romanticism*, but I summarise them here because they underpin the core arguments and coverage of this volume.

First, there is the persistence or development of a separate public sphere in Scotland. The Union of 1707 left intact most of the professions and institutions that played a major role in Scottish identity, including the Kirk, the universities, the law and the financial system. Their continuing presence secured the intellectual and cultural conditions that underpinned the development of new national institutions and professions in Scotland (in time, the National Trust for Scotland, the Scottish Football Association, the Educational Institute of Scotland and many others). Because of economic conditions in Scotland, many of the country's gentry became involved in the professions rather than living off the land. These professions and institutions were domestically controlled within Scotland; they were protected and distinctive, and their members were almost all Scots; they were linked to the institutional, associational and club culture of the major cities; and they provided a proportionately larger professional class in those cities than was the case with other cities in the British Isles outwith London (with the exception of Dublin). As the eighteenth century progressed, it was this public sphere that helped to sustain the Enlightenment and that also provided the background for the rise of a periodical culture, which in the shape of *Blackwood's* and the *Edinburgh Review*, came to dominate not only Scottish but British critical debates in the Romantic era.

The initial section of this book, 'The Scottish Public Sphere: Themes, Groups and Identities' addresses many of the particular issues raised by the presence of a distinct public sphere within Scotland. In particular, Alex Benchimol's chapter on 'Periodicals and Public Culture', Ian Duncan's on 'Urban Space and Enlightened Romanticism', Crawford Gribben's on 'Religion and Scottish Romanticism' and Thomas Clancy's on 'Gaelic Literature and Scottish Romanticism', all examine dimensions of this key component in the development of a sustaining climate for the emergence of a national Romanticism.

A second feature of such a Romanticism is the inflection of genre towards a distinctive agenda of selfhood, which I term in *Scottish and Irish Romanticism* 'altermentality', and which in its turn is linked to a third feature, the use of hybrid language and variable register to both simultaneously reveal and conceal the self, to challenge the heteroglossic hierarchies set by a metropolitan norm, and to create a tension between 'anglopetal' and 'anglofugal' representations of Scotland's place within the British polity. In the Irish case, the concept of 'auto-exoticism', developed by Joep Leerssen in *Remembrance and Imagination* (1996), describes a similar process (the glossing, editorialising and Irishing of English language texts), but there is a tension – played out in criticism of Edgeworth and Owenson in the last fifteen years – as to how far such exoticism is colonial window-dressing and how far nationalist resistance. This question can be asked of the use of variable register Scots in Scottish writing too: Ramsay produces partial and not always adequate glosses while protesting that he is a part of 'British' literature. He also inflects high cultural Latinate genres (ode, elegy, pastoral) into a deeply vernacular and unmistakably Scottish context. Burns uses Scots from different dialectal areas to produce alternate readings of the same poem. Scott allows the systemic plots of his novels to be inflected by the presence of characters who offer individuated critiques of modernity through vernacular culture, supernaturalism and subaltern status in a 'literature of combat' formulation redolent of the account of colonialism present in Frantz Fanon's *The Wretched of the Earth*, yet one that simultaneously often takes place within a closure of Unionist conformity. Hogg uses the same tension between Scottish and Anglicised speech and cultural formation as a challenge to attempts to control a narrative intended to produce that very closure. The sophisticated inflection of genre, code switching and strategic register used by Scots writers is a study still in its infancy, but it is touched on here by Steve Newman's 'Ballads and Chapbooks', Angela Esterhammer's chapter on John Galt, Caroline McCracken-Flesher's 'Walter Scott's Romanticism', Brean Hammond's 'Byron' and Fernando Toda's 'The Function of Linguistic Variety in Walter Scott's *The Heart of Midlothian*', while Hogg's masterwork is the only text to which an entire chapter is devoted in the shape of Peter Garside's '*Confessions of a Justified Sinner*', which examines the slippery cultural, religious and linguistic 'Scottishness' of the novel in the context of its textual and reception history.

The fourth feature of a national Romanticism is what can be termed the taxonomy of glory, the symbolic organisation of images and tropes (e.g. those connected with bards and the bardic) into a reading of a glorious past. This is one of the key areas for exploring the relationship between Romanticism and the Scottish Enlightenment, for just as the historiography of the Enlightenment simultaneously ignored and replaced the long tradition of Scottish patriot historiography reaching from John of Fordoun in the fifteenth century to Abercrombie's 1713 *Martial Achievements of the Scots Nation*, so that historiography surfaced again in the literary imagination.

Macpherson's *Fingal* (1761) is on one level a tribute to a glorious ancestral history denied by the dry words of William Robertson, who in the opening of his *History of Scotland* (1759) dismissed the Scottish past thus: 'Nations, as well as men, arrive at maturity by degrees, and the events which happened during their infancy or early youth, cannot be recollected, and deserve not be remembered'.[1] Scotland is childhood, Britain adulthood to Robertson; to Macpherson, Ossian recalls the splendour of the national past in intimate detail rather than discarding it as unfit for memory, and the forgetful maturity hailed by Robertson (and exemplified in the plots and closures of Scott, though not in his detailed grasp of the past) is converted into an etiolated age, decayed from the ancient strength of the Fianna and Fingal. Macpherson substituted a trope of vigour and decay for Robertson's youth and maturity, and if the Robertsonian side of Scott closed its narratives with a reconciliatory Britishness, his Macphersonian side populated them in transit with Redgauntlet, Rob Roy, Meg Merrilees and all who could not be accommodated in modernity, or resisted its pressing invitations to conform for their own reasons.

In the collection that follows, the place of the taxonomy of glory in Scottish Romanticism is touched on by Fiona Stafford in 'Romantic Macpherson' and in the discussion of Jane Porter and other writers in Andrew Monnickendam's 'The Scottish National Tale': in Scotland as in Ireland, the National Tale was largely the province of women's writing, a fact which possibly had at least something to do with the traditional characterisation of both nations in female terms.

The fifth element that contributes to a distinctively national Romanticism is the performance of the self in diaspora. The distinctive presence of national and associational Scottish culture internationally, and the continuation and development of the networks that sustained it, is central to its national quality. One of the key tests of what makes an identity national is that it survives – and indeed can be developed – in diaspora, and Scottish writing, practice and ideas certainly fulfil that criterion. Indeed, once we peel away the assumptions of conventional accounts from the careers of many writers, Scottish networking frequently shows itself. As this collection deals with Scottish Romanticism in Scottish writing, rather than in its diasporic and anti-colonial dimensions which I have labelled as 'fratriotism',[2] the chapters that follow only deal with this issue to a limited extent. Nonetheless, the national quality of Scotland's Romantic art and literature was a key component of its separate reception history abroad. Kirsteen McCue's chapter on 'Scottish Song, Lyric Poetry and the Romantic Composer' provides a taste of the international reach and appeal of a distinctly Scottish Romanticism, Nigel Leask's 'Robert Burns' investigates the 'four nations' context of the writer, while Matt Wickman's 'Travel Writing and the Picturesque' addresses the issue of how Scotland was supposed to look, and the qualities of its landscape which became, particularly in the external gaze-markers of the country's distinctiveness, 'land of the mountain and the flood' as Scott was to describe it to a market already primed for the growth of tourism as a major domestic industry.

All the chapters in this volume thus exemplify or intersect with a theoretical model that can underpin the case for a discrete national Scottish Romanticism. The study that follows does not pretend to be comprehensive, or to account for every significant Scottish Romantic writer: James Boswell and Henry Mackenzie are only two candidates who are missing. But what it does do is present a context in which such writers can be read. The social, cultural, creative and intellectual structure that underpins this context has been discussed above; what follows in the second, analytic section of the Introduction, is an exploration of the relationship of the Scottish Enlightenment to Scottish Romanticism, which has implications for the chronotope, the envelope of time and location in which we should situate the movement that is the subject of this book.

If Scottish Romanticism still requires intellectual justification for its position as a national movement and entity, increasingly the Scottish Enlightenment does not. To take only one prominent example, Arthur Herman's maximalist claims for the national Enlightenment In *How the Scots Invented the Modern World* (2001) have had a global impact, while in terms of academic research Alexander Broadie's *Cambridge Companion to the Scottish Enlightenment*, first published in 2003, has sold thousands of copies, and was translated into Mandarin in 2010. The Scottish Enlightenment has global recognition and a global reach, while Scottish Romanticism is still undergoing a process of conceptual recognition. This is an interesting reflection on the degree to which narratives of the past (in this case of contiguous eras) can appear to be self-evident while remaining radically inconsistent. As Ian Duncan has suggested, this may be in part due to the Enlightenment's interdisciplinarity. It may also reflect the apparent modernity of its universalising trope. Yet Scottish Romanticism is interdisciplinary also, which is why this book bears that title, not one that identifies its subject solely as 'literature'.

Recent writing on Scottish Romanticism has engaged with its relationship to the Scottish Enlightenment in great detail, in a debate that reached prominence in the Scottish Romanticism in World Literatures conference at Berkeley in 2006. Ian Duncan has championed a strong continuity between one and the other, while the present writer has been seen as promoting a sense of opposition between the two movements; what there is general agreement on, however, is that the nature of Enlightenment thought in Scotland leads to a prolonged periodicity for Romanticism. Ramsay's song collecting and faux mediaevalism, Macpherson's bardic epic and Fergusson's odes all predate the conventional onset of Romanticism, and, as I have argued before, render unstable concepts like 'pre-Romanticism', introduced in the twentieth century on the verge of an era of critical decline for the Scottish Romantics, increasingly inadequate to a task which they never discharged with much aplomb.[3]

So what is the nature of the relationship between the Scottish Enlightenment and Scottish Romanticism? Many of the core ideas associated with Romanticism seem to run counter to Enlightenment values. These stress the application of reason to knowledge (acknowledging the Humean arguments that cite the role of the imagination and passions in knowledge), stadial development, technological progress, standardised language and shared British norms of civility. In contrast to Enlightenment notions of such progress, Romanticism can be seen as reinscribing the importance of the primitive and isolated person, the solitary figure of genius whose insights, acquired apart from the bustle of cities and commercial modernity placed him or her beyond the reach of sociability and civility, with their numerous, distracting and shallow associations of news, gossip and daily interchange. Associationism itself, a powerful intellectual tool of Enlightenment, was linked by Coleridge in *Biographia Litteraria* (1817) with the inferior power of Fancy, in contradistinction to the creative power of the Imagination.

Yet it is this very well-known and worn account of Romanticism that itself provides the basis for many of the problems Scottish Romanticism has faced as a critical concept. An aestheticised 'Romantic Imagination', over-determined by certain interpretations of the Lake Poets and their writings, needs to be set in the context of the broader social environment of Scottish Romanticism, neglected of late years. In this context, it was more 'normal' as a Romantic movement than many accounts of the primacy of more inward Romantic values might allow. Johann Gottfried von Herder, perhaps the most notable apostle of national Romanticisms, might have distrusted Enlightenment universalism, but his strong linkage of morality to sentiment clearly derived from the world of Hutcheson, Hume and Smith, while his passionate commitment to the individuated nation was moderated by his Smithian confidence in the power of trade.

In these things, Herder as a great champion of Romantic nationalism (as Scott was later to be seen in Continental Europe) was in tune with the wider intellectual developments of his own day. As Joep Leerssen has argued, the Romantic moment really arrives when 'antiquarianism founders in the rise of historicism'. The historicist moment was in these terms not just an Enlightenment, but also a Romantic one. How could the primitive be exhibited as an ideal except in terms of the modelling that allowed it to be recognised as 'primitive'? How could mediaevalism be indulged in if it could not even be defined?[4]

Macpherson's Ossian poetry communicated the glories of ancient Scotland by speaking the teleological language of Enlightened civility, as is immedi-ately apparent when one compares the visceral violence of Homeric primary epic or even Iain Lom's Gaelic poetry of Montrose's wars with the discreetly veiled allusions to bloodshed in Macpherson's heavily edited *Fingal* (1761), itself perhaps drawing on the bolder and more violent portrayal of the Gàidhealtachd's present and future suffering in Alasdair MacMhaighstir Alasdair's *Birlinn Clann Raghnaill*, probably composed in the 1750s. Similarly,

Robert Burns presented himself, and was accepted on the European stage (particularly in Germany), as both the collectivist voice of a traditional peasant community and the individuated spokesman of a radical and progressive poetry. A separate public sphere in Scotland provided both the institutional infrastructure for the achievements of the Enlightenment and the success of the Romantic periodicals. The greatest works of Scottish Romanticism are so because they are in dialogue with the arguments of the Scottish Enlightenment, neither in outright opposition to them nor subservient to them. When Scott borrowed aspects of Byron's 'Song of the Albanian Highlanders' in *Childe Harold* (1813) for Rory Dall's song in Chapter 22 of *Waverley* (1814), both writers were utilising an Enlightenment model that encouraged the drawing of parallels between mountain peoples in one place with those of another, estimated as both were to be at the same stage of society; they were also drawing both on Jacobite and older Scottish patriot historiographical models which saw the mountaineer as a friend to liberty, itself to be a strongly marked Romantic theme, *Rauberromantik*, 'bandit romanticism'. Place was important, not just paradigm. Thus when Scott in *Rob Roy* writes that 'the effect of music arises [. . .] from association, and sounds which might jar the nerves of a Londoner or Parisian, bring back to the Highlander his lofty mountain, wild lake, and the deeds of his fathers', he endorses both the structure of Enlightenment's universal argument, and the deep particularity of the appeal of place to those who inhabit what he would like his readers to identify as a Romantic environment.[5]

Far from 'the Scottish Enlightenment' being 'Romanticism's antithesis', the Enlightenment and Romanticism are thus inextricably intertwined in Scottish Romanticism. Not only does associationism arguably give rise to an 'imaginary network' of ' "national sympathy" ', but Scottish Romantic writers are also engaged in a prolonged argument about the validity and definition of Enlightenment terms and claims, when they are not simply writing in the shadow of their historiographical values. This approach renders them often more socially engaged with these very questions, and thus less autonomously in pursuit of a Romantic aesthetic than some of their English contemporaries. To the extent that Scottish Enlightenment historiography was concerned with nation-building, national myth and the conversion of Whig party history into the apparently studied detachment of rational enquiry, it was a fit subject for both Romantic interest and Romantic contestation. Nationality was at the core of Enlightenment historiography in Scotland, since so much of it was a justificatory praxis for the teleological absorption of an older Scottish into a newer British society. It was thus a fit subject for Romantic engagement; and, moreover, its use of rhetorical strategy especially enabled that engagement, which itself – as under Napoleon – valorised a 'National Historicism'. For example, William Robertson's 'emotional allegiance to the enduring virtues of Scottish culture, such as its martial spirit of independence and self-reliance' allowed a space for sentiment and the imaginative play on feeling it aroused without any implication of political relevance. In his portrayal of Mary, Queen of Scots 'as a sentimental heroine rather than as a fully responsible political agent [. . .] Robertson laid the ground for the subsequent reinvention of Jacobitism, by Sir Walter Scott and others, as an aesthetic attitude only'.[6] Yet even this does not tell the whole story. Hume and Smith had argued for the importance of emotion and sympathy in moral judgements and sentiment and sociability were core Enlightenment values. How in such a case could an emotional appeal to the Scottish past be without any implication of moral seriousness? Emotion was often deployed to minimise the politics of the past it was true, but created sympathy for it among the moral sentiments of its conscientious Smithian bystanders, the reading public of the Romantic era. This was the paradoxical relationship of the Scottish Enlightenment to Scottish Romanticism: the latter drew on some of the former's values to critique others, and created its own national historicism in dialogue with the Enlightenment whose right to construct such a concept it refuted. Future scholarship will, I hope, see both these diverse and mighty intellectual and cultural achievements as interrelated to the point of being aspects of a single phenomenon, the desire to articulate the significance and values of Scotland's intellectual and historical inheritance in national terms within the wider British Empire. If this book can contribute to that understanding and frame some of the terms of that future structure of inquiry, it will have done its job.

The Scottish Public Sphere:
Themes, Groups and Identities

CHAPTER ONE

Ballads and Chapbooks

Steve Newman

Like Romanticism more broadly, the phenomenon recently identified as a distinctly Scottish Romanticism is unimaginable without ballads and chapbooks.[1] From Robert Burns to Walter Scott to Joanna Baillie, it is hard to find a Scottish author in the Romantic era who does not look to ballads and chapbooks for source material and who does not collect, emend and compose ballads of his or her own. This may seem odd at first glance. Since even plebeian authors like Burns and James Hogg aimed to break into the elite literary world that was the primary home of Romanticism, why would they rely so heavily on popular genres that would seem to carry with them the taint of unsophisticated views and cheap print? To answer this question is to engage with the central and complex matter of how Romanticism, including Scottish Romanticism, argued over and constructed the popular for its own ends. To understand this, in turn, it is necessary to move back before 1789, even before the publication of Macpherson's *Fragments of Ancient Poetry* (1760). For the elite collection of ballads extends back at least to the work of Allan Ramsay (1684–1758), and his work marks a starting point in drawing on the forms and energies of popular song while also redescribing or eliding those elements that might prove embarrassing to elite tastes. This fundamental move gets variously modified and reinvented over the course of the eighteenth century – sometimes intentionally to rattle conventional elite regimes of value rather than playing to them. By the time of the long career of Walter Scott (1771–1832), who, as the most influential Romantic collector of ballads is properly the touchstone of this chapter, what we see is that Scottish Romanticism is a plural formation, structured and fissured by gender and status hierarchy, inter- and intranational exchange and the messy emergence of an elite literary field from broader worlds or print and orality.

To get a taste of how ballads and chapbooks figure centrally in Scottish Romanticism, let us start with a scene from *Waverley* (1814) where an Englishman encounters ballads on Scottish ground at a critical moment. Having left his regiment to visit Baron Bradwardine, a Scottish friend of his uncle, Edward Waverley stands in front of the manor house of Tully-Veolan, waiting in vain for admittance to this 'solitary and seemingly enchanted mansion'.[2] Then, in the middle distance of this romantic scene someone appears in an 'antiquated and extravagant' dress, and as he walks toward Waverley, he keeps time to a song that the narrator identifies as 'an old Scotch ditty' beginning: 'False love, and hast thou play'd me this / In summer among the flowers?' (*Waverley*, p. 41). Waverley's question as to the whereabouts of Baron Bradwardine elicits from this 'extravagant personage' a second ditty, about an illicit tryst between 'Burd Ellen' and 'Lord William': '[L]ike the witch of Thalaba, "still his speech was song"' (p. 41).

The narrator's reference to Robert Southey's *Thalaba the Destroyer* (1801) is helpful in unpacking Scott's balladic version of Romanticism, for *Thalaba* elicited a review later taken to evidence the hostility of Scotland, home of political economy and other forms of Enlightenment rationalism, to a 'true' (Anglocentric) Romanticism.[3] In Francis Jeffrey's famously hostile review in the first issue of *The Edinburgh Review*, he classes Southey with 'a sect of poets [. . .] dissenters from the established systems in poetry and criticism' who combine among other faults Rousseau's 'antisocial principles' and the disturbing 'energy' and false 'simplicity' of Schiller.[4] The resulting representations of 'vulgar manners, in vulgar language' is redundant, Jeffrey jokes, for vulgarity has already been 'monopolized' by 'the ingenious writers who supply the hawkers and ballad-singers'. Knowing their proper place, they write for the entertainment of those 'who cannot be called readers', lacking either the basic literacy or, at least, the discrimination possessed by Jeffrey's audience (Jeffrey, review of Southey, pp. 67–8). For Jeffrey, then, authors of volumes like *Thalaba* and *Lyrical Ballads* try to overturn the 'established systems' of elite poetry by smuggling in the crude affects and effects of balladry, an aesthetic analogue of Jacobinism.

Scott, of course, is no Jacobin, and this scene from *Waverley* points up the complexity of the issues involved in the incorporation of the ballad into elite texts during the Romantic era. Davie is easily legible within an Enlightenment narrative that Jeffrey would support; like the unimproved, stagnant hamlet of Tully-Veolan, he lacks the signal commercial virtue of prudence and the modern manners that go with it.[5] And yet the Scottish Enlightenment has inscribed into it something that Jeffrey seems to miss, second thoughts about modernity that intensify in the Romantic era, a scepticism about scepticism, materialism and the advantages of commerce. With this comes an affirmation, however qualified, of the value of the primitive that favours texts ranging from Macpherson's ventriloquy of Ossian to songs like Davie's. But if Scott answers Jeffrey, he does not merely reassert Southey's position. Southey's witch is a *belle dame sans merci* who uses her unintelligible song to imprison the earnest hero of this earnest metrical romance. Davie, embroidered with 'extravagant' signs and singing of duplicity, embodies the more labile relationship between text and history in Scott. When Waverley innocently asks in response to a later song if 'the verses he sings belong to old Scottish poetry', Rose Bradwardine explains that the poems come from Davie's brother, a gifted young man whose family's attempts to raise his status were dashed by his association with the Jacobitism 'of our ground', and 'from him Davie gathered many fragments of songs and music unlike those of this country' (*Waverley*, p. 59). Rose is right that Davie's songs do not exactly belong to 'old Scottish poetry'; they are instead new-old Walter Scott-ish poetry, as here, at the inauguration of the historical novel, Scott gestures slyly at his own prior labours as a ballad collector and imitator, with Waverley enacting his typical role as the naïve English observer of a Scotland he keeps trying to stuff into his innocent preconceptions.

To see how Scottish authors variously use ballads in the Romantic era to construct their careers, this chapter will revisit Scott's stories of writerly origins, themselves Romantic internalisations of the tales of development projected by Enlightenment thought. Tracking his switch from German-Gothic balladry back to his Scottish 'roots', legitimised by an adolescent encounter with Percy's *Reliques of Ancient English Poetry* (1765), we can see how he separates his work from the cheap material supplement of minstrelsy, the broadsides and chapbooks of Jeffrey's 'ballad singers', and how he disperses the oppositional energy of Jacobite song. Tracing these strains of balladry will put us in touch with authors whose vision of the ballad anticipates or is shaped by Scott's vision but also runs athwart it: Allan Ramsay, Anne Bannerman, Robert Burns, Carolina Oliphant (Baroness Nairne), James Hogg and John Clare.

The Scandal of Gothic Balladry in Scott and Bannerman

In Scott's important 'Essay on Imitations of the Ancient Ballad' (1830), he mentions only one woman, and as significant as that fact is the way he characterises her:

> Miss Anne Bannerman likewise should not be forgotten, whose Tales of Superstition and Chivalry appeared about 1802. They were perhaps too mystical and too abrupt; yet if it be the purpose of this kind of ballad poetry powerfully to excite the imagination, without pretending to satisfy it, few persons have succeeded better than this gifted lady, whose volume is peculiarly fit to be read in a lonely house by a decaying lamp.[6]

Here, Scott situates Bannerman's work within a Gothic tableau, as the solitary reader who illuminates her eldritch pages with a guttering candle has his imagination excited but not satisfied. This is not an inaccurate representation of Bannerman's work, but it does frame her in a way that affirms the different path Scott takes and underscores why her career was foreshortened.

Bannerman specialises in the Gothic ballads associated with M. G. 'Monk' Lewis and the Coleridge of *Rime of the Ancyent Marinere*. This is precisely where Scott locates his own beginnings as an author before he returns to the more respectable model of Percy. Scott is brought into the orbit of the Gothic ballad by a series of what he calls 'quite accidental' circumstances ('Imitations' 4: p. 37). Among them are the sudden introduction of German literature into the consciousness of literary Scotland by Henry Mackenzie's 1788 lecture, 'Essay on German Literature', Anna Laetitia Barbauld's 1793 reading of a translation of Gottfried August Bürger's 'Lenore' during a visit to Edinburgh, and, above all, Scott's accidental acquaintance with Lewis, who frequently travelled to Scotland to visit the family of the Duke of Argyle ('Imitations' 4: pp. 26; 37; 34). Spurred by Lewis' high literary reputation, Scott translates 'Lenore' and then publishes it anonymously along with a translation of another ballad by Bürger, 'The Wild Huntsman' (1796). He proceeds to imitate ballads, first in the Ossianic 'Glenfinlas' and then 'The Eve of St. John' (4: pp. 44–6). Likening himself to 'a pedlar who has got two ballads to begin the world' he then meets with 'an opportunity unexpectedly' to publish his wares and others as part of a collection edited by Lewis, *Tales of Wonder* (1800) ('Imitations', 4: pp. 46; 48). But the tide of critical opinion was then turning against Lewis, thanks, among other things, to the growing impatience with the extravagances of German influence audible in Jeffrey's attack.

Scott is able 'to stand and save myself' from the harshest censures against the volume, and it is at this point that he turns instead to ballads closer to home and a safer model ('Imitations', 4: p. 51). He assembles *Minstrelsy of the Scottish Border*, 'my attempt to imitate the plan and style of Bishop Percy, observing only more strict fidelity concerning my originals' ('Imitations', 4: p. 52). In so doing, he returns to a primal scene of reading. He vividly recalls how, under a plane tree in his aunt's garden, he first encountered Percy's *Reliques*: '[I]t may be imagined, but cannot be described, with what delight I saw pieces of the same kind which had amused my childhood, and still continued in secret the Delilahs of my imagination, considered as the subject of sober research, grave commentary, and apt illustration [. . .] To read and to remember was in this instance the same thing.'[7] So, thanks to a series of accidents, Scott dallies with the Germanic-Gothic balladry of Lewis only to return to the Scottish ballads of his youth mediated by the healthier model provided by Percy, a model upon which he will himself improve. This choice allows him to peddle his balladic wares more successfully as he builds a celebrated literary career out of editing and then imitating and extending Scottish minstrelsy.

The shape of this narrative is not unlike that of a Waverley hero. Accidents lead a somewhat passive figure into peril, but he frees himself from the atavism and fetishism of the past, not by rejecting 'Delilah' outright but by figuring out a way to reframe it within a progressive narrative. In Scott's *biographia literaria* and the figure of the Waverley hero, we can see the outlines of 'the lyric subject', a Romantic self constructed by its unfolding experience with songs, in which reading and remembering become the same thing.[8] This experience is reproduced for his readers through an artful deferral and ultimate satisfaction of narrative desire that structures the ballads he edits, as well as long poems like *Lay of the Last Minstrel* and finally his novels.

This narrative system marginalises Bannerman in a number of ways, and so it is not surprising that she appears in Scott's 'Essay' as a figure, however adept, of the Gothic balladry he rejects. This has something to do with the substance of the ballads she publishes in *Tales of Superstition and Chivalry*. They do, as Scott suggests, raise an imaginative sympathy only to frustrate the reader's desire for narrative clarity and resolution. Recent scholarship on her work has focused for good reason on poems that centre around feminine figures, such as 'The Mermaid', 'The Prophetess of the Oracle of Seäm' and 'The Dark Ladie'.[9] The last poem is particularly attractive because it answers a ballad by a canonical Romantic author – Coleridge's 'Introduction to the Tale of the Dark Ladie' – by substituting his abandoned, suffering woman with one who exacts an awful revenge not only on the knight who seems to have kidnapped her while on the Crusades but also everyone who hears her strange tale. Equally interesting is a poem like 'Basil', which tells of a parentless, solitary boy who lives in a hut by the side of the sea until driven from it by someone (man? woman? murdered or dead by some other cause?) who dies unseen just outside his door. The poem thus offers an image of the Romantic Child of Nature, gifted with 'the fire of soul unseen, / Unknown, untutor'd, unrepress'd'.[10] But Basil is even eerier than, say, Wordsworth's Lucy Gray or the Boy of Winander; for he does not die only to have his story recuperated by some superior consciousness-in-development. Instead, he is arrested by a death of another, and the poem ends by telling of how Basil, exiled even from the rude hut that had been his home, is haunted by 'drearier dreams' (*Tales*, p. 87). In the final scene, the speaker describes the uncanny landmark of a 'heap of stones' raised by some unknown hand to mark the 'hollow bones' that the mariner 'can see afar, / As a beacon, on the main' (p. 87).

It would be a stretch to suggest that Basil is a figure for Bannerman herself; she possesses the self-consciousness that her 'unrepress'd' boy lacks. But his story of interrupted development does figure her own career. Her social disadvantages as a self-educated Scottish woman from an undistinguished family, combined with her unwillingness to turn toward normative themes and poetic forms, helped to ensure that none of her work was published in her lifetime after her 1807 *Poems*. Not coincidentally that same year she bowed to the advice of her better-situated friend, Dr Robert Anderson, and became a governess. Unlike Scott, Bannerman was damaged by the association of her work with Lewis's *Tales of Wonder*.[11] Unlike Scott, she also had to rely on the increasingly reluctant support of male authors in the same Edinburgh literary circle (Anderson, John Leyden and others). As Adriana Craciun observes, she is stuck on what becomes the loser's side of canonical Romanticism. Instead of 'the "authenticity" of the *Minstrelsy* and the *Reliques*, the "simplicity" of the *Lyrical Ballads*, and the historicist "maturity" of the Waverley novels', she adheres to a wilfully artificial model of poetry (Craciun, 217). This German-tinged balladry is itself an uncanny return of the poems initially exported by Percy and Macpherson, and its importance in sparking the work of Scott, Coleridge and others is one of the 'scandals of the ballad' that Scott helps to bury.[12]

Ballads with and without Music: Burns, Nairne and Hogg

So Scott turns from the Gothic ballads of the Germans and Lewis to minstrelsy modelled on Percy, consolidating the texts he had acquired through the antiquarian 'Border Raids' he had engaged in since 1792. But a well-known response from one of his informants reveals what he leaves out in his version of Scottish balladry and what alternatives exist. After being shown *Minstrelsy of the Scottish Border*, Margaret Laidlaw tartly observes: '[T]here was never ane o' my songs prentit till ye prentit them yoursell, and, ye hae spoilt them a'thegither. They war made for singin' and no' for reading.'[13] Her stinging rejoinder has often been taken to convict Scott and elite ballad collectors as a whole for freeze-drying and falsifying a living tradition of oral song. But it is more productive not to interpret Mrs Laidlaw's comment in terms of an absolute opposition between orality and literacy; her son, James Hogg, who records and perhaps embellishes this and other *Familiar Anecdotes of Walter Scott*, is himself a well-published author who does not try to save traditional songs from print but rather charts other ways to print them. Rather than a print-oral binary, the more salient absence from Scott's version of Scottish ballads is performance, music and singing, whether the ontology of the text is itself print or oral. (A persistent text-centrism continues to mislead many literature professors working on ballads.) Scott's separation of the ballad from singing is in keeping with other scandals he is keen to avoid, which can be seen more clearly in a genre adjacent to ballads, Scots songs. In their embarrassing affiliations with cheap print and those who hear and read them but 'cannot be called readers' in Jeffrey's formulation, their lack of generic prestige, and their relationship to dangerous political movements, Scots songs are for Scott the shadowy other of ballads.

Much closer to this world is Allan Ramsay. Though made faintly ridiculous in Waverley as 'the periwig-maker' who is the only poet of the last hundred years liked by Baron Bradwardine (*Waverley*, p. 61), he is a crucial precursor to Scottish Romanticism. His career is built on reworking of vernacular songs, beginning with his slender gatherings entitled Scots Songs (1718–21) and then his more substantial collections, *The Tea-Table Miscellany* (1723–37) and *The Ever Green* (1724). He also attempts to separate his work from the 'Ballad Singers' who in pirating his work sully it with 'their coarse dirty Fingers'.[14] Ramsay adapts Scots songs to clear a space for a polite yet vernacular Scottish literature within a post-1707 Union, as he indicates in his dedication of *The Tea-Table Miscellany* to 'ilka British lass'.[15] Though Scott may be among many to lament his willingness to gussy up these songs to make them more palatable to polite tastes,[16] he preserves their music in a way Scott does not. This is not to say that Ramsay is 'pre-Romantic', as if the movement from him to Burns and Scott were inevitable. His approach is closer to the sociable world of the Enlightenment tea-table than the Romantic mountaintop. But it would be a mistake to let the doxa of literary periodisation blind us to the importance of Ramsay's collection of Scots songs. In his commitment to Scots vernacular which earned him the sniffing disapproval of Adam Smith for not 'writing like a gentleman', his revision of demotic genres like Last Words ballads and ambivalence toward cheap print, and his celebration of Scotland's pastoral landscape without making it a mere joke for the amusement of the metropole, he 'anticipated many of the obsessions of the Romantic period'.[17]

Also closer to this world of cheap print than Scott was Anne Bannerman. Her father was listed as a running stationer from 1763 to 1771, licensed to sing and sell ballads. That she makes no mention of his occupation is to be expected since doing so would have only hurt her bid for literary respectability. But it is tempting to speculate how her work might have been shaped by her father's stock. Although William Bannerman's name appears on no ballad I have been able to find, the archive preserves a few chapbooks published by William Forrest of Edinburgh in 1766; among them is *Sweet William's Ghost*, which may have given Bannerman a model prior to her exposure to the literary Gothic.

With Burns, however, we do not need to speculate about a vibrant relationship to Scots songs and cheap print. Scott praises Burns' songwriting as befitting a 'high-souled plebeian'.[18] He instances 'My Heart's in the Highlands' as the clearest proof of his supremacy in reversing the bad alchemy of tradition, which converts 'gold into lead' (Scott, Review of Cromek, p. 30). This is a song Davie sings when he wakes Waverley from his Highland idyll (*Waverley*, p. 146), though in a touch Burns would appreciate Davie then ironises this romance of 'the North' with another song making fun of the Highlanders' lack of breeches. But Scott also laments Burns' 'constant waste of his fancy and power of verse in small and insignificant compositions' (Review of Cromek, p. 32), finding unaccountable Burns' devotion to furnishing songs to *The Scots Musical Museum* (1787–1803) and *A Select Collection of Scottish Airs* (1793–1818).

For his part, Burns is not dismissive of the sort of antiquarian framing favoured by Scott; he is interested in forming a canon of national songs, and 'Tam O' Shanter,' written for the Swiss antiquarian Francis Grose, winks sympathetically at the desire to collect traditional artifacts. Neither is he opposed in any simple way to Enlightenment models of development; for instance, he cites that bible of improvement, *The Statistical Account of Scotland*, when situating Ramsay's 'The Lass of Peatie's Mill' in Ayr rather than a competing locality.[19] His approach to Scots songs might be better thought of as a radicalisation of Ramsay's. Like Ramsay, his primary aim is to make the songs accessible for singing, which places him nearer to performance and cheap print. This is true of his sources, as he includes songs found in newspapers and anything else that will supply him with a text he thinks worth considering, and in the way he pictures ballads in his work, as in the broadside or chapbook the beggar-bard draws out of his pack in *Love and Liberty*.[20] It is also true in the way his songs circulate. While *A Select Collection* was marketed to a more polite audience and even *The Musical Museum*, despite its use of a cheaper method of engraving, seemed aimed more at the middling classes, Burns' songs were widely reprinted in broadsides and single sheets throughout the British Isles and beyond, and there is no record of his objecting to these acts of piracy, as Ramsay did in the more established phase of his career.[21]

This more democratic mode of circulation is echoed by the messages of the songs themselves. *Love and Liberty* offers a particularly rich set of songs that voice the sufferings and joys of a body impolitic of outcasts. One number is a Jacobite song ('Lewis Gordon') transformed into an elegy from a pickpocket for her beloved Highlandman, hanged for his crimes; and the cantata ends with a rousing denunciation of 'Courts and Churches' in favour of the pleasures of beggary. It is no wonder that Hugh Blair was horrified by *Liberty*, declaring it 'licentious' and 'altogether unfit in my opinion for publication'.[22] If polite readers sympathise with the singers in *Love and Liberty* – and the Enlightenment does, after all, value the 'untutor'd' passions of the heart – they are put in the uncomfortable position of having their models of progress challenged by low singers and their low songs.[23] Burns' embrace of 'Scots, fucking, and Song' is not a besotted reflex but a conscious choice;[24] the intertwining strands of his politics, his view of culture, and his notion of a literary career produce an alternative Scottish Romanticism.

To punctuate this point, let us look briefly at a song in *Waverley* attributed to Burns. On his way back from the Highlands in an attempt to clear his name – Davie has delivered a letter informing him that he is now presumed to be in league with the rebels – Waverley passes through a Lowland village. Suspected of being a Jacobite, even the Young Pretender himself, he is surrounded by a crowd that includes a defender he could do without:

[A] strong large-boned hard-featured woman [. . .] her cheeks flushed with a scarlet red where they were not smutted with soot and lamp-black [. . .] bran-dishing high a child of two years old, which she danced in her arms, without regard to its screams of terror, sang forth, with all her might,–
  'Charlie is my darling, my darling, my darling,
  Charlie is my darling,
                                    The young Chevalier.['] (*Waverley*, p. 160)

Burns' version of the song appears to be based on a broadside from around 1775 that tells of a 'highland jigg' between a 'bonny lass' and Prince Charlie 'in his highland dress'; her attempts to follow him are foiled by his return to exile after Culloden.[25] Happy to use sources where he finds them, Burns compresses the broadside for *The Scots Musical Museum*, taking out its most sexually-graphic elements and heightening the dramatic tension between the Chevalier and the lowland Lass by drawing on the balladic commonplace of 'tirling the pin': 'Sae light's he jumped up the stair, / And tirled at the pin; / And wha se ready as herself to let the laddie in' (ll. 12–15). However, in Scott's reframing the erotically-charged woman of Jacobite ballads takes demonic form in a grossly-embodied figure out of Hogarth's 'Gin Alley', slov-enly and a neglectful mother to boot. She is happily consigned to the dust-bin of history by the action of the novel, and she again illustrates how for Scott singing songs frequently seems close to rebellion, from Baron Bradwardine's rendition of the Jacobite Duke of Berwick's favourite song to the seductive Highland minstrelsy of Flora MacIvor (*Waverley*, pp. 51, 115–17). Scott quarantines the oppositional energy bound up in Jacobite song that Carol McGuirk in a recent article identifies as the 'imperative injunction from the Jacobites, and that was to define resistance as the ground of Scottish national consciousness'.[26] This resistance is integral to Burns' more general claim through his songs for their value beyond whatever antiquarian desire they satisfy and beyond whatever condescending historiographical scheme that would render them primitive. As he says in the preface to the second volume of *The Scots Musical Museum* (1788), 'Ignorance and Prejudice may perhaps affect to sneer at the simplicity of the poetry or music of some of these pieces; but their having been for ages the favorites of Nature's Judges – The Common People, was to the Editor a sufficient test of their merit.'[27] Burns' Scottish Romanticism is unabashed in its populism. It is therefore no surprise that while Jeffrey praises his songs as the key to his reputation and opposes his simplicity to the false simplicity of Wordsworth et al. he spends a great deal of time lamenting the faults that arise from 'the lowness of his origin', especially his professions of unbridled sensibility and political independence, which the reviewer links to 'the very slang of the worst German plays'.[28]

It is worth noting that Scott may have had another source for 'Charlie's my Darling' because it points up yet another model of a Romantic literary career built on Scots songs. Carolina Oliphant, Lady Nairne (1766–1845), who was an enthusiastic reader of Burns, also penned a version of the song.[29] As Leith Davis has observed, Nairne's lyrics bowdlerise the ballad, replacing the avid and amorous woman with the collective 'folk': 'And a' the folk came running out / To meet the Chevalier.'[30] With Nairne's concern for feminine propriety comes a difference in production and circulation. While Burns' name did not appear in *The Scots Musical Museum*, he made no secret of his contributions. Nairne, in contrast, circulated her songs only in manuscript until she submitted many of them anonymously and pseudonymously for publication in *The Scottish Minstrel* (1821–24), laundering them first through a committee of her friends. This elaborate guarding of her privacy reproduces the masculinism of the so-called Ballad Revival that Bannerman struggled with, which, even when it acknowledged the role of women in balladry tended to think of them as only passive conservators of songs (and not very dependable at that), nursemaids and beldames, not artists like Anna Gordon Brown, whose contributions were central to the Child Ballads, or songwriters like Lady Wardlaw, author of *Hardyknute*, the first ballad Scott recalls learning and a fine example of a successful forgery, and Lady Anne Lindsay, author of 'Auld Robin Gray'.

Nairne's work, however, does more than exemplify the chauvinism of the Revival. For her anonymity, as in her substitution of 'the folk' for the randy woman of 'Charlie's My Darling', is also legible as a sign of her desire to absorb her own identity in that of Scotland as a whole. This desire is evident in her 'Caller Herrin'', a turn on the balladic subgenre of Street Cries that McGuirk incisively reads as a critique of 'Whiggish displays of self-important pomp' ('Jacobite', p. 275). This form of nationhood, transmitted through the anonymous poet, is a crucial element of Romanticism that emerged with greatest influence in Scotland, though not exclusively there. It lacks the Romantic poet sublimely overcoming obstacles to claim his bardic place, but that very lack helps to make her work valuable in remapping Romanticism.[31]

Like Nairne, Hogg faced obstacles in establishing a poetic reputation, but the nature of those obstacles differed with his identity as a shepherd from the remote Borders region of Ettrick Forest rather than a well-born woman (though one whose material situation was for most of her life depressed by the effects of her family's Jacobite politics). Although Hogg suffered throughout his career from accusations of indelicacy and significant barriers to high literacies and cultural capital, he ultimately made his name as a poet; and his poetry is rooted in the songs he learned in his youth. Some of these, as indicated by Margaret Laidlaw's famous scolding of Scott, exist primarily in oral performance, but as Hogg notes elsewhere, one of the few texts to be found in the average shepherd's library in Ettrick are 'a sheaf or two of ballads', the broadsides and chapbooks sold by the chapmen who make it even to his out-of-the-way district.[32]

A good example of Hogg's reworking of Scots songs is 'Donald Macdonald', which he claims is the first he composed, and it certainly seems to be among the first that makes it into print. The evidence suggests that Hogg composed this song in 1803 while in the Highlands, and the addressee of the letters he writes out of the tour is Scott, who encouraged him to go.[33] Set to the tune 'Woo'd and married an a'', which was frequently printed in chapbooks and broadsides, the song responds to the rumours of a French invasion, and it takes up the rehabilitated image of the Highlandman as staunch British warrior rather than savage Jacobite rebel.[34] Indeed, it attributes Highland support for Bonnie Prince Charlie to hospitality and sensibility, which made them ignore 'our reason': 'Had Geordie come friendless amang us, / Wi' him we had a' gane away.' So 'Lochaber No More' will now be transformed from a song lamenting exile after the Highland Clearances to a tune for driving out Old Boney (ll. 55–6). It is important to note that Hogg elsewhere preserves the oppositional character of Jacobitism in his monumental *Jacobite Relics* (1819; 1821), assembled at the request of the Highland Society of London. Yet although the jingoism of 'Donald McDonald' may dispirit us, part of 'a sanitization [and] a domestication' of Scots songs for polite consumption,[35] it is also important to note how resourceful Hogg is here in using the form and language of Scots songs. He draws on the rolling and lively rhythms of 'Woo'd and married and a'' to carry Donald's confident declarations and punctuates them with a rousing chorus. The first chorus declares that 'Brogs and brochen an a'' (brogues and a plaid) are all he and his countrymen need to be happy. The broad Scots of his declaration, though perhaps more appropriate to a Lowlander, is here a sign not of Scottish difference-as-vulgarity but British unity-as-resolve against 'the Corsican callan'' (l. 59).

'Donald McDonald' also illuminates how Scots songs complicate distinctions in the print market as well as the songwriter's prospects for a literary career. It is printed with music in a sixpenny broadside very close to its likely date of composition by John Hamilton, a publisher specialising in cheap sheet music, and it circulates in other cheap forms, such as a Kilmarnock chapbook of c.1815–20 and another printed at Stirling in 1824 (*Minstrel*, p. 351).[36] On the other hand, the song is also featured in *The Mountain Bard* (1807) and *The Forest Minstrel* (1810), through which Hogg aimed to establish his reputation as a respectable author, a bard and a minstrel, not just a rustic informant for collectors like Scott. The bulk of the first volume, which Hogg prepared with a great deal of advice from Scott (much of which Hogg found objectionable), was devoted to 'Ballads in Imitation of the Ancients', pieces akin to those that appeared in the third volume of Scott's *Minstrelsy*. *The Forest Minstrel* is much closer to song compilations like *The Scots Musical Museum*, and Hogg accordingly observes that encountering Burns 'formed a new epoch in my life'.[37] Given Scott's scepticism toward Burns' songwriting, it is not surprising that when handing *The Forest Minstrel* to the Countess of Dalkeith, its dedicatee, he laments that it shows Hogg 'has just talent sufficient to spoil him for his own trade without having enough to support him by literature' (*Minstrel*, p. xiii). Hogg, however, continued to hew to songs throughout his career, even as he followed and revised the track of Scott's career by first writing long minstrel poems like *The Queen's Wake* (1813) and historical novels like *The Brownie of Bodsbeck* (1818). In 1831, Hogg published *Songs, by the Ettrick Shepherd*, and the headnote to 'Donald McDonald' reveals how he negotiates the advantages and traps involved in the Romantic role of the peasant-poet. He 'places it first', he says, because 'it was my first song, and exceedingly popular when it appeared. I wrote it when a barefooted lad herding lambs on the Blackhouse Heights'.[38] Although the evidence is against Hogg's claim that he composed the song during his ten-year stint as a shepherd at Blackhouse Farm, presenting it in this way allows him to set up a Romantic narrative of authorial development. This is just a first song, but its popularity betokens better things to come as Hogg transforms himself from shepherd to celebrated author who remains defiantly in touch with his rustic roots. Scott and the ventriloquisers of 'The Ettrick Shepherd' in the 'Noctes Ambrosianae' of *Blackwood's* may have tried to keep Hogg in his place. He, however, refused to stay there and rather than acceding to a view of Scots songs that would rate them as minor at best, he places them at the centre of Scottish literature and what we now call 'Scottish Romanticism'. Writing new words to old tunes, circulating them in a variety of forms (as well as those that circulate beyond his control) and editing Burns' own songs and other poems, he 'assume[s] the role of protector and evangelist of the Scottish song tradition'.[39]

Coda: John Clare's Burns

There are many important Scottish Romantic authors not touched on in this chapter who draw on Scottish singing traditions. First on the list is Joanna Baillie, whose long correspondence with Walter Scott is one of the key texts in Scottish Romanticism, whose 'Storm-Beat Maid' scoops by eight years the ballads of womanly suffering we see in *Lyrical Ballads*, and who contributed many songs to Thomson's *Select Collection*, including 'Woo'd and Married and A',' which provides a bleaker assessment of woman's lot in marriage than the traditional lyrics. Then there are, among others, Anne Home Hunter, whose 'The Cherokee Death Song' expands the borders of minstrelsy,[40] and Anne MacVicar Grant, whose 'Translations from the Gaelic'[41] adds significantly to the English translations of Scots Gaelic poetry. Also competing for our attention are other plebeian Scots like Robert Tannahill, the Paisley weaver who wrote 'The Braes of Balquhither' and other celebrated songs, and Allan Cunningham, whose expert imitations of ancient ballads fooled many readers. If we were to consider English authors who draw on Scottish song, there are candidates other than Clare who might seem more deserving. A long essay could be written comparing Hogg's 1803 tour of the Highlands with the one taken by William and Dorothy Wordsworth and Coleridge out of which emerged canonical poems like 'The Solitary Reaper' as well as 'Yarrow Unvisited' and poems set at Burns' graveside. Or we might consider the irascible antiquarianism of Joseph Ritson, who in his *Scotish* [sic] *Songs* (1794) and in other volumes intervenes forcefully against the elitism of Percy and his set.

Still, this chapter ends with Clare because the poems he produces in his latter decades reveal just how deeply Scots songs had penetrated the literary consciousness of British as well as Scottish Romanticism. Clare was steeped in cheap print and especially cheap songs. His essay, 'Popularity in Authorship', shows how intelligently he reflects on the relationship between the standards of elite literature and the 'popular fame' of the robust broadside and chapbook market of his native Northamptonshire.[42] He appears to be the first to collect songs from recitation in his region of England, and he also planned to publish his own songs before apparently being derailed by the disapproval of his patron, Lord Radstock, another powerful figure hostile to songs as trivial and/or immoral.[43] Although he mentions Scott in a couple of poems, his great model is clearly Burns.[44] He is introduced in his first volume of poems as Burns' worthy heir,[45] and he writes his own versions of 'The Cotter's Saturday Night' and other poems. It is not, however, until later in his career, during his stays in the Epping Forest and Northampton Asylums, that he evidences the force of his attachment. Indeed, he seems to have fallen into the delusion that he *was* Burns (as well as Lord Byron, Lord Nelson and a famous prizefighter). For instance, in 'Scotland', he incorporates Burns' 'My Heart's in the Highlands' in professing his love for Caledonia.[46] There are two other poems also titled 'Scotland' and many others that mention Scotland explicitly, always praising it for its 'valor' and 'worth' and for its songs. More remarkable are the scores of Scots songs. A few include the almost hallucinatory vividness of Clare's sense for natural detail separating his songs from a conventional pastoral landscape: 'The may bush smells sae very sweet / The crimson threeds sae fine'; 'Rich green & grey did seem / The pea more rich than velvet glows'.[47] But what is paradoxically remarkable about these songs is how conventionally they rehearse the simple pastoral erotics of the genre, whether Mary Ann, Mary Green or Bonny Mary is the name of the beloved. It is as if Scots songs became for Clare something like a writerly reflex, the closest poetic language to hand as he searched for some way to hold together his sense of himself as an author.

These various Romantic strains converge in *Child Harold*. As the title suggests, the poem mimics the Spenserianisms of the Scottish author who exemplified the sublime, defiant, commercially-successful Romantic poet: 'My life hath been one love – no blot it out / My life hath been one chain of contradictions / Madhouses Prisons wh-re shops – never doubt / But that my life hath had some strong convictions' (*Later Poems* 1: p. 45). But early on, it is also clear that Clare has another, Burnsian model in mind, as he claims in the first stanza that 'The life of labour is a rural song / That hurts no cause' (1: p. 41), a model of poesis that he realises in the various 'Songs' and 'Ballads' woven into the text. The presence of Burns hovers over their obsessive return to Mary, who seems to be a conflation of Highland Mary and Clare's own beloved, Mary Joyce, whom he fantasised was his second wife. So one song echoes 'My Heart's in the Highlands,' another 'Ae Fond Kiss' and a third concludes with this striking stanza: 'O when will autumn bring the news / Now harvest browns the fen / That Mary as my vagrant muse / & I shall meet again' (1: pp. 42, 52, 55).

Clare's *Child Harold* testifies to the way Scottish songs and ballads stand at the heart of the concepts, tropes and material structures that we now understand as Romantic. This is true in Scott's antiquarian rewriting of ballads to distance them from the scandals of the Gothic and of the ballads actually hawked on the streets. Extracting ballads from present performance, he can absorb them into a history that affirms personal and national development even as he elicits a nostalgic sigh for these earlier stages. But, as we have seen, there are other Romantic models of appropriating ballads. Bannerman refuses to normalise the artificial shudders of the Gothic, the shape of her narratives or her view of subjectivity. Nairne anonymously rewrites old songs to conform to the constraints on women as authors but also to her sceptical view of the progress that Scott affirms. Most influentially, Burns constructs a canon of national song that challenges the boundaries between high and low as well as genteel Enlightenment assumptions about development. Radicalising the work of Ramsay, he sets a pattern of Romantic authorship that inspires Hogg, Clare and other plebeian authors. They take advantage of an Enlightenment interest in the various forms of the primitive and the pastoral, which only intensifies in the Romantic era, to press the more democratic implications of those interests. It is no wonder, then, that ballads make Jeffrey nervous and that the more conservative canonisation of Romanticism that Scott helps to found has, until recently, overlooked or mystified the many authors who drew on Scottish ballads and songs.

CHAPTER TWO

Romantic Macpherson

Fiona Stafford

By the side of a rock on the hill, beneath the aged trees, old Oscian sat on the moss; the last of the race of Fingal. Sightless are his aged eyes; his beard is waving in the wind. Dull through the leafless trees he heard the voice of the north. Sorrow revived in his soul: he began and lamented the dead.

How hast thou fallen like an oak, with all thy branches round thee! Where is Fingal the King? where is Oscur my son? where are all my race? Alas! In the earth they lie. I feel their tombs with my hands. I hear the river below murmuring hoarsely over the stones. What dost thou, O river to me? Thou bringest back the memory of the past.[1]

If we were looking for a text to demonstrate the defining qualities of Romanticism, James Macpherson's *Ossian* would be hard to beat. The opening of 'Fragment VIII' offers readers the figure of the isolated poet in an untamed landscape, prompted to spontaneous composition by a river whose hoarse murmurs bring back moving memories. The prevailing emphasis is on feeling – both emotional and physical – while at the centre of the scene is an individual whose personal experience and perception provide the substance of the poem. Ossian, deprived of sight, like Keats listening to the nightingale or Milton feeding on his inner light, sees with his mind and speaks of what is within.

The late eighteenth-century fascination with remote time and place, with ballads, legends and native traditions is abundantly evident in Ossian's ancient Celtic tales, while the related impatience with classical kinds and conventions bursts out in this rhythmic, but irregular prose-poetry. While Gray and Collins turned to the freedom of the ode, the form of Macpherson's poetry was closer to the prophetic books of the Bible – anticipating Blake's experimental work by thirty years. Macpherson's Ossian sang to a harp suspended in a tree, which at once harked back to the psalmist by the rivers of Babylon and heralded the Romantic poet by the Aeolian Harp.[2] Indeed, the High Romantic elevation of the artist found strange confirmation in the Celtic Bard, whose traditional place at the centre of his society had been assured and who, by being left as sole survivor of that culture, had also acquired the absolute power of uncontestable narration. Ossian, who first entranced the reading public of 1760, was at once a Noble Savage, living close to nature and pouring out spontaneous songs, and a reflective consciousness, gazing nostalgically on the heroic age and saddened by knowing that he can never return. With such an array of Romantic traits, it seems strange that for much of the last century, Macpherson's *Ossian* has featured so little in anthologies and university courses devoted to Romantic Literature.

A major reason for this neglect, of course, was in itself a legacy of Romantic aesthetics. As originality and authenticity became essential to the assessment of artistic quality, a translation long since exposed as inaccurate and regarded by many as a fake, was unlikely to fare well. From its earliest appearance, *Ossian* had been greeted by doubts as well as praise, condemned by Samuel Johnson even as it was extolled by Hugh Blair. National prejudices generally tended to cloud the critical views, but even readers who were transported by the striking beauty of the poems were still inclined to doubt the translator's account of their provenance. For although numerous witnesses could be found in the Highlands to testify to the existence of Celtic legends, the idea that such a large body of poems had survived for fifteen centuries, handed down through the oral tradition, seemed a little implausible to anyone who stopped to think.

Within five years of the original publication, Blair's attempts to corroborate the translator's account were included in a new edition of *The Works of Ossian*, but after Macpherson's death in 1796, the Highland Society commissioned Henry Mackenzie to conduct a large-scale investigation into the authenticity of Ossian and the nature of traditional Gaelic poetry current in the Highlands of Scotland.[3] The extensive research was finally published in 1805, and some of the key documents and contributions to the long-running controversy have been made available to modern readers by Dafydd Moore in a magnificent collection of *Ossian and Ossianism*.[4] The conclusions of the Highland Society's *Report* were subsequently confirmed by later Gaelic scholars and Celticists, who differed in their assessments of Macpherson's work, but largely agreed about his basic practices: Macpherson had indeed drawn on traditional Gaelic materials and in some of his poems, traces of authentic ballads and tales were clearly visible. However, he had also given rein to his own imagination, so that the poems he published between 1760 and 1763 were almost as much creation as translation.

When William Sharp introduced *The Poems of Ossian* for his centenary edition in 1896, the status of the texts seemed clear. Though it still seemed necessary to review the old controversy, Sharp was equally dismissive of the view held by some patriotic Scots that Macpherson's editions represented genuine translations of a third-century Celtic bard and the 'more absurd' English opinion that they were entirely fabricated.[5] The recent work of scholars and collectors such as Alfred Nutt and J. F. Campbell of Islay had greatly enhanced contemporary understanding of Gaelic culture, but in Sharp's eyes this merely freed the poems to be properly enjoyed, since the 'stupid outcry against Ossian as no more than a gigantic fraud' could now be consigned to the past.[6] For William Sharp, as for other readers of the 1890s, when the enthusiasm for a Celtic Twilight was at its height, Macpherson's work was a 'restoration' through which 'the antique spirit' could breathe 'enduring life'.[7]

While the growth of Celtic studies meant that Macpherson's methods could be established with reasonable confidence, however, Dr Johnson's influential opinion of Macpherson's fraudulence continued to affect the reputation of Ossian throughout the nineteenth and twentieth centuries. Even after the distinguished Scottish poet, Derick Thomson, had published an authoritative analysis of the Gaelic sources of *Ossian* in 1952, Macpherson continued to be cast as an audacious forger in books, newspapers, radio and TV programmes, making his place in 'genuine' literary history problematic.[8] When the British Museum mounted a major exhibition entitled *Fake? The Art of Deception* in 1990, Macpherson's texts were on show along with the Turin Shroud and Van Meegeren's 'Vermeers'. The sheer scale of the exhibition nevertheless revealed a willingness to reconsider standard assumptions about art, as evident in Mark Jones' tentative suggestion that 'fakes' might hold 'keys to understanding the changing nature of our vision of the past' and 'as subverters of aesthetic certainties [. . .] deserve our closest attention'.[9] If placing Macpherson among history's frauds and forgers was in some ways a perpetuation of the old Johnsonian hard line, the view was now complicated by new questions about the nature and perception of art.

During the 1980s, the fortunes of Ossian had begun to turn. New ways of reading the past came into being in tandem with new ways of understanding the present. With the end of the Cold War, the co-ordinates by which the world had operated since the 1940s were no longer fixed and the ensuing global adjustments provoked intensive reconsideration of all kinds of conventional thinking. As the map of Europe was reconfigured, with smaller states re-emerging from decades of domination by larger powers, traditional ideas about the relationships between minor and major, centre and periphery no longer seemed adequate. The very idea of a United Kingdom, which had held sway for three centuries, was suddenly being replaced by a new model of devolved power and a greater awareness of regional and national distinctions. The success of Linda Colley's history of national identity, *Britons: Forging the Nation, 1707–1837* (1992), reflected both the lingering desire in some for a grand evolutionary narrative of the nation and the new awareness, signalled in her subtitle, that any such story was essentially a construction. The vigorous debates over her central thesis, by scholars in Scotland, Ireland

and Wales, rapidly demonstrated that any single account of the history of
these islands in the eighteenth and nineteenth centuries was unlikely to
meet with universal assent. In Scotland, especially, widespread dissatisfaction with Thatcher's Britain gave a powerful impetus to a longstanding sense
of national differences and a renewed appreciation of distinctively Scottish
traditions.

As Macpherson's bicentenary dawned in 1996, the atmosphere had thus
become much more accommodating to a text that did not quite fit the grand
narrative of English literary history and seemed to inhabit an unnavigable
space between objective truth and constructed narrative. Howard Gaskill's
new edition of *The Poems of Ossian* was able to treat the old issue of authenticity not as 'a stupid outcry', but rather as an instructive part of the text's
reception history, while emphasising the importance of Macpherson's work
as a foundational text for European culture. Gaskill's energetic defence of
Ossian, which stemmed from his work as a scholar of German literature,
has done much to rehabilitate Macpherson's standing in European cultural
history, especially with the inclusion of a substantial volume on *Ossian* in
the major *Reception of British Authors in Europe* series. Any idea that Ossian's
appeal was limited to those living in a newly devolved Scotland is countered
by this volume and by the numerous books, chapters and articles by scholars
from America, Canada, the Czech Republic, England, Hungary, Iceland,
Ireland, Italy, Germany, the Netherlands, Norway and Poland, that have
appeared in the last two decades.[10] Joep Leerssen has even been bold enough
to suggest that Macpherson's peculiar, antiquarian texts marked the beginning of literary historicism itself, by prompting the urge to find 'the epic
origin of separate national-literary traditions' – as seen in the successive
publications of *Beowulf* (1815), *Karel ende Elegast* (1824), the *Nibelungenlied*
(1826) and the *Chansons de Roland* (1836).[11] As the European and interdisciplinary dimensions of Romanticism have been increasingly recognised,
Ossian has re-emerged as a crucial text.

The re-appearance of Macpherson's work can fruitfully be set against the
international transformations of the later twentieth century, but it has also
been influenced by developments within the more specialised field of literary
studies. After all, the demand to reconsider Romanticism predated the fall
of the Berlin Wall, emerging in the mid-1980s in the work of critics such as
Jerome McGann and Marilyn Butler. A sense that the prevailing focus on
six major poets – Blake, Wordsworth, Coleridge, Byron, Shelley and Keats
– had led to a somewhat distorted image of a period rich in different literary
kinds began to turn critical attention towards texts that had been largely
excluded from many influential anthologies and analyses of Romantic literature. Feminist criticism, too, posed vigorous challenges to prevailing notions
of literary history: its representation of the canon as the construction of a

dominant, masculine establishment gave impetus to the wider pursuit of any text perceived to be resistant to the old norms. With the rise of the historical method, the very notion of 'Romanticism' came to be viewed with suspicion in many quarters, with the apparently neutral 'Romantic period' becoming accepted as a preferable term for describing the culture of the late eighteenth and early nineteenth centuries.

Although the initial publication of Macpherson's texts fell outside the generally agreed (albeit fluid) boundaries of the Romantic period, the move to rethink Romanticism opened the door to the serious consideration of texts previously ignored by modern scholarship. It was no longer sufficient to apply twentieth-century formalist principles to texts that had proved immensely popular in their day: if so many readers had admired the *Poems of Ossian* in the eighteenth and nineteenth centuries, the question of whether they conformed to later ideas about the quality of lyric poetry was perhaps not the most fruitful approach. Macpherson's loosely structured prose poems, with their insistent repetition of the simplest images – sun, moon, winds, hills, rocks, trees, woods, waves – might not be as obviously amenable to the kinds of sophisticated close reading afforded by Keats' great Odes, but this did not necessarily render them worthless. The historicist focus on the relationship between texts and society prompted new research into the reading habits of earlier generations, and so any text that had enjoyed huge popularity in its day offered important insights into European cultural history. As McGann argued, 'Ossian's influence on the literary scene of the late eighteenth century eclipsed all others,' and so to ignore Macpherson's contribution was to misread the sensibility of the entire period.[12]

Literary texts were attracting interest not only for their historical importance, however, but also because the new pursuit of illuminating contexts opened up fresh interpretative possibilities. Old questions about the accuracy of Macpherson's translations began to look very different once removed from a purely academic analysis of sources and methods and placed in the light of eighteenth-century Highland history. Reconsideration of Macpherson's own peculiar situation in a community convulsed by political rising and suppression led to a rather more sympathetic understanding of his project, which ceased to seem an act of self-promotion or a confidence trick and appeared rather more like a tribute to a devastated community. Once Ossian's laments for his vanished family could be read as covert elegies for the Highlanders, who had died at Culloden or been forced to emigrate during the ensuing reprisals, their sorrow took on a new meaning and Macpherson's work, as 'a rearguard act of retrieval', assumed a heroic dimension of its own.[13]

The future translator of *Ossian* was only nine when the remnants of a broken Jacobite army rallied for the last time at Ruthven, within a few hundred yards of Macpherson's home, so his entire adolescence was spent under the shadow of defeat, with his close relative, Cluny, the Clan Chief, forced into hiding in his own lands. The urge to rescue the remains of Gaelic culture from the rapid erasure of the distinctive features of Highland life seemed a more attractive motive for Macpherson's activities as a collector and translator than the earlier assumptions of duplicity and ambition. His evident desire to make a new life for himself, which the success of his poems made possible, also looks rather different when the devastation of his childhood home is taken into account. As Ossian's poems came to be seen as the voice of an oppressed people, Macpherson began to attract post-colonial readings, especially from Irish scholars for whom the common Celtic inheritance had particular significance. Luke Gibbons, for example, saw in the sentimentality of Macpherson's work a kind of Smithian sympathy that unconsciously 'cemented' the political Union and, in tracing the implications of the Scottish Ossian's insistently elegiac stance, found a telling contrast with the more hopeful treatment of the Celtic bard in Ireland.[14]

Awareness of the cultural conditions that helped to determine Macpherson's texts also shed light on their peculiar forms. The first published translations appeared in a small pamphlet entitled *Fragments of Ancient Poetry, collected in the Highlands of Scotland*, and the opening sentence of the preface presented them as 'genuine remains of Scottish poetry'. The most obvious thing about the collection was its incompletion, since the contents were variously described as 'fragments', 'remains' and 'detached pieces' and 'episodes' – but never as poems (*Poems of Ossian*, 5–6). These short passages were at once directing the reader back to a distant past, when they had been part of a more substantial whole, and towards a future moment of recovery when 'one work of considerable length, and which deserves to be styled an heroic poem' might once again be known (*Poems of Ossian*, 5–6). In other words, the fragment was caught between remembered and anticipated wholeness. If the prefatory emphasis on translation and historical provenance diverted attention from the fragment as a new literary form, Macpherson's unassuming collection was actually a forerunner of a kind of poetry that would flourish in the Romantic period, resistant to traditional ideas of closure, regularity and perfection. At the same time, the epic ambition contained within the slim volume conveyed aspirations every bit as great as the better known manifestos of Wordsworth, Coleridge and Shelley. Macpherson's pamphlet, just as much as Coleridge's *Christabel, Kubla Khan and The Pains of Sleep*, was offering a series of 'fragments', which, by remaining incomplete, evaded the kind of criticism often levelled at serious literary works, while simultaneously staking a claim on the highest form of poetry.

Although the *Fragments* was perhaps Macpherson's most 'Romantic' work, his influence in the Romantic period rested on the more elaborate, quarto volumes of ancient epic poetry that rapidly followed his initial success.

Spurred on by the excitement and financial support of the Edinburgh literati, Macpherson toured the Highlands in 1760 and 1761, collecting up
any surviving manuscripts of Gaelic poetry and whatever could be gained
from the oral tradition. The fruits of his mission were then blended into the
two 'ancient epic poems', *Fingal* and *Temora*, which appeared with a series
of shorter pieces in 1761 and 1763. These were the works that influenced so
many writers, artists and musicians, as well as transporting numerous readers
to a remote northern world of heroic battles and lost loves. The original
volumes were rapidly collected into *The Poems of Ossian* and the different editions revised by Macpherson formed the basis of a vast succession of cheaper
reprints in English and numerous translations into other languages.

Even after Macpherson assembled his fragments into the larger work he
had promised readers of 1760, however, the broken, inconsistent nature of
the epic poems meant that they still seemed reluctant to conform to neoclassical notions of correctness and literary decorum. *Fingal*, for example, begins
in true epic fashion, *in medias res*, with news of the impending Scandinavian
invasion and Cuchullin's Council of War. Even though the warriors quickly
agree to engage the enemy in combat, the force of the decision is somewhat
blunted by the inlaid tale of Duchomar, Morna and Cathbat, with its melancholy conclusion: 'He pierced her white side with steel; and spread her fair
locks on the ground. Her bursting blood sounds from her side: and her white
arm is stained in red. Rolling in death she lay, and Tura's cave answered to
her groans' (*Poems of Ossian*, 58). The narrative has hardly begun when it
takes a step back into the past, with images more striking than those of the
remembered present.

It is not just the almost pathologically anti-linear form of the poem,
however, that works against its epic surface. Even before Cuchullin's march
has been interrupted by sad recollections of Morna, the sense of the past has
pervaded the scene. The voice of the narrator, Ossian, is not only recreating
the drama of the moment, but also reflecting on its distance: 'Now I behold
the chiefs in the pride of their former deeds; their souls are kindled at the
battles of old, and the actions of other times.' Although he is ostensibly
describing the way in which the Celtic warriors draw courage from their
earlier successes, the very language used to evoke their power emphasises its
subsequent disappearance:

> They came like streams from the mountains; each rushed roaring from his hill.
> Bright are the chiefs of battle in the armour of their fathers. –Gloomy and dark
> their heroes followed, like the gathering of the rainy clouds behind the red
> meteors of heaven. –The sounds of crashing arms ascend. The grey dogs howl
> between. Unequally bursts the song of battle; and rocking Cromla echoes
> round. On Lena's dusky heath they stood, like mist that shades the hills of

autumn: when broken and dark it settles high, and lifts its head to heaven. (*Poems of Ossian*, 56)

The brightness of the Chiefs turns rapidly to imagery of rain-clouds, autumn mist and darkness. Thoughts of heroic action seem, in Ossian's world, inseparable from thoughts of brokenness and gloom. Though *Fingal* draws attention to classical ideas of epic, with its Vergilian epigraph and epic motifs, it reveals, at every turn, a dim sense of distance from the monumental inheritance of Greece and Rome. It at once claims equal status while resisting full identification with the classical epic.

Awareness of loss is everywhere, with Ossian lamenting the vanished heroes, just as his translator had reminded readers of the great Gaelic poems that are now irretrievable. Even *Fingal* itself was only a shadow of the lost original, not just by virtue of being a translation, but because of the destruction of Highland tradition. As Macpherson emphasised in the dissertation prefacing *Fingal*, the title poem 'was not the greatest or most celebrated of the exploits of Fingal', whose numerous wars had inspired the 'genius of his son', Ossian, but the great changes suffered in the Highlands meant that 'excepting the present poem, those pieces are now lost, and there only remain a few fragments of them in the hands of the translator' (*Poems of Ossian*, 51). Both Ossian (the narrator/character) and *Ossian* (the body of poems) are presented as remnants whose survival in modern Britain is little short of a miracle. Rather than allowing readers to abandon themselves entirely to an imaginary heroic past, Macpherson allowed the self-consciousness of a modern in pursuit of the ancient to pervade his texts. His focus on the poet-narrator as a suffering individual reflected an eighteenth- rather than third-century perspective and beneath Ossian's laments for his father's great deeds lay not just a personal elegy for Highland culture, but more widespread anxieties about modern society. For an age that had begun to articulate a deep longing for a nature which 'lies behind and must continually lie behind', *The Poems of Ossian* struck a deep sympathetic chord.[15]

The deep melancholy of Macpherson's work may be a further factor in the late-twentieth-century revival of critical attention. For the 1980s also saw an increasing interest in the work of Walter Benjamin, whose own efforts have been memorably presented as those of a collector, bending down 'to select his precious fragments from the pile of debris'.[16] Much light on Macpherson may be shed by Ahrendt's understanding of Benjamin's fragments, which he used not in an attempt to resuscitate the past in its original form, but rather in the belief that from utter ruin 'new crystallized forms and shapes that remain immune to the elements' might still be found.[17] Though Macpherson presented his translations as a restoration of broken pieces to their 'original purity', his own texts betrayed the sense of the past's ultimate irrecoverability at every turn.[18] Moore's reading of *Fingal* emphasises that Macpherson's annotations not only remind readers of the fragments behind the epic, but are in themselves fragmentary, often constituted from detached quotations from Vergil, Homer or Milton.[19] In Ahrendt's reading of Benjamin, too, it is fragmented quotations that furnish material for the new work, which comes into being after an irreparable break in tradition: the fragmentary form is 'born out of despair [. . .] of the present'.[20]

Benjamin's study of German Tragedy was built from a vast collection of quotations, pulled from their contexts to comment on each other, like a 'surrealist montage'.[21] At the heart of his analysis was a meditation on Melancholy, which he regarded as the condition of post-Lutheran society, for whom 'human actions were deprived of all value' and where genuine interaction was replaced by introspection.[22] As he explored early modern culture, Benjamin discovered that the 'theory of melancholy became chrystallized around a number of ancient emblems' – the dog, the stone, the sphere – while the melancholic was often depicted, as in Dürer's engraving, as an isolated figure, gazing at the earth, with the sea in the background and the signs of active life lying useless about him.[23] The form of Benjamin's own work, with its quotations plucked from an eclectic range of sources, reflected his own approach to cultural history and his willingness to find meaning crystallising around detached objects. It is an approach that may illuminate both Macpherson's melancholic poems and the revival of Ossianic interest in an age of self-styled postmodernism. Matthew Wickman, for example, has suggested that Macpherson's Fragments depict 'enlightened modernity as a tale of the traumatised witness – the witness who, in terms of consciousness, was never there, or never at the site about which he reports', while Robert Crawford has drawn a rather different analogy between Ossianic fragments and postmodern buildings.[24]

In Julian Roberts' analysis of architectural postmodernism, the bewildering array of styles that succeeded modernist building is presented as a kind of 'sceptical despair', best understood through Benjamin's theory of melancholy.[25] The devastating psychological effects of the irreparable breach between the material and divine worlds are brought helpfully to bear on the later twentieth-century scepticism about absolute truths – whether mathematical, philosophical or religious. Roberts sees the eclectic styles of postmodernism as a response to the condition of living in 'a universe of expressive systems' with no hierarchy or standard of ultimate truth by which to judge them.[26] In place of clear structures and defined forms, postmodern culture offers echoes, quotations, repetitions and correspondences, while the surfaces and interiors become increasingly interchangeable. In such a climate, a work that insistently blurred the normal distinctions between text and annotation, author and translator, past and present, quoting freely from different traditions and remaining essentially melancholic, was likely to attract new interest. Macpherson's poems can be understood as being born out of despair, his cavalier use of Gaelic, classical and English sources as much a work of montage as of restoration.

Among the most creative responses to Macpherson in recent years has been Calum Colvin's photographic series, which combines ancient materials with the most up-to-date technology to bring Ossian into the twenty-first century. Like Macpherson, Colvin works with fragments, creating unsettling new images from the juxtaposition of objects, stones, bones and broken build-ings. Through the folds, fragments and recurrent motifs, continuities are at once suggested and denied, while the face of Ossian moves in and out of the shadows. Colvin's affinity with the melancholy of Ossian is most explicit, however, in his image of 'Scota', which explicitly recalls Durer's *Melancholia*, but includes amidst a hotch-potch of traditional emblems (the pensive figure, the dog, the stone, the abacus), a trail of increasingly pixelated prints of the Reynolds portrait of James Macpherson. As Tom Normand has pointed out, 'Colvin has created a kind of visual pun, as the manipulation of Macpherson's image echoes the 'manipulated' verse of Ossian'.[27]

Although it is certainly possible to read in Colvin's *Ossian* a profound melancholy and anxiety about cultural fracture, there is also a wit and play-fulness in his work, typical of much postmodern art. Fragments can, after all, be deployed for parody as well as lamentation and, once humour enters the picture, the pervading gloom is itself fragmented. If Colvin's work is com-menting darkly on the cultural health of the newly devolved Scotland, it is also creating something strikingly beautiful, new and distinctive. Colvin's Ossian, just as much as Benjamin's source texts, suffers a sea change into something rich and strange. It is hard to see such a creative treatment of the past as a form of nostalgia, for the images seem engaged in creative dialogue rather than passive yearning.

To pierce the Ossianic gloom with parody and playfulness may seem light-years away from Macpherson's practice. As he himself observed of Ossian in a note on 'Berrathon', 'if ever he composed any thing of a merry turn it is long since lost' (*Poems of Ossian*, 472). However, it is possible to bring in yet another instructive context in the attempt to understand his elusive poems and their current appeal – and that is the emergence of the eighteenth-century novel. For while it is helpful to see Macpherson's attitudes to epic poetry as having been conditioned by the classics tutors and philosophical primitivists at the University of Aberdeen, there were other contemporary influences that might have had a bearing on his work.[28] Although many poets of the eighteenth century were haunted by the desire to scale the utmost heights of Mount Parnassus by composing a serious epic poem, some of the greatest compositions of the age were actually mock-heroic and satirical.

The satirical response to epic might be understood in terms of a sense of modern inferiority, but it can also be seen as a liberating mode. For Bakhtin, the decline of classical epic was not necessarily a sign of despair, because he traced the origins of the modern novel in the impulse to parody high, aristocratic forms and use laughter as a corrective force, breaking down barriers and allowing entry to a greater range of literary voices. The emergence of the new, flexible prose genre in eighteenth-century Britain might lead us to place Macpherson's unusual reconstructions of epic next to Henry Fielding's explicitly parodic novels, with their playful use of epic conventions, juxtapositions of high and low, imbedded tales and self-conscious narration. The tone may be strikingly dissimilar, but the essential dialogism and creation of something new from a mass of older elements is not. One of the first literary texts to incorporate Ossian explicitly was, after all, Smollett's novel, *The Expedition of Humphry Clinker*, whose epistolary juxtapositions seem every bit as disconcerting as Macpherson's fragmented epics.[29]

Keymer has pointed out that 'both *Tristram Shandy* and *The Poems of Ossian* are linked by their conspicuous violation, or fragmentation, of the polite registers and elegant structures of neoclassical convention', but concludes that this parallel fragmentation reflects a shared sense of 'disintegration and loss'.[30] However, it is also possible to read both the gaps in Sterne's texts and Macpherson's acknowledgements of an incomplete record as crucial entry points for different presences, moods, modes of perception. Colvin's postmodern photographic images are full of suggested spaces, but this is what allows for different interpretations and imaginative suggestions. The juxtaposition of Sterne and Macpherson may reveal an unexpected melancholy in *Tristram Shandy*, but it works equally to uncover the potential ironies of the *Ossian* project. To argue that a text is at once irrecoverable because of the destruction of Highland society by outside forces, while at the same time using it as evidence for the unassailable superiority of ancient Gaelic culture does, after all, require an ability to see things from a number of perspectives simultaneously. So, too, did Blair's twofold praise of *Ossian* as the voice of a simpler, more passionate society and as an embodiment of refined sentiment.

Robert Burns' admiration for both *Ossian* and Sterne has generally been seen as a sentimental enthusiasm, but it is possible that he was equally drawn by the creative possibilities opened up by texts bold enough to wrench apart and meld together diverse traditions. Burns' Luath initially seems a very different creature from the great hound who features in *Fingal* and *Temora*, but as he plucked part of Ossian from its context to use for his own distinctive purposes, Burns was perhaps following Macpherson more closely than has generally been recognised. As Burns' biographer has argued, 'the fragmented, never complete and so never finished, points not just to loss, but always to the possibility of building, growth, and renewal'.[31] The capacity to transform the

melancholy dog who haunts Ossian's dreams into 'a gash an' faithfu' *tyke*, / As
ever lap a sheugh, or dyke!' may not immediately suggest the modern witness
in despair of recovering the past, but it shares some of the parodying exuber-
ance of Fielding and the witty ironies of postmodern montage.[32] Burns is also
a key figure of the Romantic period, even though he, too, has until recently
suffered from serious scholarly neglect. As the older critical traditions have
themselves begun to fragment into a postmodern world drawn to irony
and openness, dialogism and inclusivity, both Burns and Macpherson have
offered versions of Romanticism that might not exactly conform to perceived
paradigms – and have seemed all the more exciting for that.

CHAPTER THREE

Scottish Song, Lyric Poetry and the Romantic Composer

Kirsteen McCue

In August 1829 the young German composer Felix Mendelssohn-Bartholdy, undertaking a tour of the British Isles, wrote to his father Abraham back home in Leipzig. Having just visited Blair Atholl in the Highlands, Mendelssohn had made his way across to the West Coast and his letter of 7 August was notably brief, with only one sentence: 'In order to make clear what a strange mood has come over me in the Hebrides, the following occurred to me,' and he then scribbled the first section of what became his *Concert Overture No 2: Die Hebriden* or *Fingalshöhle* ('The Hebrides' or 'Fingal's Cave') Op. 26. A second letter, written four days later, commented that this musical quotation was the only good thing about Mendelssohn's boat trip to the island of Staffa, for the most horrible seasickness rather dissuaded him from any detailed prosaic description. In this letter Felix explained to his father that he and his great friend Klingemann were having a rest before setting out for Loch Lomond and Loch Katrine, across the Trossachs, through Aberfoyle and Stirling, and down to Lanark – presumably popping in to inspect Robert Owen's 'New Lanark' – before travelling south again for London. By 25 August the pair had reached Llangollen in Wales. Mendelssohn's exhaustion was clearly getting the better of him and he vented his spleen, albeit most entertainingly, about the music that greeted them:

> Anything but national music! May ten thousand devils take all folklore. Here I am in Wales, and oh how lovely, a harpist sits in the lobby of every inn of repute playing so-called folk melodies at you – i.e., dreadful, vulgar, fake stuff, and *simultaneously* a hurdy gurdy is tootling out melodies, it's enough to drive one crazy, it's even given me a toothache. Scottish bagpipes, Swiss cow's horns, Welsh harps – all playing the Huntsmen's Chorus with ghastly variations or improvisations, not to mention the lovely songs in the lobby – it's the only real music they have! It's beyond comprehension! Anyone like myself, who can't abide Beethoven's *Nationallieder*, should come here and hear them being howled by shrill nasal voices, accompanied by doltish bumbling fingers, and then try to hold his tongue [. . .] I am going mad, and will have to leave off writing until later.[1]

This trio of letters encapsulates a number of the most important musical and literary interests of the moment. *Die Hebriden* contributed to the newly developing notion of 'programmatic' composition, whereby the musical score set out to describe landscape, weather, an emotion, or to narrate a particular story. Mendelssohn's allusion to 'Fingal' took his listener on a voyage of imagination featuring the epic adventures of the bards, for James Macpherson's *Poems of Ossian* had long since taken the European reading public by storm. The trip mentioned in the second letter is typical of most Romantic 'Highland Journeys' much circulated at the time, nearly all of which paused at 'Ossian's Hall' in Perthshire, and stopped at Loch Katrine in the Trossachs, by this time famous as the location of Walter Scott's *Lady of the Lake* of 1810. Finally, Mendelssohn's letter from Llangollen refers to another highly fashionable musical and literary development, namely a widely shared fascination for 'national song', particularly acute in the British nations at this time, but shared by his native Germany and elsewhere in Europe. His description of the cacophony of national instruments and howling singers is fodder for a Thomas Rowlandson or William Hogarth caricature, and, indeed, as is the case with their cartoons, the truth is in the detail and is much more complex than it might first appear. Allied to wider philosophical and anthropological concerns, nations, especially smaller ones on the periphery of Europe, were deeply engaged in discovering and disseminating information about their local and national musical and literary traditions. Discussions and philosophical debates about whether nations had an existing body of national music and literature, or needed to build one themselves for the future, were commonplace. The term 'Volkslieder' ('folk song') was first used formally during this period, and poets and composers were immersed in these issues.[2] Their interdisciplinary and often transnational approach to their own creations illustrates this powerfully. European composers of the period were fascinated by the opportunities provided them by Scotland's newly published poetic and musical traditions.[3] This chapter examines this area and by exploring more closely the settings of texts by James Macpherson, Walter Scott and Robert Burns by Franz Schubert and Robert Schumann, it also hopes to reveal something of the nature of the traffic of ideas about nation, song and poetry that moved between Scotland and the German-speaking world in the early decades of the nineteenth century.

Although one of the smaller nations of Europe, Scotland presented three key characteristics that were to make a huge impact on the Romantic musical imagination: sublime landscape and suitably dramatic climate; a newly emerging body of national epic and 'folk' literature; and a reactivated musical life which relied heavily on an existing and developing national tradition of instrumental music (bagpipe and fiddle). All three elements were picked up and realised creatively by contemporary musicians both at home and abroad.[4]

Landscape was directly inspirational, as we see with Mendelssohn, and it was frequently described in popular travel journals and correspondence, in pictures and paintings (Mendelssohn's letters often included sketches), as well as in imaginative literature of the period. BOSLIT (Bibliography of Scottish Literature in Translation), though not a complete resource, shows how quickly the work of Macpherson, Scott and Burns, for example, was translated into a number of European languages, thus providing composers another layer of creative interaction with Scotland.[5] Unlike Mendelssohn, most travelling performers and composers undertaking a well-worn path across Europe during the period were interested in the songs and tunes of the nations they visited, and Scots tunes were particularly noted for their 'folk' qualities as the nineteenth century dawned.[6]

Such influences were the product of much debate, discussion and collection of Scottish poetry, song and melody from the early years of the eighteenth century.[7] The sharing of materials – sometimes with musical notation but often without – between editions was common practice. Often songs were collected from performance or gathered from older broadsides and manuscript collections, but frequently contemporary editors and writers amended them and expanded them, so few were 'pure' folk songs. A large body of this material was well known by Robert Burns (1759–1796) whose involvement with James Johnson's *Scots Musical Museum* (1787–1803) and George Thomson's *Select Collection of Original Scottish Airs* (1793–1846) was to make the most substantial contribution to the movement of furnishing Scotland with a published national song tradition. And this was not just a Scottish or British activity. European composers and performers who had come as visitors and then chose to stay in the British Isles also contributed.[8] They established freelance careers as performers and teachers, and often composed, arranged and published their works. Thus Italians – including Francesco Barsanti, Pietro Urbani and Domenico Corri – and Germans, such as the cellist Johann Schetky, were all writing and publishing their own rather stylish arrangements of well-known Scottish dance and song tunes with associated lyrics.[9] George Thomson's large project of Scottish, Welsh and Irish songs even went one step further by inviting European composers on the Continent to contribute musical settings for voice and piano trio and he secured commissions from composers including the famous Joseph or 'Papa' Haydn and even from Ludwig van Beethoven.

Beethoven was particularly keen to be involved in Thomson's project and he set a large number of both Scottish and Irish songs for his collections.[10] Moreover, he and Thomson worked extensively on the idea of a collection of 'Lieder aller Völker' or 'Songs of All Nations' and Beethoven tackled the arrangement of twenty-four melodies from a variety of places including Austria (there were four Tyrolean melodies), Russia, Spain, Denmark and

Switzerland. The project was thwarted by Thomson's failure to secure decent lyrics in English for the songs, and they were not published at this time.[11] But Beethoven's interest taps into the shared notion of the importance of 'Volkslieder' both in building national confidence, and also in uniting nations. His peer Carl Maria von Weber was interested in setting Scottish airs for Thomson, because he too was fascinated by the notion of 'Volkslieder' and had already embarked, around 1810, on collecting and writing Rhenish folksongs himself (guitar in hand), with his friend Alexander von Dusch. They were inspired, as John Warrack argues, by their time in Heidelberg, 'one of the capital cities of Romanticism',[12] and, moreover, by the exciting work of Clemens Brentano and Achim von Arnim, whose collecting of some 700 songs just a few years before had resulted in *Des Knaben Wunderhorn* (1805–8). They embarked on their journey in 1802 just at the moment of Walter Scott's publication of a very similar project in Scotland, *The Minstrelsy of the Scottish Border*.

Here the importance of social networks and the influence of one fine thinker on another should not be underestimated. Scotland undoubtedly played its part in the development of Johann Gottfried Herder's ideas about 'Volkslieder' and 'Volkspoesie' which he developed from the 1760s until the 1790s.[13] He was hugely passionate about *Ossian* and was one of the first German scholars to engage closely with Macpherson's work in translation.[14] His essay 'Über Oßian und die Lieder alter Völker' ('On Ossian and the Songs of Ancient People) of 1771 was written hot on the heels of Michael Denis' first complete German translation of Macpherson's *Fragments of Ancient Poetry* of 1768–9. With Macpherson, Herder found a platform upon which he could build his arguments about the nature of 'lied' or 'song' (albeit poetically rather than musically) and its roots in popular tradition. Herder claimed that Ossian's fragments were natural, spontaneous songs simply speaking through Macpherson as the vehicle of dissemination.[15] His simultaneous discovery of the ballads and songs in Thomas Percy's *Reliques of Ancient Poetry* of 1765 left him in no doubt about what needed to be done. Herder's fascination with this material from a variety of nations, but particularly from the North, was directly related to building a sense of German confidence in their own national heritage and to encourage much the same process as that already well under way in Scotland. This was a particularly powerful aesthetic in the context of the German situation at this time, where, as Frauke Reitemeier explains, 'there was no "Germany" to speak of, but numerous principalities of various sizes and importance'.[16] It was the work of artists like Herder, she argues, that was to make a notable contribution to the intellectual revolution towards a unified Germany.

Amongst others whom Herder ignited with enthusiasm was his close friend and (in the early years) ally, Johann Wolfgang Goethe, whose use of *Ossian* in his 1774 novel *Die Leiden des jungen Werthers* (*The Sorrows of Young Werther*) was to introduce the poems to an even wider readership.[17] While there were significant differences in their theories, Goethe shared Herder's fascination with the idea of 'Volkslieder' and well before the early 1800s he too was actively involved in collecting and writing some songs himself. In 1803–4 he teamed up with Christoph Martin Wieland (1733–1813) to edit jointly a song *Almanac* or *Taschenbuch auf das Jahr 1804* (*Pocketbook from the Year 1804*) (published by Cotta). This particular publication grew out of a social activity, much the same as many of the collections in Scotland had done. Fred Sternfeld has commented that the gatherings with food and wine were 'especially devoted to group singing'. They selected 'simple and well-known melodies' and provided texts 'that could be sung at sight to popular tunes'.[18]

There is, then, an obvious correlation from the 1770s through to the early years of the 1800s between Scottish and German ideas about 'folk song' and with the active processes of collection and creation. Goethe and his colleagues Wieland, Herder and Schiller, were looking for simple settings of their folk-like poems; an easy and memorable melody repeated for each verse of the song. And this was akin to the collections of melodies that had appeared in Scotland and were used as the foundation for many newly-created or amended song texts by Burns and his contemporaries. Popular 'folk' melody was the key here and this group did not envisage free musical interpretations of their texts. While the poetry of Goethe was to be one of the major poetic stimuli for the young Austrian composer Franz Schubert (1797–1828), Goethe himself was never to warm to the idea of Schubert's imaginative musical realisations of his poetry.

Schubert was introduced to Mapherson's work in the early 1810s, apparently through his friend Anton Holzapfel, and his group of ten settings from *Ossian* date from 1815 to 1817 (published posthumously in 1830).[19] Between 1814 and 1817 Schubert composed some 320 songs, and Macpherson's texts, in translation by Edmund von Harold (1782), were amongst poetic texts by well over a dozen writers whose works he set during the three years. His friend Joseph von Spaun thought that sending the *Ossian* songs to Goethe would help Schubert's case in forming an alliance with the poet, but sadly this was not to be.[20] And there was good reason why Goethe would have so disliked the *Ossian* settings. Some of Schubert's lieder, such as his famous 'Heidenröslein' (with lyrics by Goethe) or 'Die Forelle', are strophic (using the same music for each verse) and light in texture, and thus resemble popular 'Volkslieder' in form, but the *Ossian* settings do not. Schubert's interest at this particular moment seems to have been captured by the dramatic ballad – 1815 is also the year of his superlative setting of Goethe's 'Erlkönig' or 'Earl King' with its theatrical ride through the night and with the sinister voice of death beckoning through the wind. Indeed his first *Ossian* setting,

'Kolmas Klage' or 'Colma's Lament' from 'The Song of Selma', has moments
of similarity at the beginning in the drive of its piano accompaniment.[21]
These are highly dramatic musical settings where 'the external structure of
the text has far less bearing on the musical setting than the internal structure
– the way the story is told'.[22] 'Shilrik und Vinvela' ('Shilric and Vinvela')
sounds more like an operatic duet, much of it in a recitativo style (more as
if the singers are speaking to one another), and along with 'Cronnan' and
'Lodas Gespenst' ('Loda's Ghost') John Reed has noted that they might well
have been thought of as part of a larger operatic or theatrical work based on
Macpherson's 'Carric-Thura' which Schubert never finalised. Only 'Ossian's
Lied nach dem Falle Nathos' ('Ossian's Song after the Death of Nathos') from
Mapherson's 'Dar-Thula' is a simple strophic setting like a hymn of praise.
The other settings are interested in depicting drama, emphasising the heroic
nature of the texts, the emotions of the protagonists (as is the case particularly
with Lorma's sorrow in the second of his 'Lorma' settings) and capturing the
mood of the stormy winds and rain, the rocks, torrents and floods expressed
so evocatively in Macpherson's original text and clearly brought out by von
Harold. In his use of *Ossian* Schubert clearly represents the epic rather than
the lyric so emphasised by Herder. Schubert appreciates and realises the
grandeur of *Ossian*, and captures the patriotic loyalty and energy of the poetic
texts. Far from simplifying and treating them as 'Volkspoesie' Schubert lifts
them to new heights of dramatic expression. Not surprisingly comparisons
with Wagner's later heroes have been noted in a couple of these songs.[23]
And it is noteworthy that in 1815 Schubert also set some thirteen songs by
Theodor Körner, patriotic poet and balladeer and a name now synonymous
with rebirth of German nationalism.[24]

  Elements of the grandeur Schubert found in Macpherson were shared by
the characteristics of Scott's narrative poem *The Lady of the Lake* (1810),
where the natural acoustic of the mountains surrounding its setting of Loch
Katrine provided him with an evocative soundscape as well as landscape for
his story, interspersed with thirteen songs.[25] Schubert most probably read the
poem in translation while convalescing in Steyer in 1823, and for him, as
Elizabeth McKay has commented, it opened up 'a whole new world of romantic drama and emotion, in which tenderness and sensitivity coexisted with a
larger, grander world of wide landscapes, nobility of mind, fateful action, and
often tragic outcomes'.[26]

  Duly inspired, Schubert began work on a set of seven *Fräulein vom See*
songs which were published in Vienna by Artaria in two books (Op. 52)
the following year.[27] The German text was by Adam Storck (1819) and, as
several scholars have noted it was a very free translation, thus causing no end
of difficulties for Artaria, for while Schubert wrote his settings to the Stork
text, he had decided that it was necessary to provide texts in both German

and English for the final publication of the songs.[28] Schubert picked up immediately on two elements of the opening of Scott's poem: namely the call to
arms he extends to the 'Harp of the North' which has until now been too long
silent, and the hunt which opens Canto I in such dramatic terms. Schubert's
three songs sung by Ellen feature the idea of harp accompaniment most sensitively, notably in the first and third songs, and the group of songs as a whole
makes great use of hunting calls and motifs even when the lyric captures some
other element of the narrative. The opening of 'Ellens Gesang II': 'Jäger, ruhe
von der Jagd' ('Huntsman, rest!') is a fine example with its horn call capturing
the business of the day now past. Again the drama of the story is in Schubert's
mind. The accompaniment of 'Norman's Gesang' ('Norman's Song') depicts
the galloping of Norman's horse as he sets out to call his men to battle,
and the final song 'Lied des gefangenen Jäger' ('Song of the imprisoned
Huntsman') represents the resolve of Malcolm Graeme in its dark but firmly
militaristic setting. Moreover his two choral songs 'Bootgesang' beginning
'Hail to the Chief' from Canto II for male voices and his funeral 'Coronach'
from Canto III, beginning 'He's gone to the mountains' for women's chorus
capture the theatricality of Scott's narrative. These settings by a now-mature
song-writer are polished and sophisticated in a way in which the *Ossian* settings are not. Schubert makes more of the lyrical elements of the text where
the earlier Scottish settings are epic. And here he has clearly engaged with
Scott's skill in expressing the personal emotions and connotations of wider
historical and political events.

By far the best-known and most memorable of the songs from this group
is the third Ellen song, or 'Hymn to the Virgin' from Canto III, known as
'Ave Maria' and still popularly performed today. Even at the time of creation
Schubert was amazed at how much attention this particular song attracted.[29]
Interestingly the group of *Fräulein vom See* songs are hardly ever performed
together – like the *Ossian* settings it is impossible even to find them together
on one disc – and so Ellen's 'Ave Maria' is most often performed wildly out of
context, where the references in the second verse to 'the flinty couch' becoming her bed, and the 'murky cavern's heavy air' can only be understood in
heavily allegorical terms, unless the listener is aware of the territory in which
the story takes place. Nonetheless Schubert captures Ellen's anxiety and hope
for reconciliation most powerfully with one of the finest of his melodic lines
and Allan-Bane's harp provides the stimulus for Schubert's arpeggaic accompaniment strummed out from the opening to the closing bars of the song.

One of Schubert's most important successors in the 'lieder' tradition was
Robert Schumann (1810–1856), who was fundamentally interested in lyrical
expression. It should be no surprise that the Scottish writer who inspired him
most was Robert Burns, himself much more of lyricist than a dramatist.[30]
Schumann's discovery of the poetry of Burns is linked to one of the most

touching of all love stories. He was besotted with Clara, the daughter of his
piano teacher Friedrich Wieck, but Wieck was wholly opposed to any union.
Although the couple became engaged in 1837 this was legally contested
by Wieck, and it was not until three years later that they were granted the
right to marriage. Thus, 1840 was Schumann's happiest period, and one of
his most productive as a composer. It was hailed his 'year of song' and he
created some eighteen groups of songs or fully-fledged song cycles (including *Frauenliebe und Leben* (*A Woman's Love and Life*) Op. 42 and *Dichterliebe*
(*The Poet's Love*) Op. 48) as well as many single songs. The second of those
cycles was *Myrthen* ('Myrtles' Op. 25) which was designed to celebrate this
long-awaited union with Clara. With such a prolific burst of creativity it
seems that Schumann was almost ravenous for texts that reflected all aspects
of love from both male and female perspectives – indeed this cycle has most
often been performed and recorded by two voices. Within two months he had
completed twenty-six songs for *Myrthen* using poetic texts by a dozen writers
including Goethe, Rückert, Heine, Byron and Burns.[31] The German poet
and translator Ferdinand Freiligrath provided the translations of two songs
by Thomas Moore,[32] and Schumann found his Burns texts from Wilhelm
Gerhard's volume of *Robert Burns Gedichte*, which was published in Leipzig
that very year, and included both a long biographical account of Burns
and a large number of the poet's lyrical texts.[33] Before this time only single
songs, including Herder's adaptation of 'John Anderson my Jo' in 1801 – had
appeared in translation.[34]

While Gerhard's settings are in general very sensitive to Burns' originals –
necessarily having to smooth out the linguistic idiosyncracies – Schumann's
interest in using such a diverse set of texts by British poets had little, if anything, to do with British and Irish national song.[35] It was a lyric from Byron's
Hebrew Melodies – ('My soul is dark – Oh! quickly string / The harp I yet can
brook to hear') – which attracted Schumann, and the Moore songs were his
'Venetian Airs I and II' ('Row gently here, my gondolier; so softly wake the
tide' and 'When through the Pizzetta / Night breathes her cool air') not lyrics
from his better known 'Irish Melodies'. Schumann's main aim in this collection for his new wife was to express the gamut of emotions and possibilities of
their union. Eight Burns lyrics appeared and they were scattered throughout
the four books or 'Hefte' that Schumann published under the title *Myrthen*.

The first 'Heft' included 'Jemand' ('For the Sake of Somebody') which fitted
perfectly with the other three songs in the group, all of which declare and celebrate love, and the excitement of dreaming of love. The Jacobite allusions of
the Burns text, where 'Somebody' was in fact Bonnie Prince Charlie, are not
noted by Schumann in any way. The second 'Heft' featured 'Die Hochländer-
Witwe' ('The Highland Widow'), an unusual choice alongside a couple of
short Goethe drinking songs and the allegorical 'Lotusblume' ('Lotus Flower')

of Heine and 'Talismane' of Goethe. As Fiske discusses, Schumann had mis-
interpreted the fact that the Burns lyric was a lament (due most probably to
Gerhard's removal of 'Lament' from the title) and produced a fast song with
a wailing declamatory 'O weh! o weh! o weh!' in place of 'Och-on, och-on,
och-rie!'.[36] References to the Highlands and Bonnie Prince Charlie do seem
rather out of place here. The third 'Heft' opens with Burns' 'Hochländers
Abschied' ('My Heart's in the Highlands') and 'Hochländisches Wiegenlied'
('Highland Lullaby' beginning 'Hee balou! My sweet wee Donald'). It then
features the Byron Hebrew Melody, a text by the English poet Catherine
Fanshawe (beginning ''Twas in heaven pronounced – 'twas muttered in
hell') and the two Venetian songs by Thomas Moore. Jon Finson notes that
it might well be called 'The British Collection'.[37] But rather than comprise a
group of British songs it might be argued that this group embodies a fascination for the genre of national or even transnational song. This group works
remarkably well, for Schumann's use of such a diverse range of nationalities
within his texts does much to enhance the universality of the emotions he
wishes to express musically, from the love of home and children (in the
Burns settings), the darkness and sorrow of love (particularly powerful in his
setting of Byron) to the sensuality of the atmospherics of love (so vivid in the
Moore settings). For Schumann these are emotions experienced by everyone
regardless of nationality.

The final fourth 'Heft' includes the remaining four Burns lyrics amongst
other texts by Heine and Rückert. The opening Burns 'Hauptmanns Weib'
('The Captain's Lady' beginning 'O mount and go') is one of the most dramatic and declamatory of settings in the cycle with its tense chromatic bass
line in the piano and its call-to-arms. It is then immediately followed by a
particularly beautiful melody for 'Weit, weit' ('O how can I be Blithe and
Glad'), which really enhances the poignancy of the text. It sits comfortably
with the next song, Heine's 'Was will die einsame Träne' ('Why has this
Solitary Tear Remained from Former Days'). 'Niemand' ('Naebody'), which
Schumann intended as a partner piece for 'Jemand' of Heft I is a rather nice
touch in terms of bringing the cycle to a close and finding some obvious
thematic connections. It makes a fine partner piece to the expressiveness of
'Jemand', for this is a much spikier and more spirited song. 'Im Westen' ('In
the West' beginning 'Out over the Forth') follows and, like 'The Highland
Widow' of Heft II, this song seems a little out of place, with its references
to the Forth and the Highlands. The sentiment of the lyric – the narrator is
looking to the west at sunset because that's where her lover and the father
of her child dwells – is undoubtedly the element of the lyric that attracted
Schumann. This is a very short song, quickly forgotten partly because it is followed by Heine's 'Du Bist wie eine Blume' ('You are Like a Flower'), which is
Schumann at his finest. The final three songs make detailed reference to the

title of Schumann's cycle. Myrtle was a common flower in wedding bouquets and, as Jon Finson has argued, in this cycle Schumann was making a wedding garland or bouquet for Clara.[38] Mention of flowers and roses are scattered throughout the final songs and it is sad that Burns' 'Red, Red Rose', which Schumann also set in 1840, was too late for inclusion, for the sentiments of Burns' highly stylised lyric were perfect for Schumann's intentions.

Schumann's choices of texts certainly show that he was most interested in what he could express musically about a range of specific emotions. In the case of writers from the British Isles he was thus interested in the emotional substance of the texts rather than in any ideas about nation, and he found the lyrical expression of Burns, Byron, Fanshawe and Moore an ideal fit alongside those texts by German lyricists. But it is nonetheless notable that five of his eight Burns songs make direct reference to the north or the Highlands, showing that there is still a certain attraction in the Scottish landscape and in what this northern setting suggests to the Romantic composer. What both Schubert's and Schumann's handling of Scottish texts reveal is a shift away from a focus on 'Volkslieder' and their melodies, from the preoccupation of ideas about national collections of song and poetry, to a freer imaginative musical handling of texts from the north. Sometimes their realisations enhance specific current political issues, as with Schubert's *Ossian* settings; sometimes the texts are sought and lifted purely for the ends of expressing highly personal emotional responses to life and love, as with Schumann. That said, clearly the attraction of Macpherson, Scott and Burns initially for both of these composers had to do with those popular and widely shared ideas of Highland landscape and poetry. Scotland's terrain and her epic and lyric poetic and song texts continued to play a part in European musical composition long after the period we now term 'Romantic', and a fascination for folk melodies and songs was to reappear as the twentieth century dawned and a new period of collecting and archiving began.

CHAPTER FOUR

Gaelic Literature and Scottish Romanticism

Thomas Owen Clancy

Recent work, detailed by Murray Pittock in his introduction to this volume, and well-represented by other contributions, has profoundly altered our sense of how we might employ and interrogate Romanticism within a Scottish context.[1] Two key transformations have been a widening of the chronological scope of Romanticism, to envelop and investigate its roots in the first half of the eighteenth century in Scotland, and the conversion of Scotland from object of the Romantic literary endeavours of largely anglophone practitioners, to the site and subject of the production of literature, some of which was signally influential for both English and European Romanticism. Although some critics (for instance, Pittock and Janet Sorensen) have paid close attention to aspects of the Gaelic cultural milieu, and others have studied the role of the Highlands within the evolving Romantic discourse (for instance, Peter Womack), Gaelic literature itself has been largely absent from recent work. Its place within Scottish Romanticism has chiefly featured in studies of James Macpherson and the Ossianic controversy, and Gaelic scholars have made some notable recent contributions work in that field.[2] Beyond this, critical thinking amongst Gaelic scholars on eighteenth-century Gaelic poetry has been in recent years undergoing considerable reshaping and rethinking, though largely in isolation from the wider discourse regarding Romanticism.[3]

The object of this chapter is to capitalise on both these recent critical trends, and to read Gaelic literature in the eighteenth century 'under the sign' of Scottish Romanticism. Read in this way, 'Gaelic Romanticism' (if we can allow there to have been such a thing) becomes not a mere sub-set of Scottish Romanticism, but rather a problematic counterpart to it. Earlier Gaelic literature, we will see, contained stances and perspectives, themes and genres that became characteristic modes within Romantic literature. To constitute these as anticipatory would be wrong, as we are not dealing here with straightforward evolution or influence (though some of them were arguably captured, remodelled and injected into the international literary scene via Macpherson). Likewise, we can see throughout eighteenth-century

Gaelic poetry innovations and responses to influences from Scottish and wider British literary tastes, though the nature of these responses again rarely allow us to think in terms of direct influence. Rather, within the terms of its own vernacular norms, Gaelic literature underwent its own revolution in perspective, in literary modes and in expectations, a revolution that had some of the same roots and cultural contexts as wider Scottish Romanticism, but nonetheless produced an aesthetically distinct body of work.

It will help to focus briefly on a particular case. The profile of the Scottish Gaelic poet William Ross (Uilleam Ros, 1762–1791) has been seen since his own times as fitting well the Romantic paradigm, both in his poetic works and especially in his biography. A journeying poet, most famous for his personal songs of romantic love, he died early of consumption, and had a famously tragic love affair that became the material for some of his most important poems. His works were, supposedly, burnt before he died, but later recorded from oral tradition, being published both in anthologies such as the Stewart Collection of 1804, and later in John Mackenzie's collected editions, from 1833 to 1834.[4] In his most famous poem, he forecast his own ultimate destination as being 'talla nam bàrd nach beò' ('the hall of the bards who no longer live'). No surprise, then, that Gaelic critics from the nineteenth century on should see in Ross 'the Gaelic Keats' or 'the Gaelic Burns': 'our thoughts expand and kindle with his sentiments'.[5] In an important diptych of recent articles, William Gillies has called attention to how sensitively we need to treat all aspects of Ross' profile. In particular, he notes the three-fold possibilities for critical reading of what has seemed most innovative and striking in Ross' work: that Ross draws on a deep well of Gaelic tradition, and draws on it in somewhat different ways from many of his contemporaries; that he responded both to the inspiration of the Ossianic as branded by James Macpherson, as well as to the demands of the Highlander and Gaelic bard as constructed within his work; and/or that he was an innovator responding to the *Zeitgeist* of the final quarter of the eighteenth century, aware not just of shifts in Gaelic poetry, but of the wider world of Scottish and English literary trends.[6]

The critical dilemma is well illustrated in one verse to which Gillies calls our attention, from Ross' dialogue poem between the poet and the mountain Blaven ('Còmhradh eadar am Bard agus Blàth-bheinn'):

Chaill na h-ionadan am blàth,
Is thriall gach àrmuinn àigh g'a uaigh;
Thréig a' chruit a h-inneal dána,
's leig a' chlàrsach bàs a fuaim.
(The places have lost their bloom, / and every successful warrior has departed
to his grave; / the harp has forsaken its indenture to Poetry (*or* its poetic
facility), / and the clarsach has let its sound die.[7]

Although both the Romantic credentials and the Ossianic tone of such a statement seem evident, nonetheless, as Gillies notes, the sentiments and the structure and mode of the poem itself owe much to a earlier work by Iain Mac Aoidh, am Pìobaire Dall (1656–1754). The poem is 'Cumha Coire an Easa', in which the poet engages in dialogue with the echo of a waterfall, and 'which sounds a very similar note within pre-Ossianic Gaelic literature, and would surely have been well known to its creator's grandson, William Ross'.[8] So what was Ross doing here? Was he innovating, imitating or updating?

This dilemma may be used as a mirror for a wider difficulty facing critical study of both Gaelic and Scottish literature during the eighteenth century. It is evident that Gaelic literature underwent a radical transformation during this period. But to what extent was that transformation one energised from within by historical and meta-literary factors local to the language and culture that produced it; and to what extent was this the absorption of influence from elsewhere? One way to explore this difficulty may be through the rough out- lines of Scottish Romanticism drawn by Murray Pittock in the introduction to this volume. He notes five distinctive features of Scottish Romanticism. For each of these, we may find Gaelic counterparts, but comparison is vexed by difference, and in particular by the presence of some of these characteristics in earlier, sometimes much earlier Gaelic literary tradition.

Without doubt the most distinctive and transformed aspect of the literary context for Gaelic in the eighteenth century was the nature of the networks and channels of literary production. Gone or going were the straightforward lines of professional poetic allegiance to their patrons (though in a variety of ways the aesthetics of praise and the instinct of the panegyric remained embedded in Gaelic literature's DNA right up to the twentieth century). Print, which began to work for Gaelic literature from 1751 on, gave very different access to very different audiences, and created a complex and still little explored relationship between print and oral culture, something true also of the better-studied anglophone writing in the same period.[9] There was also renewed interchange between English and Scots writing and Gaelic poets. Both Allan Ramsay and James Thomson can be seen as having a strong and lasting effect on Gaelic literature of the period, on the develop- ing genre of seasonal and nature poetry, on the strong preference for the pastoral setting of erotic poems, and even on the choice of song-settings for Gaelic poems. While notable recent contributions by Ronald Black and Christopher MacLachlan have explored the networks a poet like Alasdair mac Mhaighstir Alasdair might have plugged into, whilst in the Lowlands[10] we should not underestimate the power of the wider networks established by print. Maolcholaim Scott has noted, for instance, that John Campbell, 2nd Duke of Argyll (1678–1743), subscribed to Thomson's 1730 edition of *The Seasons*: Campbell was patron to the musician, scribe and poet Uilleam

MacMhurchaidh (c.1700–1778), whose poetry both of nature and of praise Scott has analysed as being influenced by Thomson.[11]

The role of these new networks has begun to emerge as a central theme and opportunity for interrogating this period in Gaelic literature. Work is still ongoing, but we may wish to engage in some preliminary observations about the role played by formal and informal networks. Two aspects of this stand out: elite patrons, whose financial support for poets was something crucial across the linguistic spectrum, had the capacity to change the reception and the production of poetry during this period. And we see ministers operating throughout this period as mediators, whether it be as transcribers of the poetry of Donnchadh Bàn Mac an t-Saoir, translators of Ossian or collectors of heroic ballads.[12] Both sets of individuals had considerable exposure to changing literary tastes furth of the Highlands; and they display interest in Gaelic language and literature, as also in classical learning and current taste.

As Scottish literature began to express its distinctness during this period through a variety of strategies, so too do we see a growing self-consciousness within Gaelic literature of its being Gaelic literature in contradistinction to other literatures. The final ebbing of the Classical Gaelic literary norm and the system that sustained it no doubt had much to do with this, as also with the new awareness of Scottish Gaelic's linguistic state and status. The rising genre of poetry of praise to the Gaelic languages has been explored very productively by Wilson McLeod[13] – we might, however, also set it within an emerging Gaelic discourse about the essential characteristics of Gaelic culture and literature. Such self-construction was fostered by the anti-Jacobite legislation of 1747, which spurred Gaelic poetry in praise of items that became even more closely identified with Highland culture than they had previously been (this is to gloss over somewhat the much more complex trajectories of these items and the images they created across Scotland during the seventeenth and early eighteenth century, and in particular in conjunction with the Jacobite rebellions, on which there is a growing and sophisticated historiography). Chief among these were Highland dress and the pipes, and as early as the late 1740s poetry was being created in praise of these items and in disprise of the legislation and the new modes it sought to introduce.[14] Of course, this set Gaelic literature on a convergence course with wider Scottish literature later in the century, as a now-romanticised Jacobitism, and a resignified Highland dress became part of the creation of a renewed, and more positive, stereotype of the Highlander. The rise of external literature about the Highlands can be seen as reinforcing – through ingestion, internalisation and reproduction – externally defined characteristics of the Gael, the 'auto-exoticism' mentioned, via Joep Leersen, in Pittock's introduction. So too, we might see the gradual appearance of negative reactions, played out in some of the critical introductions to various poets, to the innovations and experiments of the mid-eighteenth century, best seen in criticisms by Gaelic editors of Mac Mhaighstir Alasdair's use of English words, phrases, ideas and modes.

It is probably Alasdair mac Mhaighstir Alasdair (Alexander MacDonald, c.1695–1770) who best illustrates what Pittock has described in his introduction as the use of 'hybrid language and variable register to both simultaneously reveal and conceal the self'. The tension between high and low, between Scots and English does not map precisely onto the Gaelic situation – though the eighteenth century sees the final death of Classical Gaelic as a literary language in Scotland, and in mid-century we can see poets who are adept at adapting and employing classical modes in new vernacular contexts. Mac Mhaighstir Alasdair is probably the rangiest of the poets, his lexis flying within brief stanzas from easy English loan to dense tapestries of detailed Gaelic names for flora and fauna – the opening and middle of his 'Allt-an-t-Siucair' are good contrasts. We find high and low tone here, the smut of his 'Praise of Morag' and the vague classicism of his 'Address to the Muses'. We find experimentation with native art-forms, such as the transformation of the variations of pìobaireachd into a structure for long poems and the making of an 'art' version of a waulking song (the parallels with Ramsay and the later Burns are evident, if sporadic). But Mac Mhaighstir Alasdair is not the only poet whose work in mid-century has been seen as invested with Bakhtinian 'heteroglossia': Uilleam MacMhurchaidh likewise has been seen as fusing medieval and (Gaelic) classical inheritance with innovative and of-the-moment tropes and perspectives.[15]

Pittock's two final features of Scottish Romanticism are the ones with the longest pedigree. He invokes 'the taxonomy of glory', a feature well-developed in this period of Gaelic verse, but one with very deep roots and a highly-wrought register within the language. The evoking of past glories as a means of questioning the present can be found in key poems from the sixteenth through to the eighteenth century, its culmination being perhaps the series of poems on the withered chieftain's hall, best evinced by An Clàrsair Dall's 'Song to MacLeod of Dunvegan' (c.1694), which dramatises his dialogue with the Echo of the deserted hall of Dunvegan.[16] Here too we might see some accidental convergence of Gaelic modes with Romantic choices and preferences, with Highland bards here fulfilling both Ossianic and Romantic Jacobite types in their focus on chieftainship, ideal qualities and extinguished glories.

As for 'the performance of the self in diaspora': we may take Donnchadh Bàn Mac an t-Saoir's several meditations on his homeland Perthshire hills, and in particular his 'Final Farewell to the Mountains' as perhaps the best examples of this mode in verse of the Romantic period.[17] Donnchadh Bàn (Duncan Macintyre, 1724–1812) was a self-conscious performer of his distance from his homeland, in his Edinburgh poems and in toasting poems written for Highland societies. But the literary-self-as-exile had a very deep pedigree in Gaelic: one thinks in particular of the much-employed poetic voice of Colum Cille (St Columba), meditating on his lost Irish homelend, a literary 'moment' explored in several poems across the centuries;[18] or, indeed, the voice of the remnant, one might almost say revenant, Fenian warriors, expounding tales of past glory and meditating in verse upon the places of the past, from their chronological and theological distance. Donnchadh Bàn could not help being aware of some poetry of this sort; Anja Gunderloch and Pat Menzies have explored his employment of both Fenian ballad and the haunting and meditative 'Oran na Comhachaig' (a poem we will discuss at the end of this chapter) in his verse.[19]

The critical hinge here is undoubtedly Macpherson's Ossianic creations, which have since their publication posed critics with similar questions of their relationship to tradition. Eager to defend and incorporate Macpherson's sentimental ancient Gaelic world into Gaelic literature, poets during this period converted his Ossianisms into Gaelic poetry, made declarations about its authenticity and worth, and began to measure past and contemporary Gaelic poetry against its rather anomalous yardstick. This disabling trend has perhaps been the underlying cause of modern critics hesitating before engaging with the less straightforward traces of Gaelic tradition within Macpherson's work, keen not to invest it with a variety of stereotypical cringes, nostalgia and melancholy among them.[20] Likewise, it is difficult to hear Gaelic influence on wider Scottish literature of the period, due to the Ossianic static on the line. It is important to revisit earlier as well as eighteenth-century Gaelic literature to get a more rounded sense of the extent to which Ossian really punctuated the period for Gaelic literature. Important too to remind ourselves that Macpherson was not the first to align earlier Gaelic poetry with romantic literary ideals. Jerome Stone's preface to his version of the ballad 'The Death of Fraoch' pulls on very similar and significant strings:

> Several of these performances are to be met with, which, for sublimity of senti-
> ment, nervousness of expression, and high spirited metaphor, are hardly to be
> equalled among the chief productions of the most cultivated nations. Others of
> them breathe such tenderness and simplicity, as must be affecting to every mind
> that is in the least tinctured with the softer passions of pity and humanity.[21]

Thus, in drawing a picture of 'Gaelic Romanticism' we might invoke several key alignments with the wider Scottish Romanticism to which it relates, as well as noting some crucial differences which produced its distinct aesthetic. The rise to prominence of the reflective and emotive self within

Gaelic poetry of this period parallels that seen elsewhere, and is allied to new modes of production, in particular the publication of the poetry collections of individual poets, complete with a new focus on the (often romanticised) biographies of these bards. The literary productions of this period celebrate and curate the past, something also realised in efforts of collection and the publication of anthologies. These in turn produced a new critical mode, and the evolution of selectivity and taste. Despite this, the literature itself is, up to the early nineteenth century, only in rather particular ways inflected by Scots and English literary influences – a prominent and pervasive example might be the Scots and English songs whose tunes formed the ground on which poets built their works. The aesthetics largely conform to Gaelic modes, even when they are at their most innovative – witness the development of the experimental long poem based on the musical variants of pipe music by both Alasdair mac Mhaighstir Alasdair and Donnchadh Bàn Mac an t-Saoir.[22] And even whilst foregrounding certain stances and themes that might be seen as typical of Romantic literature, for instance, the narrative monologue, praise of nature, nostalgia for the places and people of the past, romantic love within a wild setting, these draw, as we have already noted, on very long pedigrees within Gaelic literary tradition.

The period of concentration is best book-ended by two crucial publications, each of which illustrate some of the transformations and tendencies that concern us. The year 1751 saw the publication by Alasdair mac Mhaighstir Alasdair of his *Ais-eiridh na Sean Chánoin Albannaich*. This was the first secular book to be published in Gaelic, a collection of poems by the poet himself that were bold, innovative, racy and provocative. As Ronald Black makes clear,[24] the book was dangerous, containing obscenity and sedition, alongside and within its riveting poetry. At one level his poems may be read against the political turbulence of the previous decades, and they certainly foreground, as well encode, Jacobite views. But the author's voice and his playful and receptive innovations with form and lexis (his texts bristle creatively with Scots and English words), as well as his generic choices – frank sexual encomium, praise of nature, an elegy for a pet dove – marked this debut out as a new moment for Gaelic literature. So too it was a debut for a new and overt (though arguably unfulfilled) attempted rapprochement between Gaelic and anglophone literature, signalled both by Mac Mhaighstir Alasdair's title ('Resurrection of the Old Scottish – not 'Gaelic' – Language') and by his preface in which he openly invites the consideration of the nation at large.

Mac Mhaighstir Alasdair's collection must be placed in the context of greater access to print and a newly evolving complex of patronage networks of Gaelic print literature by the elite and by the minister-class. It heralded and empowered a steady flow over the succeeding decades of the publication

of poetry collections of individual poets. These collections deserve a comprehensive study. While most to some extent perpetuate older mainstream forms
of praise and satire (as do Scots and English language collections, though this
aspect of them has largely been overlooked in favour of their more innova-
tive/lyric choices), there are nonetheless emergent genres. These include
drinking and smoking songs, poems in praise of the Gaelic language, dress
and the pipes, nature poetry, pastorals and in particular songs of romantic
love. They mark these publications out as products of a new paradigm, their
authors as emerging from different social contexts. What made collections of
this sort possible was the Romantic foregrounding of the emotional self, and
the creation of a literary type of the speaker responding to the world around
them, to events both profound and mundane.

There is a considerable range among these collections of individual poets,
with contrasting levels of access to literacy, recourse to oral or imported
modes, self-control and self-performance of their product. The networks of
support that allowed these individual collections have begun to be explored,
making clear the extent of small-scale investment in these poetic products
across the social classes.[24] One poet, Duncan Campbell, a Cowal soldier,
seems to have dragooned his fellow soldiers and commanding officers into
subscribing to his collection, published in 1798 in Cork. The book combines
local praise poetry with some wider topics, in particular love poems.[25]

The experience of Donnchadh Bàn Mac an t-Saoir is notable. As far as
we can tell he was illiterate, and several ministers participated in the record-
ing of and seeing through the press of his poems. This said, he was party to
the publication, and able to engage with further editions, augmenting them
over the course of his lifetime, and some of his final poems seem by nature
of commentary on his earlier work, and arguably address an attentive public.
He was also committed to these publications, raising subscriptions himself in
journeys through the Gàidhealtachd.[26] It is easy to compare him with Hogg,
though he shares little of Hogg's metropolitanism or sophisticated hybridity.
Nonetheless he is in one sense the first 'urban' Gaelic poet, his residency
in Edinburgh and poetry for, for instance, the London Highland Society
plugging into the newly emerging civic networks of Gaels.

By contrast, we may point to Ewan MacLachlan, librarian in King's
College Aberdeen, whose Gaelic poems are only a small part of his 1816
Metrical Effusions, which are mostly in English, but substantially also in Latin,
with some in Greek and Gaelic. Further Gaelic poems had appeared in earlier
anthologies and in later publications, including his classy suite of poems
on the seasons. Some sense of the world he came to inhabit is to be gained
from his 'Elegy on James Beattie' (Professor of History in the University of
Aberdeen, 1767–1810), the nephew of James Beattie (1735–1803), Professor
of Moral Philosopher in the same university, and important figure in the

philosophical and literary debates of the latter part of the century. The elegy itself, however, displays rather MacLachlan's knowledge of Gaelic classical conventions.[27]

A poet deserving mention in this context also is Dughall Bochanan (Dugald Buchanan, 1716–1768). Donald Meek's recent work has revealed to us Bochanan's heavy indebtedness to anglophone literature, especially to the hymn-writing of the period, as well as the way in which Bochanan's studies in Glasgow University and his mixing with the learned and literary set of the Scottish Lowlands channelled a flow of less overt influences into his poetry. Most notably, Meek has made a case for Bochanan as in many ways the most thoroughly 'romantic' poet in terms of his literary compositions themselves, albeit this is a poetry of religious conviction.[28]

A final example to round off this list might be the newly 'rediscovered' Atholl poet Mairearad Ghriogarach (Margaret MacGregor, c.1750–1820), whose poem collection was published posthumously in 1831, but whose oeuvre shows a striking range, as well as a certain self-consciousness in composition.[29] From her we have poetry on her own wedding, on her young daughter (later herself to become a poet) sick with fever, on her homesickness, away in sewing school at Perth – for all her reasonably *sotto voce* public profile, there is a crafted subjectivity to these personal poems which make clear how deep the modes of the age had penetrated.

The period is suitably closed by the 1841 publication of John MacKenzie's *Sar-Obair nam Bard Gaelach*, an anthology that did much to establish the canon of modern Gaelic poetry. MacKenzie played an interesting, if not perhaps conscious, double game in his anthology. His critical instincts drew him to much of the most impressive verse, and his judgements may be set against the staying power of most of the poets he selected within Gaelic literary studies. Yet, the introductions, and in particular the large introduction supplied by Logan, were written under the conscious influence of Ossianic and Romantic critical standards. But it also capped a century of collecting and publishing, selecting from previous collections and incorporating material from his own sources. Comment has been made elsewhere in this volume on Allan Ramsay's collecting activities as helping to energise the emergence of poetic forms based on earlier and more demotic poetry in Scots. We can see similar energies and cross currents in the Gaelic context too, partly no doubt inspired by Ramsay. Mac Mhaighstir Alasdair himself envisaged an anthology of Gaelic poetry, a vision which speaks both of his sense of Gaelic's place within a wider Scottish literary world, and also his acquaintance with and curation of earlier literature (he was, we may note, competent in earlier Gaelic script).[30] This ambition was realised by his son in the 1776 Eigg Collection, which opened a current of like-minded anthologies: Gillies (1786), Stewart (1804), MacLeod (1811), Turner (1813), for instance. The

mix in these collections is interesting. Current poets jostle with the powerful verse of the sixteenth, seventeenth and early eighteenth centuries, the
'old songs' so valued later by Sorley MacLean for their concreteness and
stark realism, but we may suspect valued by this generation for their emotive
rawness, foregrounded subjectivity and hints at romantic narrative.

Prominent too in the mix are both Ossianic imitations (that is,
Gaelicisations of Macpherson's efforts, as well as some poetry composed
under the influence, such as 'Miann a' Bhàird Aosda') and genuine Gaelic
heroic ballads. The collection of the latter predates by some measure, and
without doubt influenced, Macpherson. Although the publication of this
material was partly sparked by the vogue for Ossian and the desire to com-
plement his work in an authenticating way, in fact the considerable interest
in and collection of this sort of verse were already in evidence. The wider
motivations for this interest need to be sought elsewhere. The manuscript
collections of the period are particularly informative in this regard.

The manuscripts of Uilleam MacMhurchaidh help to show the various literary tides washing around in the middle decades of the eighteenth century.
A talented and quirky poet himself, as well as a musician, his manuscripts
see him preserving and, as I and others have argued, adapting and improving, earlier (sometimes much earlier) poetry, to which he may have had both
aural and scribal access.[31] He preserves Gaelic heroic ballads, both those
relating to Fionn, Oisean, Oscar and Caoilte (the underlying characters of
Macpherson's recreations), and also some of the dramatic poetry from the
Ulster Cycle tales, such as that of Deirdriu and most particularly the tale of
the Death of Cú Chulainn. This last is interesting given the mix of Fionn
and Cú Chulainn to be found in Macpherson's work, as also for the tone
and perspective of these poems, spoken apostrophes by characters within a
tragic narrative of glory, heroism and death. The poems appear here as fragments, 'relics' divorced from their prose narrative context, a context that
must be inferred from the allusions of the speakers themselves. This is a
mode common also to the Fenian literature. And, of course, it is a mode that
Macpherson adopts, one we may parallel in the Scots and Border ballads,
but also, of course, one characteristic of Romantic literature and of interest
within Romantic discourse. MacMhurchaidh was also someone in touch with
the times – a reader of the new periodicals if we may guess from some of his
inclusions of English verses, most likely available to him from such sources.
He is influenced in his praise poetry as in his nature poetry by Thomson's *The
Seasons* and aware early on of Mac Mhaighstir Alasdair's work.

Collectors, anthologisers, refashioners: the cultivation of earlier poetry,
whether by wholesale reinterpretation in the pages of James Macpherson,
classical inflections in stately poetry by accomplished bards, or jazzed-up versions of medieval verse *fabliaux*, make clear that, as in Scottish Romanticism

more widely, the past was part of the new present. There is not space here to explore one final important issue, the way in which Gaelic literature of earlier periods displayed some of the stances and modes that we might otherwise associate with Romanticism. We might, for example, look to the charged psychological verse monologues placed in the mouth of literary characters at watershed moments in their narrative; to dialogues between interrogators and the natural world, or visitors from the past; to meditations on the past channelled through the objects belonging to people now dead; to evocations of place and of the wilderness; to poems in which the speakers explore the multi-layered nature of perception. These are a rich part of the Gaelic literary inheritance, especially that of medieval Ireland. Importantly, almost all these features are strongly in evidence in the genre of medieval Gaelic literature with the widest currency, and the most direct influence on Gaelic and Scottish Romanticism, *Fiannaigheacht*, the literature relating to Fionn and his warrior-bands, the background literature for Ossian.[32]

In making a case for a 'Gaelic Romanticism', this chapter mainly suggests that it will be instructive for critics of both Gaelic literature and Scottish literature in Scots and English of this period to read these literatures in parallel. There are few easy ways to understand their parallel developments in tandem, few enough straightforward crossovers (though as we have seen, they are there), and the search for these can be disappointing. Macpherson's Ossian is too tight and too transformative a conduit through which to force all of Gaelic literary influence on wider Scottish literature. So also, it is too easy to attribute Gaelic innovations of the period to imitation and colonisation, whether by backdated Macphersonianism or some other process. Instead, common contexts; similar reactions to the same influences, refracted through the prisms of distinct literary traditions and modes; interwoven networks, audiences and patrons with changing tastes – all these allow us to see Gaelic literature as playing a full part in a wider Scottish Romantic century.

It is worth closing with one very specific example of crossover and translation. Anne Grant of Laggan (1755–1838) has a curious and unique position as a mediator of Gaelic culture within the networks of later Scottish Romanticism. A detached resident and observer of Highland culture, many of her works equate to an extended 'travelogue' within what became her home. Her own poems extended to effusive sub-Ossianic productions, but she also engaged in some translations of Gaelic literature. Notable among her choices are the problematic 'Miann a' Bhàird Aosda' ('The Aged Bard's Wish'), and the much older 'Òran na Comhachaig' ('Song of the Owl of Strone'). This latter poem is a strange and 'singular' creation, ascribed, probably correctly, to the sixteenth-century poet Domhnall mac Fhionnlaigh nan Dàn, and preserved in a variety of largely eighteenth-century sources.[33] The speaker (perhaps speakers) engage in a series of dialogues, in particular with the eponymous Owl of Strone. These explore, emotively, the passing of time through the revisiting of the landscape of memory, and an evocation of the perils of old age. Although Anne Grant had some peculiar notions concerning the authorship of the poem, it is clear she saw it as fulfilling in many respects a Romantic agenda: 'the power of the inventive and discriminating faculties are peculiarly exhibited;– the glowing fancy, that embellishes, with a thousand beauties of its own creation, scenes rugged and barren in the extreme to an ordinary mind.'[34] Grant supplied this poem to Walter Scott, and he makes reference to it in *The Antiquary*.

What is interesting here is not so much the Romantic interpretation and repositioning of a sixteenth-century Gaelic poem, but the fact that they converge here with vernacular Gaelic taste. 'Òran na Comhachaig' first appears in manuscripts from the mid-eighteenth century. It was, however, much anthologised and collected (we find it in both the manuscripts of Uilleam MacMhurchaidh and the anthology of John MacKenzie, at either end of our period) and imitated, as Pat Menzies has shown with examples from Donnchadh Bàn and Iain MacCodrum. The valuation of this poem has, no doubt, something to do with its apparent fulfilling of the Romantic criteria for Gaelic poetry – a bard in a desolate landscape interrogating the ruins of memory – as well as its own appropriation of the tropes of Fenian ballads. But both anglophone Romantic writers and Gaelic collectors and editors have here converged to preserve and highlight a poem that was, in fact, invested with a singular power borne of its evocation of the self in the wilderness. What is highlighted by this instance of 'Gaelic Romanticism' was, as this chapter argues was often the case, something that was actually latent, and occasionally overt, in the Gaelic literary tradition itself.

CHAPTER FIVE

Travel Writing and the Picturesque

Matthew Wickman

In a chapter entitled 'Highland Minstrelsy', Walter Scott leads his protago-nist out of a Highland castle, through a 'wild, bleak, and narrow valley', past two brooks (one 'placid', the other 'all foam and uproar'), and into a 'land of romance'. This *locus amoenus* consists of rocks of 'a thousand [. . .] varied forms', a 'forbid[ding]' crag, and a dizzying chasm with 'a rustic bridge' made of two overlaid pines, all of which form a kind of 'sylvan amphitheatre' in which the ravishing Flora Mac-Ivor charms young Edward Waverley into temporarily taking up the Jacobite cause.[1] The scene is 'roman[tic]' for it exists nowhere as such, but is instead composed of commonplaces from the growing body of eighteenth- and early nineteenth-century travel literature about Scotland. Accordingly, the scene is in some ways thoroughly typical. It unites such reputed antitheses as Highland and Lowland (in labelling Flora's bardic, Ossianic song a 'minstrel' production), Celtic and Saxon (in the 'fur[y]' of the one stream and the 'sullen' character of the other), and Jacobite and Whig (in the prospective merger of Flora and Edward). What is more, by 1814, when *Waverley* was published, these romantic fea-tures were already typical of Scott's own work, representing something of a command performance of the imagery of his popular 1810 poem *The Lady of the Lake*. Indeed, Scott's work operated here in something of a feedback loop: John Glendening remarks that it 'helped make Scotland not merely acceptable to England but powerfully desirable', fuelling a tourist industry from whose literature Scott's own poetry and fiction had initially drawn sustenance.[2]

This chapter discusses some of the key figures and dates associated with this burgeoning industry, but is ultimately most interested in the recursive loop between Scottish Romanticism and the picturesque. The key point is not merely that many texts from the Romantic period abound in striking natural imagery, but rather that the discursive structure of this imagery, this 'scene of writing' (to borrow an expression from Jacques Derrida), has come to inform the very concept of Scottish Romanticism itself.[3] Scott's chapter on 'Highland Minstrelsy' provides a fortuitous template here, for it exhibits

a curious hallmark of travel writing in the picturesque mode, abounding
in topographical types – in visual tropes, as it were – but also imparting a
sense that we behold more than meets the eye. Or rather, in this instance
and arguably in Scottish Romanticism generally, the 'more' is precisely
what the eye beholds. As Murray Pittock argues, while Scott appears to
present a 'union landscape', melding diverse historical elements with a
single stroke of the pen, and while he thus succeeds in suppressing certain
refractory political and cultural elements of this history, it is also true that
the visual features Scott describes possess a logic – and even 'voices' – of
their own: 'One can suppress the terrible, sublime, threatening, alien, and
Gaelic qualities of Jacobitism with relief and sympathy, but how does one
suppress' the Scottish landscape itself?[4] By the time Scott was writing, the
Scottish Highlands especially conjured associations less of beauty – and of
the harmonising, unionising poetics which Scott mapped onto it – than of
sublimity. Sublime imagery, however, was virtually an oxymoron inasmuch
as sublimity designated the putative limits of visual conception, an excess
of stimuli reprocessed as sentiment but also, notably, as sound. In Part Five
of A Philosophical Enquiry, Edmund Burke associated sublimity with Milton's
resonant blank verse; in Scottish writing, sublime Highland scenery – its
assemblage of mountains, heaths, winds and waters – accorded topographical
atmosphere to numerous texts, perhaps most famously the orotund Ossian of
James Macpherson.[5] Flora's theatrical song in Scott's 'Highland Minstrelsy'
episode, for example, draws upon Macpherson as well as travel-literature
references to Ossian's Hall, a viewing room over the dramatic Falls of the
Bran on the estate of the Duke of Atholl.[6] Within the context of Waverley,
then, Flora's performance amounts to Scott's narratorial illustration of a
web of sensual and cultural associations which can be neither narrated nor
illustrated – not fully: it is a presentation, Jean-François Lyotard would say,
of the fact that the unpresentable exists.[7]

   This is one of Lyotard's formulations of modern art, though it stands for
Lyotard as a figure for postmodernism which is itself an extension of the
sublime. What is most interesting here is less Lyotard's specific argument
than the mottled nature of his category, which seems less descriptive of
the sublime than the picturesque, which in the Romantic period expressly
concerned itself with the challenges of representation. 'In the early decades
of the eighteenth century,' Walter John Hipple remarks, the term 'usually
bore one of two meanings: when applied to literary style, it meant "vivid"
or "graphic", by an obvious metaphor; when applied to scenes in nature,
and sometimes when applied to imitations of these on canvas or in words,
it meant "eminently suitable for pictorial representation", as affording a
well-composed picture [. . .]'.[8] Later in the century, in the landmark treatises
on landscape and travel that brought the 'picturesque' into the lexicon of

aesthetic discourse, the term increasingly occupied a philosophical position between the beautiful and the sublime. William Gilpin, whose tours across Britain helped affix the language and customs of travel through Scotland, sought to carve an autonomous niche for the picturesque by distinguishing those objects 'illustrated in painting' from those 'which please the eye in their natural state', assigning the picturesque to the province of art.[9] His touchstone for making this case, however, was beauty – beautiful objects versus beautiful representations – whereas for Uvedale Price, who also forged a distinct place for the picturesque, the category tended more toward the sublime: 'A temple or palace of Grecian architecture in its perfect entire state, and its surface and colour smooth and even, either in painting or reality, is beautiful; in ruin it is picturesque.' The latter involves roughness, irregularity and 'intricacy', which denotes 'a partial and uncertain concealment' rather than classic hallmarks of the beautiful like 'high polish and flowing lines'.[10] Hence, for Price, what we behold in the picturesque is concealment made manifest, a vivid rendering of gloom – which is to say, in Lyotard's terminology, a presentation of the otherwise unpresentable.[11]

Such motifs informed travel narratives of Scotland (especially the Highlands) before Gilpin, though they became a fixture in the 1770s. This was the decade when a number of influential travellers made their way through Scotland, from Gilpin (1776) and Thomas Pennant (1772) to Samuel Johnson (1773) and Tobias Smollett's fictive party in *The Expedition of Humphry Clinker* (1771). In Smollett's text the irascible but articulate Matthew Bramble composes a letter describing the Highlands as a transcendent region 'beyond imagination' that strikes the gaze as though it were 'a vast fantastic vision in the clouds'.[12] He then, aptly, and for the only time in the novel, breaks into poetry – an ode, no less, the great eighteenth-century vehicle of emotional transport. The shift in literary modes is significant here, as are Bramble's declarations of virtual ineffability (i.e., of 'fantastic[al] vision[s]'), for they illustrate how gloom, or a degree of inveterate secrecy or of incommunicability, proceeded from expression itself and not only from what the (itinerant) artist failed (verbally) to paint.

Vivid obscurity; eloquent stammering: these were key features of picturesque Scottish travel narratives, and often the manner in which they were articulated. In some of them, the exigencies of description pushed their authors to catachresis, like when the Reverend Charles Cordiner wrote to Pennant and assured him that the ruins to which the latter had turned his attention would 'be faithfully copied in some of their most expressive views'.[13] Cordiner's 'expressive views', or 'speaking scenery' we might call it, exhibited the synaesthesia (or sensual confusion) which was a common feature of Highland travel narratives. James Cririe employed it as a poetic strategy in a work entitled *Scottish Scenery: Or, Sketches in Verse*, which took after James Thomson's influential paeans to nature in *The Seasons*, though adding a more overtly fanciful component:

> Entrenchments deep, and haunts of heroes old,
> The warlike champions of those barren wilds;
> The grave of Ossian, and the ruin'd halls
> Of dauntless Fingal, Morven's mighty Chief,
> Amid these mountains, now are wrapt in mist.[14]

Here the poet and the 'barren wilds' alike envelop us in a kind of vatic 'mist' inasmuch as the 'heroes old' materialise out of a landscape that is the vehicle rather than the object of vision; indeed, the 'solitary pine' and 'lofty shelving banks' recede from view once the 'grave of Ossian' comes into the imagined line of sight. William Wordsworth later and more famously performed a similar operation in the poems he wrote about his experience in Scotland, in one instance converting a 'solitary Highland lass' into a muse for his own auratic fantasy 'Of travellers in some shady haunt' – not in a Scottish glen but rather 'Among Arabian sands'.[15]

The fact that Wordsworth's muse is a labourer only makes his poem more picturesque, as rural peasantry makes up an important feature of many of the narratives and paintings of this genre. Several of Gilpin's iconic sketches display peasants at their margins, providing local colour as well as perspective for the scale of the mountains and distances. Later travellers who engaged Gilpin in his aesthetics also assimilated this identification of the landscape with peasantry. For example, in his 1800 account of a tour through the Highlands, Thomas Garnett asserted that the ruins of the fort of Dunglass 'are low and inconsiderable, and by no means so picturesque an object as represented by Gilpin', though the latter 'justly remarks' on the magnificence of Dumbarton Castle. He then proceeds one step further, commenting that 'a grotesque piece of rock' at the top of a mountain over Loch Long bears some 'resemblance to the figure of a cobler [sic] in a working attitude upon his stall'.[16] Garnett's remarks here actually duplicated those of John Lettice in his 1792 tour through the region: the 'lofty crag, on the summit of [this] mountain [. . .] presents a grotesque piece of rock, so exactly like the figure of a cobler [sic], in his working attitude upon his stall, that it never fails to suggest that resemblance to every traveller, who sees it'. (Lettice's account may also have been instrumental to Wordsworth, for Lettice later relates a conversation he had with 'a young female Highlander', who rehearsed poetry and music of a 'melancholy, and highly elegant' air. 'Hey-day! said [Lettice] to [him]self, who knows, but [he] may have been listening to a descendant of one of the old bards? Long may have been the line of her fathers, and old Ossian himself, her great progenitor!')[17] Relative to peasantry the principal point here is that what is essentially window dressing in Gilpin's work becomes the face of nature itself in Garnett's and Lettice's: picturesque language here converts human activity into the appearance of purely objective reality; it makes 'portraits' into 'nature'.

The Scottish painter David Wilkie provides a helpful point of contrast here, for he was highly attentive to peasants and the working class, illustrating in elegant and often poignant detail the lives of subjects elsewhere reduced to mere symbols.[18] Critics in the 1980s, following John Barrell's lead, appeared to share Wilkie's sensibilities more than Garnett's, remarking on how, for example, the aesthetics of the picturesque ran counter to the agricultural revolution and thus ratified rural poverty on account of its agreeable effects.[19] In his influential 1989 analysis of Highland romance, Peter Womack inflated the picturesque into a symbol of bourgeois complacency: the 'mountains of Lochaber or Assynt, the rocks of the west coast, and the treeless Hebrides, [sic] seemed to most eighteenth-century visitors to pose [. . .] a choice between abandoning the country to its hopeless sterility and intervening in vigorous and visible ways'. Proponents of the picturesque, and of Highland romance more generally, reportedly took the latter position and so promoted an 'aesthetics of Improvement', a rationale for modernising agricultural practices and the backwards habitudes of rural societies. '[S]terility', by contrast, implied an aura of sublimity which, because it was allegedly 'unimprovable', also elicited a politics of resistance, of social critique.[20]

Womack's dialectical categories – 'improvement' and the picturesque on the one hand, 'sterility' and the sublime on the other – echo texts that bear an important historical relationship with Scottish Romanticism. But together these texts tell a rather different story from Womack's. The first comes from Edmund Burt, an engineer contracted by General George Wade to build military roads in the Scottish Highlands after the 1715 Jacobite Rising, and who in the early 1720s composed a series of letters to a 'friend in London'. The letters are remembered primarily for the contempt they express for the poverty of the inhabitants and the desolation of the landscape. Writing almost a half-century prior to Macpherson, Burt finds the mountains 'rude and offensive' to the sight, characterised by 'stupendous bulk, frightful irregularity, and horrid gloom'.[21] But roughly a century and a half later, and more than fifty years after Scott's *Waverley*, Highland desolation bore a very different significance. In 1867, Karl Marx asserted that

what 'clearing of estates' really and properly signifies, we learn only in the Highlands of Scotland, the promised land of modern romantic novels. There the process is distinguished by its systematic character, by the magnitude of the scale on which it is carried out at one blow [. . .] and finally by the peculiar form of property under which the embezzled lands were held.[22]

For Marx, Highland barrenness was a function less of the landscape than of a social process of depletion exemplified by the notorious Highland Clearances of the early nineteenth century.[23] However, in large part because of Scott's influence, Marx finds this relative bleakness almost typologically romantic and thus derives meaning even from the absence of society – or, in Lyotard's language, from that which the landscape does not or can no longer present. The 'gloom' that Burt perceives, then, has the quality of a blank page on which the marks of legible (or 'improved') society have yet to appear, whereas Marx finds himself contemplating a topographical palimpsest that has fallen (as Price might say) into a comparative state of ruin, and which bears the marks of multiple erasures. And, after the visionary manner of Cririe or Wordsworth, what we can no longer 'read' in Highland scenery becomes for Marx the basis whereby we may prophetically discern the imminent doom of Western capital.[24]

If Burt's view of the Highlands is 'sublime' then Marx's is more 'picturesque'. But both, significantly (though in Burt's case retrospectively), are 'improved'. Improvement was the basis of Highland romance, as Womack rightly argues, and it provided the framework for much of the literature of travel through Scotland in the eighteenth and early nineteenth centuries. Ironically, however, Womack's critique is more Marxist than Marx', for Marx not only perceives in the 'romantic' Highlands an allegory of London and Manchester but he also grounds this vision in a picturesque conceit of eloquent ruin. Marx, in other words, does not juxtapose the sublime and the ideological, at least not in talking about the Highlands, but rather portrays the region as a 'sublime object of ideology'. This phrase names a book (and, really, a whole range of subsequent work) by Slavoj Žižek, who levels the difference between ideology and its critique: for Žižek, ideology is less a mistake to which others (e.g., Scottish travellers) are prone than a reflex of thought that habitually confounds the difference between nature and history, converting its own perspective into a concept of what universally 'is'. Because thought relies on such apparatuses, 'ideology' inflects all consciousness, critical and otherwise. Indeed, we might say, this is why Burke differentiates the sublime from 'the terrible': whereas the latter denotes 'danger or pain [which] press[es] too nearly', the sublime sublimates these dangers into digestible, conceptual forms; in mastering our fears, we convert them into pleasure (which Burke calls 'delight'). Essentially, the process of sublimation marks the difference between a fall off a cliff and a precipitous descent down the track of a roller coaster: the 'sublime' signifies fear which is always-already contained, always-already ideologised.[25] This is because the sublime is subject to the mechanics of representation, which is the special province of the picturesque. But this also means that our representations divulge more than they intend – namely the system which mediates our experience – and that even the clearest images carry with them the 'gloom' or trace of what falls outwith the mirror of self-reflection. Scott's 'Highland Minstrelsy', for example, enlists Edward in a romantic military campaign for the ultimate 'ideological' purpose of validating state power. And yet, as Pittock points out, *Waverley*'s conclusion, depicting a portrait of Fergus and Edward in Highland dress, 'illegal in Scotland after the failure of the 1745 Rising', and situating them amidst 'a wild, rocky, and mountainous pass' – in other words, in a quintessentially picturesque setting – amounts to a return of the repressed.[26] The landscape effectively testifies to undigested, unideologised remnants – Jacobite and otherwise – of Scott's British Union.

In short, if we define 'romance' as 'pure fiction' which, Ian Duncan says, signifies a 'difference from [. . .] "reality", [from] "everyday life"', and if we thus establish a connection between romantic narrative and what does not appear, or what is lacking, then the picturesque by contrast implies the freighted negotiation of all that does appear, or of what challenges the imagination by sheer force of its presence.[27] The picturesque, we may say, presents the obtrusion of the visible upon the comprehensible, or of the matter of experience upon the cognitive channels through which we mediate it.

The point here being underscored is that a peculiar phenomenological complexity inscribed itself into representations of Scotland in the late eighteenth and early nineteenth centuries. The Highlands in particular delineated an experiential threshold in much of this material: most travellers there commented on the grandeur of the landscape and the comparative strangeness of its inhabitants, but even writers from Highland regions (figures like James 'Ossian' Macpherson, the philosopher Adam Ferguson and the poet Duncan Bàn Macintyre) invoked the area as a counterpoint to a comparatively normative state of existence (for example, to British commercial society or to Highland life in ages past).[28] Picturesque sketches and accounts of Highland Scotland thus framed and at least partly illustrated phenomena of otherwise inconceivable strangeness. In doing so, they effectively reified eighteenth-century conceptions of the imagination as the cognitive agent mediating mind and world; indeed, in their way, travellers to Scotland embodied dominant conceptions of the imagination at work.[29]

This is said with an eye to the etymology of the word 'imagination', which derives from 'image'. While today the word often designates a power of conception removed from reality (making it a correlative of 'romance' – hence, the Romantic Imagination), Samuel Johnson's 1755 *Dictionary of the English Language* labels the imagination 'the power of forming ideal pictures', which was the logic of the picturesque.[30] In the eighteenth century, to think about the world was necessarily to imagine it, to create mental pictures of it; and when those pictures partly modify our understanding – when they 'compound, transpose, augment [. . .] diminish' and generally rearrange 'the materials afforded us by the senses', as David Hume says – then they function in a manner akin to the picturesque.[31]

The history of the concept of the imagination is important because it reveals how travel narratives essentially personified the operations of the mind. Indeed, the genre established itself as a key medium of *bildung*, of experience that yields a kind of enlightenment. But for many travellers there was something almost Gothic about Scotland, especially the Highlands, and hence something evocative less of understanding than desire. It was in Scotland that Ann Radcliffe set her first novel, *The Castles of Athlin and Dunbayne*, and it was this type of fiction that many travel narratives seemed to evoke:

> a most ravishing scene, unparalleled in Britain, opens suddenly upon you. A cold and fearful shuddering seizes upon your frame. Your ears are stunned. Your organs of vision, hurried along by the incessant tumult of [. . .] roaring waters, seem to participate in their turbulence, and to carry you along with them into the gulph below. Your powers of action and recollection are suspended. Though eager to be gone you become rivetted [*sic*] to the spot; and it is not till after a considerable time, that you begin to regain sufficient composure to contemplate, with any degree of satisfaction, the grand and awful objects here presented to your view.[32]

This is how James M'Nayr, in 1797, described the falls of Corra Linn near what is now New Lanark, roughly twenty miles south-east of Glasgow. But his rhetoric of 'shuddering', 'suspen[se]' and 'rivetted' attention evokes the discovery of corpses in Matthew Lewis' *The Monk* (1796), or even of concupiscent gazes in Freud's case histories. Given our conceptions of the unconscious, 'we moderns' can appreciate how especially the Highlands came to operate within Britain as an emblem of the mind's dusky, nether regions. Rugged topography evoked ('sublime') delight as a function of its superficial difference from georgic Britain, to say nothing of its cultural and political differences, conjuring an aura of danger which the dulling effects of improvement simultaneously contained. And yet the hallmarks of improvement – the replacement of peasant farms with sheep pastures; the blazing of rough tracts of land via military roads; the substitution of country retreats and fishing villages for feudal estates – acquired the virtual status of a language in that it provided travellers with access to these remote locations while also furnishing them with sufficient hallmarks of civilisation to render their experience legible. Hence, when Johnson noted in 1773 that tourists to the Highlands arrived 'too late' to see what many of them were expecting, namely, 'a people of peculiar appearance, and a system of antiquated life', he actually gave utterance to the conditions – belatedness and mediation – that made the Highlands visible in the first place.[33]

Johnson's paradoxical observation – they did not find what they were expecting, which means they had already discovered it before they left – is characteristic of the genre. Malcolm Andrews identifies two paradoxes that were particularly prominent: picturesque accounts appealed to an untouched but already somehow improved nature, and they exalted the native (that is, 'Britain') by reference to the foreign (usually France or Italy).[34] In each case, pre-existing forms (agricultural societies on the one hand, the work of Claude Lorrain on the other) mediated travellers' experience of the unknown. Not coincidentally, the very routes most travellers took were also pre-established. While the Highlands, Andrews remarks, 'were nowhere near as congested as the Lake District' during this period, there were nevertheless two Scottish tours on which most travellers embarked – a 'Long Tour' which went up the east coast 'to Aberdeen and round to Inverness' before sweeping across to the West and then looping back to Edinburgh, and a shorter tour which passed from Glasgow up to Loch Lomond and Inveraray.[35]

Correlatively, travellers themselves fell into pre-arranged types, or so claims Richard Joseph Sulivan in his cheeky *Observations Made during a Tour through Parts of England, Scotland, and Wales* (1780), which 'range[d] the several classes which are daily whirling round the world'. First, he said, 'come your men of science': '[c]hemists and musicians, [n]aturalists and tooth-drawers, [a] stronomers and quacks, [p]hilosophers and tailors, [p]oets and frizieurs, and in short a thousand others coupled in as ludicrous a manner'. The list does not necessarily grow more coherent as it expands to include adventurers of high fashion, '[c]hildren of wealthy families, [h]eirs apparent of diseases, titles, and distinction, [w]adlers astray from the courses of Newmarket, Almanack's, and St. James's, [s]pendthrifts, laughing at their creditors' and 'Dilettanti, skimming the shores of knowledge for a gaping world'. Lastly come travellers in search of health, those in search of happiness, and, at the end of the queue, those who, like himself, 'cheerfully skip along the borders of the fair field; stop where [their] fancy leads [them] to expatiate, and wander as [their] faculties and imagination may uphold [them] for the moment'.[36]

There is one significant group whom Sulivan fails to mention: women. Mary Ann Hanway, for example, was one of the first voyagers to chastise Johnson for his purported Scotophobia; Janet Schaw provided a most moving early account of Highland emigration; Sarah Murray produced an influential guidebook for subsequent travellers; and Anne Grant's seminal essay on the superstitions of the Highlanders is an early classic of what we might call Highland (or perhaps internal colonial) ethnography.[37] Had we more space we would discuss these important texts in greater detail. But for the purpose of drawing some general conclusions about the relationship of travel writing and the picturesque to Scottish Romanticism, let us stay with Sulivan's satirical, proto-Borgesian list. Its point, seemingly, is to underscore that what tourists saw (indeed, in large measure who they were) was less natural than artificial. The grand scenery they enunciated was already part of a tourist industry which, for that reason, was discursively if not geologically mass-produced. The frontier Highland landscape was *a priori* commoditised, cluttered with literary and aesthetic conventions. Scott's 'Highland Minstrelsy' was thus a relatively late arrival in a field which was literally well-travelled.

That said, this chapter has tried to make the point that picturesque travel narratives are irreducible to the sum total of their conventions, not because the Highlands defied expression *per se* but rather because narrative itself – representation – enunciated gloom under the auspice of dispelling it. This is why *Waverley* is interesting in this context: without reducing nature to artifice, it makes artifice appear uncanny. It seems fitting, then, that Scott and the picturesque should have been memorialised in literary and intellectual history through largely the same language. In 1927, for example, Christopher Hussey invoked the picturesque as a historical category occupying a transitional phase between 'classical' and 'romantic' eras.[38] When Georg Lukács revivified Scott's reputation just a few years later, he adopted similar language. Scott's work, he said, represented a 'continuation of the great realistic social novel of the eighteenth century', amounting to 'a higher development of the realist literary traditions of the Enlightenment in keeping with the new times'.[39] As Hussey might put it, Scott retained a 'classical' pose in a 'romantic' age and thus became a kind of expressive and compelling anachronism, articulating the forces of history which he simultaneously resisted and therefore placing himself at the vanguard of an era whose sweeping changes also rendered him a relic. Forty years later Tom Nairn would essentially recapitulate this argument (albeit in a deprecatory way), calling Scott a 'valedictory realist' who portrayed 'the past [. . . as] gone, beyond recall', and who therefore 'cut off the future from the past', employing in place of an authentic *Volksgeist* a garish assemblage of empty national forms, a menagerie of (mere) representations.[40] It was on this basis that Jerome McGann proclaimed Scott a romantic postmodernist – pushing the boundaries of anachronism considerably further than Lukács.[41]

But in the same volume in which that chapter was published, Ian Duncan, Leith Davis and Janet Sorensen made perhaps an even more incisive point. This is that it is Scottish Romanticism, and not just Scott's work, that 'describes rhythms of continuity, change, and disjunction quite different from the English model to which it has been subordinated' (including by Lukács, who repeatedly refers to Scott as an 'English' novelist).[42] In figures like James Macpherson, a translator/poet of romantic 'fragments' a full generation prior to their appearance in the influential writings of Friedrich Schlegel, and in Scott, a devotee of 'enlightenment' a full generation too late, one beholds a romanticism of the always-already and the never-quite-yet. We encounter, that is, a picturesque patchwork of divergent aesthetic qualities and historical types. And this means that in Scott's 'Highland Minstrelsy', we may discern, through the 'gloom' of a simple narrative about a young man coming to terms with adulthood and his place in history, the lineaments of Scottish Romanticism, and perhaps of the very horizon of the conceivable.

CHAPTER SIX

Urban Space and Enlightened Romanticism

Ian Duncan

Edinburgh became visible as a world capital of Romanticism in the first third of the nineteenth century, when an indigenous boom in literary production made the city a rival to Paris and London. Not only Edinburgh but the other Scottish university towns, notably Glasgow, had formed a major constellation of the European and North Atlantic Enlightenment in the preceding century. The post-Enlightenment cultural revival that got under way with the founding of the *Edinburgh Review* in 1802, following the hiatus of anti-Jacobin reaction, owed its more overtly 'Romantic' character to the proliferation of booksellers' genres – periodicals, poetry, novels – that constituted the emergent modern field of 'literature', in contrast to the curriculum-based genres of the human and natural sciences that characterised the republic of letters in the Scottish Enlightenment. Here in Edinburgh – now decisively the national centre of what had been a broadly dispersed network of Scottish book production – the genres that would dominate the nineteenth-century literary marketplace acquired their definitive forms and associations: periodicals – the critical quarterly (the *Edinburgh Review*), monthly magazine (*Blackwood's Edinburgh Magazine*) and weekly magazine (*Chambers's Edinburgh Journal*); popular poetry – national ballad-anthology (Scott's *Minstrelsy of the Scottish Border*) and ballad-based metrical romance (*The Lay of the Last Minstrel*); and prose fiction – the three-volume historical novel (*Waverley*), miscellany-based tale (Hogg's *Winter Evening Tales*) and local fictional memoir (Galt's *Annals of the Parish*). One person in particular, Walter Scott, contributed to almost all these genres and set the terms for at least two of them, as wartime national minstrel and post-war author of the 'Scottish novels' (as they were then called). His international fame and critical prestige, as well as his position at the centre of networks of Tory patronage, ensured that post-Enlightenment Edinburgh would be known, for better and worse, as the 'Age of Scott'.

The literary revival of the former Scottish capital accompanied its splendid architectural transformation in the decade-and-a-half between Waterloo and Reform. Lavish building projects such as the development of the Moray estates north-west of Princes Street (1822–36), the Regency triumphalism of Waterloo Place and Calton Hill to the east (1815–19) and public temples such as William Playfair's Royal Institution (now the Royal Scottish Academy, 1822–6) turned post-war Edinburgh into a spectacular, monumental and imperial urban landscape. This was a striking departure from the rational, horizontal, rectilinear conception of James Craig's residential New Town (1767). Calton Hill, its romantic prospects sketched by J. M. W. Turner for Scott's *Provincial Antiquities and Picturesque Scenery of Scotland* (1820), became the site of grandiose plans for a monumental acropolis crowned with an observatory (1818), temples to Robert Burns (1830) and Dugald Stewart (1831), a Nelson memorial (1807–16), Thomas Hamilton's Royal High School (1825–9) and a National Monument (1822–9). The foundation stone of this last was laid during the state visit to Edinburgh of George IV in August 1822. Scott himself orchestrated the 'King's Jaunt' as a fortnight-long pageant of parades and ceremonies, many of them decked out in retro-Jacobite tartan plaid, and most of them confected for the occasion. This extraordinary event, like the city's investment with a monumental architecture, expressed something more ambitious than regional municipal pride. Edinburgh was promoting itself as a new kind of national capital – one constituted not upon politics or finance but upon cultural production and aesthetic forms.[1]

This was the age of the 'Modern Athens' – a controversial title that became current at the end of the Napoleonic Wars. Literary reflections on the city's eminence made up one of the characteristic discourses of the period. A fashion for descriptions and illustrations of 'picturesque Edinburgh' formed an aesthetic hinge for the turn from a Neoclassical to a Romantic conception of the city, secured by the shift from a beautiful to a sublime vocabulary of representation. The escalating conflict between Whig and Tory parties in the post-war period made this aesthetic transformation, and the reclamation of Edinburgh's national status, inescapably political. Locked down by a Tory administration as the star of Reform rose in the south, Edinburgh became a major ideological battleground in the British press. The *Edinburgh Review*, the premier organ of opposition, upheld an oligarchic and republican ideal of citizenship based on civic virtue and a liberal commitment to electoral reform, derived from Enlightenment moral philosophy and political economy. Against this, the Tory literati of *Blackwood's Magazine* promoted an aesthetic ideology of cultural nationalism, derived from German Romanticism, in which depoliticised regional identities were the pillars of empire.

Archibald Allison jr, writing in *Blackwood's*, provides the clearest argument for Edinburgh's national status in these terms. The maintenance of ancient national distinctions in cultural terms – rather than political ones – will provide the empire with a healthy internal diversity, fending off alike the Scylla of despotic centralisation and the Charybdis of interregional fragmentation:

> But while London must always eclipse this city in all that depends on wealth, power, or fashionable elegance, nature has given to it the means of establishing a superiority of a higher and more permanent kind. The matchless beauty of its situation, the superb cliffs by which it is surrounded, the magnificent prospects of the bay, which it commands, have given to Edinburgh the means of becoming the most *beautiful* town that exists in the world [. . .] And thus, while London is the Rome of the empire, to which the young, and the ambitious, and the gay, resort for the pursuit of pleasure, of fortune, or of ambition, Edinburgh might become another Athens, in which the arts and the sciences flourished, under the shade of her ancient fame, and established a dominion over the minds of men more permanent even than that which the Roman arms were able to effect.[2]

London's status as the empire's political and commercial capital is balanced by Edinburgh's status as its cultural and aesthetic capital. (Here we glimpse the deep historical roots of the Edinburgh Festival.) While the reviewer ascribes this aesthetic status to the 'natural' harmony between Edinburgh and its setting, so that city and landscape constitute an ensemble of picturesque views, the plausibility for the claim rests on the city's evident pre-eminence as a centre of literary production – the institutional matrix of reviews, magazines, poems and novels that are restructuring the literary field and public sphere of British Romanticism.

The aesthetic distinction between a 'Classical' and a 'Romantic' Edinburgh after 1800, exacerbated by the ideological war between parties, should not however obscure the deep structural continuities between the Enlightenment city and its post-Enlightenment successor. Compared with the historical topographies of English Romanticism, Romantic Edinburgh remained an Enlightenment city – just as Enlightenment Edinburgh was in important ways already 'Romantic'. A. J. Youngson includes the city's post-war architectural developments in his account of 'Classical Edinburgh' as a matter of course, and its literary innovations reconfigure, rather than radically break from, Enlightenment discourse, from the liberal projects of the *Edinburgh Review* to the historical fictions of Scott and Galt. Scott, although a Tory in politics, was educated in the moderate Whig tradition of the late Enlightenment, and his novels have their intellectual roots in the sceptical empiricism of David Hume as well as the philosophical history of Adam Ferguson, William Robertson and Adam Smith. Even the Blackwoodian invention of a Romantic ideology set in explicit opposition to the Enlightenment legacy of the *Edinburgh Review* continued to build upon the models it ostensibly rejected, as Anthony Jarrells has recently argued.³ Henry Mackenzie, one of the leading Enlightenment literati and an influential early critic of Burns, hailed by Scott as 'our Scottish Addison' in the 'Post-script' to *Waverley*, lived long enough to preside over the generation of Scott and *Blackwood's* – the Grand Old Man of Scotland's long Enlightenment, or long Romanticism.

'I believe this is the historical Age and this [i.e. Scotland] the historical Nation,' David Hume famously declared in 1770. Writers of the next generation folded this historicism into a self-reflexive discourse of 'civic and personal memory' registering a newly felt 'historicization of everyday life'.⁴ Besides historical novels, the discourse bore literary fruit in innovative forms of cultural memoir, among them regional fictional autobiography (Galt's *Annals of the Parish*, 1821 and *The Provost*, 1822), variously satirical and elegiac hybrids of memoir and cultural criticism (Lockhart's *Peter's Letters to his Kinsfolk*, 1819; Cockburn's *Memorials of His Time*, 1856) and the antiquarian memoir of the city itself (Robert Chambers's *Traditions of Edinburgh*, 1824). Many of these works bring Edinburgh into focus as the scene of a 'change from ancient to modern manners'; as Cockburn put it, 'It was the rise of the new town that obliterated our old peculiarities with the greatest rapidity and effect'.⁵ Chambers opens *Traditions of Edinburgh*: 'The ancient part of EDINBURGH has, within the last fifty years, experienced a vicissitude scarcely credible to the present generation. What were, so late as the year 1775, the mansions of the higher ranks, are, in 1823, the habitations of people in the humblest degrees of life.' He adds, expressing a characteristic structure of feeling: 'The contemplation of this change is at once melancholy and gratifying.'⁶ Chambers, Cockburn and others evoke Old Edinburgh, before the flight of the gentry and professional classes across the North Loch to the New Town, as an 'organic' society in which the different ranks lived side-by-side, or rather on top of each other in the same tenement buildings (stratified on different floors), mingling in the streets and taverns, their eccentric types preserved (like images of a vanishing fauna) in John Kay's Edinburgh portraits. Above all this Edinburgh is evoked through a fond, vernacular literalisation of the leading Enlightenment ethos of sociability: Hume dispelling 'philosophical melancholy' in a game of backgammon with his friends, well-born ladies dancing reels in oyster cellars, judges presiding in court still drunk from their heroic toping the night before, advocates and merchants transacting business in howffs frequented by their clerks as well as thieves and whores. The organic character of this conviviality gives it a disgraceful as well as alluring charge; nostalgia for lost couthy ways is tempered with a polite disgust at their excesses.

Chambers makes the poet Robert Fergusson the *genius loci* of Old Edinburgh. Not only do Fergusson's poems supply a substantial portion of his ethnographic archive of Old Town life, with their colourful details (City

Guard, Cape Club, ten o'clock drum, trusty cadies, chamberpots emptied out of windows, etc.); at one point we catch a glimpse of the poet himself:

> In apostrophizing the capital of Scotland [in *Auld Reikie*], we might have expected some allusion to its romantic history or picturesque localities, such as that of Burns, perhaps, in his beautiful 'Address to Edina'. But, instead of this, the first and prominent idea of the poet turns out to be, that Edinburgh is a choice place for drinking and merry-making [. . .] Whenever he indulges in allusion to other matters, it is only by way of digression. He occasionally, as it were, steps out into the fresh air, to see
> ' – Morn, wi' bonnie purple smiles,
>   Kissin' the air-cock o' Saunt Giles;'
> but, quickly finding the air a little keen, and taking no interest in what he sees abroad, he turns again down the close, to his favourite tavern.[7]

Burns, the visitor, generates a polite discourse of 'romantic history or picturesque localities' amenable to Chambers' alienated generation, while Fergusson, the native, is immersed in the bliss and squalor of an extinct way of life. In making Fergusson the representative poet of Old Edinburgh Chambers takes his cue from Scott. Chambers dedicated *Traditions of Edinburgh* to Scott, and one of the book's achievements is to turn the Edinburgh Old Town into an enormous virtual monument to 'the Author of Waverley' and his works. Scott's great Edinburgh novel *The Heart of Mid-Lothian* establishes its Old Town setting with epigraphs and quotations from 'The Daft-Days', 'Hallow-Fair' and 'The King's Birth-Day in Edinburgh', while the narrator illustrates his account of the City Guard with a reference to 'Poor Fergusson,' their 'poet laureate', whose private 'irregularities' are magnified in the 'riot and irregularity' of the city streets on the public holidays celebrated in his poems.[8]

The main action of *The Heart of Mid-Lothian* takes place, however, fifteen years before Fergusson was born. Scott detaches Fergusson's career from its own historical moment and pushes it back a generation, to embed it more deeply in the lost world of a pre-modern Edinburgh. In doing so he sets the terms for Chambers' evocation of Fergusson as genius of a cosy but disreputable 'Auld Reikie', and indeed for most subsequent accounts of the matter. In fact Fergusson's poetry is acutely attuned to its contemporary horizon in the early 1770s. Fergusson was writing at the very apex of the Scottish Enlightenment, midway between Adam Ferguson's *History of Civil Society* (1767) and Smith's *Wealth of Nations* (1776), at the moment when Hume proclaimed, 'this is the historical Age and this the historical Nation'. In these years Edinburgh became a significant site of literary attention in Great Britain for the first time since the Acts of Union, anticipating the contentious apotheosis of the Modern Athens in Scott's and Chambers' era. Literary travellers, both real (Edward Topham's *Letters from Edinburgh*, 1775) and fictitious (Tobias Smollett's *Humphry Clinker*, 1771), turned their fascinated scrutiny on the city; the latter contains the famous characterisation of Edinburgh as 'a hot-bed of genius'. At the close of the decade Hugo Arnot's monumental *History of Edinburgh* (1779) made the city itself the subject of historical inquiry. Strikingly, Arnot devotes less than half the book to the chronicle of past events, from the earliest times to 1778; the rest is given over to a detailed account of the city's 'progress and present state', up to the completion of St Andrew Square and the extension of building along Princes Street. The New Town developments, architecturally realising the city's intellectual eminence, are for Arnot the main source of its interest and indeed the justification for writing its history.

More subtly and profoundly than any of these writers, Fergusson imagines a city on the threshold between Old Town and New. In the closing lines of the 1773 version (published as 'Canto I') of 'Auld Reikie', he foresees Edinburgh's wresting the laurels of urban splendour from Glasgow (adorned with the mansions of the Tobacco Lords):

Nae mair shall GLASGOW Striplings threap
Their City's Beauty and its Shape,
While our New City spreads around
Her bonny Wings on Fairy Ground.[9]

In 1767 the Edinburgh Town Council had approved Craig's plan for a residential development on the far side of the North Loch – spreading, with the fashionable South Side squares, the 'bonny Wings' of Fergusson's metaphor. The North Bridge, linking the city centre with the site, was completed in 1768, and the new Theatre Royal, at its north-eastern corner, opened to the public the following year; the foundation stone of Robert Adam's Register House, the 'Public Building' marked on Craig's plan, was laid in June 1774 – four months before Fergusson's death. His brief career thus coincided with the years when the New Town, planned, surveyed, partially feued but not yet built, was still a visionary project, on the brink of realisation, while the Old Town yet remained the dense, vital centre of Edinburgh's administrative, commercial and social life.

'Auld Reikie' is remarkable for the confidence with which it inhabits its transitional time, lovingly evoking the spectacles, noises, stinks and textures of city life and at the same time looking towards its future. Transition, temporal and spatial, sensory and metaphysical, cognitive and rhetorical, is the poem's animating theme as well as scheme, staking its claim as the masterpiece of a Scottish urban romanticism. 'Auld Reikie' finds room for Tory nationalist elegy over a dilapidated Holyrood:

For O, waes me! the Thistle springs
In DOMICILE of ancient Kings,
Without a patriot to Regrete
Our PALACE, and our ancient STATE.[10]

But it also includes the encomium of George Drummond, six times lord
provost, a notable anti-Jacobite and stirring improver: 'wale o' Men' for this
'wale o' ilka Town / that SCOTLAND kens beneath the Moon'. Drummond
was largely responsible for the surge of New Town development after his
death, and he earns his place in Fergusson's poem as the city's wizard-like ren-
ovator. Edinburgh may be the old town of 'our DADS, whase biggin stands /
A Shelter to surrounding Lands'; but it is the city's future, rather than its past,
that, as we have already noted, accommodates a visionary unfolding: 'While
our New City spreads around / Her bonny Wings on Fairy Ground.' Emerging
from the chrysalis of the ancient royalty, the city enchants the fields it covers.
The figure of metamorphosis reflexively changes register, from natural history
(a butterfly) to magic (fairy ground); in doing so it reverses the elegiac charge
of modern pastoral (as well as Enlightenment scientific history), according
to which urban development means the disenchantment of the green world.
Fergusson looks across the North Loch at a New Town which is yet – for the
last possible moment – imaginary, a marvellous threshold of possibilities.

Fergusson's poems remind us that Edinburgh always was a Romantic
town – or, if not always, that it was a Romantic town at the height of the
Scottish Enlightenment. Thomas Ruddiman's *Weekly Magazine, or Edinburgh
Amusement*, which hailed Fergusson in its pages as the city's poet laureate,
synchronised the publication of his great series of poems in Scots celebrating Edinburgh's public holidays with their appropriate dates: the Daft Days
(January 1772), the King's Birthday (June), Leith Races (July), Hallow Fair
(November). The calendrical sequence of festivities – some ancient, some
(like the king's birthday) recently established – binds specificity of place
to an immemorial, seasonal temporality, as well as to the poem's particular
historical moment, designating the riotous outbreaks as ceremonial, 'carni-
valesque', generative of a larger rhythm and economy of collective psychic
life. In short, Fergusson weaves the city into a greater natural order, just as
he weaves together past and future, ancient and modern – rather than setting
these categories in opposition to each other.

Murray Pittock has situated Fergusson's 'mythologization of the Scottish
capital' in a Tory humanist tradition of Scots poetry which sought to reclaim
Edinburgh, stripped of political sovereignty at the Union, as an abode of the
Muses.[11] In the previous generation Allan Ramsay, whose revival and synthe-
sis of ancient and popular styles of vernacular poetry made the achievements
of Fergusson and Burns possible, had founded a circulating library (1725), art

school (1729) and theatre (1736) as public resources of 'a northern metropolis which would provide an alternative cultural centre for northern England as well as Scotland'.[12] Pittock makes the case that these linked nationalist projects of literary revival and institution-building make up the early foundation of a 'Scottish Romanticism'. They were buttressed by the more durable institutions of a 'separate public sphere' in Scotland following the Treaty of Union, which provided for the country's retention of its religious, legal, financial and educational systems. In the absence of a Scottish state, these provided the institutional basis for distinctively national forms of identification, while the geographical removal of court and parliament opened space for the flourishing of an advanced civil society in the Lowland towns. Tenuous as it might often have seemed in real life, this civil society supplied a leading philosophical theme for the Enlightenment of which it was the ideological as well as sociological habitat. It was also, for all its promotion of Anglo-British and cosmopolitan styles, a distinctively national phenomenon, a medium of cultural production that would bear fruit not only in the philosophical projects of Enlightenment but in the periodicals and fiction of the succeeding era. All this meant that in Scotland a 'Romantic movement' had no need to found itself outside the city, or in opposition to the styles of Enlightenment thought associated with the city – which is not at all the same thing as saying that Scotland had no Romantic movement. In contrast, the first self-theorising wave of English Romanticism, in the writings of Wordsworth and Coleridge in the late 1790s, represented itself as seeking to 'counteract' the deleterious cultural effects of 'the increasing accumulation of men in cities' (even as recent scholarship has been recovering a broader 'urban scene' of British Romanticism).[13] What Tom Nairn claimed to be a main condition of the absence of a Scottish Romanticism – the precocious development of a bourgeois Enlightenment – was actually the condition for its rich and variegated flowering.[14]

Besides Fergusson's urban eclogues, the achievements of late eighteenth-century Scottish poetry are most comprehensively viewed in their integration with the metropolitan projects of Enlightenment, rather than in opposition to them. This includes Macpherson's simulations of an overtly pre-modern national epos – and its primitive universe – in the 'Poems of Ossian'. The Enlightenment literati virtually commissioned *Fingal* and *Temora*, and their conjectural cultural histories, from Thomas Blackwell's to Hugh Blair's, shaped the poems' production as well as their reception. Not only do the Ossian poems illustrate the tenets of Enlightenment historiography, but, as commentators noted at the time, they do not so much recreate a living world of pre-modern social relations as conjure up an elegiac wasteland haunted by modern manners and sentiments. Their revolutionary impact lay in their quality as modern poems rather than ancient ones. The most complex case is

Burns: embraced as a primitive (the 'heaven-taught ploughman') by the literati, he did not thrive in Edinburgh. A careful reading of Burns' poetry does
not however support a country-versus-city antithesis; for Burns the countryside too is a medium of civilisation, of enlightened debate, rather than of
primitivist communings with nature. The first 'Epistle to John Lapraik' opens
with a bold remapping of the eighteenth-century republic of letters. The poet
describes a Shrovetide 'sang about':

> I've scarce heard ought describ'd sae weel,
> What gen'rous, manly bosoms feel;
> Thought I, 'Can this be *Pope*, or *Steele*,
>   Or *Beattie's* wark?'
> They tauld me 'twas an odd-kind chiel
>   About *Muirkirk*.[15]

The traditional recitation of songs and poems in a Mauchline farmhouse, we
are to understand, constitutes a centre of literary production and reception
no less than do the salons of London and Edinburgh. The effusions of the
'chiel / About Muirkirk' mingle with, and rank beside, the British neoclassical works, metropolitan models of official style, by Pope (a Catholic), Steele
(an Irishman) and Beattie (the tradition's Anglo-Scots representative).[16]
Burns does not set his Ayrshire neighbourhood in imaginative opposition to
the city – instead he reimagines the 'city' as a nationwide network of cultural
making and sharing of which rural Ayrshire also is part.

The historical fictions of the post-Enlightenment develop the representation of city and countryside as dynamically integrated in a complex, evolving
world. The Edinburgh episodes in Scott's novels are as vivid and memorable
as any of those set in the Borders or Highlands – not least because of their
sensitivity to the vital connections between urban life and regions elsewhere.
The eponymous protagonist of *Guy Mannering* (1815) visits Edinburgh in
the early 1770s, the high noon of Enlightenment (and of Fergusson's career),
on the brink of that great change in local manners that would follow the
city's bifurcation between Old Town and New. Scott closely weaves this
Edinburgh into the larger cosmos of *Guy Mannering*, a novel that establishes
a modern template for the 'universal' genre of romance later theorised by the
critic Northrop Frye.[17] Edinburgh is the organic city of letters and science and
of ancient saturnalia, where the urbane advocate Pleydell (himself a merry
participant in the saturnalia) converses familiarly with the rugged Liddesdale
farmer Dinmont, an ambassador from the 'green world'; in the last chapters
Pleydell finds himself (somewhat to his own surprise) collaborating with the
gypsy spaewife Meg Merrilies to restore the lost heir to his estate. In Scott's
romance magic and fiction are the same: 'Here ends THE ASTROLOGER',

declares Mannering in the final sentence, cancelling occult powers at the same time as he closes the story.

Organic Edinburgh acquires a more troubled cast in *The Heart of Mid-Lothian* (1818), which articulates the social, political and religious antagonisms of the city around themes of criminality, injustice, riot, fornication and infanticide. The novel tracks the rhizomatic extension of these ills across the not-yet-national territory of 1730s Scotland and England, in which, for example, a seemingly ubiquitous criminal underworld makes its move in the Yorkshire countryside as well as in darkest Edinburgh. Scott reverses one of the major topoi of urban disorder by emphasising the military discipline with which the 'Porteous mob' executes its precisely considered aim: the rioters supply their own conception of the order and justice that the civil authorities have abrogated. In a third major novel of eighteenth-century Edinburgh life, *Redgauntlet* (1824: in which, like the others, Edinburgh makes up only a part of the novel's scenery), the insistently miscellaneous texture of Scott's narrative expresses the cultural discontinuities among its different worlds and subcultures – discontinuities that prevail not so much between legal Edinburgh and rural Dumfriesshire, or between civic and 'border' settings, as within the novel's various locations – all of which are fissured by internal borders: thus, the same neighbourhood affords Darsie Latimer his visits to the Laird of the Lakes' ravine, the Quakers' model estate and the 'Jolly Beggars'-like popular underworld of Wandering Willie.

Meanwhile contemporary reviewers applauded *Rob Roy* (1818) for one of its innovations, the admission of Glasgow to the topography of Scott's Romantic Scotland. The novel's Glasgow accommodates the hospitable parlour of the Baillie Nicol Jarvie, expounding Scottish Enlightenment political economy *avant la lettre* to account for the condition of the Highlands and the improvements of the city within a globalising Atlantic empire; it also accommodates the Gothic haunts of Frank's encounters with Rob Roy, whose freedom of movement belies their closed and carceral character. The intimacy between the apparently antithetical 'historical stages' of Glasgow and the Highlands, incarnate in the cousinship shared by Jarvie and Rob Roy, is perhaps the novel's ultimate secret. In his masterpiece *The Entail* (1823) John Galt set out to rival Scott – rivalling the representation of Glasgow in *Rob Roy*, eschewing Scott's fantastic flourishes for a more determined social-historical realism, as well as rivalling Scott's Edinburgh by making Scotland's western metropolis the focus of an alternative fictionalisation of national history. In *The Entail* Galt amplifies the earlier insistence on a historical integration of regional economies within the long generational span of imperial growth and world war against France in his rural and small-town fictional memoirs *Annals of the Parish* (1821) and *The Provost* (1822). Far from casting the countryside as a reservoir of symbolic resources outside history,

Galt shows it as equally subject with the city to the forces of modernisation. This vision too he shares with Scott, despite his novel's insistence on a more rigorous code of realism.

Even James Hogg, who launched his career in the guise of 'the Ettrick Shepherd', a quintessentially primitive rustic bard, turned out also to be a thoroughly urban writer. Earlier accounts of an author vexatiously divided between Ettrick and Edinburgh have yielded, in recent years, to a nuanced appreciation of the ways in which Hogg fully inhabited the Scottish metropolis – living in it, as he represented it, in close correspondence with his rural neighourhood, shuttling back and forth between them.[18] With his first venture into an avowedly urban genre, the weekly miscellany *The Spy* (1810–11), Hogg joined one of the city's vibrant democratic literary circles; the barrier he would find himself striving against was more one of rank than of region. With *The Spy* he established himself as a master of the urban print forms of miscellany, magazine fiction and satirical sketch as much as he was of rural and oral-traditional genres such as ballad, lyric and folktale. The *Blackwood's Magazine* caricature of Hogg as the 'Shepherd', a clownish mascot in the nationalist cultural pantheon assembled in the satirical dialogue series 'Noctes Ambrosianae', belies his role as one of the magazine's founders as well as one of its chief contributors.

Perhaps the most spectacularly 'Romantic' scene in early nineteenth-century Scottish fiction occurs in Hogg's *Private Memoirs and Confessions of a Justified Sinner* (1824), when young George Colwan ascends Arthur's Seat 'to converse with nature' early one summer morning. The episode takes its cue from memorable chapters in *The Heart of Mid-Lothian* in which Scott makes Arthur's Seat the location of uncanny encounters with the pseudo-satanic George Robertson. Hogg's tale goes beyond Scott's in its staging of a clash between two key topoi of British (indeed European) Romanticism: the mountaintop communion of a 'wanderer above the clouds' with sublime nature, resonating with famous treatments by Wordsworth (not all of which Hogg could have read – the description of the ascent of Snowdon was not available until the posthumous publication of *The Prelude* in 1850), versus the fatal confrontation with a demonic shadow or double, emanating from the tradition of Gothic and German terror-romance by Matthew Lewis and E. T. A. Hoffmann. (Victor Frankenstein's encounter with his 'daemon' on an alpine glacier may also be in the background.) Hogg casts the former scenario as the archetype of an 'Enlightened Romanticism'. George's refusal to deface the 'fairy web' of microscopic dewdrops that covers his hat expresses a natural piety which is rewarded with the optical phenomenon of the 'glory', provoking the narrator to interject: 'That was a scene that would have entranced the man of science with delight, but which the uninitiated and sordid man would have regarded less than the mole rearing up his hill in silence and in darkness.'[19] George's reverie is interrupted by the appalling spectre of his brother – as though the repressed energies of a Calvinist theological conviction of the depravity of nature have returned to blast the polite fiction (a thinly secularised natural theology) of a communion with it. The fiendish shadow turns out to be a truer presage of George's fate than his broken-off meditation – perhaps. Whether Wringhim's 'dark Romanticism' (Calvinist, northern, Gothic) trumps George's and the editor's version (enlightened, southern, Wordsworthian) in the larger scheme of the novel is left for the reader to find out; their incompatibility, in any case, seems clear. *The Private Memoirs and Confessions of a Justified Sinner* poses a sly challenge to those who would distinguish an authentic English Romanticism from a reprobate Scottish version – and to those who would confound the two. Wild mountain landscape though Arthur's Seat may seem, meanwhile, it is also an urban park, just a few hundred yards from the city centre.

CHAPTER SEVEN

Periodicals and Public Culture

Alex Benchimol

Recent projections of Scottish Romanticism provide a compelling illustration of the expanded temporal and geographic boundaries that increasingly characterise Romantic studies in the early twenty-first century. This work emphasises the importance of Scotland's national identity – and unique institutional history – within a necessarily extended trajectory of cultural development, from the Act of Union in 1707 up to the ascendancy of Edinburgh as the cultural capital of Britain in the early part of the nineteenth century.[1] These studies also highlight the significant role played by Scotland's national public sphere in the construction of a culturally dynamic formation of Scottish Romanticism that is in dialogue with, rather than in opposition to, its Scottish Enlightenment forerunner, and, through the 'cultural metropolis' of Edinburgh, at the centre of a wider, multi-national formation of 'British Isles Romanticism'.[2]

Ian Duncan's *Scott's Shadow* (2007) argues that the professional class that rose to institutional prominence in Scottish civil society after the Union of 1707 remained clearly marked by those national institutions given a substantial degree of autonomy in the Union settlement. 'The institutions that sustained this elite,' he writes, 'the Church of Scotland, the universities, and the law – bore a distinctively Scottish identity preserved by the Articles of Union.' He goes on to argue that 'they constituted the emergent public sphere, the field of civil society, that Jürgen Habermas distinguishes from the field of the state' (p. 50). For Duncan, the innovative forms of cultural production associated with this Scottish public sphere framed the development of literary genres that became central features of a wider British Romanticism in the nineteenth century, including the modern historical novel and the periodical review. The latter was most clearly embodied in the second *Edinburgh Review*, which, at its founding in 1802, as Marilyn Butler has noted, 'challenged the cultural status of London itself' with its selective review format that promoted an academic model of periodical knowledge based on 'the specialisms for which Scottish universities were famous'.[3] Murray Pittock's 2008 study *Scottish and Irish Romanticism* also argues for

the ideological and cultural significance of a distinctive national public
sphere in Scotland, as in Ireland, that helped contribute 'to the preservation
and development of Scottish and Irish writing' during the long eighteenth
century. He cites the general neglect of this idea of a Scottish public sphere
in British historiography, except, notably, 'the partial example of the Scottish
Enlightenment, whose clubs and clubbability are classic evidence of a public
sphere in Habermas's terms' (p. 13).

Another major contributor to the recent conceptualisation of Scottish
Romanticism has highlighted the distinctive projection of Scottish intellectual values in periodicals like the *Edinburgh Review* during the Romantic
period. Fiona Stafford's account of the formation and development of the
journal during the early nineteenth century emphasises how its editor and
contributors were able to construct a new form of cultural community for a
Scottish readership based on the nation's particular cultural needs at the time.
The *Review* was 'an expression of an emerging sense of national community,
at once reflecting and contributing to the imaginings of the Scottish people'
and in part constitutive of a new periodical-based public sphere founded on
distinctive Scottish intellectual values. 'Since the *Edinburgh Review* was also
designed to stimulate debate through its vigorous reviewing style,' Stafford
writes, 'its audience was not generally content with silent imaginings, but was
frequently provoked into active discussion with fellow readers.'[4] For Stafford,
the very intellectual modernity reflected in the format of the periodical –
where 'a great variety of style and subject matter' was accommodated through
a 'form sufficiently flexible to allow for internal difference without any danger
of wholesale collapse' – also made it a suitable cultural embodiment of the
'new United Kingdom'. 'The forum for exploring questions of nationhood
and identity,' she observes, 'was thus able to play a significant role in the creation of a new sense of Britain, and especially of Scotland's place within the
newly united islands' (p. 41).

These important reprojections of Romantic studies via the cultural
modernity of Scotland's capital display a clear awareness of the complex
development of the nation's innovative print culture within an emergent
public sphere during the eighteenth century. They also point toward the
ways this Scottish public sphere served as the primary intellectual impetus
for the emergence of a wider British periodical public sphere in the early
nineteenth century. The Scottish national public sphere, reacting to the
loss of a central force in Scotland's public life – its parliament – reflected
the ambitions of its intellectual leaders to assert the institutional autonomy
of the country after 1707, in part through new modes of cultural association
devoted to securing the nation's prosperity within the Union. Although
Edinburgh remained the cultural capital of this national public sphere
throughout the eighteenth century, the role of university cities like Glasgow

and Aberdeen in its formation and articulation demonstrate both its geographical diversity and institutional coherence, with Scotland's ancient
universities at the centre of vital local associational cultures as equally
devoted to national improvement as that of the capital.[5] Alexander Broadie
has commented:

> It is noteworthy that most of the leading contributors to the Scottish
> Enlightenment lived in the three university cities of Glasgow, Edinburgh and
> Aberdeen, cities in which there was also a rich extra-academic life, thus giving
> the professors opportunities, grasped with enthusiasm, to exchange ideas with
> lively minded people who, as agents and not just as spectators, had well-
> informed insights into people and institutions.[6]

While acknowledging the important role played by the leading cultural
institutions of Glasgow and Aberdeen, this chapter will attempt to map out
how a distinctively Scottish – if not explicitly nationalist – expression of
intellectual modernity sprang out of the unique associational culture of post-
Union Scotland embodied in the capital's intellectual clubs and societies,
and the largely autonomous national religious and educational institutions
headquartered in the city, the General Assembly of the Kirk and Edinburgh
University. The founding of the two versions of the *Edinburgh Review*, in
1755 and 1802, represent different stages of this distinctively Scottish expression of intellectual modernity. The format, topical discourse and aims of
both journals illustrate how Scotland's periodical culture emerged out of the
unique institutional structure of its national public sphere, while also reflecting its complex articulation of autonomy and assimilation in the century after
Union.

The key features of the liberal public sphere in Scotland took shape
amidst the unique political circumstances of the country at the beginning
of the eighteenth century. In a prominent recent study of the Scottish
Enlightenment Broadie has observed that after 1707

> [the] centres of political power in Scotland were major centres of patronage for
> the universities, the church, legal institutions and the arts. Scotland therefore,
> though fast becoming 'unionised' in many details as well as in the grand politi-
> cal scheme, preserved highly visible and genuinely potent symbols of its
> distinctive identity.[7]

This crucial institutional autonomy in Scottish civil society after 1707 would
help to encourage in its leaders a strong desire to demonstrate Scotland's
material and intellectual development as a principal means for asserting the
nation's cultural distinctiveness within the new Union.

Indeed, according to an influential strand of intellectual historiography most clearly represented in the work of Nicholas Phillipson, the broad-based cultural movement that would come to be known as the Scottish Enlightenment had as its primary impetus the political vacuum resulting from the constitutional settlement of 1707.[8] More specifically, Phillipson has argued that 'an alternative language of civic morality' developed in response to the Scots' loss of national political sovereignty at the beginning of the century.[9] Phillipson's wider argument, linking the new ideas of civic virtue to the modes of intellectual sociability pioneered by the Edinburgh literati in the aftermath of the Union, finds a particular resonance with Habermas' thesis from his seminal 1962 study *The Structural Transformation of the Public Sphere*.[10] For Phillipson's patriotic literati, the new forms of liberal discourse available in the post-Union capital were seen as both morally beneficial and socially useful: 'the Scots believed that coffee-house conversation could teach them the principles of civic virtue as well as of propriety'. Perhaps even more significant for the emergence of a liberal public sphere in Edinburgh, Phillipson argues that this form of Scottish intellectual practice 'was to be meshed into a complex and constantly changing network of clubs and societies devoted to the improvement of manners, economic efficiency, learning and letters'. In other words, the developing liberal public sphere in post-Union Scotland allowed for the articulation of a new vision of national material improvement wedded to the individual moral development this cultural space offered to its partici-pants. 'For it was believed,' Phillipson writes, 'that those who took part in such activities would help to secure their country's independence and acquire a sense of civic virtue.'[11]

Participants in the new Scottish public sphere were also forging a unique concept of modern national identity both in and through these intellec-tual gatherings, where the cultivation of taste helped to define a new form of cultural association in response to what Phillipson calls 'the problem of discovering alternative modes of participation to that which parliament had once provided'.[12] This response encouraged the compensatory development of an innovative practice of cultural politics; one which attempted to sustain older traditions of political leadership through the new forms of intellectual association provided by the liberal public sphere. John Dwyer has commented on the results of this peculiarly self-validating form of patriotism for the subsequent generation of Scottish literati:

> The aims of the Scottish literati were, at least on their own terms, patriotic. They wanted to shape a new vision of a harmonious, if hegemonic, British com-munity not merely in order to belong to it. Their programme was decidedly propagandistic, for they wished to proselytise their polite gospel of virtue and sentiment to a rapidly growing reading public.[13]

The new Scottish practice of cultural politics was developed in the informal network of taverns, literary societies and professional clubs where intellectual groups ranging in social status from aristocratic Tory gentlemen to middle-class Whig professionals assembled to discuss a new genre of moral journalism emerging from two of the most innovative periodicals of the age, Joseph Addison and Richard Steele's *Tatler* and *Spectator*.

One of the earliest and most important literary clubs, the Jacobite-influenced Easy Club founded in 1712 by, amongst others, the poet Allan Ramsay, 'showed unmistakable signs of the influence of the *Spectator*', according to D. D. McElroy's pioneering survey of literary clubs and societies in the period, *Scotland's Age of Improvement*. Indeed, McElroy suggests that 'without the *Spectator* there would have been no Easy Club'.[14] Its main activity was the cultivation of the new discourse of polite conversation through consideration of general topics like 'Wit', 'Friendship', 'Moderation', 'Taste' and the 'Qualities of the "Gentleman"' – unmistakable signs of its commitment to what Nicholas Phillipson calls an 'Addisonian vocabulary'. Phillipson argues that consideration of such subjects was a key illustration of the wider cultural agenda of Scots literati in clubs like the Rankenian and the Easy who

> seemed to have believed that the adaptable, modest principles of Addisonian propriety, undertaken in a patriotic spirit could be developed into a system of civic morality which was appropriate to the needs of the provincial citizen preoccupied with preserving the independence of his community.[15]

Murray Pittock has recently demonstrated how Ramsay – one of the Easy Club's leading lights – promoted 'a distinctive Scottish literature' in the early eighteenth century through literary innovations that identified 'the folk vernacular with the idea of a national literature in the present'.[16] This patriotic strategy to assert Scottish cultural autonomy after the Union settlement is also evident, as Pittock argues, in Ramsay's efforts to develop Edinburgh as a 'northern metropolis' through the establishment of cultural institutions like a circulating library, an art school and a theatre – in short providing the essential cultural infrastructure for a 'separate Scottish public sphere' in the hopes of preserving Edinburgh's identity 'as a native metropolis and cultural capital'.[17] Pittock's thesis, when juxtaposed with Phillipson's influential portrayal of the Easy Club as a key vehicle for post-Union intellectual leadership in Scotland, illustrates a wider struggle in the early eighteenth-century national public sphere between the pressures for cultural assimilation heading north from London and the assertion of domestic cultural autonomy in Scotland's capital. The appropriation of new modes of moral journalism by the Easy Club, in this context, exemplifies a distinctively Scottish formation of metropolitan politeness in complex engagement with the liberal commercial values encouraged by the Union. Hamish Mathison, in an essay about the Edinburgh version of the *Tatler*, contends that in Scotland 'the manufacture of "literary" periodicals [. . .] responded more quickly than the manufacture of newspapers to the need to accept 1707 as a watershed in the relationship between Scotland and England'.[18]

This new relationship included the recognition by Scotland's intellectual elite that Scottish national interests could be furthered by adapting the new language of civic propriety to the unique political circumstances of the country. Indeed, it was the intellectual style of openness, tolerance and moral seriousness derived from the Addisonian cultural model that would inspire the next generation of literati during their penetration and eventual control of the primary institutional strongholds of Scottish civil society. Richard Sher's seminal 1985 study, *Church and University in the Scottish Enlightenment*, maps the advancement of this second generation of Edinburgh literati in a manner that emphasises the wider cultural transformation of two key institutions of the Scottish national public sphere: the General Assembly of the Church of Scotland and the University of Edinburgh.[19] Sher's projection of the institutional basis of the Scottish Enlightenment also helps in the identification of a distinctive national periodical culture out of this public sphere; one that facilitates the exercise of moral leadership while promoting a vision of national improvement, the latter embodied in the closing lines of the preface to the first number of *The Scots Magazine* in 1739, which declared 'for as our labours, so are our wishes employed on the PROSPERITY OF SCOTLAND'.[20]

Sher's study outlines the social and political trajectory of a generation of liberal intellectuals who participated in the ideological transformation of the nation's principal cultural institutions. Characterising them as the 'Moderate literati', he argues that their institutional advancement is a core element within the wider historical development of the Scottish Enlightenment:

> Within the matrix of professional men who gave the Scottish Enlightenment its distinctive character, the Moderate literati of Edinburgh occupied a central position. Their centrality was at once geographical, in that they lived in or near the cultural capital of Scotland; social and institutional, in that they came to dominate the two most important Scottish institutions for the dissemination of knowledge and beliefs – the Church of Scotland and the University of Edinburgh – as well as important clubs such as the Poker; intellectual, in that they published works in history, moral philosophy, rhetoric and belles lettres, drama, and religion that were among the most highly acclaimed, influential, and characteristic productions of eighteenth-century Scottish polite literature; and ideological, in that they successfully employed their institutional authority and intellectual talents to make the ideals and values of Moderatism preeminent in the Scotland of their day.[21]

It is significant that these key intellectual figures – William Robertson, Hugh
Blair, Adam Ferguson, John Home and Alexander Carlyle – were of the same
generation, hailed from similarly respectable family backgrounds, and had all
studied at Edinburgh University during the 1730s and 1740s .[22]

For these young, progressive ministers open to the liberal intellectual
society available in Edinburgh student clubs like the Hen, the ecclesiastical
instability and evangelism of the Kirk in the 1730s and 1740s provided a
powerful impetus to 'direct their energies toward building a strong, unified,
orderly Scottish Presbyterian church' that culminated with the founding
of the Moderate party grouping. Their first successful intervention into the
politics of the Kirk occurred in 1752, from a response to Church debate over
the rejection of a minister by a presbytery in Dunfermline, on the grounds
of conscience. Composed chiefly by Robertson, but with the assistance of
Blair, Alexander Carlyle and John Jardine, among others, the 'Reasons
of Dissent from the Judgment and Resolution of the Commission, March
11, 1752' stressed the importance of three related organisational issues of
contemporary controversy within the Church. These were: the need to con-
strain individual freedom for the sake of institutional order in church and
civil government; the necessity for discipline and authority in ecclesiastical society; and the adjudicating primacy of the General Assembly.[23] The
document represented an explicit attempt by these rising intellectuals to
consolidate their moral and political authority through a new conception of
collective rational deliberation, establishing a model for directed publicity in
the Scottish national public sphere of which the reformed Church became
such an integral part.

The intellectually vigorous exchanges between the Moderate party and
their formidable evangelical opponents – both published in and reported on
by national periodicals like *The Scots Magazine* – manifested the high level
of official debate in the Kirk during the mid-eighteenth century. Indeed, the
debates carried on in the General Assembly contributed to the wider atmosphere of rigorous and open intellectual exchange that marked the Scottish
Enlightenment more generally. These gatherings, ostensibly to discuss theological developments and organisational issues within the Kirk, became sites
of open struggle over the ideological shape of civil society in post-Union
Scotland. In this quasi-parliamentary context, eloquent and shrewd del-
egates like William Robertson established a national reputation based on
the persuasive force and intellectual integrity of his arguments. Robertson's
performances in the General Assembly, and dexterity in managing conflicts
outside it, facilitated his remarkable institutional ascent to become both the
principal of Edinburgh University in 1762 and the moderator of the General
Assembly a year later. Sher writes: 'For the institutionalization of Moderate
authority and Enlightenment values in Scotland, the election of William

Robertson as principal of the University of Edinburgh was probably the most important single event of the eighteenth century.'[24]

As Edinburgh principal, Robertson transformed the relationship between the Senatus Academicus (consisting of the principal and professors) and the Town Council. His collegial style – honed through years of debate and negotiation during his time as leader of the Moderate faction and, eventually, the Kirk moderator – meant that his principalship represented a corporate rather than individual exercise of authority over the university's affairs, including the appointment of intellectually sympathetic friends to a number of major chairs. According to Sher, Robertson 'was less a dictator than a party leader who considered his own interest and influence to be bound up intimately with those of like-minded friends and kin. Foremost among them within the university were Adam Ferguson and Hugh Blair'.[25] All three men were members of the Select Society, an extra-academic intellectual institution that represents what could be called, borrowing from Sher's model of institutional development in the Scottish Enlightenment, the third 'pillar' of Robertson's 'Moderate Regime'.[26] It was perhaps the most explicit manifestation of a distinctive national public sphere in Scotland dedicated to cultural and material improvement.

Intellectual societies like the Select, the Literary Society of Glasgow and the Aberdeen Philosophical Society[27] – referred to by Anand Chitnis in his important social history of the Scottish Enlightenment as the movement's 'new institutions' – were the essential intermediating cultural spaces situated alongside the major urban universities in Scotland.[28] Often developing from a need to address specific intellectual controversies, philosophical interests and practical social questions, the societies were prime examples of the Habermasian ideal of a public sphere where in 'the discussion among citizens issues were made topical and took on shape'.[29] Vitally, the wide-ranging intellectual debate carried out in societies like the Select became materialised in the aims and critical style of the first *Edinburgh Review*.

The Select Society met at the Advocates' Library where David Hume was the chief librarian. Founded in 1754 by the artist Allan Ramsay (son of Allan Ramsay, the poet and leading light of the Easy Club), the society assembled some of the most dynamic intellectual figures of the Scottish Enlightenment for 'the pursuit of philosophical inquiry, and the improvement of the members in the art of speaking', as Adam Smith proclaimed at the first meeting, indicating its desire to promote a distinctive form of Scottish cultural assimilation toward the modernising values of the Union.[30] The membership came to include leading independent cultural figures like Ramsay and Hume; prominent Moderate literati like Robert Wallace, John Jardine, John Home, William Robertson, Adam Ferguson, Hugh Blair and

Alexander Carlyle; distinguished university professors from the arts and sciences like Adam Smith and William Cullen; and noted legal advocates like
Lords Monboddo and Kames and Alexander Wedderburn. Alexander Carlyle
testified to its contemporary social and cultural significance: 'In the year 1754
I Remember nothing Remarkable in the General Assembly. But this was
the year in which the Select Society was Established, which Improv'd and
Gave a Name to the Literati of this country th[e]n beginning to Distinguish
themselves.'[31] Perhaps the most important feature of the society was that it
brought together the respective leaders from the main institutional compo-
nents of the national public sphere in Scotland for a common intellectual
purpose.

Indeed, the Select Society provides a contemporary historical illustration of Habermas' concept of public reason from *Structural Transformation*,
demonstrating how, in a Scottish context, this intellectual ideal was directed
toward both individual and national improvement. In its resolutely reformist agenda the Select displayed both its practical and patriotic orientation,
with the encouragement of 'Arts, Sciences, Manufactures, and Agriculture'
in Scotland supplementing the original aims in 1755. To facilitate the realisation of these supplemental aims, the society initiated a system of what it
called 'premiums' whereby incentives ranging from medals to cash prizes
were dispersed to the 'discoverer of any useful invention in arts or sciences'.
Through this system the society hoped that 'a spirit of emulation is excited
in every artist; improvements become universally known; and merit receives
the testimony of public approbation'.[32] In short, the Select sought to demonstrate how Scotland was contributing to the greater wellbeing of the Union
through scientific and literary innovations incubated in those national
cultural institutions given autonomy by the 1707 settlement. The society
also established a crucial material context for the subsequent organisation of
intellectual discourse in the country's developing periodical culture, including the abortive effort by some of its most prominent members to establish a
new form of philosophical journalism.

The first *Edinburgh Review* was founded in 1755 by Robertson, Blair,
Smith, Alexander Wedderburn, John Jardine and James Russel. The preface
to its first number provides a clear indication of the social role that some of
Scotland's leading intellectuals envisioned for themselves as guardians of the
national public sphere nearly fifty years after the Union, together with their
hopes for an improving national periodical culture that could redeem the
country's aspirations for an equal and joint partnership in the Union. 'The
design of this work is,' the preface declares, 'to lay before the Public, from
time to time, a view of the progressive state of learning in this country'.[33]
Given this objective, it is not surprising that the preface engages in a historical review of the social and cultural development of modern Scotland,

including an assessment of those watershed political events that had led up to its present aspirational identity as 'North Britain'.

For these ascendant Enlightenment intellectuals at the centre of a cosmopolitan national public sphere within an increasingly prosperous British state, the intermittent civil and religious strife of seventeenth-century Scotland was a clear barrier to national improvement. The preface emphasises the relationship between the cultivation of nationally beneficial intellectual endeavours and national political stability, both within Scotland as well as in its relations with England. The Revolution of 1688 was a watershed event in this regard, when 'liberty was re-established, and property rendered secure; the uncertainty and rigor of the law were corrected and softened', although still insufficient because 'the violence of parties was scarce abated, nor had industry yet taken place'. 'What the Revolution had begun,' the preface argues, 'the Union rendered more compleat.'[34] This leads to one of the most revealing passages, where a distinctive post-Union notion of Scottishness is articulated, emphasising the close connection between national material improvement, the diffusion of civility and the political stability provided by the 1707 settlement:

> The memory of our ancient state is not so much obliterated, but that, by comparing the past with the present, we may clearly see the superior advantages we now enjoy, and readily discern from what source they flow. The communication of trade has awakened industry; the equal administration of laws produced good manners; and the watchful care of the government, seconded by the public spirit of some individuals, has excited, promoted and encouraged, a disposition to every species of improvement in the minds of a people naturally active and intelligent. If countries have their ages with respect to improvement, *North Britain* may be considered as in a state of early youth, guided and supported by the more mature strength of her kindred country.

A clear narrative of national progress is projected here, approximating what Pittock has called 'the teleology of civility' that became such a central feature of Scottish Enlightenment historiography.[35] Patriotism, in this North British context, is rooted in a wider process of commercial modernity facilitated by the Union; a process that encourages 'a disposition to every species of improvement in the minds of a people naturally active and intelligent'. The principal cultural vehicle for this form of national improvement is, of course, the liberal public sphere, of which the new intellectual periodical was only the most recent print manifestation.

The Scottish national public sphere is represented as both the embodiment of the nation's distinctively democratic educational traditions, and a means for a broader cultural assimilation with its southern neighbour, based on the creation of modern standards for literary discourse and the new technological opportunities for their dissemination through printing. This anticipates the regulative northern metropolitan critical imperatives of the second incarnation of the *Edinburgh Review*:

> The opportunities of education, and the ready means of acquiring knowledge, in this country, with even a very moderate share of genius diffused thro' the nation, ought to make it distinguished for letters. Two considerable obstacles have long obstructed the progress of science. One is, the difficulty of a proper expression in a country where there is either no standard of language, or at least one very remote: Some late instances, however, have discovered that this difficulty is not insurmountable; and that a serious endeavour to conquer it, may acquire, to one born on the north side of the Tweed, a correct and even an elegant stile. Another obstacle rose from the slow advances that the country had made in the art of printing: No literary improvements can be carried far, where the means of communication are defective: But this obstacle has, of late, been entirely removed; and the reputation of the Scotch press is not confined to this country alone.[36]

This passage highlights the journal's complex articulation of national identity, where ostensibly assimilationist initiatives to establish new standards for literary expression – like those carried out in the Select Society – become the basis for a much wider dissemination of Scotland's ethos of national cultural improvement. This ethos is presented as the primary motivation for the first *Edinburgh Review*. There the nation's dramatic level of cultural improvement since the Union could be showcased for a Scottish, British and international audience through the new medium of the intellectual review, firmly linking Scottish Enlightenment periodical culture to its institutional roots in the post-1707 national public sphere:

> It occurred to some Gentlemen, that, at this period, when no very material difficulties remain to be conquered; the shewing men the gradual advances of science, would be a means of inciting them to a more eager pursuit of learning, to distinguish themselves, and to do honour to their country: With this view, the present work was undertaken [. . .]

Significantly, the North British spirit of cultural emulation animating the aims of the new periodical are presented as a means to inspire further national cultural improvement, which, as the literati behind it make clear, will 'do honour to their country'.[37]

The first number of the 1755 *Edinburgh Review* presents what might be called an Enlightenment division of intellectual labour in its contents. The complementary critical efforts of the periodical's main collaborators are displayed for public benefit, mirroring – in print form – the kind of intellectual practice encouraged by the meetings of the Select Society. Critical reviews of a history of Peter the Great by William Robertson, the moral philosophy of Francis Hutcheson by Hugh Blair, Ebenezer Erskine's sermons by John Jardine, reports from the Court of Session by Alexander Wedderburn and Samuel Johnson's *Dictionary of the English Language* by Adam Smith, reflect how cultural production in this developing national public sphere constructively overlaps amongst intellectuals representing distinct but related branches of Scotland's principal post-1707 academic, legal and theological institutions.[38]

In this collective endeavour – perhaps the most ambitious periodical project of Scotland's eighteenth-century national public sphere – the practice of the critical reviewer is invested with the wider hopes of the country for intellectual and moral improvement. 'The success of the work is what they have principally at heart,' write the conductors of the first *Edinburgh Review*, 'as it may possibly be attended with a national benefit' (p. iv), prompting Sher's recent observation that 'the purpose of the *Edinburgh Review* was nothing less than to incite a national enlightenment'.[39] Despite these high hopes, the journal folded after the appearance of only its second number. Its use as a propaganda tool for the Moderates' ideological battles with the Popular party may have been partly to blame. It is more likely, however, that the first *Edinburgh Review* was the victim of its readership's unfamiliarity with the new format of the intellectual review – with juxtaposed critical accounts of contemporary academic, theological, legal and literary subjects – and the generally underdeveloped public appetite for print versions of the kind of wide-ranging topical discourse to be had in the Select Society. Chitnis observes:

> The history of the Select Society parallels the brief life of the first *Edinburgh Review* and similarly indicates that, despite the galaxy of talent and the interests represented, the 1750s may yet have been too early a stage in development for the corporate expression of high Enlightenment to have been made manifest.[40]

The year the Select Society was disbanded, 1764, witnessed the establishment of the Speculative Society, which would have a considerable influence on the editorial agenda, topical discourse and intellectual orientation of the second *Edinburgh Review*, founded almost forty years later, in 1802. This Edinburgh University debating society's stated aim was 'Improvement in Literary Composition, and Public Speaking'. As Chitnis argues more generally of the role of student societies in the Scottish Enlightenment, though, the Speculative soon became an extension of the 'distinctive Scottish university education', where students 'exposed to ideas or exercises such as debates in the classroom, took them up outside'.[41] The Speculative's meetings were held on the grounds of Edinburgh University and, like the Select Society, followed a format that informed the distinctively didactic structure of critical discourse in the second *Edinburgh Review*. During meetings a paper would be read and discussed, and then followed by a debate on another topic.[42] The intellectual range was impressive: moral and speculative philosophy, economics, politics, aesthetics, literature and history as well as specific issues of public policy.[43] This mixed topical structure also encouraged a rather liberal mixing of abstract and practical forms of knowledge, which carried over into the distinctive combination of intellectual rigour and restlessness that marked the essay style of the second *Edinburgh Review*. Society member Francis Jeffrey's lead article in the first issue of the journal in 1802 exemplifies this when he discusses the French writer J. J. Mounier's study of the *philosophes* and their impact on the Revolution from both abstract and political perspectives.[44] In this display of intellectual dexterity, as George Pottinger has commented, Jeffrey was 'inviting his readers to share in the kind of debate he had enjoyed at the Speculative Society'.[45]

Chitnis observes that the Society presented its members with lessons in 'debating, reasoning, elaborating knowledge introduced in the classroom', as well as providing an 'introduction to the passion of politics'.[46] For the generation of members that founded the second *Edinburgh Review* the applied and socially-directed forms of knowledge available at the meetings of the Speculative echoed the famed lectures in moral philosophy and political economy delivered by Dugald Stewart, Ferguson's successor in 1785 in the prestigious Edinburgh moral philosophy chair.[47] Through his classes Stewart provided students like Jeffrey, Henry Brougham and Francis Horner with a distillation of the most practical and relevant elements contained within the Scottish Enlightenment's theory of society, creatively illustrating and amplifying his lessons with references to literature, economics and ethics. One of his students, Henry Cockburn, noted that Stewart's 'generality and his indulgence in moral themes [. . .] constituted the very charm of his course', adding that 'he who, either in the business of life, or in the prosecution of philosophy, had occasion to recur to principles, always found that, either for study or for practice, Stewart's doctrines were his surest guide'.[48] Chitnis concurs with this first-hand observation by Cockburn, commenting: 'Stewart effectively equipped his students with responses to the new age: classical economics, moral seriousness and virtue, industry and sensibility'.[49] If Stewart's lectures prepared his students for the social and moral complexities of the dawning industrial age – which they later explored in the wide ranging cultural criticism of the *Edinburgh Review* – then the debates of the Speculative functioned as a necessary adjunct in which the most pressing contemporary issues could be discussed. Indeed, Cockburn – who became a member of the Speculative in 1799 – reckoned that a 'debating society was one of the natural results' of Stewart's classes.[50]

Key social institutions of the Edinburgh-based national public sphere in Scotland like the Select and Speculative societies helped to propel their members into important positions of cultural leadership during the latter half of the eighteenth century. This process of local institutional ascent had, by the early nineteenth century, overlapped with significant changes in the structure of the wider British public sphere, illustrated by the new form of cultural production and dissemination associated with the second *Edinburgh Review*. These separate but interlinked trajectories in British cultural history of the long eighteenth century elevated Scotland's capital – then regarded as the 'Athens of the North' – to a position of intellectual and cultural leadership in Britain, as Ian Duncan has recently argued in *Scott's Shadow*.

Duncan's compelling thesis about the city as a Romantic metropolis *par excellence* rests, in part, on the new forms of cultural politics played out both through and around Edinburgh's most prominent literary periodicals, the liberal Whig *Edinburgh Review* and the Tory *Blackwood's Edinburgh Magazine*. However, for the purposes of this chapter's discussion of periodical culture and the public sphere in a Scottish long eighteenth century, and the role played by both versions of the *Edinburgh Review* in its intellectual articulation, the chief concern here is with Duncan's conception of the city's post-Enlightenment metropolitan status and his contention that the second *Review* 'established the authoritative forum of cultural commentary for the age'. Duncan highlights the Scottish capital's post-Enlightenment identity through, as he puts it, the 'rise of an Edinburgh publishing industry and the reorientation of Scottish writing to periodicals and fiction', and divides the city's post-Enlightenment cultural history into three distinct phases in the early nineteenth century.[51]

Of these three post-Enlightenment stages, the one that most clearly relates to the discussion carried out here is the first, when the liberal intellectual impetus which supported the national public sphere was driven away from the primary institutions of Edinburgh's civil society and absorbed into the discourse of its leading cultural periodical. For Duncan, the key agent in this transition was the anti-Jacobin repression of the 1790s which, as he argues, 'provoked a crisis of ideological legitimation in the institutions of civil society and effectively shut down the so-called Scottish Enlightenment', isolating local academic leaders like Dugald Stewart and greatly curtailing the political autonomy of the national public sphere. 'Politics thus hastened, if it did not solely drive, the commercial devolution of the Scottish Republic of Letters,' Duncan writes. This 'devolution' led to the development of a different kind of public sphere centred around the city's periodical culture in general and the *Edinburgh Review* in particular. The founding editors of the second *Review* exemplified the transition to a post-Enlightenment public sphere, with their intellectual formation taking place within key cultural institutions of late

Enlightenment Edinburgh like the Speculative Society. This distinctively Scottish institutional experience fostered, according to Duncan, 'a liberal, professional culture of intellectual work and literary production, independent (to a limited but effective degree) from both the state and market, although enmeshed in regional patronage networks'.[52]

In Duncan's recounting, the post-Enlightenment public sphere initiated by the founding of the second *Edinburgh Review* was also facilitated by the cultural entrepreneurialism of the publisher Archibald Constable, who materialised 'Enlightenment conditions of authorship into the genres of the market'. He did this in part through an attempt to update eighteenth-century traditions of patronage, paying handsomely for the work done by the new journal's editors and contributors. This commercial innovation encouraged both the professional identity and moral autonomy of the intellectuals associated with the *Review*. It gave to these emerging leaders of the nineteenth-century bourgeois public sphere in Britain a sense of cultural legitimacy that rivalled their Enlightenment predecessors. As Duncan observes, 'Constable and the Edinburgh reviewers were thus able to reconfigure, in the early nineteenth-century press, a functional equivalent of the cultural authority of the Enlightenment philosophers'.[53] In *The Enlightenment and the Book* (2006) Richard Sher has also emphasised how Edinburgh's cultural authority in the nineteenth century was greatly enhanced by Constable's innovative publishing strategy, citing a contemporary account that remarks on how 'the establishment of the Edinburgh Review, and the enterprise of the House with which that celebrated publication originated, have procured for Edinburgh, not only the printing of works of native genius, but transferred to this city the printing and publication of books from every quarter of the empire'.[54] The young Whig lawyers who wrote for the *Review*, effectively shut out of the Tory-controlled Edinburgh legal establishment, used this enhanced cultural status to project their critical judgements with quasi-official ideological clout, masking the journal's commercial and partisan origins. As Duncan argues:

> The *Edinburgh Review* opened a new public domain of literary and scientific culture, which it defined in professional, judicial terms as a disciplinary court of judgment and evaluation rather than a marketplace of information and opinion. Jeffrey and his fellow advocates convened a critical equivalent of the Court of Session, a literary reinvention of the old Scottish Parliament-House.[55]

The second *Edinburgh Review* also reproduced, as Marilyn Butler has noted, an academic model of periodical knowledge based on 'the specialisms for which Scottish universities were famous'. In the contents of its first numbers one finds the residual material presence of the university curriculum at Edinburgh – most particularly Stewart's moral philosophy and political economy classes – which helped to shape the conceptual habits of its leading editors and contributors. But one finds also the intellectual and moral imprint of the wider national public sphere in Scotland, where critical debates about literature, politics, the natural sciences, history, economics and philosophy were often promiscuously mixed in the service of a discussion about how knowledge can serve social ends for a larger national good. In this, the conductors of the journal had as an utmost concern, as Butler has argued, a desire to 'influence a more elite stratum of opinion'.[56] This concern marked the *Review*'s policy of textual discrimination, articulated in a highly assured 'Advertisement' where the editors write that 'they wish their Journal to be distinguished, rather for the selection, than for the numbers, of its articles', with a busy and engaged professional readership clearly in mind.[57] The policy of textual selection was also a manifestation of the Reviewers' absolute sense of intellectual confidence; a confidence gained from the esteem they felt due to highly educated professional men in a national public sphere that valued informed critical debate as a primary means to social respectability. This carried over into the 'northern metropolitan' aspect of the journal's critical mission at the centre of a rapidly developing bourgeois public sphere in Britain, intellectually administered from Edinburgh rather than London.

When viewed in a discrete Scottish context that takes in the development of the national public sphere over the long eighteenth century, this critical mission demonstrates how the intellectuals in one small European country shaped its modern development through forms of cultural association that explicitly linked social progress to material improvement, while basing their leadership and authority on an intensely moral conception of public reason. This last element, whether illustrated in the literary clubs, General Assembly debates, student society forums or academic scholarship of the period, provides a particularly Scottish inflection to the ideal of public reason portrayed in Habermas' *Structural Transformation*. The success of the 1802 incarnation of the *Edinburgh Review* finally redeemed those earlier hopes for an intellectually dynamic and influential North British print culture articulated in the preface of its Enlightenment predecessor. It demonstrates how the Scottish national public sphere in the second half of the eighteenth century provided the ideological basis for the emergence of the leading British review of the early nineteenth. This wider historical trajectory allows us to see how the intellectual modernity of the Scottish national public sphere – the outcome of both the institutional autonomy of Scotland's civil society after 1707 and its particular assimilation of metropolitan and commercial values – informed an innovative new practice of periodical criticism. It made the second *Edinburgh Review* a dominant intellectual presence in the British public sphere, and Scotland's capital the new cultural metropolis of the nineteenth century.

CHAPTER EIGHT

The Scottish National Tale

Andrew Monnickendam

This chapter begins with a discussion of the term 'National Tale', before going on to examine its literary origins. It then proceeds to examine the work of five prominent practitioners: Elizabeth Hamilton (1756?-1816), Jane Porter (1776–1850), Mary Brunton (1775–1818), Susan Ferrier (1782–1854) and Christian Isobel Johnstone (1782–1854). Although it will deal with the authors individually, four common topics will be highlighted: landscape, language, romance and Ireland. Traditionally, the national tale is seen with Scott at its core, whereas these five writers occupy the periphery. All five are aware of this hierarchical difference, but it would be wrong to see their fiction as merely imitative or subservient.

The Scottish national tale comprises two basic elements: the first locates it geographically and the second locates it aesthetically. 'National' obviously means Scotland, making the national tale an example of what is often referred to as conservative romanticism, that is to say it emphasises the communal over the more individualist, rebellious Byronic strand. Conservative romanticism stresses national as opposed to classical origins: its focus turns to ancient myths and legends – Ossian, William Wallace, for example – as the essential cultural roots that should not only be conserved but cultivated in language, art and in accounts of history. However, as soon as Scotland's diversity is examined – Gaelic, Scots, Highlands, Lowlands and so on – the situation becomes more mixed. In addition, Gregory Smith's influential account of Scottish literary culture, which coined the phrase the 'Caledonian antisyzygy',[1] indicates a tricky relationship between cohesion (Caledonia) and diversity (antisyzygy) in the 'national'. The term 'tale' is equally tendentious. Scott's 1829 'General Preface' uses tale and novel as interchangeable terms, so we must accept that a tale's fantastic side does not diminish its social or political message. The novel's questionable status as a work of art is based on the widespread eighteenth-century suspicion that it might inflame its readers' imagination or blur the boundary between fact and fiction: one way of rectifying this situation is to write fiction with such a strong didactic function that these dangers never occur.

To these two elements, 'national' and 'tale', a third should be added, namely 'romance', as it is the structure on which the national tale is built. Many follow the standard pattern of a couple falling in love, who are then separated or fall out of love only to be united again in a more solid partnership based on the experience of life rather than of romantic fiction. Sometimes, this implies the rejection of a superficial for a more mature partner. *Waverley*'s double ending, the marriage and the postscript, has rendered countless interpretations of how the personal is subsumed to the public; that is, the romance is often seen primarily as a symbolic enactment which the postscript, with its exegesis on the advantages of the Union, clarifies. This may or may not be a legitimate activity, but it can suggest a pattern for national tales that is not necessarily present in all texts.

The Scottish national tale develops from two different traditions: the epic and didactic fiction. Although Milton suggested that the early modern period required no military epic, the romantic quest for non-classical cultural origins inspired just such creations, often recovering medieval texts for contemporary audiences and taste. Scott is doubtless the major exponent of this phenomenon, as his European literary reception amply demonstrates. Jane Porter's *The Scottish Chiefs* (1810), which recreates the exploits of William Wallace, is a popular example; it is contemporary to Scott's epic poetry, such as *The Lay of the Last Minstrel* (1805), *Marmion* (1808) and *The Lady of the Lake* (1810). Although the other four writers were deeply influenced by the female reformers of the late eighteenth century, such as Hannah More (1745–1833) or Mary Wollstonecraft (1759–1797), what turns their didactic fiction into a national tale is the influence of Maria Edgeworth (1767–1849) as this affects the portrayal of national character in such works as *Castle Rackrent* (1802) or *Essay on Irish Bulls* (1802) and in her more openly instructive, later fiction.

Later editions of Elizabeth Hamilton's *The Cottagers of Glenburnie* (1808) often include a brief memoir which begins 'Mrs Elizabeth Hamilton [. . .] was a native of Ireland, having been born in Belfast. She was descended from a respectable Scottish family, which had emigrated to Ireland, in consequence of the religious persecutions in the time of Charles II.'[2] At the age of six she moved to Stirlingshire and in adulthood lived in Sunning, Berkshire. Clearly, the question of defining her origins – a native of Ireland having been born in Belfast – and sense of nationality are anything but easy. It is worthwhile retaining the idea that the national tale and its authors are deeply involved in questions of identity, but these are often quite slippery to get a grip on. It is apparent from the title that the novel focuses on the domestic side of Scottish life; it might remind us of Burns' 'The Cotter's Saturday Night' or perhaps simply the iconic status of Burns' cottage as representative of essential Scottish values. The novel is episodic; it follows the life and career of Mrs Mason: first, as a servant; second, in her campaign for cleanliness; and third as an educational theorist. Mrs Mason's success as a servant is based on two fundamental principles: a belief in keeping to one's station and honesty. The various episodes are highly moralistic. Short-term advantages gained by telling white lies will always create problems: 'But liars never escape detection; sooner or later they fall into their own snares' (*Cottagers*, pp. 31–2). In the first part of the novel, it is seen as difficult to survive in a world dominated by morally corrupt aristocrats (especially vain females), spoilt children and dishonest servants who are always jockeying for position. A special emphasis is placed on the education of children; the ideal child is 'tractable and obedient' (p. 14). The fact that Mrs Mason was put in charge of the nursery – surrogate mother and therefore instructor – is irrefutable proof of her virtue, and a guarantee in the latter part of the novel that she can reform the cottagers. The distinctly Scottish episodes parallel the earlier process of being a governess: both are examples of improvement. However, the family in question is named MacClarty and 'clarty' is the Scots for filth. So, on the one hand, filth suggests that there is plenty of room for reform, while on the other, as the book progresses, the inescapable feeling is that Mrs Mason and the family she is to educate live in different worlds rather than in the same country. The reason why there is no water for washing hands (p. 75) and the problems with a dirty knife and the hairs in the butter suggest that Scotland's cottagers are almost backward. An additional problem occurs if we listen to Mrs MacClarty's words: 'I did na mind that I had been stirring fire, and my hands were a wee sooty; but it will soon scrape aff; there's a dirty knife will take it aff in a minute' (p. 65). Mrs Mason speaks Standard English whereas the cottagers speak Scots; in other words, the language of reform is English, and those in urgent need of reform speak Scots. Thus a wedge is firmly driven between the two parts. Not only is it marked linguistically, but the cottagers repeat the same phrase each time they are asked why something has not been done, namely, 'canna be fash'd', which occurs with such regularity that it becomes an irritating signpost indicating surliness and indolence. In short, they are 'internal exotica',[3] one step away from the lazy native. The novel concludes with a lengthy discussion of how best a school should be run, with an open preference for educational methods that encourage reasoning. This description of the novel might be bewildering, in the sense that it is not immediately clear if we are reading fiction or a tract, and it is precisely that middle-ground between didacticism and entertainment that it occupies. Its account of Scotland remains deeply problematic.

Two years later, Durham-born Jane Porter published *The Scottish Chiefs*, an account of William Wallace. If Hamilton's fiction focuses on the unhappy situation of rural lives, Porter opens up the national canvas to draw an epic picture. Having previously mentioned the question of language, we should note that Porter avoids it completely by using what is basically a pseudo-epic style, for example, in this dramatic description of events at Stirling Castle: 'Terrible now was the havoc; for the desperate Scots, grappling each to his foe with a fatal hold, let not go till the piercing shriek, or the agonised groan, convinced him death had seized his victim.'[4] Dialogue is also highly stylised, with oaths like 'blasphemous wretch' recurrent. What does Porter add to this legendary tale and foundational figure? Wallace has enormous vigour and strength, but he also becomes saintly, renouncing all worldly pleasure after the murder of his wife. In a reply to a taunt that his men are soft, he replies

> I seek to make them men [. . .] to be aware that they fight with fellow-creatures, with whom they may one day be friends; and not like the furious savages of old Scandinavia, drink the blood of eternal enmity [. . .] That Scotland bleeds at every pore, is sure; but let peace be our aim, and we shall heal all her wounds. (*Scottish Chiefs* I: p. 340)

As this extract illustrates, Porter's Wallace is interested in healing; this is not a revenge tragedy but something closer to a hagiography. Wallace is so different from the bloody ideology of his time that '[T]he majority of the Scottish nobles envied Wallace his glory, and hated him for that virtue' (II: p. 283). He is almost a Christ figure; his abhorrence of the evils of his world are encapsulated in the word 'tyranny' (I: p. 161), which is precisely the reason for Wallace's enormous following among the common people. Porter's reliance on epic tradition is evident in her use of other stylistic devices, for example, the soliloquy as the most recurrent form of self-examination; Wallace's scar recalls Odysseus' and the central incident of the barns of Ayr, *Beowulf*, the Edwin–Wallace relationship, David and Jonathan. In short, Porter places her epic geographically within its Scottish location but culturally within the traditions of Western warrior epics.

Porter focuses on cruelty to highlight her mystical Wallace, yet there is another reason why she details cruelty throughout the three volumes: to highlight cruelty to women. Wallace's militarism is a consequence of his wife's brutal murder. After denouncing Edward I and his followers as tyrants, she is stabbed through the chest. The horrendous nature of the murder is accentuated by the fact that she was pregnant at the time. The most salient female figure is Lady Mar, who in the end betrays Wallace after he refuses to return her rather blatant advances. So she might easily be portrayed as evil or just a femme fatale; the reverse is the case. She spends most of volume II cross-dressed as a fighter. Her sexuality is a consequence of a troubled adolescence which, in modern terms, would be identified as sexual harassment and abuse. In short, Porter's detailed portrayal of Mar – a Mary Magdalene figure – gives a female protagonist a history to tell and a voice to go with it which, if not on a par with the story of Wallace himself, does not lag far behind.

If *The Scottish Chiefs* is a national tale, is it a defence of Scottish culture and identity? If Wallace is the central figure, this would make the question rhetorical. Moreover, the aggressors are basically English; they employ every evil tactic that invading armies can use: rape, plunder, burning abbeys and castles, and Edward's scorched-earth policy, purposely designed to create the greatest misery to the greatest number of innocent people. However, in addressing the need to live together after warfare, the despicable treatment of women, Wallace's saintliness and his followers' jealousy, Porter uses both national and supra-national parameters. This begs the question as to whether, when contemplating his terrible death, we ponder more on the cruelty of Edward or on the fact that Wallace was too good for his time and country.

It might seem odd that nothing has yet been said about landscape, as initially this should be the essential ingredient of a description of a national setting. Landscape might appear in the clichéd form of misty glens and heather-clad hills or in a Burkean duality of the beautiful and the sublime, but its rare appearance or semi-absence in some of the texts may nevertheless be surprising. Two explanations are useful. The first is to recall that the eighteenth-century tradition of travel writing is not fixated by setting. Take, for example, Boswell's *An Account of Corsica* (1768), in which the author comments on great men and history, customs, society and religion; landscape is perfunctorily described. We read of the calm Mediterranean, rocks and olive trees, but little else. Second, novelists often use landscape as a metaphor. Mary Brunton's two completed novels *Self-Control* (1811) and *Discipline* (1814) are variations on the same theme: the female pursued. The pursuers are unscrupulous men who desire their bodies and unscrupulous aristocrats who desire 'new' money; a male aristocrat therefore is the most heinous combination possible. Brunton's heroines are sexually and financially desirable. In the first novel, this culminates in a snap transatlantic kidnapping, so, when Laura eventually returns to her beloved Glenalbert, it is no surprise to hear her exultant cry 'Blessed be thou among nations!'[5] but it is precisely the implication of 'blessed' that determines the otherwise sparsely articulated landscape. Laura returns on a Sunday to see Scotland at its best, yet it is at its best because it is Sunday. Hence the landscape becomes a backcloth while the soberly attired churchgoers become the object of admiration. In this particular case, Laura has just returned from a wild escapade in Canada, so nature is what she has fled from.

The storyline and conclusions to Brunton's two complete novels are similar. The familiar Gothic trope of pursuit is capped by a marriage to an elder male who may or may not be materially rich but certainly is so spiritually. The first novel concludes that the joys of domestic life cannot be described; *Discipline* adds that Scots 'wants energy' to describe such pleasure.[6] Is this nothing more than prudishness? Unlike many readers of her fiction, I do not believe so. The final pages are full of remarks about love as portrayed in fiction, using the familiar formula of informing the reader that life is not like the fiction of other authors. The ideal man writes: 'I am no weak lover now. I know you ladies are firm believers in the eternity of love'(*Discipline*, p. 469). 'Weak' means someone whose emotions override reason. Brunton's heroines are fulfilled in the role of motherhood but this does not necessarily mean that all remnants of desire have fizzled out. First, the plots of both novels are sparked by deep physical desire; in the case of the first novel, through the intense language of Laura's first suitor, Hargrave, and in the second, by the realisation that Ellen has fallen in love with the father of the child whom she educates and nurses. The novels therefore depict the transfer of desire from an unsuitable object to one which is lawful, in other words, sexuality will be contained within marriage. Ellen, at the close of *Discipline*, tells us that her husband is 'still a kind of lover' and that she 'retain[s] a little [. . .] coquettish sauciness' (*Discipline*, p. 476).

Religion features prominently in the national tale. Brunton's religiosity is as strong as that of Hamilton's Mrs Mason. In a world where the female is constantly under attack, it is difficult to imagine what can sustain an adolescent orphan untutored in the ways of the world. One answer would be the many coincidences and divine interventions in the nick of time. The second is religious fortitude, in many cases supplemented by authorial interpolation and sermonising. This might explain an otherwise curious comment that accompanies 'Helps to Devotion Selected from the Holy Scriptures' which accompany the posthumous fragment *Emmeline* (1819). Addressing her dear young friends, Brunton insists that the author of these pious pieces is 'a woman in the prime of life, as cheerful, as happy'.[7] She is aware that a heavy dose of Calvinism might not give that impression. Her fiction is the work of a thoughtful, intelligent writer, but it is difficult not to conclude that a dumbing-down of her religious Scotland emerges in the form of the Kailyard.

In stark contrast to her fiction, Brunton's correspondence is charming, lively and witty. A similar pattern is present in Ferrier's writings. The section 'The History of Mrs Douglas' from *Marriage* (1818), sets out the moral pattern by which the heroine of the novel will live and survive; it is the ideological centre. However important it is, it was described by Ferrier's great-nephew and editor of her correspondence as 'so depressingly conventional',[8] a quite common appreciation. Similarly, much closer to our time, scholars argue that her fiction contains 'great lumps of moralizing'[9] or '[i]n *Marriage* there are approximately eighteen references to religion, in *The Inheritance* there are over thirty, and in *Destiny* there are about eighty'.[10] 'The History of Mrs Douglas' was not written by Ferrier but by her friend and correspondent

Charlotte Clavering. What is curious is that their correspondence sparkles, in complete contrast to the moral biography of Mrs Douglas. Fiction was, it seems, the place for heavy moralising while correspondence permitted impishness. That said, an important distinction must be drawn between the practice of Hamilton or Ferrier, where religion and moralising play important roles, and Brunton, for whom religion is life itself and the major source of happiness.

Although Ferrier's readers and critics have expressed dissatisfaction with her moralising and interpolations, her satirical edge, defined by the great philologist George Saintsbury as 'rather a saw than a razor',[11] has entertained many readers, particularly as concerns two characters, Miss Pratt of *The Inheritance* and the Reverend Redgill of *Marriage*. As his alliterative name suggests, Redgill is red at the gills because of his love of food and drink: 'The [Scottish] people I give up – they are dirty and greedy – the country, too, is a perfect mass of rubbish [. . .] but the breakfasts! That's what redeems the land'.[12] The novel also includes a ball; whereas in Brunton's *Discipline*, the decision to attend or not attend a masked ball causes the heroine enormous emotional anxiety, in *Marriage*, what concerns this man of God is not the moral state of the youthful but the worry that the ball might delay the preparation of his breakfast the day after the night before. Saintsbury states that some of the characterisations in *Marriage* 'rank with the best originals in English fiction'. He compares her to both Edgeworth and Austen: 'None of [Edgeworth's] books is so good as *The Inheritance* and several of them are much worse than *Marriage* or *Destiny*', and sums the situation up by proposing that 'of the four requisites of the novelist, plot, character, description and dialogue, she is only weak in the first'.[13] Margaret Oliphant, writing at the same time, has similar views. She sees the three writers as sharing the same language while 'revealing the characteristics of her race in a manner as amusing as instructive'. She believes that 'there are points in which Miss Ferrier is almost superior to Miss Austen, having a touch more tender and a deeper poetic insight'.[14] Such high esteem indicates, amongst other things, a firm belief in the didactic function of the national tale in England, Ireland and Scotland. Yet, it is curious to see that the belief in a female trio enables Ferrier to be both part of a national tradition and to escape its limits.

What then, accounts for her virtual disappearance from the canon? It is often stated that her later works become increasingly moral, but, if morality was a determining factor, the vast majority of her contemporaries would have suffered the same fate, which has not happened, witness the prestige Edgeworth currently enjoys. The answer may lie in what seemed her most valuable asset: her humour.

Marriage is a *commedia dell'arte* with a large caste of female characters – 'men do not feature prominently in Ferrier's fiction'[15] – which dwells relentlessly on how Scotland has been represented. The novel starts with an elopement to the Scottish Highlands, at the thought of which 'Lady Juliana was transported with joy' (*Marriage*, p. 6). Juliana's ecstasy is the result of having read too many novels and of her profound ignorance of Scotland. One by one, all the typical markers of Scotland will confound her naivety. The castle is dreich, the bagpipes make a horrible noise on a level with the Scots language, herrings are a horrible part of a horrible diet and so on. Comedy is provided by her dressing inappropriately for the landscape; she will get wet and cold. Ferrier wags her finger at another Scot, James Thomson (1700–1748), author of *The Seasons* (1730) for supplying her with an idyllic picture of nature. Scotland is eventually too much for her, 'But in vain were creation's charms spread before Lady Juliana's eyes. Woods, and mountains, and lakes, and rivers, were odious things; and her heart panted for dusty squares, and suffocating drawing-rooms' (*Marriage*, p. 115).

Chief among Juliana's dislikes is the Scots tongue. This is exacerbated by the fact that her own daughter has been brought up in Scotland. 'Then, to hear the Scotch brogue – oh heavens! I should expire every time she opened her mouth!' (*Marriage*, p. 189). As an example of Ferrier's 'saw', this quotation foregrounds the shallowness and idiocy of its speaker, Lady Juliana, while forcing us to consider that problematic relationship between language and community. Just as her trip to Scotland introduced her to a country rather different from her expectations, so this comment implies that Scotland is not an intelligible country to its large English audience (an illustration of how extensive Scotland-in-fiction became is Sarah Green's *Scotch Novel Reading* (1824), a novel full of caricatures of both Scottish fictional subjects and gullible London readers). Ferrier's treatment of humour is close to the focus on linguistic slips and their interpretation that Edgeworth set out in her essay on Irish bulls. In the case of *Marriage*, the laughs produced by the antics of Juliana and Redgill result from a long history of inbred, anti-Scottish prejudices. However, that does not necessarily mean that Ferrier directs her satirical arsenal only towards English subjects. Her third and final novel, *Destiny*, saws apart her Scottish characters. The canny Scot, Inch Orran, is hideous, as is the lecherous, gluttonous minister; the laird's bombast is ridiculed too. In contrast, Ferrier's moral heroines look pale and dull: Juliana has some memorable lines in *Marriage* whereas the heroine, Mary, has none. But in addition to this familiar contrast between the wicked and the anodyne, *Destiny* shows that Ferrier's onslaught is relentless, no one escapes her scornful tongue. This is a result of her distaste at what she often labels vulgarity, which she sees as a defining factor of the modern world. Her satire is therefore her *Schadenfreude*, and is never mitigated by romance. *Marriage*, for example, the wittiest novel, ends as we would expect a romance to end, but the love declaration is made at a deathbed and the two lovers are hardly sprightly things; instead, they are two adults who have aged prematurely. Her *Schadenfreude* produces an outlook on life which is so misanthropic that, without the accompanying humour, it becomes unpalatable. This, as much as her moral interpolations, has contributed to the decline in her fortunes.

Johnstone's *Clan-Albin* (1815) and *Elizabeth de Bruce* (1827) come from the pen of a rather different writer, who is more openly concerned with political issues of the day, as seen from a liberal, Scottish angle. These include such things as voting reform, many aspects of the Irish question, specifically Scottish questions such as the Clearances and Presbyterianism, as well as many of the subjects that interested Mary Wollstonecraft and her contemporaries, such as marriage, education and the role of fiction. Johnstone herself was a successful career journalist, editor of *Tait's Edinburgh Magazine* between 1834 and 1846. To judge from the first of these two novels, she maintains a certain scepticism about the political class of her day, as one character has a pet parrot (a most unflattering metaphor) which repeats slogans like ' "*Rope for Pitt*," – "*Walk rogues*," – "*Coach for Fox*" '.[16] Its owner might change parties for convenience's sake, but the parrot cannot unlearn one party line and pick up another so quickly.

Johnstone's treatment of religion displays her deeper intellectual concerns. Her fervent religious figures, Gideon in *Elizabeth de Bruce* and Buchanan in *Clan-Albin* take their Calvinism seriously, which makes for both praise and criticism: Gideon stands up against the manipulative Hutchen; Buchanan does his best as a teacher. But they also have their faults, faults derived from rigidity. In the case of Buchanan, this is evident in his reliance on memorising in education, whereas Johnstone, like Hamilton, seems to favour a more rational approach, as evident in her educational books such as *The Diversions of Hollycot* (1828) or *Rational Reading Lessons* (1842). Two incidents from *Clan-Albin* – one humorous, the other suggestive – exhibit Johnstone's ambivalence. During a heated argument about religion, one villager, Hugh, tries to make peace by saying that hopefully in heaven Catholics and Protestants will all come together. 'Buchanan's eyes glowed with holy zeal while he said,- "Impossible!" ' (p. 75). Buchanan sees the peacemaker's appeal as an attack on the doctrine of Predestination. In a very strange twist of fate, Buchanan's daughter Flora converts to Catholicism at the novel's conclusion. The narrative voice stresses that she is not 'rigid or *theological*' (*Clan-Albin*, p. 548); Johnstone has opted for religious tolerance.

Johnstone is perhaps the only author who analyses the language question in an open manner, concentrating on Gaelic. *Clan-Albin* has an authoritative matriarch, but while Mrs Mason is dogmatic, prescribing how things have to be done, Lady Augusta is a polyglot, widely travelled and cultured: she is an Enlightenment philosopher. The orphan Norman is known amongst his kinsfolk as 'the Lady's child' (*Clan-Albin*, p. 31), which is not the biological truth but the cultural one: we are witnessing an experiment in education as radical as Rousseau's, but, in the narrator's eyes, much better. One platform is religious tolerance, as already mentioned, and the other is linguistic. Norman is to be bilingual:

> The Lady wished that he should converse familiarly in English from his earliest infancy [. . .] She was not however infected with the fashionable fear which now reigns in most Highland families; she was old-fashioned enough to think that there was nothing very horrible or vulgar in a mountain child lisping the language of the mountains [. . .] She even felt something like contempt for those modern renegadoes who pride themselves in real, and often on affected ignorance of all that it should be their boast to know. (p. 32)

However, the fact that her Gaelic-speaking community is so isolated and its villages have been cleared is evidence that her ideas are sadly from another era. This partly accounts for the lengthy descriptions in the novel's first volume of dying Highland life and customs.

Ferrier's last novel is sombre; the result, arguably, of an increasing unease about the question of romance, which is present in all her work. Johnstone's fiction displays similar disquiet. A novel of education instructs its characters in the harsh ways of life, leading to a more realistic view of human emotions, which, in turn, will lead to a more solid family structure. In the case of *Clan-Albin*, the spouses have gone beyond these requirements; they certainly have been buffeted by outrageous fortune, yet their knowledge of the world corresponds more to that of a world-weary philosopher than a dashing lover. The isolation that encases Johnstone's Glenalbert is more akin to Voltaire than to Scott; thus the plans for improving the material conditions of life have more to do with *Candide*'s celebrated advice for survival through withdrawal- 'il faut cultiver notre jardin'- than with the breezy confidence of the language of improvement.

Johnstone's concern with Ireland has two constituent parts. One is the description of its sorry state, summarised in Lady Augusta's highly alliterative aphorism that Ireland is a country 'which God has made, and man has marred-' (*Clan-Albin*, p. 88). Who exactly is 'man' in this instance? Johnstone is particularly harsh on absentee landlords, general ignorance and the brutal treatment meted out by the British army. This takes the form of a sub-plot in which a young, brave Irishman, who could have followed the path of the central character Norman, has been witness to such cruelty that he deserts and goes to fight for Napoleon. Ireland is also presented as a political conundrum. Norman volunteers for a Highland regiment that is sent to Ireland, before going to the Peninsular War. Bearing in mind that a regiment is defined as either fencible, stationed within the union, or line, and therefore liable for service overseas, is it more accurate to say that Ireland is really inside or outside the Union? Home or abroad? What is the role of a Highland regiment here in either case? There is little doubt that Johnstone is identifying a neo-colonialist situation rather than liminality. The conundrum is similarly phrased by Pittock in his analysis of Maria Edgeworth: 'it is a true "literature of combat", posing as a literature of reconciliation'.[17]

Elizabeth de Bruce is an outstanding novel for at least two reasons. It goes directly to the centre of the conundrum of Union by openly drawing connections throughout between the fate of Scotland and Ireland. People move continually from one country to another; the 1745 uprising in Scotland is twinned thematically with 1798 rebellion in Ireland; the eponymous heroine is a child of both countries; and so on. This underwrites the fact that in terms of time, for the national tale, the closest example of a union is the 1800 Act of Union with Ireland. In terms of literary history, for a writer like Johnstone, Scott's epic poetry and fiction is fundamental, but so too is Sydney Owenson's *The Wild Irish Girl: A National Tale* (1808), a foundational text for the way it proposes the Glorvina solution. Briefly, Owenson suggests that the marriage, the union between Glorvina and her Anglo-Irish suitor, will benefit both individuals as representatives of Ireland and England, so the love plot concludes with a marriage based on mutual desire, though not necessarily on equality. In other words, this is not, as Byron so pithily put it, a union between a shark and its prey, nor does it mean the extinction of the weaker party's personality or culture. The most easily identifiable correspondence between Ireland and Scotland is therefore cultural, the national tale itself, but Johnstone is striving to draw our attention to the fact that the relationship between the two countries is also a historical and political reality of which the textual is a portable, comfortable form. *Elizabeth de Bruce*, while simultaneously promoting these affinities, calls into question many of the national tale's literary conventions. The most important of these is the love-plot, which is of no significance at all, as the couple are already married before the essential plot device of separation takes place. The idea of a harmonious future is put on hold if not openly questioned. Johnstone's interest in Ireland is patent in all her writing. After publishing *Elizabeth de Bruce*, she dropped fiction in favour of journalism and educational writing. When she uses the word 'tale' again, it is with a different purpose: *True Tales of the Irish Peasantry, as Related by Themselves. Selected by Mrs. Johnstone for the Report of the Poor-Law Commissioners* (1839). These are truly harrowing witness accounts of poverty and starvation published before the Great Hunger.

Ferrier's third and final novel was published in 1831; Scott died in 1832. It is a tempting to conclude that these two events mark the end of the national tale, especially so as the writers analysed in this chapter are often seen as being Scott's auxiliaries. The nearness in time is indisputable, but this chapter has suggested that their national tale follows some but not all the same paths, while using different ones at certain key junctures. As *Waverley* is a pivotal text with two final chapters (Chapter 71 rounds off the love-plot, Chapter 72 traces the benefits of Union and Empire), there are, as we have seen, notable differences precisely in the treatment of the love-plot and its relation to the Union in these five writers. It is an irrelevance for Hamilton and Porter; Ferrier and Johnstone are continually bringing it into question; and Johnstone's fiction draws critical pictures of the British presence in Ireland, which rebounds back onto the question of Scotland's relationship with England and the whole question of Union. Another defining factor is the presence of religion. Hamilton, Brunton and Ferrier's moralising has troubled critics since their own day, yet it is necessary to understand its key role in the national tale: for them, Scottish religion makes Scotland distinctive; in addition, religion provides solace in an increasingly materialist, anglicised world. Even Johnstone, while not approving of much religious practice, is keenly aware of this, particularly in her detailed portraits of Scottish ministers. Of course, Scott controversially detailed Scottish religious practice in *Old Mortality* (1816), but it would be well-nigh impossible to maintain that his work is sustained by firm, active, religious beliefs. In the 'General Preface', Scott pays homage to Maria Edgeworth for promoting the Union. Edgeworth's influence over these five writers is also evident, but for a different reason: their prime concern is the didactic nature of fiction. The thorniest question of all is that of language, or more precisely, languages. Johnstone is eloquent about the value of Gaelic while realising it is waning rapidly; Porter evades the question completely; Brunton rarely touches it; and Ferrier is ambivalent. If there is such a thing as a general tendency, it takes the form of leaving the question open. In a sentence, we could say that the national tale is inevitably centred on or departs from Scott, but that is not the end of the story: it is a preface, not a postscript.

CHAPTER NINE

Religion and Scottish Romanticism

Crawford Gribben

The turn to religion in literary studies has brought with it a welcome atten-tion to the theological contexts of European Romanticism. This trend has been particularly evident in English studies, in which such canonical writers as William Hazlitt have been effectively defamiliarised by their being read within distinctive religious traditions.[1] But the same trend has been manifest in a significant number of recent publications in Scottish Romantic studies.[2] Work on Robert Burns, for example, has argued for a thorough reconsidera-tion of his reception and use of biblical and theological ideas, while work on James Hogg has argued that his best-known interrogation of Scottish Calvinism, *The Private Memoirs and Confessions of a Justified Sinner* (1824), may have almost nothing to do with satirising the religious culture it has been believed to represent.[3] As this new scholarly literature attests, there exist particular patterns of relationship between religion and the literature of Scottish Romanticism.

Scottish religion, during the Romantic period, was formed and func-tioned in ways quite different from the religious cultures of Ireland, Wales or England. In the late eighteenth and early nineteenth centuries, Scotland was overwhelmingly Christian, Protestant and Presbyterian.[4] The established Church and many of the smaller Protestant dissenting bodies still drew heavily, in theology and practice, on the legacy of the Reformation period. For Presbyterians, the Westminster Confession of Faith (1647) retained its pre-eminent place as the subsidiary doctrinal standard. Worship was con-ducted, broadly, in accordance with the liturgical structures provided by the Westminster Assembly's Directory for Public Worship (1648). Children were required to memorise the Assembly's Shorter Catechism (1648), con-gregations worshipped by singing from the Assembly's psalter (1650) and celebrations of the Lord's Supper were often conducted in the large, multi-congregational and open-air devotional festivals that had their roots in the 1660s.[5] The Confession of Faith and its supporting documents advanced a generic Calvinism that presupposed a national establishment of religion and unchanging doctrinal norms. By the end of the eighteenth century, however, this imagined hegemony of orthodoxy had been disrupted: in terms of ecclesiology, by secession from the establishment; in terms of theology, with the emergence of biblical rationalism; in terms of liturgy, with the popularisation of hymn singing; and in terms of culture, with the increasing influence of Enlightenment scepticism and print capitalism, and with the impact of democratic sentiment in the wider context of the European and American revolutions. But many Scottish Presbyterians continued to adhere to the foundational orthodoxies of their faith. Covenanters remained distinct from the established Church after the ecclesiastical settlement of 1690, which they believed failed to uphold the responsibilities into which Scottish government had freely entered with its swearing of the Solemn League and Covenant (1643). These 'United Societies' of 'Cameronians' gathered together in 1743 and gradually evolved into a national denomination as the Reformed Presbyterian Church, but they retained their radical political edge alongside a robust commitment to the confessional tradition and, ironically, their being romanticised after the popular success of Walter Scott's *Old Mortality* (1816).[6] The Secession Church, founded in 1733 by a small group of establishment clergy concerned by the General Assembly's doctrinal and ecclesiological laxity, endured a more fissiparous history. In 1747, its membership split into Burghers and Anti-Burghers over the propriety of the taking of a religious oath required of town burgesses in Glasgow, Edinburgh and Perth; then, around the turn of the century, the Burghers and Anti-Burghers each divided into Auld Licht and New Licht parties over the issue of toleration. Within the next few decades, elements of these parties moved towards reconciliation.[7] Another group, the Relief Church, constituted in 1761, maintained the doctrinal standards of the Westminster formularies while still permitting a surprising breadth of opinion and practice, including the occasional sharing of the Lord's Supper in non-Presbyterian churches.[8]

Outside the Presbyterian world, the Episcopal Church, which also traced its roots as a dissenting communion to the ecclesiastical settlement of 1690, witnessed to a quite different confessional basis, drawing upon Reformation sentiment while simultaneously exploring theological and liturgical possibilities offered in patristic and Orthodox traditions, including prayers for the dead. Rather more controversial was the fact that most Episcopalians continued to support the Stuart cause, especially in contexts influenced by the Nonjuring controversy, and the government used this enduring Jacobitism periodically to repress the denomination's adherents. In the late eighteenth and early nineteenth centuries, membership of the Episcopal Church appears to have declined numerically, and geographically it appears to have retreated to the north and north-east, and especially into its Aberdeenshire heartland. Methodism emerged in the late eighteenth century but did not exercise anything like the impact it had on English and Welsh working-class culture. Quakers, too, were holding their own, without moving far beyond their traditional base in the north-east, as their brief appearance on John Galt's *Annals of the Parish* (1821) suggests.[9] Throughout the same period, smaller Protestant dissenting groups were emerging, evolving and sometimes disappearing. Some developed distinctive theologies, including the repudiation of infant baptism that would characterise the Haldane connection of Independent churches[10] and the anticlericalism that would characterise the 'Plymouth' Brethren,[11] and others observed distinctive practices, including the foot washing and the offering of a holy kiss that would characterise the Glasites[12] and the prophesying and speaking in tongues that would characterise the followers of Edward Irving.[13] Roman Catholics, meanwhile, enjoyed a return to limited respectability after Catholic Emancipation (1793), even as their culture with its strongholds in the Highlands and Islands and the north-east (for example at Scalan, then after 1829 Blairs) was significantly influenced in urban areas by Irish immigration in the early part of the nineteenth century.[14] A tiny minority of Scots, meanwhile, maintained alternatives to these varieties of Christian commitment. Jewish life continued despite its restricted population base, without making any significant literary impact on the wider culture. A smaller number of sceptics advanced their alternatives to all forms of organised religious practice, though sometimes, as in the case of Robert Owen's social experiments in New Lanark, displaying an obvious indebtedness to it; and some, like Burns' 'Cutty Sark', continued in the ancient folkways that their contemporaries associated with the service of 'the deil'.[15] Scotland, in the late eighteenth and early nineteenth centuries, was extensively, but certainly not exclusively, Christian, Protestant and Presbyterian.

It is therefore the case that any survey of the relationship between religion and Scottish Romanticism must recognise the literary impact of the dominance of the established Church, even as it must account for the variety of faith and practice to which its hegemony was giving way.[16] It should also consider the literary impact of the salient features of the wider culture in which this movement towards modernity, plurality and tolerance was taking place, though these features will be thoroughly described in other chapters in this volume. And faith and society should certainly be closely related, for the literature of Romanticism, despite its being associated with scepticism and critical enquiry, retained a significant religious impulse, especially in Scotland, where the canon had always maintained a dynamic and often ambiguous religious concern.[17] From the vantage point of two centuries, it appears that the writers of European Romanticism did fashion their movement as 'in some respects a religion in itself, however far removed were its forms and standards from those of religious orthodoxy'.[18] But in Scotland, writers of Romanticism positioned themselves in much closer proximity to the cultural forces of belief, which they simultaneously admired, drew upon, emulated and critiqued.

This chapter, therefore, will describe a series of relationships between religion and Scottish Romanticism. It will avoid assumptions of geographical fixity and isolation by recognising both external influences on Scottish figures (for example, the influence of S. T. Coleridge on Edward Irving) and the influence of Scottish figures abroad (for example, the influence of Robert Haldane (1764–1842) on a coterie of theological students in Geneva).[19] Its reason for doing so is that the formation of distinctively Scottish approaches to the negation and negotiation of Romantic religion and religious Romanticism took place in multiple directions in an international intellectual environment. This chapter will therefore reflect a range of denominational perspectives, while focusing on what may be the most significant of the period's religious developments – the rise to dominance of a trans-denominational Protestant evangelicalism, the theology of which drew upon the Enlightenment contexts of its emergence, the identity of which was rooted in an idealised Reformation past, and the spirituality of which was reflected in the heightened supernaturalism of its theories of mission, biblical inerrancy and millennial hope. The chapter will argue that this emerging evangelical movement was formed by, at the same time as it formed, important elements of the environments of Scottish Romanticism. Donald Meek, for example, has demonstrated that Dugald Buchanan was the Gaelic poet who was by far the most thoroughly invested with literary Romanticism.[20] In addition, this chapter will concentrate on those aspects of the relationships between religion and Romanticism that may have been distinctive to Scottish cultural life. Scottish Romantic writers developed unique and conflicting literary features in a particular religious climate. Their work suggests that the established scholarly paradigm, which links European Romanticism with religious scepticism, needs to be significantly qualified. This chapter will argue that Scottish Romantic writers developed relationships with religion that were often distinctive, and sometimes unique, in the wider cultural movement of which they were a part.

In the late eighteenth and early nineteenth centuries, many Scots refused to believe that their religious faith should be or was being impacted by wider cultural change. But faith and practice were clearly evolving throughout the period and across the theological spectrum. In 1785, for example, Robert Burns and his brother Gilbert attended the open-air communion at Mauchline in Ayrshire. At this 'holy fair' they encountered a crowd of some 2,000 whose attendance was variously motivated by the demands of hypocrisy, the fears of superstition and the search for fun.[21] It was a traditional scene, for open-air communion seasons had long been a feature of Scottish Presbyterian devotional life.[22] But it was also a scene of contest, an arena in which competing parties within the Church of Scotland could recruit, for, by the end of the eighteenth century, holy fairs like that at Mauchline were providing a forum for the rival claims of Evangelical and Moderate ministers. Recent scholarship on the theological cultures of eighteenth-century Scotland has made problematic some earlier proposals for the distinctions between the competing parties in the Kirk. Both parties were conservative in their own way, and both represented significant theological and cultural novelties. The Evangelical party had emerged in the 1730s, as a new confidence in Enlightenment epistemology developed into a critique of older puritan theories of conversion. The Evangelical party was born out of mid-century friendship networks associated with the promotion of revival, and its influence quickly spread throughout the establishment.[23] The Moderates, by contrast, were sceptical of the value of revival, and their leaders, many of them prominent university men like the theologian George Hill and the literature scholar Hugh Blair, emphasised the practical over the speculative and reiterated the need for strong Church government in environments in which its value was increasingly being questioned.[24] Both parties appealed successfully to the Westminster Confession tradition; but both parties made that appeal from competing positions within the eighteenth-century intellectual world. Both were conserving, and both were innovating, but members of both parties may not have realised their shared indebtedness to the spirit of Enlightenment and, increasingly, Romanticism.

And so, at the end of the eighteenth century, as Burns knew only too well, a large section of the Scottish Presbyterian clergy believed that they were in fact fulfilling their principal duty, which, irrespective of wider cultural change, was to preserve and disseminate an inherited tradition of faith and morals. Many scholars have assumed that Burns favoured the more rational and perhaps more relaxed approach of the Moderates. The biting satire of 'Holy Willie's Prayer' certainly appears to support this claim, attacking as it does Willie Fisher, an Evangelical member of the Presbytery of Ayr who was both an opponent of Burns, in his prosecutions for fornication, and of Dr William M'Gill, a local minister and the controversial author of A Practical Essay on the Death of Jesus Christ (1786). But, perhaps surprisingly, 'The Holy Fair', the poem by Burns that best dramatises the theological conflict within the Kirk, does not seem particularly sympathetic to the Moderates. The poem's representation of the cultural baggage of the Moderates is telling. When George Smith, the minister of Galston, 'opens out his cauld harangues / On practice and on morals', the godly disappear to the beer tent, unable to endure his 'moral pow'rs an' reason' and, perhaps equally significantly, his 'English style'. The godly are brought back to their spiritual senses by the Evangelical preaching of 'Black' John Russell, the minister of Kilmarnock, whose 'piercing words', like those of Scripture, 'divide the joints and marrow'

(Hebrews 4:12). The godly return to listen to the preaching only to be figuratively dismembered with Russell's

> talk o' Hell, whare devils dwell [. . .]
> A vast, unbottomed, boundless pit,
> Fill'd fou o' lowin brunstane
> Whase ragin flame, an' scorchin' heat,
> Wad melt the hardest whun-stane! ('The Holy Fair', ll. 187, 190–4)

In the poem, the rhetoric of this preaching is immediately reduced, when the noise that frightens the audience into believing that they are listening to the roars of the fire of hell turns out to be no more than the snores of a sleeping member of the congregation. 'Sawney' Moodie, the Evangelical minister of Riccarton, is similarly described as being able to 'fire the heart devout' with 'eldritch squeel an' gestures' as he delivers 'tidings o' damnation' that are enough to scare the devil himself ('The Holy Fair', ll. 104–8). In Burns' poem, Evangelical supernaturalism is made to appeal to the religious sensibilities of the godly. It is made to sound traditional. And it is traditional – but its appeal is as much to the oral folk traditions of south-west Scotland as it is to theological traditions rooted in the Westminster Confession of Faith.[25]

While the poem makes all of the preaching ironic, therefore, its sympathy for the Evangelical party is evident. Their 'worlds of wonder', which constructed narrative spaces in which the language and the folk traditions of the Ayrshire peasantry could be preserved, were too important as a narrative source to be easily dismissed in an age of pervasive Enlightenment. Burns borrowed a great deal from the ideas – if not the values – of the Evangelical clergy. Their ideas were crucial to his imagining of the devil, for example. So far from evidencing Burns' uncomplicated sympathy for the Moderates, 'The Holy Fair' is a testament to the social and religious complexity of the culture of late eighteenth-century Ayrshire, and of Burns' aesthetic response to it. But the poem also suggests that the Evangelicals, the religious party to which Burns may have found it hardest to relate, could still function as his vehicle for a national, and even a patriotic, religious style. In the poem this is not recognised for its own sake. The poem indicates the extent to which Burns could appropriate the theological interests of the Evangelicals for his own aesthetic purpose. Burns' imagining of Scottish 'worlds of wonder' drew upon folk traditions that had been preserved in the theology and liturgical style (the 'eldritch squeel an' gestures') of the Evangelicals.

Burns, ironically, needed the Evangelicals – but many Evangelicals believed that they did not need him. His affirmation of their cultural value was met only with rebuff. James Maxwell, a poet from Paisley, prepared his *Animadversions on the Poets and Poetasters of the Present Age* (1788) as

a compilation of poetic attacks on Burns written by Evangelicals. Burns'
poetry, Maxwell believed, was nothing less than a sign of the times, evidence of a latter-day spiritual assault on Presbyterian orthodoxy. Drawing on
Revelation 20:1–10, and the tradition of millennial theories it underpinned,
Maxwell argued that Burns' poetry proved that believers were living in the
last days of human history, when

> Satan should be loos'd a while,
> And many thousands on this earth beguile.
> Now surely this appears to be the time,
> So many are deceived by jargon-rhime.[26]

Burns was 'a champion for Satan [. . .] by Satan inspir'd', Maxwell complained, 'an advocate for hell' who had been 'inspired by hell, / To captivate
the human race' (Maxwell, *Animadversions*, pp. 3, 4, 11). Maxwell believed
that Satanic inspiration was manifest in Burns' failure to take seriously the
revealed truth of Scripture, and his condemnation was both literary and
personal: 'he makes of the scriptures a ribaldry joke; / By him are the laws
both of God and man broke' (*Animadversions*, p. 4). Maxwell believed that
Burns could address Satan 'without dread, / Because in rebellion they're
jointly agreed' (*Animadversions*, p. 6). The *Animadversions* berated Burns for
his politics as much as his approach to religion. Another item in the volume,
an anonymous response to Burns' 'Here Stewarts Once in Triumph Reign'd',
promised that God would imprison Burns in the hell at which he scoffed:

> There must thou gnaw thy burning chains,
> Where Satan, thy grand master, reigns:
> Then see what satires thou can'st make,
> Amidst that black infernal lake.

As another entry put it: 'Now, B---, take back thy lies again to hell, / And tell
thy master they of sulphur smell' (*Animadversions*, p. 10).

Burns was not the only literary figure to be admonished by the religious
adherents of his age. The general dissociation of religion and creative writing
in eighteenth-century Scotland has too often and with insufficient nuance
been attributed to the anti-aesthetic instincts of the Calvinist theology which
dominated both the emerging Evangelical and Moderate parties within the
Church of Scotland as well as the various secession Churches. This explana-
tion is insufficient on many levels – and not least when it is considered that
the texts compiled in Maxwell's *Animadversions* were themselves poems, and
that many Presbyterian clergy, holding to a broadly Calvinist theology though
generally not to a definable Evangelical piety, did make literary contributions
of their own. This was true from the cusp of the Romantic era: Robert Blair,

the Church of Scotland minister of Athelstaneford, East Lothian, published a sober and influential consideration of the human predicament in his poem, *The Grave* (1743),[27] while his successor as minister of the parish, John Home, had his epic tragedy, *Douglas*, performed in Edinburgh (1756). The performance unleashed a fierce debate in Church and society on the morality of the stage, and among the most significant of the interventions was a publication by John Witherspoon, the Evangelical minister of Beith who would later gain fame as the president of the College of New Jersey at Princeton and as a signatory of the American Declaration of Independence (1776). Witherspoon's hostility was typical of the party he represented. Scottish Evangelicals continued well into the nineteenth century to be generally suspicious of creative writing across the genres. Their hesitation was only slowly overcome with the publication of Walter Scott's historical novels, which did much to raise the respectability of creative writing: the Revd Mr Charles Snodgrass' secret consumption of Scott's historical fiction is used to mark the movement of cultural epochs in John Galt's *The Ayrshire Legatees* (1823), for example.[28] But Scott's novels did not dissipate the fears of every believer. Throughout the late eighteenth and early nineteenth centuries, a significant proportion of Scottish Evangelicals continued to disavow the literary imagination. These believers were determined that cultural change should not impact on their faith, and that there should be no relationship between religion and Scottish Romanticism. But some ministers, and many writers, knew enough to disagree, for, as Maxwell's *Animadversions on the Poets and Poetasters of the Present Age* demonstrates, the strongest religious refutations of Romantic sensibility could operate on the borrowed capital of Romantic ideas.

Maxwell's *Animadversions* demonstrates that the content, values and expression of traditional religious orthodoxies, in Scotland and elsewhere, could not remain unchanged by the wider influence of Romanticism.[29] This transition towards modernity was marked in John Galt's *Annals of the Parish* (1821), the diary of a fictional clergyman whose ministry in an Ayrshire village spanned the tumultuous years from 1760 to 1810, in which the influence of a preacher 'not [. . .] gifted with the power of a kirk-filling eloquence' is pitted first against the moral revolution linked to the introduction of tea-drinking and then against democratic agitation and pressures for social and political change.[30] Ironically self-revealing, the narrator, the Revd Micah Balwhidder, documents a rapidly vanishing culture as he manifestly fails to come to terms with the later eighteenth-century world. The narrative continually undermines his frequent claims to possess the gift of prophetic foresight, that marker of early modern Presbyterian enthusiasm; and yet the narrative endorses, albeit in a limited fashion, his expectation that 'the end of the world was drawing nearer and nearer', for his world was certainly concluding (Galt, *Annals of the Parish*, p. 115). But even as Galt was constructing his version of a Scottish clerical archetype, another clerical reputation was being rooted in the sensibilities of the new age. This was the reputation of one of the most celebrated Scottish ministers of the early nineteenth century, the Presbyterian-turned-prophet Edward Irving (1792–1834). Irving, an erstwhile lover of Jane Welsh, who later married Thomas Carlyle, appeared as the very epitome of Romantic sensibility. He began his career as an assistant to Thomas Chalmers, a former professor at St Andrews whose innovations in parish economy in urban Glasgow were celebrated far beyond the Scottish Evangelical party.[31] Irving's success began with his call to the Caledonian Chapel, London, a small and struggling congregation comprised mainly of Scottish exiles, in which he took pains to develop his reputation. Hailed in somewhat Byronic terms as that 'misguided son of genius', he stepped forward from the pulpit of his increasingly fashionable church to offer an apocalyptic reading of current events.[32] His rapid move from insignificance as a pastoral assistant in Glasgow to celebrity as a lionised preacher in the capital of the Empire can be explained at least in part by his effective appeal to the spirit of the age. His preaching was sensational, highly supernatural and evidently influenced by his friendship with Coleridge. Irving was discussed in Parliamentary debates and patronised and applauded by leading members of the aristocratic and political elite. His heightened supernaturalism was manifest in the themes that characterised his ministry: primitivism in ecclesiology and spirituality; overseas missions; and prophecy, in which he predicted the end of human history in 1868. At the zenith of his popularity, between 1822 and 1824, he could preach for more than three hours at a time to audiences of many thousands. But Irving's controversial innovations in Christology led directly to his being deposed from the ministry of the Church of Scotland in 1833 and to his death in 1834. He was, Thomas Carlyle later reminisced, the 'best man I have ever [. . .] found in this world'.[33] Irving's followers had no doubt about his true significance. After his burial, in Glasgow Cathedral, a number of young women, dressed in white, remained in the crypt expecting to witness his immediate resurrection.

Irving's influence popularised his radical approach to Evangelical faith. But his support for the national establishment of religion did not feed into a distinctive nationalist sentiment. Instead, Irving theorised an alternative variety of Romantic nationalism – an incipient Zionism – which, later in the period, was developed in the preaching of another London-based Scots Presbyterian minister, John Cumming, a prophetic impresario whose preaching was admired and then ridiculed by a young George Eliot.[34] But Irving's legacy was also questioned, most significantly by David Brown, who had been his assistant in the Caledonian Chapel until the outbreak of speaking in tongues. Brown questioned his earlier commitment to Irving's eschatology in a major work entitled *Christ's Second Coming: Will it be Premillennial?* (1846).

The book was a theological sensation, and drew upon the piety of Romantic Evangelicalism to offer a robust critique of the premillennial position as it had advanced to the mid-1840s. More than any of his colleagues, Brown appeared aware of the sociological dynamic and wider cultural significance of the eschatological debate, which had arisen, he explained, 'in times of general excitement, of extensive change, of pervading uneasiness and trial, of mingled hope and fear'.[35] And so it did, across the spectrum of Scottish Protestant denominations, reflecting a general move to emphasise the supernatural as believing communities were decisively shaped by the influence of a wider cultural Romanticism.[36]

Scottish religion also made a significant impact on the Romantic movement. In many ways, of course, the principal literary figures of the Romantic movement were already attuned to the stylistic and thematic opportunities offered by religious belief. Elsewhere in Europe, Romantic writers wished for the 'forms of Christian orthodoxy [. . .] to be radically modified or even abandoned', though their 'most representative figures all favoured a religious interpretation of the cosmos, or at any rate such a spiritual view of life and the world as to leave room for the preservation of religious attitudes'. Nevertheless, the emerging Romantic aesthetic insisted that Christian orthodoxy had to be dissociated from the objective, scientific mode with which it had become associated during the Enlightenment, and that it had to be understood and represented as nothing more than an element of human experience. Across Europe, therefore, it was generally the case that any 'reaffirmation of religious values' by Romantic writers could not mean a 'straight return to the theological orthodoxies of pre-Enlightenment days'.[37]

This trend was less obvious in Scotland. Scottish Romantic writers continued to draw upon the confessional legacies they had inherited. This is most obvious in Presbyterian terms, and especially in the Romantic mythologising of Scottish Presbyterian history, which, as the nineteenth century progressed, became, ironically, a foundational element in the construction of a pan-denominational Evangelical identity.

The impact of religion on Scottish Romanticism was perhaps most obvious in literary depictions of the Covenanters. Scott's *Old Mortality* (1816) was published to popular acclaim and ecclesiastical controversy. Thomas McCrie, the Seceder minister and church historian, immediately criticised Scott's 'affectation of extensive knowledge of history' and noted the 'blunders which betray the superficiality with which it has been examined',[38] fearing that the 'encroachments of the writers of fiction upon the province of true history' had it 'in their power to do much mischief'.[39] And Scott's literary peers agreed. In *The Brownie of Bodsbeck* (1818), James Hogg appropriated the religious and patriotic myths of the 'Killing Times', elevating the voice of the folk above the voice of the élite in the novel's final unveiling of the true identity of the monster haunting the people of Ettrick – a strategy that had historical-political as well as literary significance, and one that he would pursue in his later writing on the subject. Meanwhile, John Galt, continuing the reflection on *Old Mortality*, observed that Scott had 'laid an irreverent hand on the ark of our great national cause, the Covenant', and so prepared an alternative and 'impartial' account of Covenanting history in *Ringan Gilhaize* (1823).[40] Galt's argument continued to combine the historical-political with the literary, developing the language of sentimental nationalism in his description of his Covenanter protagonists,

> sharp and vehement not only in their condemnation of the mitred Antichrist, but grieved with a sincere sorrow, that none of the nobles of Scotland would stand forth in their ancient bravery, to resist and overthrow a race of oppressors more grievous than the Southrons that trode [sic] on the neck of their fathers in the hero-stirring times of the Wallace wight and King Robert the Bruce. (Galt, *Ringan Gilhaize*, I: 61–2)

Hogg's *Private Memoirs and Confessions of a Justified Sinner* (1824) advanced another representation of the 'rage of fanaticism in former days'.[41] Hogg's novel was historically informed and appreciative of its theological subject, but Irving also entered the discussion, invoking denominational difference in his rejection of the influence of those 'Episcopalian writers and novelists who have sought to cast the scorn of vulgar ridicule, or to fasten the censure of malignant humours upon these stout resistances and masterful arguments of the Scottish people during the seventeenth century'.[42] It was hardly surprising that the first issue of *The Covenanter* (1830), the magazine of the Reformed Presbyterian Church, should want to challenge the 'unmeasured misrepresentation' of their seventeenth-century forebears in the 'Periodical press of the day'.[43]

'Holy Willie' is perhaps the most famous exponent of Scottish religion in the Romantic period. Venal and hypocritical, combining moral failings with moral censure, he is often seen as epitomising a dialectical relationship between religion and Scottish Romantic writing. But, as this chapter has demonstrated in its description of the vitality and variety of religious faith in late eighteenth- and early nineteenth-century Scotland, he does not epitomise that relationship, for the writing that damned him also drew upon his convictions to achieve its literary effect. The relationship between religion and Scottish Romanticism is complex and fraught, but always dialogic. Burns, like so many other Romantic writers, found his Scottish religious environment both disgusting and inspiring, and the exponents and defenders of Scottish religion responded to Romantic writers in similar degree.

Perhaps this was only to be expected; and perhaps future accounts of the relationships between religion and Scottish Romanticism should emphasise continuity rather than change. Throughout its history, the Scottish canon has dealt with religious themes with unusual concentration. This is particularly true of the literature produced during the Romantic period. Scotland, in the late eighteenth and early nineteenth century, was a religious country. Romantic writers responded to its culture with appreciation and critique, and both provided for and undermined the possibility of its continuing existence. As this chapter has suggested, therefore, there exist particular patterns of relationship between religion and the cultures of Scottish Romanticism.

SECTION II

Authors and Texts

CHAPTER TEN

Robert Burns and Romanticism in Britain and Ireland

Nigel Leask

In the 250th anniversary of his birth, public celebration of Scotland's national poet continued unabated. Burns' reputation in academic circles on the other hand has been less secure, although a welcome change is in the air. Over a century ago, the poet's Victorian editors Henley and Henderson described him as '*ultimus Scotorum*, the last expression of the old Scots world'. David Daiches sustained this view (albeit with qualifications attached) half a century later in his assessment of the poetry as 'a glorious Indian summer for native Scottish literature'.[1] Although such views are rarer now amongst his academic interpreters, the view that Burns' poetry is exclusively Scotocentric, traditionary and backward-looking, combined with a false perception of its linguistic unintelligibility to non-Scottish readers, has been largely responsible for its academic eclipse in university departments over the last fifty years.

Murray Pittock has recently proposed that

> the decline in Burns (who outstripped both Coleridge and Blake in critical attention at the end of the 1930s) was a bellwether to the rise of the new paradigm [in Romantic studies]: social rather than imaginative, driven by dialogism and challenges to heteroglossic hierarchies rather than idealism, Burns had virtually no place in the new Romanticism.[2]

Moreover, the 1780s, the decade of Burns' major poetical creativity, was long consigned to the period of 'pre-Romanticism', effectively obscuring its significance in relation to the poetry that preceded and followed it: the fact that Burns died in 1796 (i.e. *before* the publication of *Lyrical Ballads*) meant that he was easily excluded from the Romantic mainstream initiated by Wordsworth, despite having influenced the latter's assault on 'poetic diction'.[3] Recent critical focus on the eighteenth-century culture of sensibility and the increasing critical acceptance of a 'long eighteenth century' have gone some way to relieve this problem: Carol McGuirk's 1985 study, for example, locates Burns' poetry within the 'sentimental era', thereby also connecting it 'with the English and European literary mainstream'.[4]

A greater problem perhaps lies in the marginalisation of Scottish literature and history relative to England, although this has now begun to be effectively challenged by a 'four nations' approach to British and Irish literature. 'Scottish Romanticism' has been recently described (in relationship to an 'organic' English model) as 'an intermittent, shadowy anachronism, a temporal as well as a spatial border of Romanticism'. This holds also for its distinct chronology: (to continue the quotation) 'in Scotland, "Classical" and "Romantic" cultural forms occupy the same historical moment and institutional base, rather than defining successive stages or periods'.[5] As the present author has argued in *Robert Burns and Pastoral*, there is a distinctive difference between Burns' innovative development of 'Scots pastoral' (as inherited from Allan Ramsay and Robert Fergusson) in a Scottish lowland culture obsessed by the ideology of agricultural improvement, and the genre's more lacklustre English trajectory in the same period.[6] Because Burns was arguably the most inventive poet writing in these islands between Pope and Blake, creator of the first modern vernacular style in British poetry, such perceptions now stand in urgent need of revision.[7] This chapter will argue that Burns' poetry and song, as well as its mediation by critics and biographers, profoundly shaped the development of British and Irish Romanticism. The absence of even a single monograph dedicated to this subject, however, is astonishing, a neglect for which the present chapter can offer only a very partial recompense.[8]

Burns' influence on British and Irish Romanticism began during his own lifetime with the euphoric response to the Kilmarnock volume of 1786, as well as the three Edinburgh volumes that followed. Although it was not the first review, Henry Mackenzie's *Lounger* essay of December 1786 was the most influential in hailing Burns as a 'Heaven-taught ploughman', notwithstanding the untruth of both propositions contained in his apothegm, and the fact that 'his was a disastrously inaccurate essay in criticism, which gave rise to endless distortions of Burns's poetry'.[9] Although there were few reviews of the 1787 Edinburgh volume, and none of 1793, all three elicited admiring responses not only from the Edinburgh literati, but propelled his fame over the border to England, Ireland and Wales.[10] Famously, William Cowper struggled with Burns' Scots but nevertheless believed the volume to be 'a most extraordinary production', hailing Burns as the first British poet 'in the lower ranks of life since Shakespeare (I should rather say since Prior) who need not be indebted for any part of his praise to a charitable consideration of his origin'.[11] Cowper instantly grasped the fact that Burns had broken the mould of the conventional eighteenth-century labouring class poet.

Burns' deep and enduring influence on Wordsworth is probably his most significant legacy to the Romantic mainstream; Duncan Wu's reconstruction of the English poet's reading reveals that he first 'became acquainted with [Burns' poems] almost immediately upon their first appearance in the volume printed at Kilmarnock in 1796' [a mistake for 1786].[12] Wordsworth had no difficulty with Burns' language, because, he later recalled, 'familiarity with the dialect of the border countries of Cumberland and Westmoreland made it easy for me not only to understand but to feel [Burns poems]'.[13] Criticism has begun to demonstrate the debt of influence to Burns in Wordsworth's poetry up to and including *Lyrical Ballads*, although much work remains to be done.[14]

Wordsworth's first published poem 'A Sonnet on Seeing Miss Helen [Maria] Williams Weep at a Tale of Distress' conveys some sense of (the Anglo-Scots) Williams' national popularity as a poet of sensibility in the 1780s (although amusingly, twenty years later, Williams – long since resident in Paris – claimed never to have heard of Wordsworth). In June 1788 Williams wrote to Burns exclaiming that she 'had fully felt the power of your genius', as 'my mother's family is Scotch, and the dialect has been familiar to me from infancy'.[15] Williams later published a 'Sonnet on Reading Burns' Mountain Daisy' and in 1788 sent him copy of her 364–line *Poem on the Bill Lately Passed for Regulating the Slave Trade*. Unusually, the poet responded with a lengthy and appreciative critique in a letter of July/August 1789, providing a rare glimpse of his real sentiments concerning the slave trade.[16] There is no evidence that William Blake had read Burns, although there is no doubt that the two poets 'are deeply compatible',[17] whether we consider the concluding lines of 'Love and Liberty' ('COURTS for Cowards were erected / CHURCHES built to please the Priest'), or the pastoral/bardic dialectic structuring Blake's *Songs of Innocence and Experience*.

Yet as Liam McIlvanney has suggested, Burns' most immediate impact was 'transperipheral' to the extent that it inspired readers and writers in Wales and Ireland. Mary-Ann Constantine has recently demonstrated the extent of his influence on Welsh Romanticism, especially on the *Poems, Lyrical and Pastoral* (1794) of Edward Williams ('Iolo Morganwg'). Although Welsh writers lacked a non-Celtic 'vernaculum' equivalent to Burns' Scots, Iolo embedded traditional Welsh metrical forms in his English poetry, much of it inspired by Burns' political pastoral in the revolutionary decade.[18] This was of course less of a problem in Ireland, especially in Ulster with its strong links with Lowland Scotland. It is no surprise that the first edition of Burns' poems published outside Scotland was by James Magee in Belfast in 1787, and a staggering sixteen editions appeared in Ulster from 1787 to 1826.[19] Burns' popularity with Ulster Scots built on the earlier influence of Ramsay and the eighteenth-century Scots vernacular revival. Burns' satires on the Presbyterian 'unco guid' appealed to the Moderate temper of Ulster Presbyterians, and his stress on 'independence' chimed with the highly politicised Ulster Dissenters in the revolutionary decade of the United Irishman. His poems and songs were widely circulated in the moderate reformist *Belfast*

Newsletter and (more sparingly) in the radical *Northern Star*; his influence is acknowledged in Samuel Thomson's *Poems, on Different Subjects, partly in the Scottish Dialect* which appeared in 1793, James Orr's *Poems* (1804) and other poetry collections. In 1794 Thomson (who had sent Burns a verse epistle in Scots) visited the poet in Dumfries, followed by his friend Luke Mullan in 1796. When in October 1795 the *Belfast Newsletter* published Burns' loyalist song 'The Dumfries Volunteers', however, the *Northern Star* countered a fortnight later with a reply, taking Burns to task for political inconsistency, 'dipp[in] I' th' dish with slee D[undas]', and reminding the bard of the fate of the 'Scottish Martyrs' Muir and Palmer.[20]

The Burns cult was not confined to Presbyterian Ulster, however: a Dublin edition was published by William Gilbert in 1787 and reprinted in 1789 and 1790.[21] The Ennis-born teenage prodigy Thomas Dermody included 'An Odaic Epistle' written in 'stage Scots' entitled 'Tam to Rab' in his 1792 *Poems*, parading his learning with quotations from Virgil. Dermody invited the Ayrshire bard to 'quaff stout whiskey, at our ease, / Drive fools, before our verse, like geese'.[22] But a more palpable Burnsian influence on Irish Romanticism was Thomas Moore's *Irish Melodies* (1808–34), the hugely popular collection of national songs that earned Moore the epithet of 'the Minstrel of Erin'. Dermody and Moore shared a patron in Charles Rawdon-Hastings, Lord Moira, whose family owned huge estates in County Down.[23] This represents another Burnsian link: in 1804 Moira was married to Flora Mure Campbell, orphaned daughter of the 5th Earl of Loudoun, laird of Mossgiel Farm, and himself became the 6th Earl through marriage. Later, as the Marquis of Hastings, Moira served as governor general of India, where he and his Ayrshire-born wife Flora supported the careers of Burns' sons in the East India Company army. Although many critics have endorsed Hazlitt's scathing attack on Moore for turning 'the wild harp of Erin into a musical snuff-box', the *Melodies* did much to establish the mood of Romantic Ireland by articulating a muted yet unmistakable Irish nationalism.[24] In a letter to Sir John Stevenson quoted in the preface to the first, 1808, volume of *Irish Melodies*, Moore insisted that his lyrics expressed the true Irish character, 'that rapid fluctuation of spirits, that unaccountable mixture of gloom and levity', adding that 'if [Robert] Burns had been an Irishman (and I would willingly give up all our claims to Ossian for him), his heart would have been proud of such music'.[25] This 'transperipheral' influence will be returned to briefly at the end of the present chapter in considering the importance of this account of Hibernian affect and its Burnsian resonance, in Moore's analysis of his friend Lord Byron's 'mobilite' in his 1831 biography.[26]

Burns' poetic legacy for his Romantic successors was, however, heavily mediated by the debate ignited by his premature death on 21 July 1796. The obituaries, poems and biographies that immediately poured from the press harped obsessively on the poet's genius, his alleged moral frailty, alcoholism and sexual incontinence, as well as the indigence into which he and his family had been reduced by the time of his death. Lurid accounts of Burns' decline into seedy inebriation in the Dumfries years flowed from the pens of George Thomson and Robert Heron shortly after the poet's death, and were broadcast in the popular press; an ineffectual defence by his friend Maria Riddell did little to redeem the situation.[27]

English commentators, especially those of a radical stamp, blamed Scotland's detested 'Dundas despotism' for failing to patronise the humbly-born genius in their midst. The fact that Burns' Edinburgh edition had been dedicated to the Caledonian Hunt, the flower of the Scottish gentry and nobility, made his subsequent neglect at their hands seem all the more unpardonable. In Liverpool, the fate of Burns became something of a *cause célèbre* in liberal circles, resulting in a spate of poems by his friend and collaborator William Roscoe (author of *Life of Lorenzo de Medici*), the blind abolitionist poet Edward Rushton and others. Often they adopted the 'habbie' stanza in tribute to Burns, although employing English diction. These poems were originally published in the *Liverpool Phoenix*, but later collected in an 1800 subscription volume dedicated to Burns' family, entitled *Liverpool Testimonials to the Departed Genius of Robert Burns*.[28] Behind all these dark visions of the half-starved Scottish exciseman/poet hovered the spectres of Thomas Muir and the 'Scottish Martyrs' exiled to Botany Bay in 1794 on exaggerated charges of sedition, although ironically the Scotophobia of some of the poems echoed the cadences of Charles Churchill and the anti-Bute campaign of the 1760s. Most agreed that the Excise Commission was an utterly inadequate form of patronage, ignoring Burns' stated desire for independence from the trammels of farming: for example, Coleridge concluded his 1796 poem 'To a Friend who had Declared his Intention of Writing no more Poetry' (addressed to Charles Lamb, who idolised Burns) by asking:

Is thy Burns dead?
And shall he die unwept, and sink to Earth
'Without the meed of one melodious tear?'
Thy Burns, and Nature's own beloved Bard,
Who to the 'Illustrious of his native Land
So properly did look for Patronage'.
Ghost of Maecenas! Hide thy blushing face!
They snatched him from the Sickle and the Plough –
To gauge Ale-Firkins.[29]

This was the context for Dr James Currie's (1756–1805) anonymously published 1800 *Works of Robert Burns; with an Account of his Life, and a Criticism of his Writings, to which is Prefixed, some Observations on the Character and*

Condition of the Scottish Peasantry. This first authorised edition of Burns' poetry after his death, prefaced by a 335–page critical biography of the poet which makes up the first of its four volumes, was immensely popular in its time, going through five editions and about 10,000 copies by 1805, and at least twenty editions by 1820.[30] By comparison, the combined sales of the three editions of *Lyrical Ballads* between 1798 and 1802 amounted to a maximum of 2,000 copies, although we should recall that at the upper end of the poetry market, Scott's *Lay of the Last Minstrel* sold about 19,000 copies in eleven editions in the five years following its publication in 1805.[31] Currie's edition was the main portal through which Burns' life and poetry reached the Romantic reader, and its depressing account of his decline into alcoholism and dissipation in the Dumfries period continued to influence the reception of Burns' poetry well into the twentieth century. In establishing an official Burns 'canon', Currie was undoubtedly guilty of what Walter Scott described as 'a fastidious and over delicate rejection of the bard's most spirited and happy effusions' in omitting poems like 'Holy Willie's Prayer' and Love and Liberty' for fear of offending polite taste.[32] Currie's Burns has in consequence long been vilified by Burns scholars and marginalised in Romantic studies, notwithstanding the fact that, in the light of contributions from men like Dugald Stewart, Henry Mackenzie, Walter Scott, George Thomson, Baron David Hume (nephew of the philosopher), Alexander Fraser Tytler and the Earl of Buchan, it represents a composite production of the late Scottish Enlightenment, assembled under the auspices of its anonymous editor.[33]

The Dumfries-born, Edinburgh-educated Dr Currie practised as a physician in Liverpool; a political liberal and abolitionist, he was a member of the Roscoe circle that published *Liverpool Testimonials* in an effort to raise a subscription for Burns' widow and children, a charitable endeavour to which his edition was also dedicated. In his introductory volume, Currie noted the degree to which Burns' 'reputation has extended itself beyond the limits of that country, and his poetry has been admired as the offspring of original genius by persons of taste in every part of the sister islands', drawing from this observation a desire 'to write the memoirs of his life, not with the view of their being read by Scotchmen only, but also by natives of England, and of other countries where the English language is spoken or understood'.[34] Sensing, however, that the tone adopted by his liberal English friends would do little service to the project of raising a subscription for Burns' family (Roscoe had provocatively hailed Burns as 'Thy Country's glory, and her Shame'),[35] Currie wrote in a letter of 8 February 1797, when his biography was already under way:

> To speak my mind [. . ..] fully, it appears to me that [Burns'] misfortunes arose chiefly from his errors. This it is unnecessary and, indeed, improper to say; but

his biographer must keep it in mind, to prevent him from running into those bitter invectives against Scotland, &c., which the extraordinary attractions and melancholy fate of the poet naturally provoke.[36]

Despite his avid unionism, Currie needed to blame Burns in order to exonerate Scotland; and the rhetoric of moral blame that subsequently attached itself to the narrative of the poet's life is without doubt the most regrettable and most enduring legacy of his biography. 'The fatal defect in [Burns'] character lay in the comparative weakness of his volition, that superior faculty of the mind,' he wrote: 'the occupations of a poet are not calculated to strengthen the governing power of the mind, or to weaken that sensibility which requires perpetual controul, since it gives birth to the vehemence of passion as well as to the higher powers of imagination' (I: pp. 236–7). Currie drew upon his vocational training as a 'mad doctor' to diagnose the psychopathology of Burns' genius: 'temptations to *the sin that so easily beset him*, continually presented themselves; and his irregularities grew by degrees into habits' (I: p. 205). This led Charles Lamb to complain in 1800 that Currie's 'Life of Burns' was 'very confusedly and badly written, and interspersed with dull pathological and *medical* discussions',[37] although Coleridge (who may have recognised features of his own psychopathology in Currie's diagnosis) described it as 'a masterly specimen of philosophical Biography'.[38]

Currie's cautionary tale sounded a warning blast to other would-be geniuses from humble life. Gifted a copy of Currie by a patron, the English labouring-class Robert Bloomfield, whose poem *The Farmer's Boy* sold a staggering 26,000 copies between its publication in 1800 and 1803, wrote in July 1800 that 'I cannot read three pages of his life without walking across the room to relieve my stomach.' In a letter to the Earl of Buchan (whose patronage Burns had himself struggled to brush off a decade earlier) Bloomfield complained '*Remember Burns* has been the watch word of my friends. *I do remember Burns*, but I am not Burns, neither have I his fire to quench, nor his passion to controll'.[39] (This resonates with Wordsworth's later comment on reading Currie 'here is a revolting account of a man of exquisite genius, and confessedly of many high moral qualities, sunk into the lowest depths of vice and misery!')[40] Such visceral reactions to Currie's sorry tale reveal something of the power of Burns' charisma for Romantic readers, while also showing the extent to which it coloured their enjoyment of his poetry. In an entirely different social register, Jane Austen's Charlotte Heywood, a character in her posthumously published *Sanditon*, likewise reacts to Sir Edward Denham's admiring observation that 'Burns is always on fire': 'I have read several of Burn's [sic] Poems with great delight', said Charlotte as soon as she had time to speak, 'but I am not poetic enough to separate a Man's Poetry entirely from his Character; – & poor Burns's known Irregularities, greatly interrupt

my enjoyment of his Lines.' [41] As Fiona Stafford comments, 'responses to literature, as Austen knew only too well, were determined as much by thoughts
of an author's death as by knowledge of his life'.[42] Once again it is Currie's
biography that casts a huge shadow over the Romantics' Burns.

If Burns' psychopathology of genius was one critical element of Currie's
'Life', his analysis of the poet's humble social background was also delivered
with something like missionary zeal. Reminding his readers that 'Robert
Burns was in reality what he has been represented to be, a Scottish peasant',[43]
Currie proceeded to dismantle Mackenzie's myth of his 'heaven-taught
genius'. There was nothing 'heaven-taught' about Burns, Currie insisted,
because the Scottish peasantry 'possess a degree of intelligence not generally
found among the same class of men in the other countries of Europe', and
in this respect Burns was utterly representative of his class (I: p. 3). Currie's
prefatory 'Observations on the Scottish peasantry' provides a historical analysis of Scotland's 'popular enlightenment' – the matrix of Burns' genius – in the
history of Scotland before and after the Union, particularly the excellence of
Scottish parochial education, and the 'self-help' mentality (uncontaminated
by Poor Laws or statutory welfare provision) that had nurtured the domestic affections of the Lowland peasantry. Currie especially celebrated the
'strength of the domestic affections of the Scottish peasantry [. . .] which it is
hoped will not be lost' (I: p. 26). The *Gemeineschaft* of Scottish rural society
(as portrayed in poems like 'Scotch Drink', 'Halloween', 'The Holy Fair' and
'Cotter's Saturday Night') is here proposed as a regulative idea for Scotland
within the Union, rather than as a discourse of nationalism, which, as Tom
Nairn suggests, was the goal of similar mobilisations of 'ethnic and historical
differentiae' in nearly all other small European countries.[44]

Currie promoted the moral community upheld in poems like 'The Cotter's
Saturday Night' as a form of naturalised civil society operating harmoniously
with minimum state intervention. Despite the exemplary nationalist appeal
to the Scottish people contained in Burns' poetry, Currie's anomalous concern
was to exorcise the spectre of an 'independence' (personal or national) which
he believed had proved fatal to the poet himself.[45] Enshrining a cultural
memory at once infantile and posthumous, Burns' poetry 'displays, and as it
were *embalms*, the peculiar manners of his country; and it may be considered
as a *monument* not to his name only, but to the expiring genius of an ancient
and once independent nation' (my italics).[46]

Conceived as an act of charitable recuperation, it is easy to underestimate
the enormous influence of Currie's 'embalming' of Burns on the Romantic
generation. Part of the problem, even in the case of Wordsworth, lies in the
depth at which Burns' poetry and example were assimilated (after Currie, the
two were inseparable). Wordsworth generously acknowledged the extent of
Burns' influence in his poem 'At the Grave of Burns', written in the Habbie

stanza; 'whose light I hailed when first it shone, / And showed my youth / How verse may build a princely throne / On humble truth'.[47] Daniel Sanjiv Roberts has shown that Wordsworth and Coleridge were reading Currie's edition of Burns in September 1800, the very month in which they were composing the preface to *Lyrical Ballads*.[48] Whereas the advertisement to the 1798 edition of *Lyrical Ballads* declares the linguistic model for its poetic 'experiments' to be 'the language of conversation in the middle and lower classes of society', the 1800 preface (composed after reading Currie's 'Observations on the Scottish Peasantry') specifies 'low and rustic life' as the social locus of 'the real language of men in a state of vivid sensation'.[49] Burns was far from being the only 'peasant poet' enjoying huge popularity in 1800 (see the remarks on Bloomfield above); nonetheless, in this respect the preface appears to respond quite specifically to Currie's 'philosophical' attribution of Burns' genius to the manners of the Scottish peasantry as a class. The abstract idiom of the preface makes more sense if we read Wordsworth's 'real language of men in a state of vivid sensation' as a response to Currie's 'Observations', an attempt to deterritorialise Burns' exemplary genius, a species that could hardly flourish on English soil. Judging from verbal echoes alone, Wordsworth (as is shown above, long an admirer of Burns' poetry) appears to have been particularly attracted to Currie's account of the *amor patriae* of the Scottish peasantry in their austere upland environment. But Wordsworth was also responsible for a more covert act of ideological assimilation: for as Leith Davis puts it, 'Scotland and Burns symbolize a difference within Britain, which Wordsworth both acknowledges and attempts to deny by incorporating it into a universal scheme.'[50]

Francis Jeffrey's distaste for Wordsworth was famously expressed in the first number of the *Edinburgh Review*, but it was not until his 1809 review of Cromek's *Reliques of Burns* that the leading reviewer of the age had an opportunity to express his views on Burns, and the Wordsworthian 'appropriation' of Burns, to which his ear was evidently highly sensitive. Jeffrey was in many ways indebted to Currie's 'Life' in its Whiggish demystification of Burns' genius, which he viewed as an encouraging symptom of Scottish popular enlightenment and the 'spirit of the age'. In Jeffrey's hands, however, Currie's 'psychopathological' diagnosis of Burns' character was coarsened into a moralising rant that regretted the poet's 'contempt [. . .] for prudence, decency and regularity; and his admiration of thoughtlessness, oddity, and vehement sensibility [. . . that] communicated to a great part of his productions a character of immorality, at once contemptible and hateful'.[51]

In this strangely inconsistent essay, Jeffrey decried Burns' plebeian independence and insubordinate spirit, while at the same time extolling his use of the Scots language. As much of an angliciser as any of the Edinburgh literati, Jeffrey nevertheless insisted that Scots was not a 'provincial dialect' but 'the language of a whole country, – long an independent kingdom, and still separate in laws, character and manners [. . .] it is an ignorant, as well as a illiberal prejudice, which would seek to confound it with the barbarous dialects of Yorkshire or Devon'. In the final paragraph he set up a comparison between the 'authentic rustics' of Burns' 'Cottar's Saturday Night' and Wordsworth's 'fantastical personages of hysterical schoolmasters and sententious leech-gatherers': 'these gentlemen are outrageous for simplicity; and we beg leave to recommend to them the simplicity of Burns'.[52] Seen through the partisan lens of the *Edinburgh Review*, Burns was the national poet, Wordsworth the provincial, a judgement that had the unfortunate effect of making Burns (and Scottish writing generally) a hostage to fortune in the subsequent Romantic offensive against the Whiggish literary values of Jeffrey and his ilk.

Wordsworth was justifiably infuriated by Jeffrey's review, and (as Leith Davis has pointed out) his subsequent hatred of the Scottish literati like Jeffrey further complicated his relationship with Burns.[53] Wordsworth's 1816 *Letter to a Friend of Burns* was inspired by (and boldly endorsed) Alexander Peterkin's well-meaning bid to contest the charges of alcoholism and dissipation levelled against Burns by Currie, Jeffrey, Scott and others.[54] Wordsworth argued that literary biography had its limits and that, regarding poets, 'our business is with their books, – to understand and to enjoy them [. . .] if their works be good, they contain within themselves all that is necessary to their being comprehended and relished'.[55] Given the nature of the charges against Burns, this was an evasion rather than a rebuttal, however, and in consequence, as James Mackay suggests, Wordsworth 'unwittingly left the reader with the impression that the charges were essentially correct'.[56] And unfortunately Wordsworth further weakened his defence of Burns by employing him as a stalking horse for a savage retaliatory attack on Jeffrey. As John Wilson noted in a *Blackwood's* article the following year, 'all the while he is exclaiming against the Reviewer's injustice to Burns, he writes under the lash which that consummate satirist has inflicted upon himself'.[57] Ironically, both Peterkin's *Review* and Gilbert Burns' timid exoneration of his brother's character appeared (respectively) as prefaces to the 1815 and 1820 republications of Currie's four-volume *Works*, in which the introductory 'Life' remained intact.

Space permits, by way of conclusion, only a brief survey of Burns' influence on the younger generation of British Romantics. Passing over Shelley's witty preference for Burns' over Wordsworth's naturalism in his powerful satire 'Peter Bell the Third', the startling contrast between Burns' genius and the seedy Dumfries environment as portrayed by Currie affronted the 'Cockney' poets, whose attitudes to Scotland were soured by the barbed satire of *Blackwood's Magazine*. Drunk on whisky toddies in Burns's birthplace cottage at Alloway in July 1818 (by now a tavern benefiting from the poet's posthumous fame),[58] John Keats penned a 'flat sonnet' and wrote to his friend Reynolds:

> One song of Burns's is of more worth to you than all I could think of for a whole year in his native country. [Burns's] misery is a dead weight upon the nimbleness of one's quill – I tried to forget it – to drink Toddy without any Care – to write a merry Sonnet – it won't do – he talked with Bitches – he drank with Blackguards, he was miserable – We can see horribly clear in the works of such a man his whole life, as if we were God's spies.[59]

For Keats Burns was a romantic genius despite, not because of, the poet's 'anti-grecian' Ayrshire environment. This view was reiterated later in the century by Matthew Arnold when he wrote that 'Burns's world of Scotch drink, Scotch religion and Scotch manners is a harsh, a sordid, a repulsive world.'[60]

Dissenting from such a view, however, was Lord Byron, one of Burns' greatest champions in the Romantic era, and perhaps, despite the huge social differences dividing the two, his truest poetic heir. It was Byron's close friend Thomas Moore (whom we saw offering to exchange *Ossian* for an Irish Burns) who first underlined Burns' poetic importance for Byron in his authorised *Life, Letters and Journals of Lord Byron*.[61] Byron's *Corsair* (1814) had been dedicated to Moore, and drew parallels between Ottoman domination in the Levant and British rule in Ireland: Murray Pittock has recently drawn attention to the 'fratriotism' of both poets, their shared solidarity with colonised small nations and trenchant opposition to empire.[62] Although a fashionable figure in Regency London society, Moore was a life-long antagonist of the 1800 Union with Ireland, and as we have seen, much of his poetry was a more or less concealed lament for a lost Irish *patria*. Moore dilated on the Anglo-Scottish Byrons' Aberdonian childhood, and his difficult relationship with his mother, Catherine Gordon of Gight. He quoted Byron's lines from *Don Juan*; 'but I am half a Scot by birth, and bred/ A whole one; and my heart flies to my head /As "Auld Lang Syne" brings Scotland, one and all –'.[63] Moore also made much of Byron's passionate and personal identification with Robert Burns, whose poetry he read in Currie's edition, describing his reaction to reading some of Burns' *Merry Muses* in manuscript (songs that certainly did not make it into Currie); 'What an antithetical mind! – tenderness, roughness – delicacy, coarseness – sentiment, sensuality – soaring and grovelling, dirt and deity – all mixed up in one compound of inspired clay!'[64]

Richard Cronin has noted that 'the impossibility of adequate biography' is 'an unlikely but common theme' [amongst Byron's many biographers], a consequence of the extreme 'mobility' that [they] all [. . .] recognise in him'.[65] But Byron's own description of an 'antithetical' Burns does offer a clue to

Moore's own attempt to pin down his subject. Because the delicate matter of Byron's own divorce is such a central episode in his biography, the story of his parents' failed marriage is often overlooked. For Moore, however, Lord Byron, despite his noble pedigree, was the product of a spectacular failure of Anglo-Scottish union, the disastrous marriage of Catherine Gordon and English 'Mad Jack' Byron. In fact, Byron's whole hyphenated identity seems to be based in that failure: 'So various indeed, and contradictory, were [Byron's] attributes, both moral and intellectual,' Moore continued, 'that he may be pronounced not one, but many.'[66]

Insightfully, Moore fastened on Byron's commentary on Burns as the basis for his own interpretation of *Don Juan*, Byron's 'most characteristic work'. In a long passage at the end of Chapter 32 he characterised *Don Juan* as the perfect reflection of its author's versatile mind, fugueing upon Byron's 'dirt and deity'; 'the two extremes [. . .] of man's mixed and inconsistent nature, now rankly smelling of earth, now breathing of heaven, – such was the strange assemblage of contrary elements, all meeting together in the same mind, and all brought to bear, in turn, upon the same task [. . .] the most powerful and, in many respects, painful display of versatility of genius that has ever been left for succeeding ages to wonder at and deplore'.[67] In this passage, Moore seems aware (with remarkably modern insight) that the 'scorching and drenching' effect of *Don Juan*, rather than the egotistical gloom of a Conrad or a Harold, was the key to Byron's poetic greatness.

For this very reason, Moore refused to foreclose on his subject by explaining away (as Currie would have done) poetic versatility in terms of 'weakness of volition'. Although downplaying Byron's sexual licentiousness and his religious heterodoxy, Moore's influential biography in the end rejected the closure of a regulative moral framework or the application of organicist aesthetics to the work itself. The Irish Moore thus permitted Byron to stand apart from the unifying and centripetal impulse of romantic imagination as influentially defined by Coleridge and Wordsworth: diagnosing his genius as the brilliant but tragic effect of a flawed act of union, Byron remained 'not one but many'. To this extent the agency of a 'transperipheral' Burns, in the hands of Byron or Moore, can be seen as actively deconstructing the interpretative legacy of mainstream British Romanticism.

CHAPTER ELEVEN

Walter Scott's Romanticism: A Theory of Performance

Caroline McCracken-Flesher

Nothing in him —
But doth suffer a sea-change.

Tempest (epigraph to *The Pirate*)

Walter Scott poses a problem in our understanding of Romanticism: as a poet, he was one of the most successful writers of the Romantic era, and he went on to stratospheric success as a novelist; yet Scott's place as a Romanticist is alternately denied and pleaded, and in no case has it proved certain. This chapter suggests that Scott's absence among the 'big six' of Romanticism (Blake, Byron, Keats, Shelley, Wordsworth and Coleridge) derives not so much from the character or quality of his work, but from the ways in which Romanticism gradually has been constructed by critics. In fact, Scott brought a unique sensibility to the movement during the period of its formation – a scepticism that foregrounded Romantic identity, brought it into question and recast it in terms that meet yet exceed the usual run of Romanticism. Looking back, he stands forth as a crucial player in the development of Romanticism and in its meaning today.

Critics have long argued over what constitutes Romanticism. Still, if we were to hold Walter Scott against a check-list, we could do worse than draw our terms from *The Lyrical Ballads* (1798). Here, Coleridge privileges Gothic supernaturalism, and we can track Wordsworth's predilection for figures in a landscape, both manifesting an investment in what Coleridge termed 'the dramatic truth of [. . .] emotions'.[1] Whose emotions were these? In his preface to the volume (1802), Wordsworth emphasised 'incidents and situations from common life' related in 'language really used by men'.[2] Essential to this presentation is the proto-Romantic poet, who brings 'a certain colouring of imagination' to reveal 'the primary laws of our nature' in 'a state of excitement' (Wordsworth, 'Preface', pp. 392–3). Whatever the emphasis on ordinary men, in that 'all good poetry is the spontaneous overflow of powerful feelings', the feelings at play are those of the poet: 'the feeling [. . .] gives importance to the action and situation' (pp. 393, 395).

But whether we focus on people, places or poets, it is important to note that Walter Scott was held to meet these criteria in his own time. As a student of Kant, Goethe and Schiller, Scott shared the intellectual credentials of other putative Romantics; as a translator of Bürger's *Lenore*, with its spectral bridegroom, he early matched Coleridge's Gothic supernaturalism (1796).[3] Compiling and writing *The Minstrelsy of the Scottish Border* (1802), he could be aligned with Romantic precursors such as James Macpherson and later practitioners like Keats; his landscapes lured Wordsworth north of the border – the poet admired *The Lay of the Last Minstrel* (1805) for its 'clear picturesque descriptions'.[4] Speaking through the gaberlunzie Edie Ochiltree, or the ploughman Cuddie Headrigg (*The Antiquary* and *Old Mortality*, both 1816), Scott easily overmastered a Wordsworth insistent on the 'language really used by men', but not, as Murray Pittock observes, given to provincialisms.[5] Most importantly for our purposes, Thomas the Rhymer (1802) and Michael Scott (in *The Lay*) stand as powerful manifestations of the Romantic poet and his illuminating gaze – Thomas with his inspiration from fairyland and the wizard, even when buried, streaming light and clasping his 'Book of Might' (*Lay*, canto 2, verses 18–19). Scott, indeed, could challenge Coleridge and Wordsworth together by the numbers and intensity of his impassioned seers – often in the form of that 'Wordsworthian' figure, the mad mother.

It seems logical, then, that M. H. Abrams turns twice to Scott, in his authoritative *The Mirror and the Lamp*, to express the crucial elements of Romantic poeticism: the inspiration of the author and the communication of passion. Scott, Abrams notes, testified to 'an experience of unwilled and unpremeditated verse', claiming that: 'writing good verse seems to depend upon something separate from the volition of the author'.[6] Moreover, Scott insisted that all artists served to excite 'in the reader, hearer, or spectator, a tone of feeling similar to that which existed in his own bosom [. . .] It is the artist's object [. . .] to communicate [. . .] the same sublime sensations which had dictated his own composition'.[7] There is no lack of Romantic terminology or sensibility here.

And not surprisingly, Scott's more self-consciously Romantic contemporaries recognised his work as akin to theirs. Byron mistakenly blamed a hostile review on Scott and responded acerbically in *English Bards and Scotch Reviewers* (1809), but by 1812 the two were on terms of mutual compliment: Byron openly admired Scott, declaring of the critics and canon makers who would gradually oust his fellow poet from the charmed circle of Romanticism: 'I only wish they would not set me up as a competitor [. . .] I like the man – and admire his works'.[8] Others turned to Scott as the arbiter for their compositions – and thereby, we might think, for the Romanticism they espoused. Even William Godwin, credited as a radical founder of the movement, asked Scott to support him, and when Scott declined, lamented, 'The most obvious reason for your declining to recommend me is my unworthiness.'[9] Scott, then, in his own times was recognised both for his writing (as poet and novelist) and as a leader in the literary movement in formation.

Yet subsequent critical evaluations could make us believe that Scott's role in Romanticism was only a coincidence in chronology. M. H. Abrams, in fact, proves both insightful and rare in his designation of Scott as Romantic, for since Scott's death, his critics, whether friends or enemies, typically determine otherwise. J. G. Lockhart, in *Memoirs of the Life of Sir Walter Scott, Bart.* (1837–8), begins with a pedigree, and ends with a sentimental deathbed scene: '"Lockhart," he said [. . .] "be a good man – be virtuous – be religious – be a good man. Nothing else will give you any comfort when you come to lie here."'[10] Committed to the social and moral romance by which he reads Scott's life and work – a romance he later completed by being buried at Scott's feet – son-in-law Lockhart situates Scott apart from the unpredictable personalities essential to Romanticism. Picking up on Lockhart's tone, in 1838 Thomas Carlyle congratulated Scott because, 'in the sickliest of recorded ages, when British literature lay all puking and sprawling in Werterism, Byronism, and other sentimentalism, tearful or spasmodic (fruit of internal *wind*), Nature was kind enough to send us [Walter Scott]'.[11] Yet Lockhart's Scott was too much of a romancer and a romance for an authorship Carlyle nonetheless imagines in Romantic terms. Carlyle wonders that 'Scott is altogether lovely' to Lockhart; that 'Scott's greatness spreads out for him on all hands'; that 'Scott is to Lockhart the unparalleled of the time' (Carlyle, 'Review', pp. 301–2). Taking the Transcendentalists as his yardstick, Carlyle laments that Scott was not 'possessed with an *idea*'; worse, Scott cared not 'for the spiritual purport of his work' ('Review', pp. 304, 318). Leaping ahead to 1965, Georg Lukács, by contrast, celebrated Scott's 'middle way'. That was an idea in itself: 'He finds in English history the consolation that the most violent vicissitudes of class struggle have always finally calmed down into a glorious "middle way".'[12] Thus Scott portrays 'the struggles and antagonisms of history by means of characters who [. . .] represent social trends and historical forces' (Lukács, p. 34). But this was an anti-Romantic idea: 'What is expressed here, above all, is a renunciation of Romanticism, a conquest of Romanticism' (Lukács, p. 33). Small wonder, then, that with Scott's supporters and detractors so keen to place him apart from Romanticism, Scott until recently has failed to figure in that critical tradition.

The terms by which F. R. Leavis left Scott out of the 'Great Tradition' of the novel, that form in which he had played so large a part, point to what is at stake in Scott's exclusion. Leavis declared: 'not having the creative writer's interest in literature, [Scott] made no serious attempt to work out his own form and break away from the bad tradition of the eighteenth-century romance'.[13] Scott does not rise to the level of the author as defined by Romanticism: straddling Enlightenment and Romanticism, he is aligned with the obverse of both, that lowly form, 'romance'; and as either cause or effect of this literary *faux pas*, he is said to lack an aesthetic.

How could a writer who so aligned with the persons, locations and tech-niques of Romanticism, and who was also an accomplished critic of the moment and his place within it, be so perceived? Scott's placement has little to do with either his similarity to or difference from Romantic mores in his or later times. Of course, critics have helpfully worked to retrieve Scott's reputation in Romanticism on the grounds of parallel interests and talents: Nancy Goslee focuses on his poetry; Katie Trumpener situates Scott within the history of the Romantic novel according to his literary debts.[14] Others participate in the important project that Murray Pittock character-ises as 'broadening [the] space and deepening [the] time' of Romanticism.[15] Fiona Robertson tracks Scott and Romanticism through the Gothic; Ian Duncan connects the Gothic to the Victorian through Scott and by way of Romanticism; Ina Ferris pursues Scott's role in gendering the novel and the period; Murray Pittock foregrounds national difference as an engine for the shifting literary dynamic we call Romanticism.[16] But the fact is that Scott's assigned place with regard to Romanticism derives from no aesthetic criterion of past or present.

However much Scott's contemporaries and later critics talked in terms of aesthetic value, that phenomenon is always constructed in opposition to another to which it bears no actual relation: popularity. Wordsworth famously commended 'fit audience [. . .] though few';[17] today, Robert Miles slyly argues that 'the notion of the "romantic misfit" is about all that now popularly survives of the literary culture of the Romantic period [. . .] together with its virtual synonym, "neglected genius"'.[18] And where Wordsworth aligned aesthetic quality with limited sales, Scott, for all his other virtues, unfortu-nately proved a commercial success. Worse, with his four jobs (lawyer, poet, novelist, president of the Royal Society of Edinburgh), lively social life and connections to the great and the good, he seemed incapable of appreciating the refined and elevated role of the Romantic author, never mind suffering adequately to fulfil it. This is where Romanticism parts company with Walter Scott.

Thomas Carlyle makes the case clear. Assertively anti-Romantic, but with a decidedly Romantic idea of the author, Carlyle insisted: 'our greatest [. . .] are perhaps those that remain unknown!' (Carlyle, 'Review', p. 314). No doubt refracting his own anxieties at the time as a relatively unrecognised genius, Carlyle implies that great writing actually produces obscurity. Thus if one is popular, one cannot be a genius. Walter Scott, Carlyle reminds us over and over again, is very popular – therefore inadequate as an author: 'Popularity is as a blaze of illumination, or alas, of conflagration kindled round a man [. . .] often abstracting much from him; conflagrating the poor man himself into ashes' (p. 302); 'Shorn of this falsifying *nimbus*', Scott is 'reduced'. 'There is nothing spiritual in him' (p. 303). Indeed, Scott is barely a writer at all: because his books are 'faster written and better paid for than any other books in the world', he manifests only 'the perfection of extemporaneous writing', not the artistry of a thinking aesthete (pp. 334–5).

This overdetermination of Scott as less of a writer because more of a seller tells us more about the social and historical construction of Romanticism than it does about the author. That the idea of the inspired and elite author can only be sustained by recoding aesthetics as unpopularity, that this strategy excludes one of the most significant writers of the period, and that generations of confirming and corrective arguments only cut additional demarcating lines between Romanticism and its others, reveals that the critical construction of Romanticism is, in Foucault's terms, a kind of violence – dominating and carving up the literature it would address.[19]

This is where Walter Scott most problematises and informs the discourse that is Romanticism. Scott, of all his cohort, recognised, questioned and recast the perplexity that was the Romantic author.

Notably, if Romantic criticism has experienced difficulty placing Walter Scott, he himself showed no desire to be so placed. Scott, we have seen, was perfectly capable of concepts, techniques and criticisms that might locate him as a Romantic, but the man who disliked collaboration as a 'literary picnic' was not one to be confined to a literary school.[20] Indeed, when Scott yielded poetry to Byron, he assertively slipped out from under the discourse that was in the process of defining Romanticism (Grierson, *Letters*, VI: p. 506). Thus, the introductory chapter to *Waverley* (1814) begins with a statement about discourse and its limits: 'Had I, for example, announced in my frontispiece, "Waverley, a Tale of other Days", must not every novel-reader have anticipated a castle [. . .] had my title borne, "Waverley, a Romance from the German", what head so obtuse as not to image forth a profligate abbot'.[21] Scott instead tells us what the book is not: 'I would have my readers understand that they will meet in the following pages neither a romance of chivalry, nor a tale of modern manners' (*Waverley*, p. 4). This author is alert to, and set to reveal, the violence of inclusion and exclusion inherent in any discourse – and Romanticism is the discourse of the day, claiming dominance through the figure of the elite, inspired author.

As a Romanticist, Scott set out to query the terms he himself informed. *The Pirate* (1822), researched as Scott waited to see how *Waverley* would take and pondered his role as anonymous author, and the 'Introductory Epistle' to *The Fortunes of Nigel* (1822), developed alongside *The Pirate*, show Scott investigating the idea of the author as a figure of inspiration and oddity.[22] Scott puts the notion of the 'neglected genius' under pressure to reveal the romance of the Romantic author. Interestingly, he suggests that in the performance of authority, it is the reader who really matters.

The Pirate offers an appropriate test case, for in many respects it is exactly the kind of story Scott's detractors claimed was the site of his popularity and limitation: a romance. It is a veritable swashbuckler that has bequeathed persons, poses and piratical outfits to *Treasure Island*, J. M. Barrie's Captain Hook and *Pirates of the Caribbean*. In fine romance style, the pirate Cleveland is washed ashore on Zetland, where he falls in love with a dark lady and sets the locals in a spin. Moreover, in the introduction to the Magnum edition (1831), Scott affirms this is a romance – numerous times.[23] But as a successor to Byron's stupendously successful pirate poem, *The Corsair* (1814), this novel is also cued in to Romanticism. Edgar Johnson notes that 'None of Scott's novels are richer in atmosphere and the vivid creation of setting'; contemporary critics agreed, William Hazlitt declaiming 'Ah! [when Scott is gone] who will then call the mist from the hill? Who will make the circling eddies roar?'[24] Further, the novel is loaded with Scott's typically obstreperous common people, in the persons of Bryce Snaelsfoot the jagger (packman) and Swertha the housekeeper. The family dynamics, with their hints of incest, multiplied sibling rivalries, reclusive father and crazed mother would please Romantics as disparate as Byron and Jane Austen – who recommended in *Love and Freindship* (sic) 'run mad as often as you chuse; but do not faint'.[25]

Predictably, this package of romance and Romanticism translated easily to the stage in the form of melodrama, where Tom Dibdin aligned romance plot with Romantic characters and landscape in a visual spectacular: 'one finds [. . .] the barren waste of moor, with the house of Mertoun resting gloomily, like its owner [. . .] the landscapes in sunshine, rain, and moonlight, shifting back and forth like drops in the theatre [. . .] Finally, one [canvas reveals] the fight between the revenue cutter and the pirate craft'.[26] But, notably, Scott sets up Cleveland and the 'mad mother', Norna, as opposed figures of romance and Romanticism. And each is critiqued on the grounds of their discourse – their construction through display and performance. Most notably, that critique occurs through a 'reader's' eye.

Cleveland is an undoubted figure of romance. Aboard his ship, he is immediately in command: 'resolved to take upon him, with spirit and without loss of time, the task of extricating his ship's company from their perilous situation'.[27] This Cleveland is read in terms of romance and Romanticism by Minna Troil, who lives out her own version of both in a dream of Zetland's liberation (*The Pirate*, p. 210). But in Cleveland, piracy is exposed as a romance of sartorial style. Essential to Cleveland's 'gallant' role are 'a blue coat, lined with crimson silk, and laced with gold very richly, crimson damask waistcoat and breeches, a velvet cap, richly embroidered, with a white feather, white silk stockings, and' (eat your heart out, Captain Hook!)

'red-heeled shoes' – not to mention his various warlike accoutrements (p. 318). Scott pushes home the point that the romance of piracy is founded in performance by paralleling Cleveland with the strolling player Jack Bunce, now swaggering as the pirate 'Frederick Altamont' (p. 289). Unfortunately, a naïve audience can translate this comedy of manners into their own tragedy. This is what happens to Minna. Piracy requires brutality: 'a revenge so severe, that it was of itself sufficient to stamp [Cleveland] with the character of [. . .] inexorable ferocity' (p. 216). For Minna, to know this is to be 'awakened and undeceived' – and to end up an old maid (p. 217).

Equally, Norna manifests the dangers of Romanticism as a delusive performance. Norna has been lured by romance, and her misreading of that situation has converted her into a Romantic author, of sorts. She has had the requisite vision located in tradition and the folk: it promised great gifts at great cost. Subsequently, sneaking out to see a lover, she closed her father in his room and inadvertently suffocated him; now, she figures as the 'Reim-kennar', and seems able to control the weather and prophesy for those around her. She declaims in particular on behalf of young Mordaunt Mertoun – Cleveland's supposed rival in love.

Norna thus appears to meet the checklist of Romanticism – the chapter in which she appears in the dark of night to prophesy to the sisters Minna and Brenda even bears an epigraph from 'The Rime of the Ancient Mariner':

I pass like night from land to land,
    I have strange power of speech;
So soon as e'er his face I see,
I know the man that must hear me,
    To him my tale I teach.

(*The Pirate*, p. 174)

However, Norna's Romantic qualifications are overdetermined: Scott tracks her to a wilderness hide-away not once, but twice, with each location more rugged than the last; she is not just figuratively a mad mother, but literally so, believing Mordaunt to be her illegitimate and lost son (not recognising her actual son, the pirate Cleveland) (pp. 237–58, 381). In *The Pirate*, Scott reveals that the Romanticism that insists on itself through its signal of inward passion and outward prophecy is only a performance – and a flawed one.

Walter Scott persistently turned a winking eye toward that figure of Romanticism in full fling, the madwoman. In *The Heart of Mid-Lothian* (1818), he remarks: 'Of all the mad-women who have sung and said, since the days of Hamlet the Dane, if Ophelia be the most affecting, Madge Wildfire was the most provoking.'[28] Norna is surely the most theatrical. For her as much as for Cleveland, Scott specifies the conflation of literary sensibility and dramatic performance: Norna is 'as striking in appearance as

extravagantly lofty in her pretensions and in her language. She might well
have represented on the stage [. . .] the Bonduca or Boadicea of the Britons
[. . .] or any other fated Pythoness', and Scott goes on to give the full account
of her theatrical wardrobe, as he did for the pirate (*The Pirate*, pp. 49–50).
So not surprisingly, those for whom Norna would prophesy doubt her power
because of her performance.

Even as Norna cites her dreadful qualifications, and exercises her talents
on Mordaunt's behalf, the young man doubts her reality:

> 'Bear me witness, Mordaunt Mertoun, – you heard my words at Harfra – you saw
> the tempest sink before them – Speak, bear me witness!'
>   To have contradicted her in this strain of high-toned enthusiasm, would
> have been cruel and unavailing, even had Mordaunt been more decidedly con-
> vinced that an insane woman, not one of supernatural power, stood before him.
> (*The Pirate*, p. 94)

And when Norna discloses herself as his parent, thus aligning mother and
madness, he is fully convinced: 'disposed to ascribe this burst of passion to
insanity' (p. 307).

Norna insists that her suffering has made her solitary and significant – a
neglected genius. Certainly, that is how she presents herself, and locates
herself in landscape and society. When she comes to Brenda and Minna, her
song relates:

> One hour is mine, in all the year,
>   To tell my woes, – and one alone;
> When gleams this magic lamp, 'tis here, –
>   When dies the mystic light, 'tis gone. (p. 177)

But Norna is a bad reader of her own circumstances. Instead of casting light,
she accomplishes light effects only, mistakenly shining the spotlight on
Mordaunt as her son, and misrecognising Minna as his love interest. Bound
up in her performance as Romantic genius she is, both by her fortuitous
choice of domain and as Scott ironically terms her, only 'Norna of the Fitful-
head' (p. 50).

Importantly, in his Magnum introduction, Scott insists on this reading of
Norna. Unlike some of his other wild and wise women, she is 'the victim of
remorse and insanity, and the dupe of her own imposture' (Magnum, p. x).
'Yet, amid a very credulous and ignorant population, it is astonishing what
success may be attained by an impostor, who is, at the same time, an enthusi-
ast' (Magnum, pp. x–xi). The problem lies both in reader and in author. But
notably, Norna eventually learns to see herself in a more sceptical reader's
eye, wailing to Mordaunt:

'Your voice joins that of the daemon which [. . .] whispers to me, "Norna, this is but delusion – your power rests but in the idle belief of the ignorant, supported by a thousand petty artifices of your own" [. . .] I must either cease to be, or continue the mightiest as well as the most miserable of beings!' (*The Pirate*, pp. 310–11)

In the end, 'She [refuses] the [assumed] name of Norna [. . .] She appeared deeply to repent of her former presumptuous attempts to interfere with the course of human events [. . .] and expressed bitter compunction' (p. 389). That is, she realises her responsibility in the falsification of reality and the damage thereby to those around her. Through Norna, Scott cuts to the problematic heart of the impassioned relation between Romanticised author and the reader as Romantic.

In the 'Advertisement' to *The Pirate*, Scott began 'The purpose of the following Narrative is to give a detailed and accurate account of certain remarkable incidents'; he concluded: 'It is to be supposed [. . .] that the last circumstance [. . .] and other particulars of the commonly received story, are inaccurate, since they will be found totally irreconcileable with the following veracious narrative, compiled by materials to which he himself alone has had access, by THE AUTHOR of WAVERLEY' (*The Pirate*, pp. 3, 4). Yet 'he himself alone' tells the tale of an unwitting fraud between Norna and those around her – between self-Romanticising 'writer' and 'readers'. This dangerous inter-relationship swirls, too, between the aggrandised 'AUTHOR OF WAVERLEY' and his readers, and those readers and Walter Scott.

Scott pursued the problem in his 'Introductory Epistle' to *The Fortunes of Nigel*.[29] Jerome McGann rightly notes that Scott's difficulty for romance and Romanticism lies in the self-reflexivity at play (most obviously) in his introductions and his role as 'The Author of Waverley' – 'Scott's "post-modernity": the ironic awareness with which he constructs and pursues his Romantic quest, the awareness that forbids him from turning his poetic tale into a form of worship'.[30] In particular, Scott refused to pose, himself, as an object for worship. In this 'Introductory Epistle', following hard on the heels of his critique of Romantic authority in *The Pirate*, he makes a direct attack on the discourse of the neglected/inspired author and the co-dependent relation between self-Romanticising writer and the reader's romance. At last, 'The Author of Waverley' appears in his own text: Captain Clutterbuck, one of Scott's narrative personae, penetrates into the back of the publisher's shop where he meets: 'the person, or perhaps I should rather say the Eidolon, or Representation, of the Author of Waverley' (*Nigel*, pp. 4–5). Overwhelmed by this afflux of Romantic authorship, Clutterbuck can only worship: 'I at once bended the knee, with the classical salutation of, *Salve, magne parens!*' (p. 5). Yet, for all he is loaded with the signs of the impassioned seer – hidden, solitary, indistinct and thus, presumably, inspired – the Author will have none of it.

Clutterbuck grovels, then critiques: Scott's White Lady (*The Monastery*) ought to be 'uniformly noble' in her actions; stories should be 'natural and probable', not 'huddled up' – they should be organic and Romantic (*Nigel*, pp. 6, 8). Most of all, Clutterbuck grooms the Author in the Romantic role. Scott is 'not now [. . .] so impersonal as heretofore'; Scott should 'care for your reputation [. . .] for your fame' (p. 8). In particular, he should not write so sloppily or publish so fast – in order to maintain his role as Romantic author: 'Respect to yourself [. . .] ought to teach you caution' (p. 9).

In response, the Author disabuses Clutterbuck of his illusions. Refusing the Romantic role, he declares:

> For the critics, they have their business, and I mine [. . .] I am their humble jackall, too busy in providing food for them, to have time for considering whether they swallow or reject it. – To the public, I stand pretty near in the relation of the postman who leaves a packet at the door of an individual [. . .] the bearer of the dispatches is [. . .] as little thought on as the snow of last Christmas. The utmost extent of kindness between the author and the public which can really exist, is, that the world are [sic] disposed to be somewhat indulgent to the succeeding works of an original favourite, were it but on account of the habit which the public mind has acquired; while the author very naturally thinks well of *their* taste, who have so liberally applauded *his* productions. (p. 9)

The 'Author' parodically declares that any author is, in fact, is a 'productive labourer'; everything else is 'cant' (pp. 9, 14). Deliberately, Scott foregrounds that horror Carlyle would later debase as the 'cash nexus', and thus, step by step, he reduces the critics' romance of the Romantic author.[31] Furthermore, Scott disrupts the relation between writer and romancing reader. The 'Introductory Epistle' coaches Clutterbuck up off his knees and into a direct, clear-eyed relationship between his reading and reality. Scott jokingly alludes to his own Romantic re-creation in the public eye: 'having been [. . .] made a dramatist whether I would or not. I believe my muse would be *Terrified* into treading the stage, even if I should write a sermon' – referring to Daniel Terry, who did indeed stage the novels (*Nigel*, p. 12). Encouraged by Clutterbuck to produce 'a volume of dramas like Lord Byron's', he declines (p. 12). 'I do entreat you my son,' he declares, on the one hand instructing, on the other undermining his authority by mockingly aligning himself with Dr Johnson, 'Free your mind from cant' (p. 9). Scott will not be Romanticised by himself or by others. Rather, he encourages readers to make what they will of his texts – knowing that the Author is a constructed and rather suspect subject. 'Well, you must take the risk and act only on your own principles,' Clutterbuck gives in; 'Do you act on yours,' the author ripostes (p. 17). Instead of celebrating 'fit audience [. . .] though few', Scott aims to fit all his readers to act for themselves, outwith the charmed circle cast by the Romantic writer.

Thomas Carlyle, we may recall, claimed that Scott lacked an 'idea' (Carlyle, 'Review', p. 304). It is more accurate to note that he refused an idea, particularly the romance of the Romantic author. He found significance, indeed, in its obverse; instead of performing as the impassioned seer, he actively resisted being made present in the Romantic myth of the author. Clutterbuck, worshipping at the Eidolon's feet, ultimately collapses into confusion, for 'Whether she man or woman inly were, / That could not any creature well descry' (p. 5). This Author, though Eidolon, is so indistinct even its gender cannot be sure. And this is what marks Scott's role as author: he resists being determinable. As indeterminable, he implies significance, but cannot dominate. He makes it impossible for himself to participate in the excluding violence that is Romantic discourse.

Scott, then, constitutes authorship not as a role that sorts out the fit from the few, but as a site of negotiation between writers and readers – a place of Romantic production. Thomas Carlyle denigrated Scott as 'not of the sublime sort' ('Review', p. 308). Recognising, questioning and recasting the idea of the Author, Scott would likely have been pleased to hear this acerbic reader's response.

CHAPTER TWELVE

Byron

Brean Hammond

There is a widely held impression that George Gordon, Lord Byron, was one of the stars of the English poetic galaxy. The truth about Byron's nationality is, however, more complicated. That Byron was a Scottish writer is arguably a more defensible proposition. His own account of the matter of nationality, succinctly supplied in *Don Juan* X.17, is as follows: 'I am half a Scot by birth, and bred /A whole one.'[1] This is partly a matter of fact, or at any rate a matter of partial fact. Byron's mother, Catherine Gordon, was a Scot; and although her son was born in London, by the time he was eighteen months old he was living in a furnished apartment in Queen Street, Aberdeen. The poet lived for most of his first ten years in Aberdeen and visited the Highlands of Scotland in successive summers. Before he left with his mother in 1798 to claim his title and inheritance in Newstead Abbey, he seems to suggest above that he had absorbed the elements of a 'Scottish sensibility'. If the contours of the personality are formed, as is now thought, in early childhood, then Byron's personality was a Scots one; the poet Moore's biography was the first to notice his slight but perceptible Scots accent. As Jerome McGann writes:

> Visits during the school holidays to his great-grandmother Lady Gight at Banff, and to the Dee valley where he was taken to convalesce after an attack of scarlet fever in 1795 or 1796, introduced Byron to the splendours of highland scenery to which he formed a lifelong attachment, and which formed a sublime ideal in the landscape of his imagination.[2]

In the preface to his first published book of poems, *Hours of Idleness* (1807), the identity of a Scotsman was one that he adopted – though amongst the several postures of that ill-fated preface, it is hard to say with what degree of commitment. Sideswiping at the poets identified with the Lake District seems a more immediate objective:

> Though accustomed, in my younger days, to rove a careless mountaineer on the Highlands of Scotland, I have not, of late years, had the benefit of such pure air,

or so elevated a residence, as might enable me to enter the lists with genuine bards, who have enjoyed both these advantages. (Byron, *Poetical Works* I: p. 33)

In the same introduction, Byron's coy but insistent hopping up and down upon his rank and title betrays an insecurity about his lineage, mercilessly exposed by Brougham in the *Edinburgh Review*, that might be symptomatic of the difficult Anglicisation process he was then undergoing.[3] Several poems in a collection suffused with an elegiac and nostalgic Caledonianism manifest at least one defining characteristic of a national culture, as recently discerned by Murray Pittock: 'the taxonomy of glory, the symbolic organization of images (e.g. bards), and the reading of history as a continuous struggle for liberty, by which the national past is reclaimed'.[4] In 'Lachin y Gair', for example, the poet apostrophises the ghostly 'forms of my fathers' (*Poetical Works*, p. 23) in the following crypto-Jacobite terms:

'Ill-starred, though brave, did no visions foreboding,
Tell you that Fate had forsaken your cause?'
Ah! were you destin'd to die at Culloden,
Victory crown'd not your fall with applause;
Still were you happy in death's earthy slumber,
You rest with your clan in the caves of Braemar;
The Pibroch resounds, to the piper's loud number,
Your deeds, on the echoes of dark Loch na Garr. (ll. 25–32)

The collection boasts a prose-poem in imitation of Ossian, 'The Death of Calmar and Orla'; while in the lyric 'I would I were a careless child', Byron explicitly contrasts Highland freedom to the slavery associated with 'The cumbrous pomp of Saxon pride' that 'Accords not with the freeborn soul' (pp. 5–6). Elsewhere, as in 'When I Rov'd, a Young Highlander', the connection between Scottish scenery, primitivism and passionate love for his Highland Mary is cemented into an elegy for lost youth and irretrievable memories of its carefree condition. This is an early and self-conscious homage to Robert Burns, whose secretive affair with Margaret Campbell, whom he called Highland Mary, was already the stuff of legend as the nineteenth century began. The Ossianic posture of a line such as 'As the last of my race I must wither alone' (p. 27) is obvious as, more generally, is the indebtedness of the collection's structure of feeling to the poems of Gray and Scott. In Byron's prefatory understatement: 'I have not aimed at exclusive originality.'

Less than two years later, however, the publication of *English Bards and Scotch Reviewers* (1809) furnished evidence that Byron's earlier deployment of what Pittock calls 'the taxonomy of glory' was strategic rather than deeply felt. This poem, whatever its other merits, plays a part in occluding Byron's place in any Scottish tradition of Romantic writing or in a Scottish

national culture. In its Manichean structure, 'bards' are English and are virtuous, whereas reviewers – critics – are Scottish and are uncreative parasites.
Picking up some pieces of Pope's ideology of duncehood created in his later
poems from the early *Dunciad* to the *Epistle to Dr Arbuthnot*, Byron tries to
create a similar unholy alliance of bad poetry and bad politics, deploying
Southey's writing and Francis Jeffrey's criticism as embodiments of degenerate culture – as Pope had done with such earlier figures as Lewis Theobald and
Colley Cibber. Pope's Goddess of Dulness who presides, in *The Dunciad*, over
the fate of the entire literarium – hacks, scribblers, booksellers and publishers
– dons a kilt in Byron's poem to become 'Caledonia's goddess'. Byron takes
advantage of a Popean line in anti-Scottish humour (Scotland as 'ultima
Thulè', fabled as the most northerly land in the world, a frozen, uncultured
wasteland) to set England and Scotland at odds with one another: 'For long
as Albion's heedless sons submit', the goddess advises:

> Or Scottish taste decides on English wit,
> So long shall last thine unmolested reign,
> Nor any dare to take thy name in vain.
> Behold, a chosen band shall aid thy plan,
> And own thee chieftain of the critic clan. (pp. 503–7)

Despite the possible allusion to Burns' famous line 'Great Chieftan o' the
Puddin' race' in 'To a Haggis' and its relatively positive view of his writing,
the poem is not kind to the Scots. The 'chosen band' of Byron's targets
included, of course, some of the most celebrated poets of the time – and still
of ours – to more than one of whom he was forced to apologise later. Lacking
Pope's cultural authority, never being capable of replicating the depth of
Pope's political analysis or the circumstantiality of his mentor's attack on
the subliterary swarm of print-befuddled nonentities, Byron did not produce
a masterpiece in *English Bards and Scotch Reviewers*. Its re-enactment on the
cultural field of the Anglo-Scottish wars was a major aspect of the poem's
false consciousness.

Byron's 'step on your grandmother for a good joke' betrayal of his cultural
heritage in this poem is the more disappointing in that, on his European
travels over the next two-year period (1809–11), he sometimes gazed on
foreign lands through a Scots telescope. Given the conceivable commonality
of derivation between 'Alba', the Gaelic word for Scotland and Albania, it
is hardly surprising that Byron saw that wild country, 'rugged nurse of savage
men!' (*Childe Harold's Pilgrimage, Poetical Works* 2.38.6), as analogous to the
land of his upbringing. In a letter to his mother, Byron observed that his entry
into Ali Pasha's palace at Tepelene called to mind, in its feudal aspect, Scott's
description of Branksome Castle (in his *Lay of the Last Minstrel* [1805]). Byron

writes: 'The Albanians in their dresses (the most magnificent in the world, consisting of a long *white kilt*, gold worked cloak, crimson velvet gold laced jacket & waistcoat, silver mounted pistols & daggers)'.[5] The bloodthirsty chant in *Childe Harold* that the warrior-Suliotes 'half sang, half screamed' (interpolated after 2.72), resembling the anapaestic if not the tetrameter measures of Scott's *Lay*, came full circle when Scott adapted it as the song of Rory Dall of Alba as translated by Flora McIvor in chapter 22 of *Waverley* (1814). Andrew Nicholson cites Byron's note to the Albanian section of *Childe Harold* canto 2, where again the resemblance between Albania (which was the medieval Latinised name for Scotland) and Scotland is remarked:

> The Arnaouts, or Albanese, struck me forcibly by their resemblance to the Highlanders of Scotland, in dress, figure, and manner of living. Their very mountains seemed Caledonian with a kinder climate. The kilt, though white; the spare, active form; their dialect, Celtic in its sound; and their hardy habits, all carried me back to Morven.[6]

Subsequently, Byron's attitude towards Scotland was frequently that of sentimental exceptionalism. Scotland was an exception, that is, to a general principle espoused elsewhere in his writing: the tendency of powerful nations to behave badly, perhaps because Scotland could not be regarded as powerful. The 'message' of much of *Childe Harold's Pilgrimage* and of the satire on military glory and the siege of Ismail in cantos 7 and 8 of *Don Juan* is profoundly anti-war. Yet in canto 3 of *Childe Harold's Pilgrimage* against a context of deeply pessimistic scepticism about war and military glory on the field of Waterloo, the narrator can pause to praise the Cameron Highlanders in a passage sufficiently attention-grabbing for Scott to use it as an epigraph to chapter 13 of *The Fair Maid of Perth* (1828):

> How in the noon of night that pibroch thrills,
> Savage and shrill! But with the breath which fills
> Their mountain-pipe, so fill the mountaineers
> With the fierce native daring which instils
> The stirring memory of a thousand years,
> And Evan's, Donald's fame rings in each clansman's ears. (III: p. 26)

Eliot thought this the finest stanza in the entire poem, precisely because it memorialised Byron's 'mother's people'.[7] Earlier, Byron has excoriated Lord Elgin, despoiler of the Acropolis, as an affront to his nation: 'Blush, Caledonia! such thy son could be!' (II: p. 11) – as if there were few or no other Scottish despoilers and empire-builders. Arguing as he did for the restoration of the marbles, Byron was considerably ahead of his time; ideologically, very far away from the colonising mentality that acquired them. Where, after

all, did Byron come by his sympathy for the struggling Greek nation? It must
derive in some measure from the analogous situation in which he perceived
the Scottish Highlands and Scotland herself to exist. Once in Greece, Byron
found things very different from his expectation. He speaks of their 'present
burglarious and larcenous tendencies', but is understanding enough to write
in his journal that 'when the limbs of the Greeks are a little less stiff from
the shackles of four centuries – they will not march so much "as if they had
gyves on their legs"' (*Letters*, p. 298). Greece perceived through a template of
Shakespeare's *Henry IV, Part One*: a Byronic conjuncture.

It was not until much later in his poetic career that Byron acknowledged
the intensity of his Scottish attachment – intense despite its somewhat
erratic trajectory. As Bernard Beatty notes, it was as part of a conversation
with Medwin, whom he first met in late 1821, that Byron 'tidie[d] the whole
thing up'.[8] He lost his early affection for Scotland, Byron reports, because
of the *Edinburgh Review* critique of *Hours of Idleness*, so that 'I transferred a
portion of my dislike to that country; but my affection for it soon flowed back
into its old channel'.[9] His 1823 poem *The Island* goes on to pay Scotland
more than passing compliments on its natural beauty. Scottishness is factored
into the deep artistic structure of the work. A highly idiosyncratic account
of the mutiny on the *Bounty*, the poem features a Caledonian hero, Torquil,
to offset its brooding protagonist, Fletcher Christian, a gloomy, isolated presence tortured by self-reproach. By means of a typically Byronic narrative
intrusion, the poet celebrates his heritage in a conception of his past that
throws a Caledonian plaid over his subsequent classicism:

> He who first met the Highlands' swelling blue
> Will love each peak that shows a kindred hue [. . .]
> Long have I roamed through lands which are not mine,
> Adored the Alp, and loved the Apennine,
> Revered Parnassus, and beheld the steep
> Jove's Ida and Olympus crown the deep:
> But 'twas not all long ages' lore, nor all
> *Their* nature held me in their thrilling thrall;
> The infant rapture still survived the boy,
> And Loch-na-gar with Ida look'd o'er Troy,
> Mixed Celtic memories with the Phrygian mount,
> And Highland linns with Castalie's clear fount. (II: p. 12, ll. 280–1, 284–92)[10]

Ida and Olympus are fine mountains, but they 'are not the hills of home', in
Andy Stewart's immortal lyrics. *Heimatsweh* is, however, a minor aspect of
this. The more significant point is that the poet's Scottish upbringing and
education has laid the foundations, not only for his receptivity to a good
classical education (although *Childe Harold*, IV: 73–7 suggests the limits

to book-learnt classical erudition), but for a modern pan-Europeanism and philhellenism. Byron sees his citizenship of the world as a product of his early Scottish environment. Nigel Leask's reading of *The Island* helps us to understand how important the poem from which the above extract is taken actually is in Byron's *oeuvre*.[11] Whereas Byron's early oriental tales, *The Giaour* (1813) and *The Corsair* (1814), may be read as direct enough expressions of what Said termed 'orientalism',[12] the slightly later *Lara* (1814) represents a condensation or displacement of that – not quite a stripping away. The figure of Kaled/Gulnare in the poem can be seen as a mirror image of her master Lara: an embodiment of his fear, which is of 'turning Turk', of becoming the despised oriental Other. This, of course, still postulates the orientalist dichotomy between European illuminism and Asiatic darkness. Leask sees in *The Island* (1823) the closest thing to resolution of that orientalism. Byron's partiality is reflected in the poem's narrative. Whereas Fletcher Christian's rebellion against Bligh's authority is severely censured, young Torquil, just as much a mutineer however Scottish, secures a utopian alliance with the South Sea Island princess Neuha. In Leask's words:

> The stereotypical 'Byronic hero' is still present in the figure of Fletcher Christian, the 'ruddy, reckless, dauntless' leader of the mutineers, but his influence in the *Tale* is eclipsed by Torquil, the 'blue-eyed northern child', who has been 'civilized' by the voluptuous Neuha, and the paradisical delights of the Pacific island.

The idyllic merging of Torquil and Neuha offers the possibility of a racial resolution that is not some form of miscegenation, based neither on the subduing of the other by a military and economic domination hinted at in Fletcher Christian's mock-heroic last stand, nor on the process of 'going native' – an ingesting of the other through fear. Torquil's position as a Hebridean commoner, the representative, that is, of an internally colonised country, enables an ideal blend with Neuha of rank and race.

By the time this poem appeared, Byron had already written the stanzas in *Don Juan*, Canto X (11–19) in which he made lasting peace with his sometime enemy Francis Jeffrey. Reflecting on his old feud with Jeffrey and the *Edinburgh Review* first patched up in 1816, Byron deploys Burns' anthemic phrase 'Auld Lang Syne' metonymically, to stand for a chain of associations that captures the essence of his childhood, forming the bedrock of his romantic caledonianism:

> And when I use the phrase of 'Auld Lang Syne!'
> 'Tis not addressed to you – the more's the pity
> For me, for I would rather take my wine
> With you, than aught (save Scott) in your proud city.

But somehow, – it may seem a schoolboy's whine,
And yet I seek not to be grand nor witty,-
But I am half a Scot by birth, and bred
A whole one, and my heart flies to my head,-

As 'Auld Lang Syne' brings Scotland, one and all,
Scotch plaids, Scotch moods, the blue hills, and clear streams,
The Dee, the Don, Balgounie's Brig's *black wall*,
All my boy feelings, all my gentler dreams
Of what I *then dreamt*, clothed in their own pall,
Like Banquo's offspring;- floating past me seems
My childhood in this childishness of mine:
I care not – 'tis a glimpse of 'Auld Lang Syne.' (*Don Juan* X.17–18)

If the passage as a whole anticipates a Tennysonian sense of 'the days that are no more' as a kind of death-in-life – even if memories of 'Auld Lang Syne' must inevitably be tempered with melancholy – a debt to both Burns and Scott as his literary mentors is acknowledged. However he may have, 'in a fit / Of wrath and rhyme' attacked 'Scotch Reviewers' in the past, nevertheless, he says, 'I "*scotched* not killed" the Scotchman in my blood, / And love the land of "mountain and of flood"' (*Don Juan* X: 19). This is a highly-wrought passage, punningly alluding to *Macbeth* possibly via Wordsworth's *Tintern Abbey* and certainly, as acknowledged by the quotation marks, via Scott's *Lay of the Last Minstrel* – a literary confection that nevertheless discovers Byron's deep allegiance to Scotland.[13]

Byron's autobiographical and poetically-expressed sense of being 'bred a whole [Scot]' suggests that his Scottishness is not superficial, not merely a single sonority in his rich soundscape. Scottishness is, on the contrary, the timbre of Byron's poetic voice. He is, as Bernard Beatty has proposed, not merely a Scottish but actually a 'Celtic' poet. What remains of this chapter will contend, supplementary to the work of such as Nicholson, Beatty and Pittock, that this case can and should be argued. Part of the argument is a stronger account of Burns' influence on Byron than is usually given, strengthened by the observation that the reception of both poets was analogous. Like Burns, Byron was un-English. This showed in his growing unacceptability to wide sections of his readership in his own time and in his subsequent imperviousness to home-grown English literary classification; on the other hand, he became increasingly valued, indeed worshipped, by European audiences. The history of Burns' reception was not dissimilar, and for some of the same reasons: antinomianism, enthusiasm for lost or minority causes, apostleship of toleration, brotherhood and freedom, unparalleled 'warmth' of expression. Byron was half a Scot by birth and this, we are saying, comes to be expressed in his developing poetic temperament. Of course, it is not easy to discern what, in Byron's peculiar composition, is the result of a national inflection and what derives from, for example, his consciousness of status. In combination, however, those elements imparted a directness, a distinctive warmth of expression, a refusal to be gagged and its obverse, a fatal propensity to speak his mind, at the same time as he would, infuriatingly, deny that it was his mind he was speaking, that adds up to being un-English. Even if there are limits to the comparison with Burns, there is enough in it to establish affinities that position both credibly enough in a Scottish tradition.

An insight into how one notable Scots contemporary read Burns and Byron is provided in the opening to *Quentin Durward* (1823), where Scott is considering the diabolical character of one of the story's protagonists, Louis XI of France. Scott emphasises the 'cold-hearted and sneering' anti-chivalric aspect of that monarch's nature, and is led to make the following observations:

> In this point of view, Goethe's conception of the character and reasoning of Mephistophiles, the tempting spirit in the singular play of Faust, appears to me more happy than that which has been formed by Byron, and even than the Satan of Milton. These last great authors have given to the Evil Principle something which elevates and dignifies his wickedness; a sustained and unconquerable resistance against Omnipotence [. . .] all those points of attraction in the Author of Evil, which have induced Burns and others to consider him as the Hero of the Paradise Lost.[14]

Scott is possibly referring to a letter of 1787 in which Burns, anticipating William Blake, says that he has 'bought a pocket Milton which I carry perpetually about with me, in order to study the sentiments – the dauntless magnanimity; the intrepid, unyielding independance [*sic*]; the desperate daring, and noble defiance of hardship, in that great Personage, Satan'.[15] Whether Byron's Lucifer in *Cain* (1821) is any object of hero-worship is open to debate: assuredly, Byron's Lucifer is earnest and persuasive in his debates with Cain rather than suave and humorous, or sneering. What is significant, though, is the alternative Scoto-European romantic pantheon constructed by Scott: Milton, Burns, Goethe (whom Byron called the 'undisputed Sovereign of European literature') (*Letters*, p. 294) and Byron, a group of writers not in agreement about the characteristics of evil but certain that its nature is a central question for cultural representation. Rebellion, anti-authoritarianism, disregard for the conventional pieties of morality – these are the attitudes that this literary grouping might be thought to share. Scott could discern the characteristics the more easily because he did not share them.

What Scott did share with Byron, however, was a love of recited Scottish poetry. So well known was Byron's predilection that the musical publisher George Thomson, who had issued very many songs written and collected by Burns in his *Select Collection of Scottish Airs* (published between 1793 and 1841), spent time trying, even if ultimately unsuccessfully, to recruit Byron for the project. In 1815, Byron's publisher John Murray sent him a volume of Percy's *Reliques* containing 'Hardyknute. A Scottish Fragment', by Sir John Bruce of Kinross, first published in Edinburgh in 1719 and collected in Allan Ramsay's *Tea-Table Miscellany* (1724). This had been recited to Byron by Scott, who claimed that it was the first poem he (Scott) ever learnt by heart.[16]

The issue is the hoary one of Byron's status as a 'Romantic' writer. Readers tempted to think of Byron as in any straightforward sense a 'Romantic' poet might be surprised by the vehemence with which he attacked most of the other poets so considered:

> All are not moralists, like Southey, when
> He prated to the world of 'Pantisocracy';
> Or Wordsworth unexcised, unhired, who then
> Season'd his pedlar poems with democracy;
> Or Coleridge, long before his flighty pen
> Lent to the Morning Post its aristocracy;
> When he and Southey, following the same path,
> Espoused two partners (milliners of Bath) (*Don Juan* III st. 93).[17]

At one time or another, Byron attacked all of the so-called 'Big Six' Romantic poets, except Shelley – even if we need to set the record straight by conceding that he provided direct pecuniary and other assistance to several of them, notably Coleridge, whose *Christabel* was published by John Murray at Byron's insistence. (Again, it was Scott who educated Byron's ear to the beauties of this poem (*Letters of John Murray*, p. 146)). His refusal to be placed in any grouping of the outstanding poets of his era has been echoed down the ages by readers who have found him impossible to pigeon-hole. Aestheticised definitions of Romanticism that make a fetish of the subjective sensibility – the creative self – are not easily applied to a writer who, like Alexander Pope, speaks out on public occasions 'with an ironic counter-voice and deliberately opens a satiric perspective on the vatic stance of his romantic contemporaries'.[18] One of the chasms separating Byron from his contemporaries was his admiration for the cultural achievements of the preceding century. In a *Letter to John Murray Esqre* (1821), Byron set out the terms of his defence of Pope in opposition to the strictures of William Lisle Bowles, first expressed in his ten-volume edition of Pope's *Works* (1806). Bowles objected both to the kind of poetry that Pope wrote and also to his personal morality.[19] The issue was revived in a pamphlet controversy following publication of Thomas Campbell's *Specimens of the British Poets* (1819), where Campbell denied that there was anything intrinsically 'poetical' about specific kinds of subject-matter.

In contrast to Wordsworth, whose way of making his own poetry new was in part to attack aspects of Pope and Gray that he considered outmoded, Byron was steeped in eighteenth-century achievement, and not only that of Pope. His greatest persona, Don Juan, clearly derives more from Fielding's Tom Jones than from any Juan available in the mainstream tradition of sexual adventurers to which the amatory conqueror ostensibly belongs. Claude Rawson emphasises the passivity of both, 'the relaxed composure, the availability to experience, and the easy openness with which these heroes typically let love come to them rather than expend emotional substance in pursuit of it'. As he wittily summarises, they are 'more wooed against than wooing'.[20] The combination of warmth and moral relaxation to be found in *Tom Jones* was thought by early biographers and readers also to typify the poetry of Burns: and in Byron's admiration for Burns is to be found an important facet of his un-Englishness.

Offering a definition of Romanticism inflected towards a national culture, Murray Pittock foregrounds the importance of clashing and coalescing linguistic registers; of dialect against standard English, of metropolitan against urban and village localisms. He refers to the way in which hybridised language deploying variable registers causes 'metropolitan' language to occupy the same linguistic space as localised dialect, to 'create a tension between what at times seems deliberately 'anglopetal' and 'anglofugal' representations of the meeting-point between language and culture'.[21] Not conversant with Scots, Byron could not be said to deploy 'anglofugal' speech in anything like the same way as did Burns. Nevertheless a Bakhtinian heteroglossic element is clearly present in the combination of registers so often responsible for comic effect in poems such as *Beppo* and *Don Juan*. One example may suffice, in which Byron alludes to Burns, the stanza benefiting, perhaps, from some of Burns' context for readers who pick up the allusion. In *Tam O' Shanter*, the narrator is itemising the grim appurtenances with which 'Auld Nick' is surrounded at the witches' dance. Here, the Prince of Darkness appears in his folkloric garb, presiding over an anatomical chamber of horrors that includes murderers' bones still encased in the gibbet irons, the corpses of tiny newborn babies and that of a thief with his throat sliced open by the hanging rope, blood-encrusted toma-hawks and scimitars. The passage reaches a climax of self-censorship where the poet's imagination, or Tam's, can be presumed to have failed him or where he is too eager to get on with the story to include more local colour. As so often in Burns' poetry, it is the energy released by the clash between the grammatical structures and vocabulary of standard English on the one hand, and Scots syntax and lexical items on the other, that enacts the relationship between the narrator and the focalised consciousness of Tam. The latter's naïve horror is controlled by the narrator's knowing superiority. There is a performativity, an implied hand-waving gesture of dismissal, in the last couplet:

A garter which a babe had strangled;
A knife a father's throat had mangled –
Whom his ain son o' life bereft –
The grey-hairs yet stack to the heft;
Wi' mair of horrible and awefu',
Which even to name wad be unlawfu'. (ll.137–42)

The rhyme words 'awefu'/ 'unlawfu' are picked up by Byron in *Don Juan* III.12:

Haidée and Juan were not married, but
The fault was theirs, not mine: it is not fair,
Chaste reader, then, in any way to put
The blame on me, unless you wish they were;
Then if you'd have them wedded, please to shut
The book which treats of this erroneous pair,
Before the consequences grow too awful;
'Tis dangerous to read of loves unlawful.

Here the effect is the result, again, of an implied split between the narrator and his fictional creations, enabling the narrator's Fieldingesque teasing of the invoked reader designated 'chaste'. Refusing to take responsibility for his fictional characters or to acknowledge them as such, the narrator manages to absolve himself of blame for their immoral conduct and to render any reader who construes their conduct thus as prudish and inadequate. Meanwhile, the poem's unconventional amatory amorality marches on.

What is at stake in the local instance discussed above – relationships between narrators and characters narrated and the differing linguistic registers deployed to create those – is at issue in the wider evaluation of both poets. Elusiveness in the nature of the poetic self is echoed on the (auto) biographical plane and forms part of the critical ecology surrounding them both. In the verbal self-portraits that Byron has left us, he claims for himself a shape-shifting absence of psychological continuity, an evanescent self of which gentlemanly diabolism was an aspect. The conversations with Byron reported by Lady Blessington record this self-portrait:

Now, if I know myself, I should say, that I have no character at all [. . .] what I think of myself is, that I am so changeable, being everything by turns and nothing long, – I am such a strange *mélange* of good and evil, that it would be difficult to describe me.[22]

Byron's posturing claim to uniqueness here, the aristocratic *sprezzatura* with which he advertises the Manichaean mixture of his personality, is developed through two allusions – to Pope's *Epistle to a Lady* wherein the poet notoriously says that 'Most women have no characters at all'; and to Dryden's

Absalom and Achitophel where Zimri is said to be 'Everything by starts and nothing long'. Byron's identity is, he claims, a *pentimento*, a layered self of which a conversancy with the great achievements of earlier couplet verse is an aspect. Lady Blessington was sufficiently convinced to echo him in her own appraisal. He is, she said, 'a perfect chameleon' who assumes 'the colour of whatever touches him. He is conscious of this, and says it is owing to the extreme *mobilité* of his nature, which yields to present impressions' (*Lady Blessington's Conversations*, p. 71). Taken at his own estimate, Byron's character type might be an example of what G. Gregory Smith dubbed 'antisyzygy', the term later given the helium of publicity by Hugh MacDiarmid's essay of 1936 entitled 'The Caledonian Antisyzygy'.[23] This quality consists in a colloidal suspension of incompatible personality traits that MacDiarmid argued had been altogether typical of the Scots before they permitted themselves to dwindle into the dour, 'canny' beings, 'almost wholly assimilated to the English', that they now are.[24]

In his verse, Byron makes himself his own subject just as much as does Wordsworth in *The Prelude*. That self, though, is exasperatingly protean.

> If people contradict themselves, can I
> Help contradicting them, and every body,
> Even my veracious self? – But that's a lie:
> I never did so, never will – how should I?
> He who doubts all things nothing can deny. (*Don Juan* XV.88)

The Byron who narrates himself in *Childe Harold* and in *Don Juan* does so without Wordsworth's drive towards the sincere and exacting encapsulation of the stages of poetic development.[25] Sometimes the narrator espouses a firm purpose in writing: 'I mean to show things really as they are, / Not as they ought to be' (XII.40). Much more often, he denies that he has any such purpose, his improvisatory manner resulting in his having no idea what he will say next:

> Some have accused me of a strange design
> Against the creed and morals of the land,
> And trace it in this poem every line:
> I don't pretend that I quite understand
> My own meaning when I would be *very* fine;
> But the fact is that I have nothing plann'd. (IV.5)

and:

> I ne'er decide what I shall say, and this I call
> Much too poetical. Men should know why

They write, and for what end; but, note or text,
I never know the word which will come next. (IX.41)

In Byron's poetic representations of the self there is what Susan Manning has
dubbed an 'aversiveness', a steering away from all enduring senses of selfhood.
The point is succinctly put by Peter Manning: 'By displaying the unavoidable
inauthenticity of language, he liberates its fictiveness and sets in motion the
self created by it.'[26] 'Inauthenticity', relativity, paradox: those appear to be
the anti-values of a poet who could tease his readers with the observation
– nowadays much more familiar than it once seemed – that politicians 'live
by lies, yet dare not boldly lie'; unlike women who 'can't do otherwise than
lie, but do it / So well, the very truth seems falsehood to it'. The next stanza
opens with a declaration as shocking to many readers as anything Byron ever
wrote: 'And, after all, what is a lie? 'Tis but / The truth in masquerade' (*Don
Juan* XI.36–7). No lines can better measure the degree of separation between
Byron on the one hand and Wordsworth and Southey on the other.

Burns and Byron had both received unfavourable attention from *The
Edinburgh Review* within a year of each other: Brougham savaged *Hours
of Idleness* in 1808, while in March 1809, Francis Jeffrey, reviewing R. H.
Cromek's *Reliques of Robert Burns*, coined a telling phrase that he might also
have applied to Byron: he speaks of 'the *dispensing power* of genius and social
feeling, in all matters of morality and common sense'.[27] Antinomianism –
disregard for the moral law – would be a vital component of the reception of
both poets thenceforward. Indeed, perceptions of the two poets, particularly
in Europe, have often elided the considerable differences between them,
regarding both as apostles of freedom and toleration – representatives of
the greatness of the self-sufficient individual genius. There were, as Richard
Cardwell points out, two sides to Byron's European reputation: political and
social revolt on the one side; personal, existential revolt expressed in such
works as *Manfred* and *Cain* on the other. Byron expressed, for many European
readers, the tendency of the age:

> Despite the avowed Christian and rationalist beliefs of the age and the reaction
> against the corrosive ideas of Voltaire and others, Byron's writings expressed the
> view that there were no abiding values, no absolute standards for belief or judge-
> ment. If anything, rather than the presence of a Benevolent Providence, there
> could only be a God of Injustice and Vengefulness if there was any God at all.
> Man was the victim of cosmic injustice; life a prison house where the oppressed
> was guilty without guilt.[28]

Readers' fascination with the figure of the Byronic hero often bled into the
identification of that hero with the poet himself. Like Burns, Byron was at

the centre of his own epic. As the *Edinburgh Review* of June 1831 expressed the matter: 'He was himself the beginning, the middle, and the end of all his poetry, the hero of every tale, the chief object of every landscape.' Burns and Byron, through their principal poems, become synonymous with the cause of freedom and democracy. Their lives are seen to be the living embodiments of their causes. Alcoholic and sexual excess, disregard for conventional morality, in Burns' case an affection for Jacobitism and alleged republicanism and in Byron's his espousing of the causes of the Italian Carbonari and Greek independence, ensure that the two poets walk hand in hand to posterity. Thanks to recent work by Murray Pittock, we now know a great deal more about the Scottish network that supported the cause of Greek independence, into which Byron tapped extensively.[29] What Pittock calls the 'fratriot' mentality of Scots who supported the nationalisms of small proto-nations was shared by the members of this network and by Byron.[30]

Burns was perhaps the only writer who could actually shock Byron. Defending Pope's letters from a charge of indecency in his *Letter to John Murray Esqre* (1821), Byron offers Burns' letters as an example to anyone who really wants to read indecent epistles:

> I have myself seen a collection of letters of another eminent – nay – pre-eminent deceased poet – so abominably gross – and elaborately coarse, that I do not believe they could be paralleled in our language – What is more strange is – that some of these are couched as *postscripts* to his serious and sentimental letters- to which are tacked either a piece of prose – or some verses – of the most hyperbolic indecency.[31]

What Byron responds to is the way in which Burns could combine structures of feeling and linguistic registers normally considered incompatible – exactly, of course, what he himself had achieved in *Don Juan*.

Before there was Byromania, there was Burnomania; and Byron shared it.[32] There is not the space to document the full extent of Byron's indebtedness to Burns. Grounds exist, though, for saying that Byron hero-worshipped Burns: that his sense of Burns' selfhood was a layer that he wished to add to the *pentimento* of his own. Antinomianism is an aspect of the wider, more important commitment that Burns and Byron shared to the cause of liberty – arguably the most important aspect of their poetic legacies. From the foregoing discussion, however, we derive a paradox. Byron, we have seen, is an 'aversive' poet: in other words, a poet who performs the self. Susan Manning has made a similar claim for Burns. She speaks of his

> rhetorical attitude, a challenge to settled 'beliefs' of all kinds. It's why he can write Hanoverian poems and Jacobite ones, poems devout and sceptical,

sentimental and scurrilous; why he can express convincing outrage at the obscenity of slavery, and think of becoming a slave-driver in Jamaica. It's simultaneously true that Burns has one of the strongest, most instantly recognizable poetic 'signatures,' and that in an almost Keatsian sense, he has *no* poetic self.[33]

Burns and Byron have in common that their poetic voices are entirely distinctive, and that this distinction resides in having no distinctive*ness*. Byron is similarly 'aversive', similarly committed to nonce attitudes and rhetorical postures; yet his great legacy to poetry and drama is, paradoxically, the 'Byronic hero' – the entirely possessed, fully self-present ego that requires no vindication of his identity from others. However depressively afflicted by a cathected sense of a tragic or criminal past, the Byronic hero has no needs that others can satisfy. In that mould, the poet himself was so often constructed. The place of both poets in the history of anglophone poetry has often been secured by the 'facts' of their extraordinary lives, rather than by any adequate sense of their achievement in verse.[34]

One last example might serve to indicate both the proximity and the distance that exist between Byron and Burns as exemplars of a Scottish Romantic tradition. In 1820, Byron completed his tragedy of the Venetian republic, *Marino Faliero*, premièred on the Drury Lane stage on 25 April 1821. The play takes its plot from the historian Sanuto's account of a fourteenth-century duke who was decapitated on the steps of his palace for conspiring with the people. As Caroline Franklin observes, events occurring in England in 1820, when a group of Spencean radicals planned to assassinate cabinet members dining at Lord Harrowby's house in Grosvenor Square but were betrayed by one of their number, are lurking in the background.[35] The play is therefore an example of the 'parallel history' dramatic mode popular in Restoration and eighteenth-century England. Its neoclassical theme and structure imparts to the drama a conservative, nostalgic, retrogressive colour, assisted by the structural references to Shakespeare. Marino Faliero and his story are developed by Byron to try to resolve, ultimately unsuccessfully, a deeply personal dilemma. Can an aristocrat who has, if not merely personal, certainly class-based reasons for becoming a leader of a popular conspiracy, do so with any credibility? Throughout the action, the doge is a difficult and oblique conspirator whom the men he leads are unable to fathom. Shakespeare's Julius Caesar and Macbeth mark the polarities of the action. The 'Scottish play' represents the possibility that Faliero could simply be offering a different form of personal, charismatic tyranny – perhaps a kind of Bonapartism *avant la lettre* – whereas *Julius Caesar* offers by allusion to Brutus the possibility of high-minded, if failed, idealism. The play includes the lines from *Macbeth* that were to recur, as noted above, in *Don Juan* X, where the poet refers to his attempt to suppress his Scottishness. In 3.2.268–9, the conspirator Calendaro exclaims: 'Would that the hour were come! we will not scotch, / But kill.'[36] Calendaro is improving upon the doge's promise to execute genocide upon the entire patrician class.[37] This serves as a reminder that Byron did not become a spokesman for the common people because, like Burns, he shared their experiences. More convincingly he wanted like Malvolio to have revenge on the whole pack of his peers, those who had insulted and besmirched his name as Faliero's enemies had his wife's. In a famous passage from *Childe Harold's Pilgrimage* 3.113, Byron sounds more like Coriolanus than either Macbeth or Caesar:

> I have not loved the world, nor the world me;
> I have not flattered its rank breath, nor bow'd
> To its idolatries a patient knee –
> Nor coin'd my cheek to smiles,– nor cried aloud
> In worship of an echo; in the crowd
> They could not deem me one of such; I stood
> Among them, but not of them.

Burns could never have written like this, but a Scottish aristocrat could, and did.

CHAPTER THIRTEEN

John Galt's Fictional and Performative Worlds

Angela Esterhammer

John Galt (1779–1839) was a familiar figure in literary and business circles in his day, circulating almost as widely in person as through his voluminous literary works. He travelled the Mediterranean at the same time as Byron in 1809–11, produced reams of travel writing, biography, geography, history and school texts in London during the following decade, and rose to prominence as a novelist during the early 1820s. He had a hand in numerous mercantile, legal and governmental ventures, culminating in a role as land agent in Upper Canada that also installed him as a significant figure in Canadian literary history. A best-selling and widely reviewed author, Galt was especially popular for his humorous chronicles of Scottish life, but his fiction also exhibits a remarkable range over historical periods from the medieval to the Napoleonic and geographical locales from the west of Scotland to London, the West Indies, North America, the Mediterranean and Asia Minor.

Galt's posthumous reputation and reception, by contrast, have been ironically restrained. Recently, works such as *The Entail*, *Ringan Gilhaize* and *Bogle Corbet* have begun to receive serious consideration in studies of the Scottish and the Romantic novel.[1] Yet Ruth Aldrich's observation, made in 1978, that 'Galt is one of the truly experimental novelists of the early nineteenth century'[2] still merits much more attention. The current critical climate seems propitious for highlighting Galt's innovations in fiction, given the wealth of new research on print culture and on various inflections of the concept of performance during the Romantic period. Galt's experimentation is heavily conditioned by both these contexts. He was thoroughly involved in the periodical-writing and book-making world of London and Edinburgh, and his experience of this print-culture milieu permeates his writing. The theatrical culture of the Romantic era also registers in Galt's fiction through frequent allusions to theatre as well as insights into what is now termed cultural performativity: identity-construction, disjunctions between intention and appearance and the formative effect of social discourses. The influence of print culture and performance gives Galt's fiction a texture through which his presence as author and storyteller can clearly be felt. His fiction, that is to say, calls attention to itself as narrative construct and straddles the boundary between real and imaginary worlds. Performance and performativity are evident in Galt's construction of fictional narrators who manifest their subjection to history by echoing received idioms and expressing traditional ideologies. Yet his narrators also relate their stories in idiosyncratic ways, blending chronicles with subjective perceptions, using flashbacks, flashforwards and other distortions of temporality, and reflecting different views of providence, accident or progress. While all these features serve to characterise Galt as a product of early-nineteenth-century print and performance culture, they also give his fiction a distinctly modern and even postmodern inflection.

Throughout his career, Galt had a very basic reason to stay in close touch with the publishing milieu of London and Edinburgh: he wrote to make money. It was usually the only way he had of supporting his family given the failure of his multifarious ventures in business, trade and government lobbying. Galt's financial exigency tinctures his writing in many ways, sometimes even breaking into the fiction in the form of explicit authorial asides. Towards the end of the first volume of his 1820 novel *The Earthquake*, for instance, the narrative about sensational adventures in Sicily is suddenly interrupted by the narrator's comment that he needs to finish the book quickly because of his publisher's demand that it get onto the market in the right season, and because he stands in need of the agreed-upon payment.[3]

While such a disruption of verisimilitude (to the extent that verisimilitude exists in the implausible narrative of *The Earthquake*) might seem excessive, allusions to a reality beyond the covers of the novel feature in all of Galt's fictional works. His novels of Scottish life and history are interwoven with cross-references to each other's characters and incidents. This kind of cross-referencing is unsurprising, given that Galt thought of these novels as an interrelated series and would have preferred to publish them under the unified title 'Tales of the West', had his publisher William Blackwood not vetoed this marketing concept. Cross-references among works of the early 1820s such as *The Ayrshire Legatees*, *The Steam-Boat*, *Annals of the Parish* and *The Provost* tend to contribute to verisimilitude by delineating a self-contained fictional world of characters and locations in the west of Scotland. Yet the same texts also contain other kinds of cross-referencing that has exactly the opposite effect, disrupting verisimilitude by exposing the constructed nature of the fiction and thereby blurring the boundary between the fictional world Galt creates and the real world in which he lives and writes.

Even *The Entail; or, the Lairds of Grippy* (1823), Galt's most self-enclosed and tightly plotted three-volume novel, contains extra-textual allusions of this kind. A family saga set in Glasgow and the west of Scotland and extending from the mid-1700s to 1815, *The Entail* follows three generations of the Walkinshaw family through the economic machinations, marriage alliances and legal manoeuvring with which they seek to enrich themselves and tighten their hold on property. In addition to the usual cross-references that readers of Galt's earlier novels might recognise, *The Entail* contains allusions to books he has not yet written, as when Leddy Grippy refers to 'my cousin, Ringan Gilhaise'[4] – that is, to a character conceived by Galt as the protagonist of a future novel. *The Entail* also contains more tendentious allusions, at one point appropriating a character from Walter Scott's *Rob Roy* and briefly alluding to her future beyond the part that Scott wrote for her (*Entail*, pp. 45–6). At the end of *The Entail*, the narrator characteristically offers to produce a sequel 'as soon as ever we receive a proper hint to do so, with ten thousand pounds to account' (p. 363).

Other 'Tales of the West' include similar references to the circumstances of publishing and print culture; in *The Ayrshire Legatees*, for instance, the Pringle family sojourns in an Edinburgh hotel 'next door to one Mr Blackwood, a civil and discreet man in the bookselling line'.[5] Sometimes fictional characters propose to negotiate with real-world publishers to produce the book in which they themselves appear. This occurs in the introduction to *The Provost*, and more ostentatiously in *The Last of the Lairds*, where the Laird aspires to sell his memoirs to the publisher Blackwood for even more money than the (fictional) Reverend Balwhidder of Dalmailing got for *Annals of the Parish* or the Provost's widow for her husband's papers. Metafictional allusion of this kind is common in the world of Scottish Romantic writing, on display above all in the hoaxes and the quasi-real, quasi-fictionalised personae that appear in *Blackwood's Edinburgh Magazine*, to which Galt was a regular contributor. But Galt's use of metafictional play predates his involvement with *Blackwood's* and often goes further. Ironically, when Galt's novels were published in book form, real-world references and in-jokes that appear in his manuscripts and in the original serialised publications were sometimes removed by Blackwood and other editors in an attempt to 'turn the book into a self-contained novel as opposed to a work which constantly crossed and re-crossed different levels of reality'.[6] While it is endemic to Galt's print-culture milieu, the blurring of boundaries between the imaginary world inside the book and the outside world of writing, publishing and marketing also resonates interestingly with postmodern techniques.

The Last of the Lairds (1826) extends these allusions to literal book-making into a more elaborate experiment with narrative perspective. The novel's subtitle, *The Life and Opinions of Malachi Mailings Esq. of Auldbiggings* – echoing Sterne's *The Life and Opinions of Tristram Shandy, Gentleman* – sets up an expectation that the narrator will be the 'Last of the Lairds' himself, Malachi Mailings. While this was Galt's original plan, he later revised it to include himself, or at least a self-representation in the form of an unnamed writer, as the first-person narrator. Astounded to find the Laird engaged in writing his autobiography in half a dozen school copy-books, the narrator questions him about his motives and undertakes to correct his methodology. As becomes clear from the sample chapter of the Laird's manuscript that the meddling narrator secretly copies out for his readers, the Laird is a hopeless speller and historiographer, although his lack of aptitude by no means deters him from his project. Near the end of the novel he even determines to adapt to the contemporary book market by publishing his memoirs in serialised form in an Edinburgh journal: 'I'll publish my book in numbers and mak [sic] a monthly income by that'.[7] Aided by the presence of a self-conscious writer-narrator within the novel, *The Last of the Lairds* thus foregrounds the process by which Malachi Mailings' 'life and opinions' emerge from a discussion about strategies of writing and publishing.

If metafictionality is one aspect of Galt's achievement that deserves greater recognition, another is the performativity that pervades his fiction. The performative dimension of Galt's writing takes a variety of forms, including actual references to the theatrical culture of his day, the depiction of characters who construct their own social, economic and class identities (or even assume a new identity through fraud) and the author's 'performances' of fictional narrators with distinctive idiolects, preoccupations and ways of telling their stories. Most of the critical discussion about Galt has, with good reason, focused on his representations of local, national, international, social, religious and economic history, but his fictional historiography is inseparable from his experiments with performance and identity-construction.

Persistent allusions to dramatic performance throughout Galt's fiction testify to his lifelong involvement with the world of theatre. Although he never achieved success as a playwright, he continued writing dramas throughout his career; he also wrote theatrical reviews and dramatic criticism, edited a series of his own and other writers' plays (*The New British Theatre*, 1814–15) and published a volume of brief biographies of actors and actresses (*The Lives of the Players*, 1831). In his novel *The Earthquake*, the protagonist Castagnello, illegitimate son of a Neapolitan actress, gains an entrée to the theatre worlds of Paris and London by way of his sister, a celebrated opera singer. Castagnello's theatrical heritage manifests itself in an adventurous lifestyle that involves playing many roles in widely varying social contexts throughout Europe and Asia Minor; it culminates in his fraudulent impersonation of a Sicilian nobleman, in which guise he successfully deceives even the nobleman's relatives and servants for many years. The small towns of Galt's Scottish novels, such as *Annals of the Parish* and *The Provost*, are inevitably visited by travelling players; in *The Member*, the narrator-protagonist Archibald Jobbry wins an election by hiring an acting troupe to distract the townspeople from his popular rival. Even brief references to the theatre

generate reflections on the performative quality of individuals and institutions. At the end of *The Entail*, the formidable Leddy Grippy, in her late
seventies, decides to follow up the unexpected success she has had in personal
lawsuits by undertaking a more formal study of the law. She asks her grandson
James to take her to the Parliament House in Glasgow so she can observe
legal proceedings, but 'by some mistake' he leads her 'to that sink of sin the
Theatre' instead, where they witness a performance of *Othello* (*Entail*, p. 354).
The legal profession whose machinations have been on display throughout
the novel is thus superimposed for a moment onto Shakespearean drama,
as if to reveal the interchangeability of the law-court and the theatre – two
institutions of which Galt had extensive personal experience.

The *Autobiography* and *Literary Life* that Galt published during the 1830s
also testify to his awareness of living in an age of ostentation and public
spectacle. When he reminisces about the coronation of George IV in 1820,
for instance, he calls it 'the show' and uses the terms 'performance', 'spectacle', 'exhibition', 'pageantries', 'tricks of state' and even 'tomfoolery'.[8] In a
cluster of fictional writings Galt imagines the responses of Scottish observers
to these spectacles in order to stage a contrast between rural Scottish and
urban English customs. The observers in *The Ayrshire Legatees; or, the Pringle
Family* (1821) are the minister Dr Zachariah Pringle, his wife Janet, daughter
Rachel and son Andrew, who travel to London to sort out the legalities surrounding a legacy. The events they witness include the funeral of George III
in 1820 and the ensuing scandal and divorce trial of Queen Caroline at the
time of George IV's accession, in addition to fashionable entertainments like
'Almack's balls, the Argyle-rooms, and the Philharmonic concerts' (*Ayrshire
Legatees*, p. 240). The Pringle family's responses to these events are presented
in a way that is itself (in Galt's words) 'undoubtedly dramatic' (*Literary Life*
I: p. 227). Manifesting impressions, interpretations and modes of expression
that correspond to their individual characters, each of the Pringles writes
letters to friends back home in Ayrshire, where their accounts are shared
around and discussed within the community. Galt followed up the success
of *The Ayrshire Legatees* with two sequels in which Scottish characters again
witness royal spectacles: the coronation of George IV in *The Steam-Boat*
(1822) and the king's visit to Edinburgh in *The Gathering of the West* (1823).
All three of these works were first serialised in *Blackwood's* and *The Steam-
Boat* in particular engages in the metafictional play typical of the magazine:
the characters who come together during the steam-boat voyage and in
London include newly created fictional personalities, characters from existing Galt novels (the Pringles), real people (Walter Scott, Lord Castlereagh)
and people who are both real and quasi-fictionalised due to their regular
portrayal in *Blackwood's* (the 'Odontist' Dr James Scott).

Galt's attraction to performative modes and his skill in working with them are also evident in the short novel *Andrew of Padua, the Improvisatore* (1820). Until recently, this text was not even recognised as Galt's because it advertises itself as an anonymous translation from an Italian author named 'Francisco Furbo' – and because Galt, seriously or not, maintained in his memoirs that he could not remember writing it, even when a friend insisted he had (*Literary Life* I: p. 349). However, the tale is unmistakably Galt's invention: the title character already appears in *The Earthquake* under the slightly altered name 'Andrea' and Galt later republished most of *Andrew of Padua* verbatim as a short story entitled 'The Improvisatore' and annexed to his historical novel *Rothelan* (1824). The invented Italian author and the fake documentary paratexts of *Andrew of Padua* show Galt deftly fusing performance and metafiction. The title character Andrew is an *improvisatore* who claims to have charmed theatre audiences from Palermo to London with his ability spontaneously to create and perform poetry. In fact, though, he has fabricated his entire 'autobiography' in order to take advantage of his listener Francisco Furbo, as the surprise ending reveals. The character Furbo (whose name means 'trickster'), the novel's first-person narrator and its purported author, is Galt's device for extending this hoax to a meta-level and putting one over on his own readers.[9]

The apparently ephemeral *Andrew of Padua* casts a revealing sidelight on the fiction Galt produced during the next decade. Many of his books are, as he called them, 'imaginary autobiographies'[10] featuring a first-person narrator-protagonist who relates his own experiences together with those of his family or community. The imaginary autobiography is a performance of self on the part of the narrator, but it can also be understood as the performance of a persona on the part of the author, and sometimes – superimposing these two levels – as a self-depiction of Galt the market-conscious, improvising author in the form of a shrewd and pragmatic narrator-protagonist. Making use of distinctive speech patterns, psychological obsessions and chronologies, Galt's experiments with the genre of fictional autobiography foreground the practice of storytelling, the construction of history and the performance of identity.

These performances are especially effective when the narrator-protagonist is a 'self-made man', a successful agent in the socio-economic marketplace who is also highly aware of the self-construction on which his success is based. A prime example is *The Provost* (1822), which begins with a typically metafictional frame. In a brief introduction, the author explains that he came into possession of the memoirs of Provost James Pawkie from Pawkie's widow after she heard that he had edited 'that most excellent work, entitled, "Annals of the Parish of Dalmailing"'.[11] Galt is thereby cast as an editor whose role is to give 'historical coherency' to the 'detached notes' left by the Provost (p. 2). The remainder of the book, narrated in Provost Pawkie's own voice, skips quickly over his economic rise from apprentice to prosperous shopkeeper in order to concentrate on his strategies for success in the local government of Gudetown. The Provost combines pride, self-confidence and an aptitude for Machiavellian machinations with an explicit awareness of the importance of performance. He carefully gauges the effect of his words on listeners; he is always conscious of the appearance he makes, and often of the gap between appearance and inward intention. From the beginning, a key to achieving his goal of public office is his willingness to adapt to situations and appear to play the part that others expect: thus, he relates, 'I [. . .] assumed a coothy and obliging demeanour towards my customers and the community in general' (p. 4) and 'maintained an outward show of humility and moderation' (p. 6). Paradoxically – although typically for Galt – Provost Pawkie is a sincere performer, one who narrates with engaging frankness how he employed trickery, manipulation and pretence to achieve basically responsible goals in his community. A central theme of the Provost's memoir is progress, more specifically the general improvement in political morals that results in public officials becoming more disinterested and less corrupt over the course of his half-century in office. Thus, he can claim near the end of the book that 'my third provostry was undertaken in a spirit of sincerity, different, in some degree, from that of the two former' (p. 140). Nevertheless, the Provost employs his theatrical tactics until the moment of his retirement, an event that he stage-manages by manipulating a young fellow-councillor into making sure he is honoured with a farewell speech and gift, effectively casting, scripting and rehearsing with him what he must say in the council chamber to bring about this desired dénouement. Summing up the performative practices by which the Provost has advanced and maintained himself in public office, this final scene also shows him passing on his acting skills to a carefully chosen member of the next generation of politicians.

Galt's more extended portrayal of a self-made man and a sincere performer, written at the same time and published in the same year as *The Provost*, is the three-volume *Sir Andrew Wylie, of that Ilk* (1822). This novel depicts Andrew, the son of a Scottish peasant, achieving economic and social success in London and returning to his home town as a rich and titled baronet to marry his childhood sweetheart, the daughter of the local laird. Like Provost Pawkie and Francisco Furbo (whose last names mean 'wily' in Scots and Italian respectively) and like the eponymous protagonist of Galt's 1830 novel *Lawrie Todd* (which is dialect for 'sly fox'), Andrew Wylie wears his dominant character trait in his name. Indeed, when he makes his fortune, acquires a title and buys the hereditary Wylie estate, he becomes 'Sir Andrew Wylie, Baronet, of that Ilk, or of the same'[12] – that is, 'Sir Wylie of Wylie', as if to indicate his compounded cleverness. Yet Andrew's most memorable trait is a combination of naïvety and wiliness, manifested in his ability to act the frank, natural, unaffected rural Scotsman in a manner that plays extraordinarily well among London's *beau monde*. At his first introduction to London society, the joke is on the newly arrived Andrew: he is invited to a masked ball at the Earl of Sandyford's mansion but deliberately given the impression that he is being taken to the theatre. Completely unacquainted with London manners, Andrew believes that the aristocratic party-goers are hired entertainers while they all derive amusement from his unwitting performance in 'the part of a Scottish lad' (I: p. 116). Andrew, however, quickly turns the tables by learning from this incident that he can ingratiate himself with high society by, in effect, playing himself as a simple Scotsman. Meanwhile, he shrewdly observes the manners and language of others so that he can imitate these when appropriate. Throughout the novel's varied scenes of action – from upper-class dinners to the offices of London newspapers, a gypsy encampment and a morning walk with King George III at Windsor – Andrew excels in adapting to circumstances and mediating between different classes and worlds. Alternately fulfilling and manipulating others' expectations, he progresses to extremely elaborate stage-managing projects including a sensational murder trial and an election that brings him into Parliament.

Andrew makes his way in the world without the advantages of looks, birth or fortune and without any real skill at his supposed profession, the law. Throughout the novel, it remains ambiguous whether people react so positively to him because of his personal qualities – as the Earl of Sandyford implies by calling him 'a singular being' (II: p. 37) and 'a human being' (I: p. 146) – or for exactly the opposite reason, because he reassuringly fulfils a national stereotype. The novel's final sentence sums up the source of his success as a combination of character and circumstances ('prudence and good fortune united', III: p. 310), but other descriptions of Andrew suggest a more explicit discrepancy between his actual cleverness and the appearance of naïvety: he is a 'sly simpleton' (I: p. 285) who manifests 'supposed rustic simplicity' (I: p. 287), yet maintains 'a degree of system in the simplicity of his manners' (III: p. 99). More than any other of Galt's characters, Andrew Wylie wilily performs candour and profits from an economy that values both stereotype and reputation.

In several other novels the primary performer is Galt himself, as he takes on the role of a fictional narrator whose perspective is determined by his subjection to historical, religious and economic discourses. Galt's first successful experiment in this genre of imaginary autobiography is *Annals of the Parish* (1821). The historical orientation signalled in the title 'Annals' is borne out by the subdivision of the book into fifty short chapters, each one corresponding to a year of the Reverend Micah Balwhidder's tenancy as pastor of the rural parish of Dalmailing from 1760 to 1810 – a term that, as Balwhidder points out, corresponds exactly to the reign of George III. The narrative's high degree of verisimilitude, achieved through accuracy as to local detail and dialect, credibility of characterisation and the authentic representation of the repercussions of historical events, led many readers to accept it as the actual chronicle of a retired minister – and encouraged Galt to perpetuate the fiction of the chronicle's truth through intertextual references to the world of Dalmailing in several later novels. Yet *Annals* represents his extended performance of a fictional narrator, in this case a conservative but pragmatic elderly pastor who observes and interprets the history of his parish.

Balwhidder's retrospective narrative and his maturing psyche both work against the strict linear chronology suggested by the 'Annals' structure. The narrative begins proleptically with an introduction in which Balwhidder quotes his farewell sermon of 1810, before jumping back to begin his history with the year 1760. In the process of introducing characters for the first time, he often flashes forward to anticipate their death or their present state. When he brings his first wife home, they are accompanied by 'her little brother Andrew, that died in the East Indies';[13] at the birth of his daughter Janet, he thinks of her 'now in the married state [as she] makes a most excellent wife' (p. 54); when the first Mrs Balwhidder dies, he anticipates the shifting of her headstone at the time the second Mrs Balwhidder is buried in the same grave, and then stops himself: 'But I must not here enter upon an anticipation' (p. 24). Local temporal disruptions of this kind create a tension between the chronological order of history and the achronological patterns that emerge when memory records events in terms of their causes, consequences and affective associations. Later in the *Annals*, Balwhidder becomes increasingly aware of the achronological perspective he developed even at the time events were occurring. He refers increasingly to his 'prophetic powers', which is to say his mature ability to reflect on his observations of parish life and extrapolate from the local to the global level. This partly recollective, partly proleptic narrative serves to express Balwhidder's faith in divine providence as well as Galt's more secular interest in Scottish Enlightenment concepts of the progress of civilisation or 'theoretical history'.[14]

Galt's more strictly historical novels, those that portray epochs and episodes in Scottish history, also experiment with different narrative perspectives and chronologies. These three-volume novels include *The Spaewife* (1823; about the early-fifteenth-century assassination of James I of Scotland), *Rothelan* (1824; set in the fourteenth century under Edward III) and *Southennan* (1830; depicting the first four years of the reign of Mary, Queen of Scots), but the best known of them is *Ringan Gilhaize; or, The Covenanters* (1823). *Ringan Gilhaize* achieves its powerful and disturbing effect from the I-narrator Ringan, who relates how three generations of his family – his grandfather Michael, father Sawners and he himself – fought for the Presbyterian cause during the religious wars in Scotland from 1558 to 1696. Ringan's heavily biblical, sectarian idiom betrays his partisan rendering of historical events:

becoming increasingly fanatical and intolerant as he tells his story, he borders on being an unreliable narrator. Yet he is also a credible product of the familial, national and religious history he experiences and recounts. Thus, while Ringan Gilhaize is a (tragically) sincere narrator, on Galt's part this historical novel represents the performance of a psyche formed by indoctrination on the part of his forefathers, his religious faction and his historical moment. Even when deliberately imitating a genre – the historical novel in the style of Scott – because it had proven so successful in the literary marketplace, Galt did so in an innovative manner. 'Excellence is his [Sir Walter Scott's] characteristic', Galt commented when comparing one of his own historical novels to Scott's, 'and, if I may say so, originality is mine, and the approbation of time is required to the just appreciation of that quality' (*Literary Life*, I: p. 262).

Like Ringan Gilhaize, the narrator-protagonist of *Bogle Corbet, or The Emigrants* (1831) is the product of performative discourses, particularly economic and colonial ones.[15] The character of Bogle Corbet reflects a good deal of Galt's own background, from his father's role in trade with the West Indies to his own recent experience as (failed) land agent in Canada. Once again, the novel's framing devices blur the boundary between truth and fiction: an epigraph from Thomas Gray's *The Bard* on the title page of each of *Bogle Corbet*'s three volumes reads 'Truth severe by fairy fiction dressed', and after its notably inconclusive ending the narrative segues into an appendix consisting of a statistical account of the physical geography of the Upper Canadian townships. This elision of the novel with a scientific gazette is evidence of Galt's intention to include actual 'truth severe' about settlement in Canada for the information of prospective emigrants. The truth/fiction boundary gets pushed in the other direction as well: within the novel, Corbet's decision to emigrate to Canada is influenced by the advice of Mr Lawrie Todd, 'a shrewd Scotchman, recently from America'.[16] 'He has since published some account of himself, and of his adventures and experience as a settler in the woods of the Genesee Country' Corbet adds (II: p. 181) – that is to say, Galt's novel *Lawrie Todd, or The Settlers in the Woods*, which appeared the year before with the same publisher.

Corbet's narrative about his apprenticeship and unsuccessful business ventures in Glasgow, his trip to the land of his birth, Jamaica, and his return to Scotland and subsequent emigration to Canada generally lacks plot and direction; instead, it is loaded with coincidences and with what the narrator himself calls 'accidents'. These include actual physical mishaps, such as an overturned carriage that leaves Corbet with a cut on the forehead. 'This accident coloured the tissue of my subsequent life', he reports (I: p. 257), because he is taken into the nearby house of a Mr Ascomy and meets his daughter Urseline, who will later become the second Mrs Corbet. While 'accidental narrative' as (in Ian Duncan's terms) 'the narrative mode of common life: the empirical, material domain of here and how'[17] is the typical form of agency in many of Galt's novels, Bogle Corbet as narrator shows a particular fascination with the term 'accident'. His perspective merits contrast with the Reverend Balwhidder's providential view of accidents in *Annals of the Parish*, where seemingly trivial or chance events unfold far-reaching consequences in the fullness of time – a view represented rather unconvincingly in *Bogle Corbet* by the long-winded Mr Moth who opines, 'accident is one of the main weapons with which Providence, or Destiny, achieves its greatest results' (II: p. 93). Corbet, however, fails to achieve anything like Balwhidder's 'prophetic' sensitivity to progressive connections between events and outcomes. Despite his awareness of the double perspective involved in writing a retrospective narrative ('When we describe in retrospect our first impressions, we are little aware how much they have been insensibly modified by intervening circumstances', III: p. 5) and his strong interest in omens, the events of Corbet's life continue to be so many accidents that never coalesce into meaningful patterns. His vocabulary and the lack of pattern in his retrospective narrative reflect his sense of subjection to history, a perspective quite different from those of Galt's other narrators who thrive by adapting to circumstances and pursuing a vision of personal and societal progress. Corbet, instead, sees himself as 'a man fighting with adversity, and tracing, in all the movements of a variegated life, how truly he has ever been but a cog on one of the great wheels of the social system, directed by no effort of his own' (II: p. 69). Rather than learning from the past, he is haunted and even tortured by it, lamenting that his memories are 'like those gnawing insects and reptiles which are said to fasten themselves in the flesh and will not be shaken away' (II: p. 189).

Bogle Corbet comes to a sudden metafictional end in a scene where the characters begin to feel that they are, or might as well be, in a novel. After a number of highly coincidental meetings take place in their new Canadian settlement, Mrs Corbet comments that a romance might be written about their adventures: 'I do think we shall soon have matter for a novel in three volumes of our own [. . .] Who ever thought that I would be a heroine, and live in a midnight turret in America?' (III: p. 282). Her remark is addressed to the mysterious Scottish visitor Mr Jocelyn (himself a character out of the world of romance), who thereupon reveals that he is engaged in 'writing his life' (III: p. 283) – as, of course, is Bogle Corbet. Mrs Corbet's opinion about the relative merit of the two books is ironically self-reflexive in the context of Galt's fiction. Jocelyn's book, she exclaims, 'will be worth seeing', but her husband's 'is whey and water: he never met with a right novel-like adventure in all his days – what he has read to me of it, is as common as an old newspaper' (III: pp. 283–4). Throughout his career, Galt was uncomfortable about applying the term 'novel' to his own fiction, being conscious of his shortcomings as to plot, resistant to the three-volume format demanded by the literary marketplace and inclined to experiment with mixed genres including the chronicle form suggested by Mrs Corbet's reference to 'an old newspaper'. Mrs Corbet's acerbic comment on her husband's writing brings his memoirs (and hence the novel *Bogle Corbet*) to an abrupt end, as she commands him to 'Finish your book, Bogle, outright' (III: p. 296) so that Jocelyn can carry the manuscript back to England for publication.

Ruth Aldrich has summed up Galt's typical (male) protagonists as 'worldly minded, shrewd, adaptable, [and] confident of turning circumstances to their advantage'.[18] This chapter has suggested that Galt's imaginary autobiographies display such characters both in their successful incarnation (Andrew of Padua, Sir Andrew Wylie, Provost Pawkie, Reverend Balwhidder) and in the more tragic form of subjects at the mercy of circumstances (Ringan Gilhaize, Bogle Corbet). In dramatising their varied experiences and versions of history, Galt creates hybrids of real and imaginary characters, settings and events, experimenting throughout his career with different forms of factual fiction. Often his narratives derive their factual dimension from his own experience amidst the literary marketplace of his day, which required him to be as shrewd and adaptable as his protagonists in order to make a living as a writer. Public spectacle and innovative forms of entertainment featured prominently in early-nineteenth-century urban culture, and the literary milieux of London and Edinburgh generated experiments with the kind of boundary-crossing between fictional and real-world characters at which the Blackwood's group excelled. Galt's adaptation to his contemporary literary field, therefore, also renders him well versed in themes and techniques that would come to the fore in a later age: the performativity of everyday social life, the construction of character by social discourses and the blurring of real and imaginary worlds. These preoccupations of twenty-first-century fiction and criticism should bring about a new appreciation of Galt's originality in chronicling material and theoretical history.

CHAPTER FOURTEEN

The Private Memoirs and Confessions of a Justified Sinner

Peter Garside

There can be few works of literature whose current reputation and popularity contrast so markedly with their earlier publication and reception history as does James Hogg's *Private Memoirs and Confessions of a Justified Sinner* (1824). Whereas in the 1950s copies of the text were hard to find, by the 1990s a number of rival editions were vying for a share of a growing market both in universities and among general readers. The turn of the century has also seen the first fully scholarly edition produced as part of the Stirling/South Carolina Edition of the Collected Works of Hogg,[1] as well as a useful Broadview Press edition (2001), edited by Adrian Hunter, which provides valuable contextual materials in support of its text. The eagerness of publishers to stay at the head of the market with what is now clearly considered to be a key item in their lists is also evident in the revamped editions published by Penguin (2006), Canongate Press (2008) and World's Classics (2010), with fresh editorial material provided (respectively) by Karl Miller, Ian Rankin and Ian Duncan. While differences obviously exist between all the above-mentioned editions, there are nevertheless signs of a new tendency to regard Hogg's masterpiece foremost as a work of Scottish literature, and usefully interpretable in a number of Scottish contexts. As Duncan asserts, not only is it 'an intensely Scottish work of the imagination', but 'its Scottishness buoys up rather than detracts from [its] status [. . .] as a "world's classic"' (p. ix). The distinction being made here is carefully considered, and offers a reverse position compared with previous critical practices which, while acknowledging a Scottish component, generally moved away from such a position to claim other forms of significance. At the same time *Confessions* has been acknowledged as an inspirational text by a number of contemporary Scottish novelists, including Irvine Welsh and James Robertson, while its popular standing as one of the greatest Scottish books has been confirmed by several polls, with Hogg's work now enjoying a secure place as one of '100 best Scottish books of all time'.[2]

A marked contrast to this is found in the hesitancy with which the London publishing firm of Longman & Co. brought out the relatively small first edition of 1,000 copies in June 1824. Longmans had also published

Hogg's previous two novels, the *Three Perils of Man* (1822) and *Three Perils of Woman* (1823), in similarly modest impressions, after Hogg had found himself outcast as a writer of fiction amongst Scottish publishers. The firm was relatively lenient in their dealings with Hogg, allowing him advance payments and the use of an Edinburgh printer, but so far had been insistent on the appearance of his name on the titles, not wishing to lose the connection with Hogg's earlier celebrity as (notably) the author of *The Queen's Wake* (1813). His appeal as novelist was also no doubt boosted in their eyes by the huge success being enjoyed by the Waverley novels of Walter Scott, of whose earlier titles Longmans had enjoyed a share, and beyond that the wider craze for the 'Scotch novel' then at its height. In the build-up to publication there are several signs of Hogg manoeuvring the situation so as to escape some of the restrictions connected with these expectations, one significant aspect of this being his engagement (apparently contrary to Longmans' directions) of the little-known Edinburgh printer James Clarke, potentially allowing him autonomous control over the text.

If these negotiations were meant to enhance the novel's chances of success, however, they can hardly be said to have worked. The Longman records show that only about 350 copies cleared in the vital first year of marketing, after which sales ground virtually to a halt, with five copies being sold between 1825 and 1826, and with the rest being remaindered in 1828 at a knockdown price, Hogg himself at the end receiving nothing for his labours. The sale in Scotland seems to have been especially poor, with just a hundred of the shipment being held back for Longmans' Edinburgh agent, Adam Black, about whose performance Hogg later complained. Of the ten or so contemporary journals that have been identified as carrying reviews on the work, all are evidently English publications; and where Scottish elements are mentioned, this is usually done so pejoratively. Hogg's efforts to be noticed in *Blackwood's Edinburgh Magazine*, as well his plea to its publisher to take a share in the work, were both effectively disregarded, in the face of the Blackwoodian line that Hogg should best concentrate on his poetry. An attempted reissuing of the work in Edinburgh in 1828, under the new lead title of *The Suicide's Grave*, almost certainly never reached the general market.

A distinctly different version of the text, retitled as 'The Private Memoirs and Confessions of a Fanatic', which subsequently appeared as part of the fifth volume of the posthumous *Tales and Sketches by the Ettrick Shepherd* (1836–7), published by the Glasgow firm of Blackie & Son, has all the marks of a hatchet-job. In addition to making fairly sweeping standardisations of style and grammar, this version tends to remove any hint of 'indelicacy' or blasphemy; it also expunges much of the original theological content of the work, as well as several 'oral' intrusions (notably the Auchtermuchty tale) which are now seen as vital to its meaning and structure. As a whole, it seems likely that the perceived anti-Calvinism of Hogg's original text, its apparent satire of saving faith, represented a considerable threat to a publisher whose main market lay amongst a chiefly 'artisan' readership in Glasgow and its immediate environs, then a heartland of evangelical Presbyteriansm. Another feature of this version is the removal of the figure of Hogg from within the tale, and a general shifting (partly through the uniformity of presentation) to a position where the 'Editor' and Author are aligned, and as such equally condemnatory of the 'fanaticism' exhibited by the 'Sinner'. All in all, as is suggested in the introduction to the Stirling/South Carolina edition, it is hard to think of a manifestation of a literary work more influenced by its publishing colours, or of a later edition that loses so much of the quality of the original text.[3] Yet it was in this form that Hogg's novel was chiefly known (or not known) to the end of the nineteenth century, with the 'Confessions of a Fanatic' in largely unaltered form generally appearing somewhere close to the end of the Ettrick Shepherd's *Tales*.

It was not until 1895 that an unbowdlerised version of the original 1824 text was made available, by J. Shiells & Co., in an edition published from London but printed in Edinburgh, with *The Suicide's Grave* adopted as the main title. To some extent one might associate this revival with the more open view of Hogg encouraged by Mrs Garden's humane treatment of her father in *Memorials of James Hogg* in 1885, as well as a generally more 'democratic' climate of opinion in the 1890s. There are also some signs of a renewed interest in the original *Confessions* amongst some contemporary Scottish writers, as evident in the unsuccessful recommendation made early in 1895 by the novelist S. R. Crockett to the publisher Macmillans that it was worthy of reprinting in its original form as 'one of the very greatest books in Scottish literature'.[4] A more tangible trigger, and one less flattering to Hogg's reputation, however, is found in a disclaimer in the prefatory 'Publishers' Note' to this edition, relaying a suspicion of Andrew Lang and others that the book was 'not wholly written by Hogg', but that J. G. Lockhart 'had some part in its production'. This alludes to the controversy begun in 1889–90 by the English critic George Saintsbury, who conjectured that the imaginative core of the work was Hogg's but that its design originated from Lockhart: a point of view with which Lang concurred, while accepting there was no proof, in a contribution to the *Illustrated London News* in November 1894. Here one might sense more than a whiff of the social condescension that had bedevilled Hogg throughout his career as an author, accompanied by a kind of reiteration of past literary hierarchies, with Scott's Waverley Novels unassailably at the head, and Lockhart and contemporaries such as John Galt representing a competent species of 'secondary' Scottish fiction beyond the reach of Hogg by himself.

This hypothesis of co-authorship, notwithstanding a powerful intervention by Mrs Garden followed by Lang's recantation, carries over to the next first edition-based text, published in 1924 as part of the Campion Reprint series, where T. Earle Welby, in an introduction favourably likening Hogg to the American writers Poe and Hawthorne, considers the idea '[t]hat Hogg owed something of such success to Lockhart' (pp. 7–8) as indisputable. Almost forty years later, Louis Simpson still felt obliged to counter such suggestions in his *James Hogg: A Critical Study* (1962), which commendably (and for its time unusually) uses the work's Scottish contexts and parallels with other works by Hogg as part of its argument.

A fuller recognition of Hogg's achievement in *Confessions* might be said to date from the Cresset Press edition in 1947, whose text is from the Bristol-printed Campion edition, but which is distinguished owing to its introduction by the eminent French novelist and critic, André Gide. He had come across the work when in Algiers, and subsequently found it to be virtually unknown when making enquiries about it. In broad terms it is possible to trace from Gide two distinct lines of approach that have directed criticism of the novel since, and which might be roughly characterised as 'Scottish' and 'universal' approaches. On the one hand, Gide quotes at some length comments by his translator, Dorothy Bussy, who had been brought up partly in Scotland, on the book's specially Scottish provenance and character: 'This book is Scotch to its very marrow; no Englishman could possibly have written it. Its whole atmosphere, the very form and substance of its Puritanism, is essentially Scottish' (p. x). At the same time, the main drift of Gide's own commentary is towards dimensions 'not peculiar to Scotland': to 'Shakespeare and the Elizabethan dramatists' (p. xi), and to the larger European experience of puritanism (to which he was able to relate personally) and the Antinomianism of Johannes Agricola. Yet it was Gide's focusing on the unusual psychological intensity of the narrative, especially in its dichotomous form, that did most to ensure a place for Hogg in a modern context. His words concerning Gil-Martin, Hogg's devil figure who might or might not be a projection of Robert Wringhim's (the Sinner's) own mentality, have been immensely influential:

> The personification of the Demon in Hogg's book is among the most ingenious ever invented, for the power that sets him in action is always of a psychological nature; in other words – always admissible, even by unbelievers. It is the exteriorized development of our own desires, of our own pride, of our most secret thoughts. (p. xv)

Gide's immediate point of reference here is to Henry James' *The Turn of the Screw* (1898), where in his view the supernatural is in similar ways 'psychologically explicable' (p. xv); and this is matched by a tendency in English criticism from the 1960s to treat Hogg's work as a proto-modernist text, inviting parallels with works such as Conrad's *The Heart of Darkness* (1902). As Cairns Craig has also suggested, Gide's observations were well pitched to appeal to a European intellectual scene in the aftermath the Second World War, itself viewable as a bloodbath stemming from the triumph of fixed ideology in individual minds.[5]

If Gide's highlighting of *Confessions* gave it new credentials in 'world literature' terms, John Carey's influential edition of 1969 represented an important moment in the novel's repositioning close to the centre of a more specifically British Romanticism. With a freshly clean text based on the 1824 first edition, it made its first appearance in the Oxford English Novels Series, whose general editor, James Kinsley, had himself wide interests in Scottish literature. This had the effect of placing the work alongside a number of other 'secondary' Scottish novels of the period, considered then to be worthy of critical reappraisal, as well as a variety of Gothic titles, now regarded as main exemplars of the genre, such as M. G. Lewis' *The Monk* (1796) and Charles Robert Maturin's *Melmoth the Wanderer* (1820). Carey's introduction is notable for helping make several important critical advances. It stresses the significance of the dual narrative frame, clearly distinguishing Hogg from the Editor, characterising the latter as 'a bluff Tory, Lockhart's college-friend' (p. xiii). It likewise draws attention, albeit briefly, to the centrality for the work of Hogg's ambivalent experiences with *Blackwood's Magazine* (notably his own suffering of a 'second self' through the creation of 'the Shepherd' in its *Noctes Ambrosianae* series), while finding a Gothic parallel in the German writer E. T. A. Hoffmann's *Die Elixiere des Teufels*, translated by Hogg's friend R. P. Gillies as *The Devil's Elixir* and published virtually contemporaneously in 1824.

Carey also touches on the issue of Antinomianism, though tellingly it is a controversy regarding the Plymouth Antinomians in 1823 rather than the 'Marrow Controversy' involving Thomas Boston, minister at Ettrick, in the early eighteenth century, that he chooses to foreground. Carey's sparse annotation comments on historical events, such as the Scottish Parliament of 1703 (as alluded to in parts of the narrative), but only selectively; and mention of topographical elements in the story is infrequent, and in one instance (the reported gravestone slab found on Fall Law by the Bursar of St John's College, Oxford!) somewhat egregiously second-hand. The impact of the Carey edition was also immeasurably increased by its reappearance in 1981 as a paperback in *World's Classics*, followed by frequent reprints in this form (including reissuing with a glossary in 1990 and a new bibliography in 1995), this reflecting its wider currency as an academic set text, on mainstream courses relating to Romanticism, Gothic and the history of the English novel.

Somewhat similar tendencies are found in a rival paperback edition, edited by John Wain, first published in the English Penguin Library in 1983, where one senses conflicting priorities in the effort to outline 'background' in Scottish terms while stimulating a readership figured as essentially English. On the one hand, the theological and historical dimensions of the work are found to have an 'intensely Scottish flavour', with Wain showing a particularly good sense of the element of enclosure or entrapment that this brings with it: 'Not only do its characters exhibit a psychology and a motivation very rarely met with among the English, it is also anchored to a period of Scottish history [. . .]' (p. 10). On the other hand, the introduction soon concedes that the 'modern English reader' is likely to 'skate over' (p. 12) such elements; and, by its end, 'flavour' has diminished to something more optional and potentially discardable: 'Not that the oppressive atmosphere of Hogg's novel is *merely* [my emphasis] a matter of national flavour, or traceable to Scottish literary tradition' (p. 21).

A correlative to the anglocentric/generalist tendencies in Carey and Wain can be found in a number of critical interpretations belonging to the same period. L. L. Lee in an article in *Studies in Scottish Literature* of 1966 cites both Kurt Wittig on *Confession*'s continuation of a long-standing theme of duality in the Scottish literary tradition, and Walter Allen's claim in his *The English Novel* (1954) that it represents a work that 'only a Scot could have written', before turning to his own noticeably more diffuse commentary on the ambiguity of the representation of Gil-Martin in the novel.[6] While according to David Eggenschwiler, in an article in the same journal of 1971, Hogg addresses one of the 'central problems of English [*sic*] romanticism' in focusing on the disharmony of self and society – a major preoccupation also in his view of Wordsworth, Coleridge and Blake – and the split between spiritual and corporeal worlds.[7] Not dissimilarly, Robert Kiely's *The Romantic Novel in England* (1972) – which provides a chapter on *Confessions*, though dealing predominantly with standard 'English' Gothic novels, starting with Walpole's *Castle of Otranto* (1764) – is mainly formalist in its approach, emphasising paradox, tension and irreconcilability as distinguishing features of the period's fiction.

The complex narrative patterns of *Confessions* made it especially amenable to interpretation in theoretical terms, as post-structuralist approaches began to dominate Anglo-American criticism from the late 1970s onwards. Three prevalent strands, often interlinking, might be distinguished here.

Narratological. In its earlier phase this approach is characterised by an increased attention to the text's conflicting narratives, Douglas Gifford in his 1976 full-length study of Hogg noting an endless sequence of *double entendres* generated by conflicting polarities, and David Groves in an article of 1982 observing a sustained structural parallelism in the two main accounts, with glimpses of an implied 'middle way' in 'choric' interruptions from subordinate voices.[8] Later analysis tended to view the work in deconstructionist terms, according it in the process some of the attributes of a post-modernist novel. Magdalene Redekop, in noting the novel's stubborn resistance to closure, claimed nevertheless positive elements in the 'process of misreading' itself; while Douglas Jones, endeavouring to go further than dual-narrative interpretations, saw the text as a whole not only as denying meaning, but exhibiting in its closing stages 'a general distrust of literary creation itself'.[9]

Gothic. At much the same time, the reputation of *Confessions* gained a huge boost from the rapidly burgeoning field of Gothic Studies, actively competing with Romanticism as a centre of academic activity. General studies of the mode, such as David Punter's *The Literature of Terror* (1980), often incorporated *Confessions* as a significant point in the genealogy of the Gothic novel, either tracing a line of masculinist 'horror' fiction running from Lewis' *The Monk*, or aligning the work with a more consciously 'intellectual' second phase of Gothic involving writers such as William Godwin, Mary Shelley and Maturin. The indeterminacy of *Confessions* also invited fresh interpretation in terms of Todorov's category of the 'fantastic', lying between the uncanny (supernatural explained) and marvellous (the apparently other-wordly), and marked by reader uncertainty.[10] Another main channel of interpretation concentrated on 'doubling' in the novel, this often involving attention to the role of the *doppelganger* in the Gothic tradition, as well as more detailed attention to Hoffmann's *Devil's Elixir*, though primarily as a parallel text showing remarkable affinities in its narrative ambiguities.[11]

Psychoanalytical. Following on from Gide's lead, and often interlinking with Gothic interpretations, some commentaries provided informed analyses of *Confessions* as a seminal psychodrama, with Robert Wringhim the sole patient under examination, and Gil-Martin fully interpretable in terms of Wringhim's own accelerating mental confusion. A landmark essay of 1983 by Barbara Bloedé in this way offers an examination 'in the light of modern understanding of the etiology of mental illness', with special reference to the condition of 'depersonalisation'.[12] While in this instance comparison is invited with another celebrated pre-Freudian fictional text by a Scottish writer, R. L. Stevenson's *Jekyll and Hyde* (1886), this approach along with the two other main approaches outlined above, at least in their purer forms, naturally had an effect of militating against any concerted effort at reappraising Hogg's novel in its original Scottish context.

From the 1990s onwards there has been a more clearly focused interest in the peculiarly national qualities mentioned only at second-hand by Gide and others. A considerable milestone in this respect is to be found in David Groves' claim, in his 1991 edition in the Canongate Classics series, that '[p]erhaps no other novel presents a more balanced and multifarious picture of Scottish life', the work as a whole representing 'one of the great novels of Scottish and world literature' (pp. vii–viii). This represents a shift in priorities that had already been signalled in Groves' earlier 1988 critical study of the author: 'Although the *Confessions* has a universal and modern significance that makes it popular with many readers around the world, it is also very deeply rooted in the traditions and history of southern Scotland.'[13] Though textually insignificant (being primarily based on the Carey text), the Canongate edition was the first to reproduce the 1824 spoof dedication to the Provost of Glasgow, an important ingredient in Hogg's effort to project his work at his contemporary audience. It also not only includes the original engraved frontispiece, purporting to give a sample of the Sinner's writing, but manages to trace its commissioning by Hogg from the Edinburgh engraver Robert Scott, whose premises were in Parliament Square (close to those of James Clarke off the High Street, and indeed to the workshop of the printer James Watson within the story, though Groves was unable to follow through these links, themselves indicative of the depth of the text's roots in the Edinburgh print industry).[14]

In his introduction to this edition, Groves also finds a fresh and more immediate model for the dual narrative scheme in Charles Kirkpatrick Sharpe's 1817 edition of James Kirkton's *Secret and True History of the Church of Scotland*, which Hogg had reviewed unfavourably for *Blackwood's Magazine*, and where there is a clear contrast between Kirkton's theologically-centred first-person account of events and the often caustic secular anti-Covenanting view imposed on this by Sharpe's paratextual materials as editor.[15] Groves's notes also touch on a number of other possible Scottish sources, relating to both main temporal frames in the story, which can appear all the more collapsible as a result. This reflected a number of key articles published by Groves at this time, opening up possibilities such as an origin for the prostitute Bell Calvert in the story in Mary M'Kinnon, executed in Edinburgh in 1823 for stabbing a client, before a crowd estimated at 20,000, prior to the dissection of her body and the use of a plaster cast of her head as an exhibit by the Phrenological Society.[16] Another major source of such materials can be found in the transactions of the James Hogg Society, which published regular Newsletters from 1982, as well as the Papers of Conferences held in 1983 and 1985, leading ultimately to the establishment in 1990 of the annual journal, *Studies in Hogg and his World*, now a major repository of critical essays, having reached its twentieth number in 2009.

Whereas re-establishment of Hogg in his original Scottish setting represented a considerable advance, the tendency to treat *Confessions* in isolation as a largely unexplained 'one-off' masterpiece still threatened to have an unbalancing effect, denying among other things a fully considered understanding of affinities with his other work. In an article in the first number of

Studies in Hogg and his World, titled 'Are We Still Underestimating Hogg?', Douglas Mack called for a concerted effort to rescue Hogg from the poor printed versions in which he had often appeared, as a means of countering the impression that his *oeuvre* was hugely uneven in quality. This provided the blueprint for the Stirling/South Carolina Research Edition of the Collected Works of James Hogg, whose first three volumes appeared in 1995. Its edition of *Confessions* appeared as the ninth in the series, published in 2001, and provides a fully revised text based on the original 1824 version. An extensive introduction places the work in a variety of contexts. Following earlier prompting by Ian Campbell and others,[17] the annotation also offers an especially full record of allusions to the King James Bible and the sung Metrical Psalms of the Church of Scotland, which Hogg knew intimately, initially through oral means as a child. Another feature of this edition is its attention to place names and topography, ranging from the semi-fictional world of Dalcastle at the start of the novel, through the maze-like confusions of Edinburgh, to stable yet shifting localities in Hogg's own Ettrick. In a number of respects, Hogg's text is revealed to be unremittingly Scottish in its main fabric, almost perversely, it might seem, withholding from the English reader the interpretational signposts and glosses provided by novelists such as Scott, just as it denies the Sinner his ambition to enter England, when the only available way out is effectively blocked off, forcing him up back towards Ettrick.

Subsequent volumes in the Collected Edition, such as Thomas C. Richardson's two-volume retrieval of the full scope of Hogg's contribution to *Blackwood's Magazine*, will have the effect of further illuminating such aspects. Another direct offshoot of the Edition is the *Collected Letters* of Hogg, edited by Gillian Hughes in three volumes (2004–8), which together supply a plenitude of fresh information about Hogg's rich social and literary relationships. This in turn has fed into Hughes' *James Hogg: A Life* (2007), the first authoritative modern biography, which usefully counters views of a victim-like ingénue in favour of a more proactive figure, capable of participating in a range of literary activity in Scotland, much of which has been obscured in traditional historical accounts in favour of the more 'primary' scene commanded by the likes of Francis Jeffrey and Scott.

An awareness of the novel's intrinsically Scottish characteristics has also fed positively into much literary criticism in recent years, sharpening in the process the broad approaches previously outlined. General studies of narrative method, following in the path of overviews of Romantic Fiction and the Scottish Novel by Gary Kelly and Cairns Craig,[18] have viewed Hogg's fiction as actively disrupting the conventions of Enlightenment discourse, or more especially the grand linear design of the Scottish historical novel, with its supposition of a beneficial endpoint to the barbarous if partly attractive past in a consensual and more rational social present. Other recent investigations have attempted to demonstrate a more vital interchange between Scott and Hogg as novelists, defusing older notions of a Laurel-and-Hardy type relationship, with Scott himself even in some instances responding to the challenge offered by Hogg's titles.[19] Critics, notably Murray Pittock,[20] have pointed more recently towards the influence on *Confessions* of a specifically 'Scottish Gothic', productively viewable in conjunction with Irish counterparts, in which the uncanny connects with an unusual degree of historical specificity to an ancestral/national identity alienated from modern life. Psychoanalytical criticism has also turned in some instances to events knowable to Hogg in his own time, such as a report of 'divided consciousness' presented to the Royal Society of Edinburgh in 1822, or the activities of his friend Dr Andrew Duncan in setting up a public lunatic asylum in Edinburgh.[21] Ian Duncan has also combined psychoanalysis and theories of the body as a means of disentangling Hogg's uncertain representations of a national literature, in key articles for *Studies in Hogg and his World*[22] that have since helped form the backbone of his major study *Scott's Shadow* (2007), which includes the fullest and most challenging contextualisation of Hogg in his Scottish literary and cultural environment to date.

One especially fertile field in recent discussions of *Confessions* has been the relationship in Hogg's make-up between the oral/folk world of his native Ettrick and print culture in Edinburgh. A valuable template here is provided by Penny Fielding's *Writing and Orality* (1996), which points to an intermixture of elements belonging to both worlds in Hogg's work:

> In his oral stories for a readership obsessively and self-consciously interested in printed material, Hogg both effects the continuation of oral techniques into print, and exposes ideologies which mark the division into a rural working class identified with the low status of orality, and an urban middle-class readership.[23]

Much work has gone into re-evaluating the impact of the rich storehouse of oral tradition Hogg experienced in his earliest years, through sources such as his mother, herself the daughter of Will Laidlaw of Phaup, famed in the region for having been the last mortal to converse with the fairies. Several main features of Hogg's multi-dimensional text – its circular patterning, blurring of truth and fiction, denial of literal meaning and sly insinuation of alternative possibilities – have been sought in the tradition of oral story-telling. Equally a strong folkloric element has been traced in Hogg's devil in the novel, marked not for the most part by Miltonic grandiosity, but a more familiar and insidious figure, capable of causing disruption in the natural world while also integrally bound up with human fallibility. Hogg's experience as an autodidact has also been seen as having given him an especially acute sense of the artificiality of various forms of written discourse, informing alike the parodies of Romantic poetry in his *Poetic Mirror* (1816) and the construction of the two main opposing narrative registers in *Confessions*.

In his middle years, Hogg has been depicted as straddling two worlds, with the new metropolitan 'polite' literary culture he embraced more fully in 1810, in settling in Edinburgh to make his way as an author, sometimes bearing down intolerably on his efforts to create a distinct and genuine literary identity. As several commentators have observed, it is not coincidental that the devil in the story should make one of his most disruptive appearances in the printing house where the Sinner's memoirs are being printed. In Karen Fang's words, the Sinner's consequent flight 'significantly reverses the trajectory of Hogg's own life'.[24] As a journey this noticeably involves both a process of social deconstruction, as Wringhim finds refuge successively with a yeoman farmer, a publican and a poor hind (leading to his own adoption of a shepherd's clothing and employment as a herdsman), and a parallel retreat from printed book through fragmentary diary to oral report.

Another associated area of investigation has focused on Hogg's output in relation to the surrounding publishing scene, at a time when Edinburgh was rapidly developing as a rival centre to London, with notable successes in the production of fiction and periodical literature. While comparison with Scott's historical fiction continues to attract attention, a number of recent critics have turned instead rather to Hogg's complex relationship with *Blackwood's Magazine* and its main circle of contributors, tracing his contributions as a founding editor, disenchantment as the younger Oxford-educated J. G. Lockhart and John Wilson took over the reins, followed by feelings of destabilisation and betrayal, the latter particularly as a result of Wilson's savage dismantling of his literary identity (and claims to be a successor of Burns) in a review of the 1821 version of his 'Memoir of the Author's Life'.[25] Also deserving attention is the phenomenon of the Blackwoodian novel, which became a central element in output in Scotland during the 1820s, and from which Hogg felt himself effectively excluded. Dominated by authors such as Lockhart and Wilson, this was heavily puffed in the *Magazine* as constituting a new school of Scottish fiction, and is distinguishable from Scott by a number of characteristics such as a preference for west of Scotland settings. Obliged to witness this from the sidelines, Hogg in letters to the publisher Blackwood made a number of adverse comments, singling out for special criticism the sentimental depictions of the Scottish working class. As the present writer has argued, *Confessions* can be seen as reflecting (or darkly mirroring) this phenomenon, in a number of ways, both in physical and thematic terms.[26]

Above all, the final sequence in *Confessions*, involving the Editor's journey to Ettrick to visit the Sinner's grave (itself prefaced by a transcript of Hogg's own 1823 'A Scots Mummy' contribution to *Blackwood's*), has been seen as enacting a savage counter-response to the Blackwoodian's claim to represent a coherent Scottish culture. Notable features as observed by several commentators[27] include the much closer proximity of the Editor to John Wilson at this stage; the securing of a pony rather than a horse when Lockhart is enlisted on the Abbotsford estate; the bumbling way in which the tourists proceed over a landscape whose functions they fail to understand; the discovery of James Hogg at Thirlestane market, and his refusal to engage in the enterprise; an echoing of the reopening of Burns' grave at Dumfries in 1815 when the corpse is unearthed;[28] and a parodying of Enlightenment materialism (perhaps too of the Blackwoodian tale of terror) in the detailing of the physical remnants found. In such ways, Hogg's attempted neo-Blackwoodian novel, having turned into an anti-Blackwoodian novel, might be said to end up as a resolutely non-Blackwoodian novel, constituting in this Hogg's most concerted (and at the same time almost consciously self-defeating) attempt to produce a truly Scottish novel.

CHAPTER FIFTEEN

The Function of Linguistic Variety in Walter Scott's *The Heart of Midlothian*

Fernando Toda

In this chapter, taking *The Heart of Midlothian* as a paradigmatic case of the intention underlying Walter Scott's use of linguistic variety in dialogue, it is argued that his foregrounding of the linguistic situation of Scotland has a didactic nature with a historical and political purpose. The effort to reflect different languages or varieties in the dialogues and, through authorial comment, to draw attention to the characters' speech is not just a stylistic breakthrough in the use of dialogue in the nineteenth-century novel; it is a major component in Scott's construction of the message to his readers, both in Scotland and in England. This 'double readership' needs to be kept in mind when trying to ascertain the function of the use of Scots and other varieties in the novels. Many explanations and comments contained in them are clearly aimed at readers with little knowledge of Scotland's culture and history, while some terms or references left unexplained would seem to be meant especially for those who do have that knowledge. J. M. D'Arcy's distinction between a 'literary competent' British reader who is 'in the role of an English or anglicised Scottish narratee' and a 'textually competent' Scots reader who is the 'ideal or implied reader', that is, the one who can understand things that the British reader cannot, is very useful for the purpose of this chapter, where the adjectives British and Scots, when applied to readers, are to be taken in this sense.[1] Naturally, this aspect affects the use of Scots, which is made accessible to the British readership to a greater or lesser degree at different moments, depending on the author's intention. Scott makes a calculated use of 'indicators' of Scots, especially in spelling and vocabulary; through them, he establishes what we can call, following J. D. McClure, the 'degree of Scotsness' of his characters' speech.[2]

The multilingual setting in which they take place is a factor that pervades the Scottish Waverley Novels. Writing about his country after the Treaty of Union of 1707, Scott depicts Scotland as a multilingual, multidialectal nation, now part of a larger state, the United Kingdom. This kingdom has as its citizens people who, like some of the Highlanders in *Rob Roy*, 'have no English' and speak only Gaelic, and others who use Lowland Scots, not always understood in England, as in the case of Jeanie Deans in *The Heart of Midlothian*. Scott aims to make his readers aware of this state of affairs and of the cultural and historical differences it represents, and the highlighting of this multilingualism and the situations of language contact derived from it becomes part of the message underlying the Scottish novels. How this message is to be interpreted, in terms of Scott's historical and political point of view, is still a matter of debate, but the aim of this chapter is to emphasise that the use of Scots and other varieties in *The Heart of Midlothian*, as in all the Scottish novels, was instrumental in conveying his vision, and that interpretations of it should take this into account.

D'Arcy remarks that most criticism since the 1950s has been heavily influenced by what he calls the 'Daichean' view of Scott, the vision presented by David Daiches and Duncan Forbes that Scott was a defender of the Union from a rational standpoint, though perhaps not sentimentally, and that he wished to reconcile the Scots to the idea that the loss of national independence had been compensated for by the benefits obtained from the Treaty of 1707 .[3] Most of the ensuing criticism, he affirms, seems to have accepted this notion that the purpose of the Waverley Novels was to support the United Kingdom and make it acceptable to Scots. D'Arcy does not hold with this, and in fact claims that the Scottish novels contain a subtext that is subversive, in that it actually questions whether there really have been such benefits from the Union, and in doing so implies that Scott's point of view was far more favourable to Scots nationalism than has hitherto been acknowledged.

With regard to Scott's point of view and the role that Scots play in it, the starting point for this chapter is the present author's 1983 essay, where, with reference to Jeanie Deans' interview with the queen in *The Heart of Midlothian*, it was argued that the historical lesson conveyed by the novel is that

> If a fruitful and powerful union between Scotland and England is to be achieved, it is important that those who rule the United Kingdom should have a fair and just attitude towards Scotland. This implies accepting that there are national differences that must be respected. Jeanie's Scots is a symbol of Scotland's national identity.[4]

The conditional nature of the first part of this statement, applicable not only to *The Heart of Midlothian* but to all the Scottish novels, takes it beyond the Daichean view, and challenges the idea that the novels were written solely to reconcile the Scots to their post-Union fate. It implies that they were mostly (or at least also) meant to show British readers that Scotland's rights had to be respected and the country treated more fairly than had often been the case after the Union. If this message is aimed at the British readers, the function of Scots in the novels must be approached from that point of view. In that case, ideological or political criticism based on the accuracy of the linguistic forms employed in the dialogues or the implications of the concessions made to Standard English spelling becomes less relevant; the objective is not so much to write 'genuine Scots' as to put the message across in an effective manner. When Norman Blake discussed Scott in *Non-Standard Language in English Literature* in 1981, for the Scottish novels he focused on *The Heart of Midlothian*. After dealing with Lowland and Highland Scots he also comments on the representation of English dialects, and makes the following statement: '[Scott] was not so worried about creating an accurate dialect as giving the impression of a non-standard speaker.'[5] In the case of Scots, he is usually quite accurate, but there is no doubt that he manipulates it with his British readership in mind; in that way he can use it to underscore his point of view about the place of Scotland in the Union. The following study of *The Heart of Midlothian*, which includes the interview between Jeanie and the queen, is based on these premises.

The Heart of Midlothian contains most of the varieties that Scott used in his linguistic depiction of Scotland. Standard English is used by educated characters from England and Scotland, and the novel also includes non-standard English dialects. Lowland Scots is used by most of the Scottish characters. Highland Scots is Scots as spoken by Highlanders whose mother tongue is Gaelic. It appears in the last third of the novel. In this novel there are no speakers of what was termed 'Ossianic English' in my 1985 essay,[6] a rather high-flown, metaphoric and formulaic Standard English, the product of the translation into English, in the speakers' minds, of thought conceived in Gaelic by those who do not use Highland Scots. Helen McGregor speaks it in *Rob Roy*, for example, and it is also used as a rendering of what some characters are actually supposed to be saying in Gaelic in stories such as 'The Highland Widow'. The differences are not always clear-cut, and Scott shows a good perception of the socio-linguistic situation around him. His manipulation of the different varieties, or of the changes from one to the other, in presenting his historical point of view is masterly, and *The Heart of Midlothian* is an excellent example. Graham Tulloch (1980) extensively described the way in which Scott carries out the representation of linguistic variety in the Waverley Novels.[7] Before him (and before Blake), Norman Page, in his ground-breaking *Speech in the English Novel* (1973),[8] focused on *The Heart of Midlothian* for his brief but revealing section on Scott's use of dialogue. The idea that Scott's representations of linguistic variety help to consolidate a post-1707 multicultural and multilingual vision of Great Britain was approached in Robert Crawford's *Devolving English Literature* and Leith Davis' *Acts of Union: Scotland and the Literary Negotiation of the British Nation*. Analysing the role given to Scots, Janet Sorensen focused on the implications of its written representation in *The Heart of Midlothian*.[9] She argues that, contrasted with the Standard English in the narrative and the dialogues, the 'strange orthography and singular diction' of the Scots leaves it in an inferior position when considering 'this text's intervention in the discourse of British nationalism' (p. 63). Her analysis, which in effect accepts the Daichean view, differs from the interpretation of the function of Scots presented here.

The Heart of Midlothian is set at the time of the Porteous Riots and their consequences, which constitute the historical background. In 1736 the people of Edinburgh stormed the prison known as 'The Heart of Midlothian' and seized and lynched Captain Porteous, who had been sentenced to death for ordering his troops to shoot upon the crowd after a public execution, killing several citizens, but had later been granted a royal reprieve. The ensuing tension between London (the Crown and government) and Scotland (especially the city of Edinburgh) becomes entangled with the story of Jeanie Deans, a devout Presbyterian woman faced with the moral dilemma of having to commit perjury in order to save the life of her sister, accused of having murdered her new-born child. Unable to do so due to her religious beliefs, Jeanie travels to London to obtain the king's pardon when Effie is sentenced. As in *Waverley* and *Rob Roy* (set in 1745 and 1715), in this novel the historical setting chosen is a key moment of tension between England and Scotland after the Union, a testing ground for the functioning of the new United Kingdom. Using this historical setting, *The Heart of Midlothian* emphasises the idea that the rights and peculiarities of Scotland need to be respected and preserved. Also as in *Waverley* and *Rob Roy*, this notion includes the two cultures and languages of Scotland, Lowland and Highland. With his depiction of characters from both parts, identified through their language, Scott conveys a message that can be summarised, at least, as a plea for equal justice and respect for diversity within the Union.

In *The Heart of Midlothian* the people of Edinburgh are given a major role, due to the nature of the historical event in which the fiction is embedded, the Porteous Riots. The refusal of the people to testify in the enquiry following the lynching of Captain Porteous and the feeling that the subsequent measures taken by the government in London had been an aggression against Scotland are both presented in the novel. Scott's narrator, Peter Pattieson, recounts that an Act of Parliament was passed offering a two-hundred pound reward to whoever might inform against any person concerned in the deed, and stipulating that those who harboured the guilty could be subjected to the death penalty. Moreover, a clause was included which obliged the officiating clergyman (of the Kirk of Scotland) to read out the Act publicly on the first Sunday of every month for a period of time, with severe reprisals for those who refused. He then makes the following comment:

Very many [. . .] of different political or religious sentiments [. . .] thought they saw, in so violent an act of parliament, a more vindictive spirit than became the legislature of a great country, and something like an attempt to trample upon the rights and independence of Scotland.[10]

In the historical context, 'a great country' must be taken to mean the United Kingdom. Apart from statements like this, we are also allowed to hear the opinions of the citizens of Edinburgh in their native Scots. The way in which Scott introduces their complaints is very interesting as an example of linguistic didacticism aimed at his British readers.

The origin of the Riots, we are informed, had been the execution of a smuggler, Andrew Wilson, for robbing a Collector of the Customs. Part of the crowd present at the public hanging, though they had not acted violently before, after the execution started to shout and throw stones at the Guard commanded by Porteous; one person climbed up to the gallows and cut down the body. At that point, Porteous ordered his troops to fire, and six or seven citizens were killed; many were hurt. For this action he was tried and condemned to death, but on the day of the execution the reprieve from London arrives. This brings about a series of comments on the part of the people who had gone to see the hanging (the positive references to Wilson refer to the fact that he had generously given his accomplice the chance to escape from their guards, remaining captive himself). The remarks are in direct speech, attributed to a plural, nameless speaker:

'This man [Wilson],' they said, 'the brave, the resolute, the generous, was executed to death without mercy for stealing a purse of gold, which in some sense he might consider as a fair reprisal; while the profligate satellite [Porteous], who took advantage of a trifling tumult, inseparable from such occasions, to shed the blood of twenty of his fellow-citizens, is deemed a fitting object for the exercise of the royal prerogative of mercy. Is this to be borne? – would our fathers have borne it? Are we not, like them, Scotsmen and burghers of Edinburgh?' (*Heart*, pp. 35–6)

The people are here given voice in English, not Scots. The narrator states the case, or the opinions about it, in a way similar to that of an interpreter. It is as if someone who understood Scots well was explaining the tenor of the arguments to someone who did not. And then, after this general introduction, we are allowed to hear the voices of some of the individuals in the crowd, in their native Scots. Once the execution has been suspended, comments like these are made:

'An unco thing this, Mrs Howden,' said old Peter Plumdamas to his neighbour the rouping-wife, or saleswoman [. . .] 'to see the grit folk at Lunnon set thir face against law and gospel, and let loose sic a reprobate as Porteous upon a peaceable town!' (*Heart*, p. 37)

The narrator's gloss of *rouping-wife* is also part of Scott's technique for making readers aware of national differences through language. Plumdamas then makes open reference to the situation after the Union: 'I am judging this reprieve wadna stand gude in the auld Scots law, when the kingdom was a kingdom.' His longing for the past situation is echoed by Mrs Howden, who can see other advantages to having the institutions closer to home: 'I ken, when we had a king, and a chancellor, and parliament-men o' our ain, we could aye peeble them wi' stanes when they werena gude bairns – But naebody's nails can reach the length o' Lunnon' (*Heart*, p. 37). Apart from national feeling, we hear other post-Union complaints. A seamstress regrets that rich Edinburgh citizens now have their clothes made in London: 'Our gentles will hardly allow that a Scots needle can sew ruffles on a sark, or lace an owerlay.' Plumdamas himself complains about the great amount of taxes to be paid, and the number of 'idle English gaugers and excise men as hae come down to vex and torment us' (*Heart*, p. 37), and nearly justifies the fact that Wilson had robbed one of them. Some economic and administrative consequences of the Union are presented as part of the unrest.

Comments from some of these citizens are also heard about the case of Effie Deans, accused of infanticide. Mrs Saddletree, in whose harness-shop Effie had worked, is willing to defend her and refuses to believe she might be guilty of the crime, or, in any case, thinks she must have been out of her mind at the time:

'How she was abandoned to hersell, or whether she was sackless o' the sinfu' deed, God in Heaven knows; but if she's been guilty, she's been sair tempted, and I wad amaist take my Bible-aith she hasna been hersell all the time.' (*Heart*, p. 44)

This Scots that we hear from the mouths of the citizens is the variety that the heroine of the novel normally speaks, as do her father and sister. Jeanie Deans, Scott's only Scots-speaking heroine, can also use Standard English, but Scott ensures that she uses her native vernacular in highly dramatic situations. One of these is the interview between the two sisters when Effie is in prison awaiting trial. Under the pre-Union Scots law of 1690, if a witness could swear in court that Effie had informed her of her pregnancy, it would be assumed that she had not intended to commit infanticide, and the charges would be dropped; were Jeanie to do this, she would save her sister's life. But her religious beliefs prevent her from lying, and the dialogue between the sisters turns tense and dramatic. Both speak Scots, and we find lines like these, after Jeanie tells Effie that she has spoken to George Staunton, her English seducer. Effie asks:

> 'And he [Staunton] wanted you to say something to yon folks that wad save my young life?'
> 'He wanted,' answered Jeanie, 'that I suld be mansworn.'
> 'And you tauld him,' said Effie, 'that ye wadna hear o' coming between me and the death that I am to die, and me no aughteen year auld yet?'
> 'I told him,' replied Jeanie, who now trembled at the turn which her sister's reflections seemed about to take, 'that I dared na swear to an untruth.'
> 'And what do ye ca' an untruth?' said Effie, again showing a touch of her former spirit – 'Ye are muckle to blame, lass, if ye think a mother could, or would, murther her ain bairn [. . .]' (*Heart*, pp. 188–9)

The frequency of indicators is high. In a scene like this, Scott appears to wish to give back to Scots part of the all-purpose character it had enjoyed earlier in Scottish literature, before the Union of Crowns and the Union of Parliaments made it lose its status in the face of Standard English. David Murison claims that the first blow had in fact been the absence of a translation of the Bible into the Scots vernacular.[11] Here, in this dramatic moment, Scots is the language of tragedy.

Another key moment involving the use of Scots is the interview between Jeanie and Queen Caroline, George III's queen. When Effie is condemned to death, Jeanie travels to London on foot to obtain the king's pardon. With the aid of the Duke of Argyle, the most important Scottish nobleman and a Member of Parliament, she obtains an interview with the queen (though Jeanie is only told is that she is an important lady). The dialogue has drawn the attention of a number of critics. W. J. Hyde[12] quotes several who in the past had pointed out not only the importance of the scene itself but also the key role of Jeanie's eloquence which, according to them, is what wins the pardon for Effie. Hyde's own argument is that in view of several clues in the narrative perhaps that is an exaggeration, since the granting of the reprieve seems to have been a foregone conclusion. In any case, after Jeanie's speech the queen does make the comment 'this is eloquence' (*Heart*, p. 398). And, as the readers perceive it, it is eloquence in Scots. Behind Jeanie's personal plea lie the historical tensions that Scott wants to highlight: the harsh law on child murder (applied to Scotland but not England) does not reflect equal treatment for British citizens, and the strict measures imposed on Scotland after the Porteous Riots (which are referred to by the queen) encroach unduly on the rights of post-Union Scotland. Jeanie's use of Scots in the interview acts as a reminder of Scottish national identity, and the narrator's references to her speech ensure that readers never lose sight of this. Two days before the interview the Duke of Argyle instructs her: 'just speak out a plain tale, and shew you have a Scotch tongue in your head' (*Heart*, p. 320). On the same day he recommends her to 'speak out as boldly to this lady, as you did to me the day before yesterday; and [. . .] I'll wad ye a plack, as we say in the north, that you get the pardon from the king' (*Heart*, p. 329). The implication seems clear: Jeanie is to speak Scots and not the kind of Standard English that we already know she can use.

Before this interview, readers have had more than one taste of Jeanie's linguistic range. On her way to London she talks English to the English highwaymen who try to rob her (*Heart*, pp. 259–60). Later she arrives at the parish held by George Staunton's father and meets the beadle, a man who speaks in a Lincolnshire dialect. Jeanie speaks to him in Standard English with words like these: 'I do not wish to burthen anyone [. . .] I have enough for my own wants, and only wish to get on my journey safely' (*Heart*, p. 286). Here, the absence of Scots indicators that have appeared before in her speech is obvious: we find *do not* instead of *dinna*; *to*, not *tae*; *have*, not *hae*; *own* instead of *ain*. In the interview with the queen, however, the case is different. When Jeanie is introduced by the duke, we learn that the queen smiled 'at her broad northern accent' and her first answer given in direct speech contains three indicators: *Leddyship*, *mony* and *ain* (*Heart*, p. 338). This shows that she is speaking Scots, precisely because we have heard her use Standard English before, as in the example quoted. Later, a gloss is required when Jeanie mentions 'the cutty stool' as a reason that may lead young Scots women to infanticide and Lady Suffolk, also present, does not understand:

'The what?' said Lady Suffolk, to whom the phrase was new, and who besides was rather deaf.

'That's the stool of repentance, madam, if it please your Leddyship,' answered Jeanie, 'for light life and conversation, and for breaking the seventh command.' (*Heart*, p. 338)

Soon after this, the queen needs to have Jeanie's speech interpreted. Impressed by the fact that Jeanie has walked most of the way to London, she asks her how far she can walk in a day. The answer is 'Five-and twenty miles and a bittock.' The queen turns to the duke: 'And a what?' His version: 'And about five miles more' (*Heart*, p. 339). Once more, the readers' attention is called to linguistic differences.

In terms of the degree of Scotsness, it should be borne in mind that the use of a higher frequency of English forms in parts of this scene is justified by two socio-historical factors. One affects the language of the law. When asked by the queen about her attitude to the Porteous Riots, Jeanie's speech becomes more anglicised. Her use of words like 'lawfully' or 'civil magistrate' recalls Effie's trial, where all the speeches are in English. But readers have also seen that some of the characters involved in the administration of justice change from Scots in private conversation to English when acting as public figures, so it seems natural for Jeanie to use English when referring to legal matters too.

The second factor has to do with religious contexts, and then the predominance of English is due to the influence of the English Bible. As mentioned earlier, the absence of a Scots translation had its effect on the speech of the Lowlands, and this shows in Jeanie's language. When she speaks of her father, she tells the queen, with obvious biblical echoes, that he regularly prays 'that his majesty might be blessed with a long and prosperous reign, and that his throne, and the throne of his posterity, might be established in righteousness' (*Heart*, p. 340). Scots words like *wi'* or *lang* are normally used by Jeanie, but the use of English forms here is not so much a conscious effort to anglicise her speech as the influence of English biblical language. James Murray, describing the situation in the Lowlands in the nineteenth century, wrote that 'as a rule, English is the liturgical language even among the illiterate'[13] and David Murison remarks that 'this is the second language of Scotland, the heritage of [. . .] the English Bible [. . .] with which every Scottish peasant was familiar' and adds that Jeanie's speech is worded in this style.[14] In spite of this, the second part of the plea to the queen, a more emotional appeal to her better feelings and moral principles with religious overtones, becomes increasingly Scots. Murray Pittock states that this passage expresses 'in (albeit light) Scots [. . .] the deep-sounding bell of autochthonous sincerity, rung as loudly as Burns ever could'.[15] Compared to some Burns poems, the Scots is possibly lighter, but what the reader perceives in this final part is an increase in the degree of Scotsness. At the end of her speech, Jeanie makes the reflection that when things are going well for us we tend to forget the sufferings of others, and then adds:

> 'But when the hour of trouble comes to the mind or to the body – and seldom may it visit your Leddyship – and when the hour of death comes, that comes to high and low – lang and late may it be yours – Oh, my Leddy, then it isna what we hae dune for oursells, but what we hae dune for others, that we think on maist pleasantly. And the thoughts that ye hae intervened to spare the puir thing's life will be sweeter in that hour, come when it may, than if a word of your mouth could hang the haill Porteous mob at the tail of ae tow.' (*Heart*, p. 341)

The construction of this final part brings together the personal story and the historical narrative. Jeanie reminds the queen that her intervention in Effie's favour will grant her peace of mind when her time comes, and expresses this in the form of a comparison, thus bringing back the subject that the queen had brought up earlier; she had questioned Jeanie's position with regard to the riots and the ensuing enquiry, and Jeanie now presents her with a moral dilemma of her own. But the implications are not merely personal. Jeanie's final words recall the historical issue underlying the scene, the tension between England and Scotland after the riots. And this is brilliantly done through the use of Scots, especially in the very last words 'the tail of ae tow'. The choice is surely not accidental. Due to the context, there is not much doubt about what they mean (the end of a rope), but the Scots forms would not normally be recognisable to British readers (or to the queen). As the closing words, they are a sharp reminder that Jeanie, a British subject of the queen, does not speak like her, and her language here becomes representative of Scotland and its rights.

The representation of Highland Scots in *The Heart of Midlothian* also turns out to be a well-calculated device when one compares it to other instances of that variety in earlier novels like *Waverley* and *Rob Roy*. In portraying it, Scott draws on a literary tradition in Scotland which often used this dialect for comedy. Tulloch gives a list of traits attributed to what he calls 'pseudo-Highland Scots'.[16] Some of them seem to be based on reality and appear to be interferences from the speakers' native language. For example, phonemes not found initially in Gaelic like the voiced and voiceless affricates in *gentleman* and *chase* are represented as *shentleman* and *shase*. There is also the devoicing of *b*, *d* and *g*; for instance, 'bed' is *ped*. Initially, *t-* is used for *th-*, giving cases of *tat* for *that* and *ta* for *the*. In grammar, a striking feature is the use of *she* as a general all-purpose pronoun. It was in literary use since the fifteenth century, although it seems to have no basis in reality. Highlanders are made to say *her nainsell*, ('her own self') for 'I' or 'me', and often use *she* for 'he'. In *The Heart of Midlothian* the only character who uses this variety, Duncan of Knockdunder, speaks a modulated version of Highland Scots that does not include the last two features mentioned here.

Duncan is the Duke of Argyle's agent and the main authority in his lands on the 'island' of Roseneath (actually a peninsula), where Jeanie settles with her family after Effie has been pardoned. Scott's choice of an 'island' that is only nearly an island, territory on the frontier of Highlands and Lowlands, where the Gaelic and Scots languages are in liminal proximity, is certainly not accidental. Our attention is drawn to Duncan's clothing; we are told that it was his pleasure 'to unite in his own person the dress of the Highlands and the Lowlands' and that his wig and hat corresponded to the latter. We learn that he 'superintended a district which was partly Highland partly Lowland, and therefore might be supposed to combine their habits, in order to show his impartiality to Trojan or Tyrian'. Yet after this humorous description there comes a macabre comment: 'as someone said who had seen the executions of the insurgent prisoners in 1715, it seemed as if some Jacobite enchanter, having recalled the sufferers to life, had clapped [. . .] an Englishman's head on a Highlander's body' (*Heart*, p. 394). This is a sombre reminder of recent

civil strife within the United Kingdom, so that, in spite of his 'feudal' attitude, this Highland-Lowland Duncan is perhaps the only possible guarantee
of peace between peoples on the lands of the duke, who in turn is presented as
a champion of the rights of Scotland in its co-existence with England. Scott
chose to give Duncan a variety of Highland Scots that lacks two indicators
which he had previously used in *Waverley* and *Rob Roy*; again, this shows
his conscious manipulation of language to underline his message. Duncan's
Highland Scots, though identifiable as such, is closer to the Lowland variety.
His speech is like his attire. Here is a sample of it, and of his attitude. Faced
with the possibility that some of the elders of the local parish might not agree
with the duke's decision that Jeanie's husband should be the new minister, he
tells David Deans, her father:

> 'Never fash your peard about it, man [. . .] Leave it a' to me. Scruple! de'il o'
> them has been bred up to scruple onything that they're bidden to do. And if sic
> a thing suld happen as ye speak o', ye sall see the sincere professor [. . .] towed at
> the stern o' my boat for a few furlongs. I'll try if the water of the Holy Loch
> winna wash off scruples as weel as fleas – Cot tamn! – ' (*Heart*, p. 395)

The first person pronoun is used correctly; *the* and *that* are employed, not
ta and *tat*. This happens consistently in his speech. Most of the features are
Lowland Scots, but *peard* for 'beard' and *Cot* and *tamn* for 'God' and 'damn'
are Highland. Scott has modified the dialect to coincide with the clothing.
As for Duncan's feudal attitude, it may well serve as an instance of why a
reappraisal of the 'Roseneath section' of the novel in the line suggested by
D'Arcy may be necessary. Where critics have usually remarked that this last
third of the book is inferior to the rest in literary worth, he argues convincingly that as far as the structure of the novel is concerned this is not the case:
there are a number of parallelisms and matching structures that seem to close
the story in a carefully planned manner. But what is more to the purpose, he
argues that the idyllic vision of life in Roseneath as a symbol of a better, more
peaceful life in post-Union Scotland, a Daichean view that most critics have
not questioned, is not what Scott had in mind:

> The meaning and purpose of the last section of *The Heart of Midlothian* is [. . .]
> to present an ironic rather than idyllic picture of mid-eighteenth century
> Scotland; far from being a wishful model of a law-abiding, unified 'Scott-land',
> the Roseneath of the 1750s is as fundamentally prone to lawlessness, violence,
> and moral corruption as the Scotland of the early eighteenth century.[17]

Duncan is an example of this. This unified Scotland partly represented by
him and his mixed clothing and dialect has not turned out as might have
been expected when the Treaty of Union was signed. Nearly fifty years

later, things have not improved much. The vision conveyed is not really the Daichean one; in D'Arcy's view, it would rather seem to be that 'Roseneath is a more grimly pessimistic picture of eighteenth-century Scotland: the individual Scotsman could gain all the profits from the British Empire, but the Scottish nation had lost its soul'.[18] The implication is that Scott is sending a message that applies not just to the 1750s but to his own day and age, and it seems to be that the Union has not been so good for Scotland. To what extent this implies a fully nationalist view in terms of a political stance may be harder to establish; as D'Arcy reminds us, the times were not easy for such a positioning. But some years later, in 1826, rejecting any possibility of violent action on the part of Scotland in relation to England, Scott would write in *The Letters of Malachi Malagrowther*:

> We had better remain in union with England, even at the risk of becoming a subordinate species of Northumberland, as far as national consequence is concerned, than remedy ourselves by even hinting the possibility of rupture. But there is no harm in wishing Scotland to have just so much ill nature [. . .] as may keep her good-nature from being abused; so much national feeling as may determine her to stand by her own rights, conducting her assertion of them with every feeling of respect and amity towards England.[19]

Again, what seems undeniable is the implicit conditional nature of these statements: if the Union is really to prosper, the terms of the Treaty of 1707 at least must be respected, and in this Scotland needs to stand firm. This was not the case in the past, as *The Heart of Midlothian* shows, and was still not happening in Scott's own time, which is the basic argument in *Malachi*. This point of view is skilfully expressed, especially with the British readers in mind, through the use of Scots and other varieties in the Scottish novels, and *The Heart of Midlothian* is a fine example of Scott's masterly attribution of a historical and political function to linguistic variety in literature.

Endnotes

Abbreviations

EHSL: *The Edinburgh History of Scottish Literature*
ER: *The Edinburgh Review*
RES: *Review of English Studies*
SGS: SGS
SHW: *Studies in Hogg and his World*
SLJ: SLJ
SSL: SSL
SSR: *Scottish Studies Review*

Introduction – Pittock

1. William Robertson, *The History of Scotland*, 2 vols (London: Jones, 1827), I: xviii, 1. See also Colin Kidd, *Subverting Scotland's Past* (Cambridge: Cambridge University Press, 1993); Karen O'Brien, *Narratives of Enlightenment* (Cambridge: Cambridge University Press, 1997); Pittock, 'Historiography', in Alexander Broadie (ed.), *The Cambridge Companion to the Scottish Enlightenment* (Cambridge: Cambridge University Press, 2003), pp. 258–79.
2. See for example Pittock, 'Byron's Networks and Scottish Romanticism', in *The Byron Journal 37:1* (2009), pp. 5–14 and 'Dissolving the Dream of Empire: Fratriotism, Boswell, Byron and Moore', *Journal of Irish and Scottish Studies* 1.1 (2007), pp. 127–44.
3. See Pittock, *Scottish and Irish Romanticism* (Oxford: Oxford University Press, 2008); 'Robert Fergusson and the Romantic Ode', *British Journal of Eighteenth-Century Studies* 28.1 (2005), pp. 55–66.
4. See Pittock (ed.), *The Reception of Sir Walter Scott in Europe*, (London: Continuum, 2007); *Scottish and Irish Romanticism* (Oxford: Oxford University Press, 2008), chapter 1; Joep Leerssen, unpublished address, Wales–Ireland Symposium, Cardiff, 23 October 2008. For Romantic Mediaevalism, see Michael Alexander, *Medievalism* (New Haven: Yale University Press, 2007);

Alice Chandler, 'Sir Walter Scott and the Medieval Revival', *Nineteenth-Century Fiction* 19.4 (1965), pp. 315–32.

5. Walter Scott, *Rob Roy*, ed. Ian Duncan (Oxford: Oxford University Press, 1998), pp. 5, 20, 25, 37, 51.

6. Ian Duncan in *Modern Language Quarterly* 70.4 (2009), pp. 405, 409; for 'National Historicism', see Joep Leerssen, *National Thought in Europe* (Amsterdam: Amsterdam University Press, 2006), p. 119 ff.; Karen O'Brien, 'Historical Writing', in David Womersley (ed.), *A Companion to Literature from Milton to Blake* (Oxford: Blackwell, 2000), pp. 530–1; Pittock, 'Historiography'.

Chapter 1 – Newman

1. See Maureen N. McLane's persuasive argument that Romantic poetry is minstrelsy: *Balladeering, Minstrelsy, and the Making of Romantic Poetry* (Cambridge: Cambridge University Press, 2008), pp. 140–80. On Scottish Romanticism, see Davis, Duncan and Sorensen (eds), *Scotland and the Borders of Romanticism* (Cambridge: Cambridge University Press, 2004); Pittock, *Scottish and Irish Romanticism* (Oxford: Oxford University Press, 2008).

2. Walter Scott, *Waverley*, ed. Peter Garside (Edinburgh: Edinburgh University Press, 2007), p. 40.

3. Ian Duncan, *Scott's Shadow* (Princeton: Princeton University Press, 2007), p.4.

4. Francis Jeffrey, 'Review of Southey, *Thalaba the Destroyer: A Metrical Romance*', *ER* 1.1 (October 1802): pp. 63–4.

5. Deirdre McCloskey, *The Bourgeois Virtues* (Chicago: University of Chicago Press, 2006), pp. 252–63.

6. Walter Scott, 'Essay on Imitations of the Ancient Ballad', *Minstrelsy of the Scottish Border*, ed. T. F. Henderson, 4 vols (Edinburgh: William Blackwood and Sons, 1902), IV: pp. 16–17.

7. J. G. Lockhart, *Memoirs of the Life of Sir Walter Scott, Bart.*, 2nd edn, 10 vols (Edinburgh: Robert Cadell, 1839), I: p. 53.

8. Steve Newman, *Ballad Collection, Lyric, and the Canon* (Philadelphia: University of Pennsylvania Press, 2007), pp. 185–228.

9. See Andrew Elfenbein, 'Lesbianism and Romantic Genius: The Poetry of Anne Bannerman', *ELH* 63.4 (1996), pp. 929–57; Adriana Craciun, 'Romantic Spinstrelsy: Anne Bannerman and the Sexual Politics of the Ballad', in Davis et al. (eds), *Scotland and the Borders of Romanticism* (Cambridge: Cambridge University Press, 2004), pp. 204–24; Ashley Miller, 'Obscurity and Affect in Anne Bannerman's "The Dark Ladie"', *Nineteenth-Century Gender Studies* 3.2 (2007), www.ncgsjournal.com

10. Anne Bannerman, *Tales of Superstition and Chivalry* (London: Vernor and Hood, 1802), p. 80.

11. Craciun, 'Spinstrelsy', pp. 215–17.

12. Susan Stewart, *Crimes of Writing* (Oxford: Oxford University Press, 1991), pp. 102–31.

13. James Hogg, *Familiar Anecdotes of Sir Walter Scott* (New York: Harper Brothers, 1834), pp. 124–5.

14. Allan Ramsay, 'To the Right Honourable, The Town-Council of Edinburgh, The Address of Allan Ramsay', *The Works of Allan Ramsay: Volume 1 – Poems, 1721*, ed. Burns Martin and John M. Oliver (Edinburgh: Scottish Text Society, 1972), p. 208. Ramsay complains about the pirating and sullying of his pastoral elegy on Joseph Addison, 'Richy and Sandy' – starring 'Richy' Steele and 'Sandy' Pope speaking 'Doric' Scots.

15. Allan Ramsay, *The Tea-Table Miscellany*, 2 vols (Glasgow: J. Crum, 1871), I: p. x.

16. Walter Scott, 'Introductory Remarks on Popular Poetry', *Minstrelsy of the Scottish Border*, ed. T. F. Henderson, 4 vols (Edinburgh: William Blackwood, 1902), I: p. 25.

17. Amicus, 'Anecdotes tending to throw light on the character and opinions of the late Adam Smith, LL.D' (1791), in Adam Smith, *Lectures on Rhetoric and Belles Lettres*, ed. J. C. Bryce (Oxford: Clarendon, 1983), p. 230; Pittock, *Scottish Romanticism*, p. 58.

18. Walter Scott, 'Review of Cromek, ed., *Reliques of Robert Burns*', *Quarterly Review* 1.1 (1809), p. 26.

19. Robert Burns, 'Annotations to The Scots Musical Museum,' rpt. in Peter J. Westwood (ed.), *The Definitive Illustrated Companion to Robert Burns*, 5 vols (Kilmarnock: Distributed National Burns Collection Project, 2004), V: p. 2732.

20. Robert Burns, *Poems and Songs of Robert Burns*, ed. James Kinsley, 3 vols (Oxford: Oxford University Press, 1968), I: p. 207.

21. For one sign of Burns' strong broadside and chapbook presence, the Bodleian Library Broadside Ballads Index lists 157 for Burns (second among named authors only to Charles Dibdin) and 22 for Scott (http://www.bodley.ox.ac.uk/ballads/ballads.htm). Kirsteen McCue kindly forwarded findings from the National Library of Scotland, which include cheap single sheets of Burns' songs, including some music for German flute or guitar.

22. Donald Low (ed.), *Robert Burns* (London: Routledge, 1974), p. 82.

23. Newman, *Ballad*, pp. 79–83.

24. Jeffrey Skoblow, *Dooble Tongue* (Newark: University of Delaware Press, 2001), p. 123.

25. As Kinsley observes in Burns, *Poems and Songs* (III: p. 1503), Otto Ritter made this link in *Neue Quellenfunde zu Robert Burns* (1903). The broadside itself, 'Charly is my darling', is available on *Eighteenth Century Collections Online*.

26. Carol McGuirk, 'Jacobite History to National Song: Robert Burns and

Carolina Oliphant (Baroness Nairne)', *The Eighteenth Century: Theory and Interpretation*, 47.2/3 (2006), p. 253.

27. James Johnson (ed.), *The Scots Musical Museum*, 2 vols (Hatboro, PA: Folklore Associates, 1962), II: p. iii.

28. Francis Jeffrey, 'Review of Cromek, ed., *Reliques of Robert Burns*', ER 13.26 (1809), pp. 256, 276, 252–6.

29. Peter Garside, editor of the Edinburgh University Press edition of *Waverley*, forcefully identifies Burns as the source but admits Scott 'may have known of [Nairne's version] through mutual personal acquaintances in Edinburgh' (p. 572). He is perhaps reacting to Claire Lamont's attribution of the song to Nairne in the 1986 Oxford World's Classics edition (p. 434).

30. Leith Davis, 'Gender, Genre and the Imagining of the Scottish Nation: The Songs of Lady Nairne', in Nancy Kushigian and Stephen Behrendt (eds), *Scottish Women Poets of the Romantic Period*, http://asp6new.alexanderstreet.com/swrp/swrp.index.map.aspx, pp. 11–12.

31. For an influential Romantic attempt to balance femininity and the bardic, see Felicia Hemans' critically and commercially successful poems and songs; her *Welsh Melodies* includes songs set to music and sold as well as 'The Rock of Cader Idris', which tells of poetic election on a sublime mountaintop.

32. James Hogg, 'A Journey through the Highlands of Scotland [. . .]', *Scots Magazine* 64 (1802), p. 815.

33. James Hogg, *The Forest Minstrel*, ed. P. D. Garside and Richard Jackson (Edinburgh: Edinburgh University Press, 2006), pp. 348–9.

34. For the complicated origins of 'Woo'd and Married and A'', see Hogg, *The Forest Minstrel*, pp. 350–2. By 1803, the tune had been printed with various sets of verses in many forms, including song collections like Oswald's *Caledonian Pocket Companion* (c. 1759) and the first volume of *The Scots Musical Museum* (1787), antiquarian collections like Herd's *Ancient and Modern Scotish Songs* (1776) and Ritson's *Scotish Songs* (1794), broadsides and chapbooks. *Eighteenth Century Collections Online* lists a broadside version conjecturally located in Edinburgh and dated 1776 and a version in a chapbook printed in 1783, probably in Glasgow.

35. Murray Pittock, 'James Hogg: Scottish Romanticism, Song and the Public Sphere', in Sharon Alker and Holly Faith Nelson (eds), *James Hogg and the Literary Marketplace* (Burlington, VT: Ashgate, 2009), p. 111.

36. Thanks again to Kirsteen McCue for information on Hogg's appearance in cheaper print.

37. Hogg, *Altrive Tales*, ed. Gillian Hughes (Edinburgh: Edinburgh University Press, 2004), p. 18.

38. Hogg, *Songs by the Ettrick Shepherd* (Edinburgh: William Blackwood, 1831), p. 1.

39. Kirsteen McCue, 'Singing "More Songs than ever Ploughman could": The songs of James Hogg and Robert Burns in the Musical Marketplace," in

Sharon Alker and Holly Faith Nelson (eds), *James Hogg and the Literary Marketplace* (Burlington, VT: Ashgate, 2009), p. 124.

40. McLane, *Balladeering*, pp. 104–12.

41. In Anne MacVicar Grant, *Poems on Various Subjects* (Edinburgh: privately published; Mundell and Son, Manners and Millers, Arch, 1803), pp. 349–93. Reproduced in Anne MacVicar Grant, *The Highlanders: And Other Poems* (London: Longman, 1808).

42. John Clare, 'Popularity in Authorship', *European Magazine, and London Review* 1.3 (1825), p. 301.

43. George Deacon, *John Clare and the Folk Tradition* (London: Sinclair Browne, 1983); Sam Ward, 'Melodies in the Marketplace: John Clare's 100 Songs', *John Clare Society Journal* 25 (2006), pp. 11–30.

44. Scott is paired with Byron in 'Genius', in *Poems of the Middle Period, 1822–37*, ed. Eric Robinson, David Powell and P. M. S. Dawson, 5 vols (Oxford: Clarendon, 2003), V: pp. 10–11; 'The Heart of Midlothian' (*Later Poems* 2: p. 888) appears to be a song in honour of Jeanie Deans.

45. John Clare, *Poems Descriptive of Rural Life and Scenery* (London: Taylor and Hessey, 1820), p. xix.

46. John Clare, *The Later Poems of John Clare*, ed. Eric Robinson, David Powell and Margaret Grainger, 2 vols (Oxford: Clarendon, 1984), I: p. 280.

47. The first quote is from 'Song – White Thorn Tree' (*Later Poems* I: pp. 219–20); the second is from 'Song [Twas i' the morning early]' (*Later Poems* II: pp. 897–8).

Chapter 2 – Stafford

1. 'Fragment viii', *Fragments of Ancient Poetry* (1760), in *The Poems of Ossian and Related Works*, ed. Howard Gaskill (Edinburgh: Edinburgh University Press, 1996), p. 18.

2. Pittock notes the omission of Macpherson from M. H. Abrams' celebrated discussion of the Romantic metaphor, see *Scottish and Irish Romanticism* (Oxford: Oxford University Press, 2008), p. 80; see also Katie Trumpener, *Bardic Nationalism* (Princeton: Princeton University Press, 1997), pp. 3–34.

3. *The Works of Ossian*, 2 vols (London, 1765) contained letters regarding this as well as Hugh Blair's influential 'Critical Dissertation on the Poems of Ossian'. *The Report of the Committee of the Highland Society of Scotland, appointed to inquire into the nature and authenticity of the Poems of Ossian*, ed. Henry Mackenzie was published in 1805 and reviewed by Walter Scott in *ER* 6 (1805), pp. 429–62.

4. Dafydd Moore (ed.), *Ossian and Ossianism*, 4 vols (London: Routledge, 2004).

5. *The Centenary Edition of the Poems of Ossian*, ed. William Sharp (Edinburgh: Patrick Geddes, 1896), p. xvi.

6. Ibid., p. xxiv; J. F. Campbell of Islay, *Leabhar na Féinne* was published in 1872 and *Popular Tales of the West Highlands* appeared in 1860 with a new, revised edition in 1890.

7. *Poems of Ossian*. For Sharp's connection with the Celtic Twilight, see Robert Crawford, *The Modern Poet* (Oxford: Oxford University Press, 2002), pp. 158–61.

8. D. S. Thomson, *The Gaelic Sources of Macpherson's Ossian* (Edinburgh: Oliver and Boyd, 1952).

9. Mark Jones (ed.), *Fake? The Art of Deception* (London: British Museum, 1990), p. 16.

10. See e.g. Fiona Stafford and Howard Gaskill (eds), *From Gaelic to Romantic* (Amsterdam: Rodopi, 1998); Terence Brown (ed.), *Celticism* (Amsterdam: Rodopi, 1996); Gauti Kristmannson, *Literary Diplomacy*, 2 vols (Frankfurt am Main: Peter Lang, 2005); Leith Davis, *Acts of Union* (Stanford: Stanford University Press, 1998).

11. Joep Leerssen, 'Ossian and the Rise of Literary Historicism', in Gaskill (ed.) *The Reception of Ossian in Europe* (London: Thoemes Continuum, 2004), pp. 114, 125.

12. J. McGann, *The Poetics of Sensibility* (Oxford: Oxford University Press, 1996), p. 33. See also Moore, *Ossian and Ossianism*, introduction.

13. Thomas Keymer, 'Narratives of Loss: *The Poems of Ossian and Tristram Shandy*', in Stafford and Gaskill (eds), *From Gaelic to Romantic*, p. 88. See also my *The Sublime Savage* (Edinburgh: Edinburgh University Press, 1988).

14. Luke Gibbons, 'The Sympathetic Bond: Ossian, Celticism and Colonialism', in Brown (ed.), *Celticism*, pp. 273–91, 289; 'From Ossian to O'Carolan: The Bard as Separatist Symbol', in Stafford and Gaskill (eds), *From Gaelic to Romantic*, pp. 226–51.

15. Friedrich von Schiller, *Naïve and Sentimental Poetry*, trans. Julius Elias (New York: Frederick Ungar, 1966), p. 101.

16. Hannah Ahrendt, introduction to Walter Benjamin, *Illuminations*, trans. Harry Zorn (London: Jonathan Cape, 1970), p. 49.

17. Ahrendt in *Illuminations*, pp. 54–5.

18. Mackenzie, *Report*, p. 44; Stafford, *Sublime Savage*, pp. 124–5.

19. Moore, *Ossian and Ossianism* I: p. lxi.

20. Ahrendt in *Illuminations*, p. 43.

21. Ibid., p. 51.

22. Walter Benjamin, *The Origin of German Tragic Drama*, trans. John Osborne (London: Verso, 1998), pp. 138–9.

23. Benjamin, *German Tragic Drama*, p. 151.

24. Matthew Wickman, *The Ruins of Experience* (Pennsylvania: University of Pennsylvania Press, 2007), 114; Crawford, *Modern Poet*, p. 68.

25. Julian Roberts, 'Melancholy Meanings: Architecture, Postmodernity and Philosophy', in Nigel Wheale (ed.), *The Postmodern Arts* (London: Routledge,

1995), pp. 130–49, 137. See also Charles Jencks, *What is Post-Modernism?* (Chichester: Wiley, 1996).

26. Roberts, 'Melancholy Meanings', p. 139.

27. Tom Normand in Calum Colvin, *Ossian* (Edinburgh: Scottish National Portrait Gallery, 2002), p. 31.

28. Stafford, *Sublime Savage*, pp. 24–39.

29. Trumpener's analysis of Macpherson's influence on the Romantic novel begins with Smollett, *Bardic Nationalism*, pp. 101–2.

30. Keymer in *From Gaelic to Romantic*, pp. 84–5, 87.

31. Crawford, *Modern Poet*, p. 68. Crawford emphasises the importance of Macpherson's bardic figure for Burns in *The Bard: Robert Burns* (London: Cape, 2009).

32. Robert Burns, 'The Twa Dogs', 29–30, James Kinsley (ed.), *The Poems and Songs of Robert Burns*, 3 vols (Oxford: Clarendon, 1968), I: p. 138.

Chapter 3 – McCue

1. The three letters from 7 August, 11 August and 25 August 1829 are given in Rudolph Elvers (ed.), *Felix Mendelssohn: A Life in Letters*, trans. Craig Tomlinson (London: Cassell, 1986), pp. 87, 89. See also David Jenkins and Mark Visocchi, *Mendelssohn in Scotland* (London: Chappell and Co., 1978).

2. Johann Gottfried Herder first used the term in his essay *Von Deutscher Art und Kunst: einige fliedgende Blätter* published in Hamburg in 1773. See also Matthew Gelbart, *The Invention of "Folk Music" and "Art Music"* (Cambridge: Cambridge University Press, 2007), pp. 102–10.

3. See Gelbart, *Invention*. Gelbart provides an in-depth study of Scotland's role, also discussing in much more detail what is meant by the labels/categories and genres of 'folk' and 'art'. This chapter has no space to examine these terms' complex contexts, but in it 'folk' represents the notion of the songs coming from 'the people'.

4. A key text here is Roger Fiske's *Scotland in Music: A European Enthusiasm* (Cambridge: Cambridge University Press, 1983).

5. See Howard Gaskill (ed.), *The Reception of Ossian in Europe* (London/New York: Continuum, 2004); Pittock (ed.), *The Reception of Sir Walter Scott in Europe* (London/New York: Continuum, 2007). BOSLIT is available through the website for the National Library of Scotland: http://www.nls. uk/catalogues/resources/boslit/. See Christopher Small, 'Ossian in Music', in *The Reception of Ossian in Europe*, pp. 375–92; Jerome Mitchell, *The Walter Scott Operas* (Alabama: University of Alabama Press, 1977); Jeremy Tambling, 'Scott's 'Heyday' in Opera', in *Reception of Scott in Europe*, pp. 285–92; also Roger Fiske, *Scotland in Music*, pp. 80–115; Robert Giddings 'Scott and Opera' in Alan Bold (ed.), *Sir Walter Scott* (London: Barnes and Noble, 1983), pp. 194–218.

6. Gelbart, *Invention*, pp. 111–52.

7. Allan Ramsay's *Scots Songs* appeared in 1718–19 and his *Tea-Table Miscellany* (from 1724 throughout the century in numerous editions). William Thomson's *Orpheus Caledonius* was published in London in 1725 and was reissued in 1733. David Herd's *The Ancient and Modern Scots Songs, Heroic Ballads, &c.* was published in Edinburgh in 1769 and Joseph Ritson's *Scotish [sic] Songs* [With an Historical Essay on Scotish Song] appeared in London in 1794. James Beattie's *Essay on Poetry and Music as they Effect the Mind* appeared in Beattie's *Essays* published in Edinburgh in 1776; John Aiken's *Essays on Song-Writing: With a Collection of English Songs as are most Eminent for Poetical Merit* [. . .] was published in London in 1772; William Tytler's 'Dissertation on the Scottish Music' appeared in *Transactions of the Society of Antiquaries of Scotland* (Edinburgh and London, 1792), pp. 495–6. Many collections of Scottish songs included 'dissertations' or 'historical surveys' by way of introductions.

8. Jenny Burchell, *Polite and Commercial Concerts* (London: New York: Garland, 1996).

9. See Sonia Tingali Baxter, 'Italian Music and Musicians in Edinburgh c.1720–1800: An Historical and Critical Study', unpublished PhD Thesis, Glasgow, 1999; David Johnson, *Music and Society in Lowland Scotland in the Eighteenth Century* (Oxford: Oxford University Press, 1972). Both Urbani and Schetky collaborated directly with Robert Burns.

10. See Barry Cooper, *Beethoven's Folksong Settings* (Oxford: Clarendon, 1994). Cooper accounts for some 179 settings, p. 7.

11. See McCue, 'George Thomson (1757–1851): His Collections of National Airs in their Scottish Cultural Context', unpublished DPhil thesis, Oxford, 1993, pp. 243–7. Breitkopf and Härtel eventually published the songs in 1941.

12. See John Warrack, *Carl Maria von Weber* (Cambridge: Cambridge University Press, [1964] 1976), p. 88.

13. See Alexander Gillies, *Herder und Ossian* (Berlin: Junker und Dünnhaupt Verlag, 1933); Johann Gottfried Herder, *Selected Early Works 1764–1767*, ed. Ernest A. Menze and Karl Menges, (Pennsylvania: Pennsylvania State University Press, 1992), pp. 13–14; also Alexander Gillies, *A Hebridean in Goethe's Weimar* (Oxford: Blackwell, 1969), pp. 58–9.

14. See Gaskill, *Reception*.

15. Alexander Gillies, *Herder* (Oxford: Blackwell, 1944), p. 39. For further discussions of the reception history of Macpherson's work see Stafford, *The Sublime Savage* (Edinburgh: Edinburgh University Press, 1988) and Howard Gaskill (ed.), *Ossian Revisited* (Edinburgh: Edinburgh University Press, 1991).

16. See Frauke Reitemeier, 'The Reception of Walter Scott in German Literary Histories, 1820–1945', in Pittock, *Reception of Scott*, p. 95.

17. See Caitríona Ó Dochartaigh, 'Goethe's Translation from the Gaelic *Ossian* in Gaskill, *Reception of Ossian*, pp. 156–8.

18. Frederick W. Sternfeld, *Goethe and Music* (New York: New York Public Library, 1954), p. 13.

19. Fiske, *Scotland in Music*, p. 84.

20. See Elizabeth Norman McKay, *Franz Schubert: A Biography* (Oxford: Clarendon, 1996), p. 58.

21. Later in 1827 Schubert set Herder's translation of the Scottish ballad 'Edward', which Herder had found initially in Percy's *Reliques*. It was entitled 'Eine Altschottische Ballade' (D923). This was one of many ballads Herder translated and included in his *Volkslieder* of 1774 and 1778–9. See *Johann Gottfried Herder Volkslieder Übergragungen Dichtungen*, ed. Ulrich Gaier (Frankfurt: Deutscher Klassiker Verlag, 1990).

22. Marjorie Wing Hirsch, *Schubert's Dramatic Lieder* (Cambridge: Cambridge University Press, 1993), p. 84.

23. See John Reed, *The Schubert Song Companion* (Manchester: Manchester University Press, 1985). Reed gives a detailed account of each song. He notes Wagnerian overtones in particular in 'Cronnan' and 'Loda's Gespenst'. See also Roger Fiske, *Scotland in Music*, p. 85.

24. See Susan Youens, *Schubert's Poets and the making of Lieder* (Cambridge: Cambridge University Press, 1996). See chapter 2, pp. 51–149.

25. Fiske, *Scotland in Music*, pp. 90–5.

26. McKay, *Schubert*, p. 214

27. The first edition is entitled *Sieben Gesänge aus Walter Scott's Fräulein vom See mit Begleitung des Pianoforte . . . von Franz Schubert Op. 52* (Vienna: Artaria). The copy used was that housed at the British Library: Hirsch IV 30.

28. See John Reed, *The Schubert Song Companion*, p. 215; Roger Fiske, *Scotland in Music*, p. 95 and Richard Capell, *Schubert's Songs* (London: Duckworth and Co. Ltd, [1928] 1966), p. 209; also Elizabeth Norman McKay in *Schubert*, p. 230.

29. Capell, *Schubert's Songs*, p. 210; McKay, *Schubert*, p. 229.

30. John Daverio suggests that Schumann saw *Ossian* as 'Northern' and was interested primarily in Macpherson's work through the works of his Danish composer friend Niels Gade. See John Daverio, 'Schumann's Ossianic Manner', in *19th Century Music* 21.3 (1998), pp. 247–73.

31. See Richard Cardwell (ed.), *The Reception of Byron in Europe*, 2 vols (London; New York: Continuum, 2004), I: chapter 10: Frank Erik Pointner and Achim Geisenhanslüke, 'The Reception of Byron in the German-Speaking Lands'. They support the claim that, next to Shakespeare, Byron was the most popular British writer with the Germans.

32. Freiligrath produced his *Gedichte* in 1845 including translations of Moore, Scott, Thomas Campbell, Felicia Hemans and Burns. They were also in

Freiligrath's volume of translations of British and Irish poets, *The Rose, Thistle and Shamrock* or *Rose Distel und Kleeblatt [. . .]* published in 1863.

33. Gerhard's interest in Burns appears not to have been in isolation. In 1853 he published *Minstrelklänge aus Schottland* including his translations of 'Sir Patrick Spens', 'The Douglas Tragedie' and 'Edward', amongst other ballads and a small group of songs, thus looking back to Herder's earlier translations of Scottish ballads.

34. See Margery Palmer McCulloch, 'German Responses to Robert Burns', in *SSL* XXXIII (2004), pp. 30–41. Herder apparently possessed a copy of the first three volumes of Johnson's *Scots Musical Museum*.

35. See Fiske, *Scotland in Music*, pp. 156–86. See also Eric Sams, *The Songs of Robert Schumann* (London/Boston: Faber and Faber, [1969] 1993) for accounts of each song in the cycle.

36. *Scotland in Music*, p. 161.

37. See Jon W. Finson, *Robert Schumann: The Book of Songs* (Cambridge, MA; London: Harvard University Press, 2007), p. 29.

38. See ibid. This Heft was entitled *Myrthen. Liederkreis von Göthe* [sic], *Rückert, Byron, Th. Moore, Heine, Burns & J. Mosen für Gesang und Pianoforte von Robert Schumann. Op. 25 Heft III*. The publisher was Fr. Kistner of Leipzig. The copy used was at the British Library: Hirsch M.1198.(8.)

39. Finson, *Schumann*, p. 21.

Chapter 4 – Clancy

1. See Janet Sorensen, *The Grammar of Empire in Eighteenth-Century British Writing* (Cambridge: Cambridge University Press, 2000); Davis, Duncan and Sorensen (eds), *Scotland and the Borders of Romanticism* (Cambridge: Cambridge University Press, 2004); David Duff and Catherine Jones (eds), *Scotland, Ireland and the Romantic Aesthetic* (Oxford: Oxford University Press, 2007); Pittock, *Scottish and Irish Romanticism* (Oxford: Oxford University Press, 2008).

2. See Dafydd Moore, *Enlightenment and Romance in James Macpherson's* The Poems of Ossian (Aldershot: Ashgate, 2003); Stafford, *The Sublime Savage* (Edinburgh: Edinburgh University Press, 1988) and in this volume for further references; Donald E. Meek, 'The Sublime Gael: The Impact of MacPherson's *Ossian* on Literary Creativity and Cultural Perception in Gaelic Scotland', in H. Gaskill (ed.), *The Reception of Ossian* (London: Coninuum, 2004), pp. 40–66; Derick S. Thomson, 'James Macpherson: The Gaelic Dimension', in F. Stafford and H. Gaskill (eds), *From Gaelic to Romantic* (Amsterdam: Rodopi, 1998), pp. 17–26.

3. Ronald Black, 'Alasdair Mac Mhaighstir Alasdair and the New Gaelic Poetry', in S. Manning (ed.), *EHSL*, 3 vols (Edinburgh: Edinburgh University Press, 2007), II: pp. 110–24; for earlier overviews, see Derick S. Thomson,

'Gaelic Poetry in the Eighteenth Century: The Breaking of the Mould', in A. Hook (ed.), *The History of Scottish Literature*, 4 vols (Aberdeen: Aberdeen University Press, 1987), II: pp. 175–89.

4. See William Gillies, 'Merely a Bard? William Ross and Gaelic Poetry', *Aiste* 1 (2007), pp. 123–69, esp. fns 1–3, for full details of Ross' publication history and (problematic) treatment at the hands of editors and translators.

5. John Mackenzie, *Sar-Obair nam Bard Gaelach. The Beauties of Gaelic Poetry and the Lives of the Highland Bards* (Edinburgh: John Grant, [1841] 1907), p. 302; for the comparisons, see Gillies 'Merely a Bard?', p. 124; The quote from Ross is from his 'Òran eile', most conveniently now in R. Black, *An Lasair. Anthology of Eighteenth-Century Scottish Gaelic Verse* (Edinburgh: Birlinn, 2001), pp. 316–18, l. 48.

6. Gillies, 'Merely a Bard?'; Gillies, 'The Poetry of William Ross', in C. MacLachlan (ed.), *Crossing the Highland Line* (Glasgow: ASLS, 2009), pp. 195–215.

7. See Gillies, "Merely a Bard?', p. 153.

8. Ibid., p.154. For 'Cumha Coire an Easa', see C. Ó Baoill and M. Bateman (eds), *Gàir nan Clàrsach/The Harp's Cry. An Anthology of 17th-Century Gaelic Poetry* (Edinburgh: Birlinn, 1994), pp. 206–13.

9. Ronald Black offers a convenient snapshot in 'A Handlist of Gaelic Printed Books, 1567–1800', *SGS* 25 (2009), pp. 35–93; see the same author's forth-coming contributions in S. W. Brown and W. McDougall (eds), *The Edinburgh History of the Book in Scotland* (Edinburgh: Edinburgh University Press, forthcoming), II.

10. Ronald Black, 'Sharing the Honour: Mac Mghr Alastair and the Lowlands', in MacLachlan, *Crossing the Highland Line*, pp. 45–56; C. MacLachlan, 'Literary Edinburgh in the time of Alexander MacDonald', in ibid., pp. 57–66.

11. M. Scott, 'Poetry and Politics in Mid-Eighteenth-Century Argyll: *Tuirseach andiugh críocha Gaoidhiol*', in C. Ó Baoill and N. McGuire (eds), *Rannsachadh na Gàidhlig 2000* (Aberdeen: An Clò Gaidhealach, 2002), pp. 149–62.

12. See particularly Donald Meek, 'The Pulpit and the Pen: Clergy, Orality and Print in the Scottish Gaelic World', in A. Fox and D. Woolf (eds), *The Spoken Word* (Manchester: Manchester University Press, 2002), pp. 84–118.

13. Wilson McLeod, 'Language Politics and Ethnolinguistic Consciousness in Scottish Gaelic Poetry', *SGS* 21 (2003), pp. 91–146.

14. See Black, *An Lasair*, pp. 186–91, 455–58, for what may be oldest of such poems and general background.

15. For 'heteroglossia' in these poets, see Scott, 'Poetry and Politics'; Sarah Fraser, 'The Wheat / Grows Tallest in Well-Dug Fields': Influence and Innovation in Some Early Poems by Alastair Mac Mhaighstir Alastair', in Ó Baoill and McGuire, *Rannsachadh na Gàidhlig*, pp. 171–81.

16. Most conveniently in Ó Baoill and Bateman, *Gàir nan Clàrsach*, pp. 198–207.

17. See A. MacLeod, *Òrain Dhonnchaidh Bhàin/Poems of Duncan Ban Macintyre* (Edinburgh: Scottish Gaelic Texts Society, 1952), pp. 386–91.

18. Máire Herbert, 'Becoming an Exile: Colum Cille in Middle-Irish Poetry', in J. F. Nagy and L. E. Jones (eds), *Heroic Poets and Poetic Heroes in Celtic Tradition* (Dublin: Four Courts, 2005), pp. 131–40.

19. A. Gunderloch, 'Donnchadh Bàn's *Òran do Bhlàr na h-Eaglaise Brice* – Literary Allusion and Political Comment', *SGS* 20 (2000), pp. 97–116; P. Menzies, 'Òran na Comhachaig', in M. Byrne, T. O. Clancy and S. Kidd (eds), *Litreachas & Eachdraidh: Rannsachadh na Gàidhlig 2, Glaschu 2002* (Glasgow: Roinn na Ceiltis, 2006), pp. 83–96.

20. This in contrast to the emphasis laid on the availability of and his use of Gaelic sources, for which see Derick S. Thomson, *The Gaelic Sources of Macpherson's Ossian* (Edinburgh: Edinburgh University Press, 1952), and note 2 above; for a rather different recent approach, see Mícheál Mac Craith, 'Fingal: Text, Context, Subtext', in Stafford and Gaskill, *From Gaelic to Romantic*, pp. 59–68. For the effect on Gaelic literature, see Meek, 'The Sublime Gael'; William Gillies, 'On the Study of Gaelic Literature', in Byrne, Clancy and Kidd, *Litreachas & Eachdraidh*, pp. 1–32, esp. pp. 4–12.

21. Jerome Stone, *Scots Magazine*, 1756, reprinted in D. Moore, *Ossian and Ossianism*, 4 vols (London: Routledge, 2004), I: p. 8 and see pp. xxx–xxxvii for discussion.

22. See most conveniently Black, *An Lasair*, nos 24 and 49.

23. R. Black, 'Alexander MacDonald's *Ais-Eiridh*, 1751', *Journal of the Edinburgh Bibliographical Society* (forthcoming).

24. See M. Byrne and S. Kidd, '"Vintners and Criminal Officers": Fo-sgrìobhaichean leabhraichean Earra-Ghàidhealach ann am meadhan na 19mh linn', in W. McLeod, A. Burnyeat, D. U. Stiubhart et al. (eds), *Bile òs Chrannaibh* (Ceann Drochaid: Clann Tuirc, 2010), pp. 29–44.

25. D. Campbell, *A New Gaelic Song-Book* (Cork: John A. Cronin, 1798); on the author see Joseph A. Flahive, 'Duncan Campbell: A Scottish-Gaelic Bard in Eighteenth-Century Cork', *Journal of the Cork Historical and Archaeological Society* 113 (2008), pp. 80–9.

26. See Anja Gunderloch, 'Donnchadh Bàn mac an t-Saoir and his Subscribers', forthcoming in proceedings of seminar on Gaelic Networks in the Eighteenth and Nineteenth Centuries.

27. For the poem and background, see most conveniently Donald E. Meek, *Caran an t-Saoghail: Wiles of the World* (Edinburgh: Birlinn, 2003), pp. 210–17 and 432–3; also Black, *An Lasair*, pp. 340–51, 518–21.

28. D. Meek, 'Evangelicalism, Ossianism and the Enlightenment: The Many Masks of Dugald Buchanan', in MacLachlan, *Crossing the Highland Line*, pp. 97–112.

29. D. Mac an Tòisich, *Co-Chruinnechadh dh'Òrain Thaghte Ghaelach* (Edinburgh:

John Elder, 1831); Michel Byrne, 'Mairearad Ghriogarach: Súil Thòiseachail air Bana-bhàrd air Dìchuimhne', *SGS* 23 (2007), pp. 85–122.

30. See particularly Black, 'Sharing the Honour'.

31. Scott, 'Poetry and Politics'; T. O. Clancy, 'Mourning Fearchar Ó Maoilchiaráin: Texts, Transmission, and Transformation', in W. McLeod, J. E. Fraser and A. Gunderloch (eds), *Cànan & Cultar/Language and Culture. Rannsachadh na Gàidhlig 3* (Edinburgh: Dunedin Academic Press, 2006), pp. 57–71; Pádraig Ó Macháin, 'Scribal Practice and Textual Survival: The Case of Uilliam Mac Mhurchaidh', *SGS* 22 (2006), pp. 95–122. A sample of his work can be assessed from A. Cameron (ed.), *Reliquiae Celticae*, 2 vols (Inverness: Northern Chronicle, 1892–94), I: pp. 151–66; II: pp. 310–420.

32. There is a copious literature on this material. See, for instance, Meek, 'The Sublime Gael'; J. F. Nagy, *Conversing with Angels and Ancients* (Dublin: Four Courts, 1997). Regarding the essential 'romanticism' of earlier Gaelic literature, the argument here chimes with Meg Bateman's recent 'The Environmentalism of Donnchadh Bàn: Pragmatic or Mythic?', in MacLachlan, *Crossing the Highland Line*, pp. 123–36, at 135: 'I think we are wrong to dismiss all romantic stances in Gaelic as a projection of Lowland and European Romanticism. Gaelic literature can demonstrate the possession of many such features from the earliest times.'

33. Mrs Grant of Laggan, *Poems on Various Subjects* (Edinburgh: J. Muir, 1803), pp. 395–402; and *Essays on the Superstitions of the Highlanders of Scotland*, 2 vols (London, 1811), II: pp. 230–62.

34. Menzies, 'Òran na Comhachaig', see esp. pp. 88–9 where she discusses Grant's rendition of the poem; a modern edition and translation is in W. McLeod and M. Bateman, *Duanaire na Sracaire/Songbook of the Pillagers* (Edinburgh: Birlinn, 2007), pp. 392–405. Pat Menzies is scheduled to produce a new edition for Scottish Gaelic Texts Society.

35. Grant, *Superstitions*, 234; quoted and discussed by Menzies, 'Òran na Comhachaig', p. 88.

Chapter 5 – Wickman

1. Sir Walter Scott, *Waverley*, ed. Claire Lamont (Oxford: Oxford University Press, 1986), pp. 104–5.

2. John Glendening, *The High Road* (New York: St Martin's Press, 1997), p. 174.

3. The Derrida essay referred to is 'Freud and the Scene of Writing', in *Writing and Difference*, trans. Alan Bass (Chicago: University of Chicago Press, 1978), pp. 246–91.

4. Pittock, *Scottish and Irish Romanticism* (Oxford: Oxford University Press, 2008), pp. 192, 190.

5. Trumpener calls Macpherson's *Ossian* an 'echo chamber'. See *Bardic*

Nationalism (Princeton: Princeton University Press, 1997), p. 70. Cf. Edmund Burke, *A Philosophical Enquiry into the Origin of Our Ideas of the Sublime and Beautiful*, ed. James Boulton (London: Blackwell, 1987), pp. 161–77.

6. Dorothy Wordsworth recounts the visit she and William made to Ossian's Hall in terms at once rapt and amused. Before viewing the falls, she and William were 'conducted into a small apartment, where the gardener desired us to look at a painting of the figure of Ossian, which, while he was telling us the story of the young artist who performed the work, disappeared, parting in the middle, flying asunder as if by the touch of magic, and lo! we are at the entrance of a splendid room, which was almost dizzy and alive with waterfalls, that tumbled in all directions [. . .] We both laughed heartily [. . .]': *Recollections of a Tour Made in Scotland* (New Haven: Yale University Press, 1997), pp. 173–4.

7. Lyotard, *The Postmodern Condition*, trans. Geoff Bennington and Brian Massumi (Manchester: Manchester University Press, 1984), p. 78.

8. *The Beautiful, the Sublime, and the Picturesque in Eighteenth-Century British Aesthetic Theory* (Carbondale: Southern Illinois University Press, 1957), p. 186.

9. 'On Picturesque Beauty', in Gilpin, *Three Essays* (London: Printed for R. Blamire, 1792), p. 3.

10. Price, *An Essay on the Picturesque, as Compared with the Sublime and the Beautiful* (London: Printed for J. Robson, 1794), pp. 46, 18, 17.

11. Richard Payne Knight, responding to Price in 1805, insisted further on this point that the picturesque is a quality of art – and criticism – rather than nature: '[T]he great and fundamental error, which prevails throughout [Price's] otherwise able and elegant *Essays on the Picturesque*, is seeking for distinctions in external objects, which only exist in the modes and habits of viewing and considering them.' Knight thus locates in the mind – in associationism – what Price (through Burke) locates in objects. Price 'unfortunately suffered himself to be misled by the brilliant, but absurd and superficial theories of' Burke's *Inquiry*. See *An Analytical Inquiry into the Principles of Taste* (London: Printed by Luke Hansard, 1805), p. 196.

12. Tobias Smollett, *Humphry Clinker*, ed. Shaun Regan (London: Penguin, 2008), pp. 276–7.

13. *Antiquities and Scenery of the North of Scotland* (London, 1780), p. 3.

14. *Scottish Scenery: Or, Sketches in Verse, Descriptive of Scenes Chiefly in the Highlands of Scotland* (London: Printed for T. Cadell, 1803), p. 44.

15. 'A Solitary Reaper', in *William Wordsworth: The Poems*, ed. John Hayden, 2 vols (London: Penguin, 1977), I: 659.

16. *Observations on a Tour through the Highlands* (London: T. Cadell, 1800), 2 vols, I: pp. 10–11, 68.

17. *Letters on a Tour through Various Parts of Scotland, in the Year 1792* (London: T. Cadell, 1794), pp. 228, 255, 257–8.

18. On Wilkie, see Nicholas Tromans, *David Wilkie* (Edinburgh: Edinburgh University Press, 2007).

19. See especially Ann Bermingham, *Landscape and Ideology* (Berkeley: The University of California Press, 1986), pp. 65–6; cf. John Barrell, *English Literature in History, 1730–80* (London: Hutchinson, 1983).

20. Peter Womack, *Improvement and Romance* (Basingstoke: Macmillan, 1989), pp. 68–9, 62.

21. *Burt's Letters from the North of Scotland*, ed. Andrew Simmons (Edinburgh: Birlinn, 1998), p. 157.

22. Karl Marx, *Capital*, trans. Ben Fowkes, 3 vols (London: Penguin, 1976), I: p. 890.

23. See Eric Richards, *The Highland Clearances* (Edinburgh: Birlinn, 2000), esp. chapters 8–11.

24. See Wickman, *The Ruins of Experience* (Philadelphia: University of Pennsylvania Press, 2007), chapters 3 and 4.

25. Burke, *A Philosophical Enquiry*, p. 36. See Žižek, *The Sublime Object of Ideology* (London: Verso, 1989).

26. Pittock, *Scottish and Irish Romanticism*, p. 190.

27. Scott, 'Romance', in *Miscellaneous Works of Sir Walter Scott*, 3 vols (Edinburgh: Robert Caddell, 1850), I: 560; Ian Duncan, *Modern Romance and Transformations of the Novel* (Cambridge: Cambridge University Press, 1992), p. 2.

28. On the subtle form of this engagement in Macintyre's work in particular, see my article 'Gaelic Poetry's Province of Stone: Iain Crichton Smith and the Hebridean Echoes of Paul de Man's Late Work', *SSR* 6.2 (2005), pp. 99–112.

29. On the concept of the imagination in the eighteenth century see Dennis Todd, *Imagining Monsters* (Chicago: University of Chicago Press, 1995).

30. Johnson, *A Dictionary of the English Language*, 3rd edn, 2 vols (London: Printed for A. Millar, 1766), I: no pagination.

31. David Hume, *An Enquiry concerning Human Understanding*, ed. Antony Flew (La Salle, IL: Open Court, 1988), p. 64.

32. James M'Nayr, *A Guide from Glasgow to Some of the Most Remarkable Scenes in the Highlands of Scotland, and to the Falls of Clyde* (Glasgow: Printed in the Courier Office, 1797), pp. 242–3.

33. Samuel Johnson, *A Journey to the Western Islands of Scotland*, ed. Peter Levi (New York: Penguin, 1984), p. 73.

34. See Malcolm Andrews, *The Search for the Picturesque* (Aldershot: Scolar, 1989), p. 3.

35. Ibid., pp. 200, 206

36. *Observations Made during a Tour through Parts of England, Scotland, and Wales* (London: printed for T. Becket, 1780), pp. 4–6.

37. The reference here is to Hanway, *A Journey to the Highlands of Scotland* (London: Fielding and Walker, 1776); Schaw, *Journal of a Lady of Quality*, ed. Evangeline Walker Andrews, in collaboration with Charles McLean Andrews (Salem: Higginson, 1997); Murray, *A Companion and Useful Guide to the Beauties of Scotland* (London: George Nicol, 1799); and Grant, *Essays on the Superstitions of the Highlanders of Scotland* (London: Longman, 1811).

38. Hussey, *The Picturesque* (Hamden: Archon, 1927), pp. 4–5.

39. George Lukács, *The Historical Novel*, trans. Hannah and Stanley Mitchell (London: Merlin Press, 1962), pp. 31, 33.

40. Tom Nairn, *The Break-Up of Britain* (London: New Left Books, 1981), pp. 114, 115, 116.

41. Jerome McGann, 'Walter Scott's Romantic Postmodernity', in Davis, Duncan and Sorensen (eds), *Scotland and the Borders of Romanticism* (Cambridge: Cambridge University Press, 2004), pp. 113–29.

42. Davis et al., *Scotland and the Borders of Romanticism*, p. 3.

Chapter 6 – Duncan

1. For a full account see chapter 1, 'Edinburgh: Capital of the Nineteenth Century', in Duncan, *Scott's Shadow* (Princeton: Princeton University Press, 2007), pp. 3–45.

2. 'On the Proposed National Monument at Edinburgh', *Blackwood's Edinburgh Magazine* V (July 1819), p. 385.

3. Anthony Jarrells, 'Provincializing Enlightenment: Edinburgh Historicism and the Blackwoodian Regional Tale', *Studies in Romanticism* 48.2 (2009), pp. 257–77.

4. Mark Salber Phillips, *Society and Sentiment* (Princeton: Princeton University Press, 2000), pp. 310, 320; see also Pittock, 'Historiography', in *The Cambridge Companion to the Scottish Enlightenment*, ed. Alexander Broadie (Cambridge: Cambridge University Press, 2003), pp. 258–79.

5. Henry Cockburn, *Memorials of His Time*, ed. Karl Miller (Chicago: Chicago University Press, 1974), pp. 25–6.

6. Robert Chambers, *Traditions of Edinburgh*, 2 vols (Edinburgh, 1825), I: p. 1.

7. Chambers, *Traditions*, II: pp. 239–40.

8. Sir Walter Scott, *The Heart of Mid-Lothian*, ed. Tony Inglis (Harmondsworth: Penguin, 1994), pp. 32–3.

9. 'Auld Reikie', in *The Poems of Robert Fergusson*, ed. Matthew P. McDiarmid, 2 vols, (Edinburgh: Scottish Text Society, 1954–6), II: p. 119.

10. *Poems of Fergusson*, II: p. 117.

11. Pittock, *Scottish and Irish Romanticism* (Oxford: Oxford University Press, 2008), p. 121.

12. Ibid., pp. 47–8, also pp. 32–4.

13. See James Chandler and Kevin Gilmartin (eds), *Romantic Metropolis* (Cambridge: Cambridge University Press, 2004).
14. Tom Nairn, *The Break-Up of Britain* (London: New Left Books, 1981), pp. 114–18.
15. Robert Burns, *Poems and Songs*, ed. James Kinsley (Oxford: Clarendon, 1970), p. 68.
16. See Leith Davis, 'At "Sang About": Robert Burns, Music and the Scottish Challenge to British Culture', in Davis, Duncan and Sorensen (eds), *Scotland and the Borders of Romanticism* (Cambridge: Cambridge University Press, 2004), pp. 195–6.
17. See my discussion in Duncan, *Modern Romance and Transformations of the Novel* (Cambridge: Cambridge University Press, 1992), pp. 113–35.
18. See Gillian Hughes' recent biography, *James Hogg* (Edinburgh: Edinburgh University Press, 2007) and her edition of *The Collected Letters of James Hogg*, 3 vols (Edinburgh: Edinburgh University Press, 2005–8).
19. James Hogg, *The Private Memoirs and Confessions of a Justified Sinner*, ed. Ian Duncan (Oxford: Oxford University Press, 2010), p. 33.

Chapter 7 – Benchimol

1. See Duncan, *Scott's Shadow* (Princeton: Princeton University Press, 2007); Pittock, *Scottish and Irish Romanticism* (Oxford: Oxford University Press, 2008); and Stafford, 'Scottish Romanticism and Scotland in Romanticism', in Michael Ferber (ed.), *A Companion to European Romanticism* (Oxford: Blackwell, 2005), pp. 49–66.
2. Duncan, *Scott's Shadow*, pp. 3–45; Pittock, *Scottish and Irish Romanticism*, pp. 2, 10.
3. See Marilyn Butler, 'Culture's Medium: The Role of the Review', in Stuart Curran (ed.), *The Cambridge Companion to British Romanticism* (Cambridge: Cambridge University Press, 1993), pp. 130, 131.
4. Fiona Stafford, 'The *Edinburgh Review* and the Representation of Scotland', in Massimiliano Demata and Duncan Wu (eds), *British Romanticism and the Edinburgh Review* (Basingstoke: Palgrave-Macmillan, 2002), p. 40.
5. See Roger Emerson, 'The Contexts of the Scottish Enlightenment', in Alexander Broadie (ed.), *The Cambridge Companion to the Scottish Enlightenment* (Cambridge: Cambridge University Press, 2003), pp. 20–4.
6. Broadie, *Cambridge Companion*, p. 5
7. Alexander Broadie, *The Scottish Enlightenment* (Edinburgh: Birlinn, 2001), p. 8.
8. See Nicholas Phillipson, 'The Scottish Enlightenment', in Roy Porter and Mikulas Teich (eds), *The Enlightenment in National Context* (Cambridge: Cambridge University Press, 1981), pp. 19–40. Anand Chitnis has developed another historical view of the Scottish Enlightenment – one emphasising

institutional reform in Scotland as a continuous process that predated Union. See Anand Chitnis, 'The Eighteenth-Century Scottish Intellectual Inquiry: Context and Continuities versus Civic Virtue', in Jennifer J. Carter and Joan H. Pittock (eds), *Aberdeen and the Enlightenment* (Aberdeen: Aberdeen University Press, 1987), p. 78.

9. Phillipson, 'Scottish Enlightenment', p. 22.
10. See Jürgen Habermas, *The Structural Transformation of the Public Sphere*, trans. Thomas Burger with the assistance of Frederick Lawrence (Cambridge: Polity, [1962] 1989).
11. Phillipson, 'Scottish Enlightenment', p. 27.
12. Ibid., p. 26.
13. John Dwyer, 'Introduction – "A Peculiar Blessing": Social Converse in Scotland from Hutcheson to Burns', in John Dwyer and Richard B. Sher (eds), *Sociability and Society in Eighteenth-Century Scotland* (Edinburgh: Mercat, 1993), p. 6.
14. See D. D. McElroy, *Scotland's Age of Improvement* (Pullman: Washington State University Press, 1969), pp. 14–15.
15. Phillipson, 'Scottish Enlightenment', p. 27.
16. See Pittock, 'Allan Ramsay and the Decolonisation of Genre', *RES* 58 (2007), p. 329.
17. Pittock, 'Allan Ramsay', pp. 328–9.
18. See Hamish Mathison, 'Robert Hepburn and the Edinburgh *Tatler*: A Study in an Early British Periodical', *Media History* 11 (2005), p. 47.
19. See Richard B. Sher, *Church and University in the Scottish Enlightenment* (Princeton: Princeton University Press, 1985).
20. See 'Preface', *The Scots Magazine* 1 (1739).
21. Sher, *Church and University*, p. 14.
22. Sher, *Church and University*, pp. 24–5.
23. Sher, *Church and University*, pp. 32, 52–3; see also 'Reasons of Dissent from the Judgment and Resolution of the Commission, March 11. 1752, resolving to inflict no censure on the presbytery of Dunfermline for their disobedience in relation to the settlement of Inverkeithing', *The Scots Magazine* 14 (1752), pp. 191–7.
24. Sher, *Church and University*, pp. 114–15.
25. Ibid., p. 139.
26. Ibid., p. 147.
27. See McElroy, *Scotland's Age of Improvement*, pp. 40–67; see also 'Minutes of the Select Society, 1754–63', National Library of Scotland, Manuscript Adv. MS. 23.1.1, p. 33; 'Minutes of the College Literary Society, Glasgow University, 1790–99 (7 November 1794–26 April 1800)', Glasgow University Library, Manuscript MS. Gen. 4; and Lewis H. Ulman (ed.), 'Minutes of the Aberdeen Philosophical Society, 1758–1773', *Aberdeen University Studies* 158 (Aberdeen: Aberdeen University Press, 1990).

28. See Anand Chitnis, *The Scottish Enlightenment* (London: Croom Helm, 1976), pp. 199–201.

29. Habermas, *Structural Transformation*, p. 4.

30. McElroy, *Scotland's Age of Improvement*, pp. 48–9.

31. Alexander Carlyle, *Anecdotes and Characters of the Times*, ed. James Kinsley (London: Oxford University Press, 1973), pp. 149–50.

32. McElroy, *Scotland's Age of Improvement*, pp. 49, 50.

33. 'Preface', *ER* 1 (1755), p. i.

34. *ER*, p. ii.

35. See Pittock, 'Historiography', in *The Cambridge Companion to the Scottish Enlightenment*, p. 260.

36. *ER*, p. iii.

37. Ibid.

38. See '[William Robertson], 'History of Peter the Great', *ER* 1 (1755), pp. 1–9; [Hugh Blair], 'Hutcheson's Moral Philosophy', *ER* 1 (1755), pp. 9–23; [John Jardine], 'Mr. Eben. Erskine's Sermons', *ER* 1 (1755), pp. 32–9; [Alexander Wedderburn], 'Decisions of the Court of Session', *ER* 1 (1755), pp. 48–50; [Adam Smith], 'Johnson's Dictionary', *ER* 1 (1755), pp. 61–73.

39. See Richard B. Sher, *The Enlightenment and the Book* (Chicago: University of Chicago Press, 2006), p. 66.

40. Chitnis, *Scottish Enlightenment*, p. 201.

41. See McElroy, *Scotland's Age of Improvement*, p. 111; and Chitnis, *The Scottish Enlightenment*, p. 196.

42. See Chitnis, *The Scottish Enlightenment and Early Victorian English Society* (London: Croom Helm, 1986), p. 59.

43. See 'List of Questions for the Speculative Society' in Minute Book – Speculative Society, 21 November – 15 April 1784–5 (6?), Glasgow University Library, Manuscript MS. Gen. 723.

44. See [Francis Jeffrey], '*De l'Influence attribuée aux Philosophes, aux Francs-Maçons, et aux Illuminés, sur la Revolution de France. Par. J. J. Mounier*', *ER* 1 (1802), pp. 1–18.

45. See George Pottinger, *Heirs of the Enlightenment* (Edinburgh: Scottish Academic Press, 1992), p. 95.

46. Chitnis, *Scottish Enlightenment and Early Victorian English Society*, p. 62.

47. For an illuminating discussion of the relationship between Stewart's innovative pedagogy and the distinctive intellectual style of the second *Edinburgh Review*, see Donald Winch, 'The System of the North: Dugald Stewart and his Pupils', in Stefan Collini, John Burrow and Donald Winch, *That Noble Science of Politics* (Cambridge: Cambridge University Press, 1983), pp. 23–61.

48. See Henry Cockburn, *Memorials of His Time* (Edinburgh: Adam and Charles Black, 1856), pp. 25–6.

49. Chitnis, *Scottish Enlightenment*, p. 176.

50. Cockburn, *Memorials of his Time*, p. 27.

51. Duncan, *Scott's Shadow*, pp. 21, 23.

52. Ibid., p. 24.

53. Ibid., p. 25.

54. See John Stark, *Picture of Edinburgh* (Edinburgh, 1819), pp. 233, 221, quoted in Sher, *The Enlightenment and the Book*, p. 431.

55. Ibid., p. 26.

56. Butler, 'Culture's Medium', p. 131.

57. 'Advertisement', *ER* 1 (1802).

Chapter 8 – Monnickendam

1. G. Gregory Smith, *Scottish Literature, Character and Influence* (London: Macmillan, 1919), p. 4.

2. Elizabeth Hamilton, *The Cottagers of Glenburnie* (London and Edinburgh: Chambers, [1808]1859), p. i.

3. Pittock, *Scottish and Irish Romanticism* (Oxford: Oxford University Press, 2008), p. 63.

4. Jane Porter, *The Scottish Chiefs*, 3 vols (London: Bentley, [1810] 1839), I: p. 183.

5. Mary Brunton, *Self-Control* (Lakewood, CO: Revive Publishing, [1811] 1999), p. 338.

6. Mary Brunton, *Discipline* (London: Bentley, [1810] 1849), p. 476.

7. Mary Brunton, *Emmeline* (Edinburgh: Manners and Miller, 1819), p. 79.

8. John A. Doyle, *Memoir and Correspondence of Susan Ferrier, 1782–1854* (London: 1897), p. 47.

9. Vineta Colby, *Yesterday's Woman* (Princeton: Princeton University Press, 1974), p. 102.

10. Marian Lilley Warren, 'Life and Works of Susan Edmonstone Ferrier', unpublished PhD thesis, Cornell University, 1942, p. 222.

11. George Saintsbury, 'Miss Ferrier,' in *The Collected Essays and Papers of George Saintsbury 1875–1920* (London and Toronto: J M Dent, 1923), vol. 1, pp. 302–29.

12. Susan Ferrier, *Marriage*, ed. Herbert Foltinek (Oxford: Oxford University Press, [1818] 1997), p. 237.

13. Saintsbury, 'Miss Ferrier', pp. 314, 329.

14. Mrs Oliphant, *The Literary History of England in the End of the Eighteenth and Beginning of the Nineteenth Century*, 3 vols (London: Macmillan, 1882), III: pp. 202, 247.

15. Mary Cullinan, *Susan Ferrier* (Boston: Twayne Publishers, 1984), p. 24.

16. Christian Isobel Johnstone, *Clan-Albin*, ed. Andrew Monnickendam (Glasgow: Association for Scottish Literary Studies, [1815] 2003), p. 460.

17. Pittock, *Scottish and Irish Romanticism*, p. 185.

Chapter 9 – Gribben

1. Tom Paulin, *The Day-Star of Liberty* (London: Faber and Faber, 1998). See also Robert M. Ryan, *The Romantic Reformation* (Cambridge: Cambridge University Press, 1997); Morton D. Paley, *Apocalypse and Millennium in English Romantic Poetry* (Oxford: Clarendon, 1999); Ian Balfour, *The Rhetoric of Romantic Prophecy* (Stanford: Stanford University Press, 2002).

2. See the pioneering work of Gerard Carruthers and Alan Rawes (eds), *English Romanticism and the Celtic World* (Cambridge: Cambridge University Press, 2003) and Murray Pittock, *Scottish and Irish Romanticism* (Oxford: Oxford University Press, 2008).

3. See, for Burns, J. Walter McGinty, *Robert Burns and Religion* (Aldershot: Ashgate, 2003); Liam McIlvanney, *Burns the Radical* (East Linton: Tuckwell, 2002); and relevant chapters in Frank Ferguson and Andrew R. Holmes (eds), *Revising Robert Burns and Ulster* (Dublin: Four Courts, 2009); and, for Hogg, Crawford Gribben, 'James Hogg, Scottish Calvinism and Literary Theory', *SSR* 5.2 (2004), pp. 9–26 and 'The *Justified Sinner* and Presbyterian Demonology', *SHW* 17 (2006), pp. 127–31; Ismael Velasco, 'Paradoxical Readings: Reason, Religion and Tradition in James Hogg's *Private Memoirs and Confessions of a Justified Sinner*', *SSR* 7.1 (2006), pp. 38–52; H. B. de Groot, 'The Labourer and Literary Tradition: James Hogg's Early Reading and its Impact on Him as a Writer', in Sharon Alker and Holly Faith Nelson (eds), *James Hogg and the Literary Marketplace* (Aldershot: Ashgate, 2009), pp. 81–92.

4. On Scottish Christianity's general history during the late eighteenth and early nineteenth centuries, see A. L. Drummond and James Bulloch, *The Scottish Church 1688–1843* (Edinburgh: St Andrew Press, 1973) and relevant chapters in Stewart J. Brown and George Newlands (eds), *Scottish Christianity in the Modern World* (Edinburgh: T. and T. Clark, 2000) and Nigel M. de S. Cameron (ed.), *Dictionary of Scottish Church History and Theology* (Edinburgh: T. & T. Clark, 1993) [hereafter *DSCHT*].

5. Marilyn J. Westerkamp, *Triumph of the Laity* (New York: Oxford University Press, 1988).

6. Matthew Hutchison, *The Reformed Presbyterian Church in Scotland* (Paisley: J. and R. Parlane, 1893). For more recent discussion of the Reformed Presbyterian Church of Scotland's early history, see Gordon J. Keddie, 'The Reformed Presbyterian Church of Scotland and the Disruption of 1863: I. Disruption and Recovery', *Scottish Bulletin of Evangelical Theology* 11.1 (1993), pp. 31–49.

7. *DSCHT*, s.v.

8. Kenneth B. E. Roxburgh, *Thomas Gillespie and the Origins of the Relief Church in 18th Century Scotland* (Bern: Peter Lang, 1999).

9. G. B. Burnet, *The Story of Quakerism in Scotland, 1650–1850* (Cambridge:

James Clarke, 1952); Paul Burton, *A Social History of Quakers in Scotland, 1800–2000* (Lewiston, NY: Edwin Mellen, 2007).

10. D. W. Lovegrove, 'Pope Haldane, Bishop Ewing and the Troubled Birth of Scottish Independency', *Records of the Scottish Church History Society* 29 (1999), pp. 23–38; Deryck Lovegrove, 'The Mirage of Authenticity: Scottish Independents and the Reconstruction of a New Testament Order of Worship, 1799–1808', in R. N. Swanson (ed.), *Continuity and Change in Christian Worship* (Woodbridge: Boydell Press, 1999), pp. 261–74.

11. Neil Dickson, *Brethren in Scotland, 1838–2000* (Carlisle: Paternoster, 2002).

12. John Howard Smith, *The Perfect Rule of the Christian Religion* (Albany, NY: SUNY Press, 2009).

13. Columba Graham Flegg, *Gathered under Apostles* (Oxford: Clarendon, 1992).

14. *DSCHT*, s.v.; *Peter F. Anson, Underground Catholicism in Scotland, 1622–1878* (Montrose: Standard Press, 1970); S. Karly Kehoe, 'Irish Migrants and the Recruitment of Catholic Sisters in Glasgow, 1847–1878', in Frank Ferguson and James McConnel (eds), *Ireland and Scotland in the Nineteenth Century* (Dublin: Four Courts, 2009), pp. 35–47; Clotilde Prunier, '"Aliens and Outlaws rather than Subjects and Citizens"? (The Image and Identity of) Catholics in Eighteenth-Century Scotland', *SSR* 1.1 (2000), pp. 39–46.

15. Abel Phillips, *A History of the Origins of the First Jewish Community in Scotland: Edinburgh, 1816* (Edinburgh: John Donald, 1979). While the history of atheism is notoriously difficult to write, religious scepticism was given substantial assistance by the writings of David Hume. The history of Scottish folk religion has still to be prepared.

16. Deryck Lovegrove, '"A Set of Men whose Proceedings Threaten No Small Disorder": The Society for Propagating the Gospel at Home, 1798–1808', *Scottish Historical Review* 79.1 (2000), p. 61.

17. See, for example, Crawford Gribben, 'The Literary Culture of the Scottish Reformation', *RES* 57.228 (2006), pp. 64–82 and chapters in Crawford Gribben and David G. Mullan (eds), *Literature and the Scottish Reformation* (Aldershot: Ashgate, 2009).

18. Bernard M. G. Reardon, *Religion in the Age of Romanticism* (Cambridge: Cambridge University Press, 1985), p. 2.

19. See Kenneth J. Stewart, *Restoring the Reformation* (Milton Keynes: Paternoster, 2006).

20. Donald E. Meek, 'Evangelicalism, Ossianism and the Enlightenment: The Many Masks of Dugald Buchanan', in Christopher MacLachlan (ed.), *Crossing the Highland Line* (Glasgow: ASLS, 2009), pp. 97–112.

21. 'The Holy Fair', ll. 37–40, in *The Canongate Burns*, ed. Andrew Noble and Patrick Scott Hogg (Edinburgh: Canongate, 2001), p. 29.

22. Westerkamp, *Triumph of the Laity*.

23. D. W. Bebbington, *Evangelicalism in Modern Britain* (London: Unwin Hyman, 1989).

24. Richard B. Sher, *Church and University in the Scottish Enlightenment* (Princeton: Princeton University Press, 1985) and I. D. L. Clark, 'From Protest to Reaction: The Moderate Regime in the Church of Scotland, 1752 – 1805', in N. T. Phillipson and Rosalind Mitchison (eds), *Scotland in the Age of Improvement* (Edinburgh: Edinburgh University Press, 1996), pp. 200–24.

25. See E. J. Cowan, 'Calvinism and the Survival of Folk: Or, "Deil Stick Da Minister"', in E. J. Cowan (ed.), *The People's Past* (Edinburgh: Polygon, 1980), pp. 32–57.

26. James Maxwell, *Animadversions on the Poets and Poetasters of the Present Age* (1788), p. 20. For a survey of the millennial tradition, see Crawford Gribben, *Evangelical Millennialism in the Trans-Atlantic World, 1500–2000* (Basingstoke: Palgrave, 2011).

27. Eric Parisot, 'Disinterring *The Grave*: Religious Authority, Poetic Autonomy and Robert Blair's Fideist Poetics', *SSR* 8.2 (2007), pp. 24–35.

28. Bebbington, *Evangelicalism in Modern Britain*, p. 131.

29. See, especially, Mark Hopkins, *Nonconformity's Romantic Generation* (Milton Keynes: Paternoster, 2004).

30. John Galt, *Annals of the Parish, The Ayrshire Legatees, The Provost*, ed. Ian Campbell (Edinburgh: The Saltire Society, 2002), p. 74.

31. Peter Gray, 'Thomas Chalmers and Irish Poverty', in Ferguson and McConnel, *Ireland and Scotland*, pp. 93–107.

32. William Reid, *Plymouth Brethrenism Unveiled and Refuted* (Edinburgh, 1875), p. 296.

33. A. L. Drummond, *Edward Irving and his Circle* (London: J. Clarke, 1937), p. 277.

34. David Hempton, *Evangelical Disenchantment* (New Haven, CT: Yale University Press, 2008), pp. 19–40.

35. David Brown, *Christ's Second Coming* (Edinburgh: Johnstone and Hunter, 1846), p. 3.

36. The influence of Romanticism continued to shape the formation of a later Evangelicalism; see Crawford Gribben, '"The Worst Sect a Christian Man can Meet": Opposition to the Plymouth Brethren in Ireland and Scotland, 1859–1900', *SSR* 3.2 (2002), pp. 34–53; Donald E. Meek, 'The Literature of Religious Revival and Disruption', in *EHSL*, ed. Susan Manning, vol. 2 (Edinburgh: Edinburgh University Press, 2007), pp. 360–70.

37. Reardon, *Religion in the Age of Romanticism*, pp. vii–viii.

38. Thomas McCrie, Review of *Tales of My Landlord* (1817), in Thomas McCrie, *Miscallaneous Writings*, ed. Thomas McCrie, jr (Edinburgh: John Johnstone, 1841), p. 251.

39. Ibid., p. 269.

40. John Galt, 'The Covenanter', *The Steamboat* (1822), p. 318; John Galt, *Ringan Gilhaize* (1823), in D. S. Meldrum and William Roughead (eds), *The Works of John Galt*, 10 vols (Edinburgh: John Grant, 1936), II: p. 178.

41. James Hogg, *The Memoirs and Confessions of a Justified Sinner* (1824; reprinted Oxford: Oxford University Press, 1969), p. 93.

42. Edward Irving, 'The Spiritual Economy of Scotland' (1826), in G. Carlyle (ed.), *The Collected Writings of Edward Irving*, 5 vols (London: Alexander Strahan, 1864–5), III: p. 476.

43. *The Covenanter* 1.1 (December 1830 [wrongly printed 1831]), p. 1. This tradition continued into the later nineteenth century, with Robert Pollok's *The Persecuted Family* (1846) and R. M. Ballantyne's *Hunted and Harried* (1892), and into the twentieth century, in such texts as John Buchan's *Salute to Adventurers* (1915) (in which John Gib, leader of the mystical antinomian group the Sweet Singers, is transplanted to Virginia and almost succeeds in leading a massive native invasion of the Tidewater communities). See, more recently, James Robertson's *The Fanatic* (2000) and his rewriting of Hogg's *The Memoirs and Confessions of a Justified Sinner* in *The Testament of Gideon Mack* (2006).

Chapter 10 – Leask

1. *The Poetry of Robert Burns*, ed. W. E. Henley and T. F. Henderson, 4 vols (London: Blackwood, 1896), I: p. x; David Daiches, *Robert Burns* (London: G. Bell and Sons, 1952), p. 363.

2. Pittock, *Scottish and Irish Romanticism* (Oxford: Oxford University Press, 2008), p. 9. See also Raymond Bentman, 'Robert Burns's Declining Fame', *Studies in Romanticism*, 11.3 (1972), pp. 206–24.

3. Pittock, 'Robert Burns and British Poetry', The Chatterton Lecture on Poetry 2002, *Proceedings of the British Academy* 121 (2003), p. 192.

4. Carol McGuirk, *Robert Burns and the Sentimental Era* (Athens: University of Georgia Press, 1985), p. xxvi.

5. Editors' introduction to *Scotland and the Borders of Romanticism*, ed. Davis, Duncan and Sorensen (Cambridge: Cambridge University Press, 2004), p. 3.

6. Leask, *Robert Burns and Pastoral* (Oxford: Oxford University Press, 2010).

7. Robert Crawford claims Burns as 'the most brilliantly distinguished eighteenth-century example of a British poet', *Devolving English Literature*, 2nd edn (Edinburgh: Edinburgh University Press, 2000), p. 106.

8. But see also Stafford, 'Burns and Romantic Writing', in Gerald Carruthers (ed.), *The Edinburgh Companion to Robert Burns* (Edinburgh: Edinburgh University Press, 2009), pp. 97–109.

9. Donald Low (ed.), *Robert Burns*, the Critical Heritage (London: Routledge, 1974), p. 17. Mackenzie's review was contested by John Logan who insisted on Burns' literary artfulness and sophistication.

10. Low, *Burns*, p. 18.

11. Ibid., p. 91.

12. Duncan Wu, *Wordsworth's Reading, 1800–1815* (Cambridge: Cambridge University Press, 1995), p. 254.
13. Low, *Burns*, p. 162.
14. Russell Noyes, 'Wordsworth and Burns', *PMLA* lix (1944), pp. 813–32; Mary Jacobus, *Tradition and Experiment in Lyrical Ballads* (Oxford: Clarendon, 1976); Leith Davis, *Acts of Union* (Stanford: Stanford University Press, 1998), chapter 5; Andrew Noble, 'Wordsworth and Burns', in Carol McGuirk (ed.), *Critical Essays on Robert Burns* (New York: G. K. Hall, 1998), pp. 49–62.
15. Deborah Kennedy, *Helen Maria Williams and the Age of Revolutions* (Lewisberg and London: Bucknell University Press, 2002), p. 39.
16. *The Letters of Robert Burns*, ed. J. de Lancey Ferguson and Ross Roy, 2 vols (Oxford: Oxford University Press, 1985) I: 427–31; see my 'Burns and the Poetics of Abolition', in Carruthers (ed.), *The Edinburgh Companion to Robert Burns*, pp. 52–3.
17. Editors' Introduction, Patrick Scott Hogg and Andrew Noble (eds), *The Canongate Burns* (Edinburgh: Canongate, 2001), p. lxxxvii; Thomas Crawford, *Burns*, 3rd edn (Edinburgh: Canongate, 1994), p. 145.
18. Mary-Ann Constantine, *The Truth against the World* (Cardiff: University of Wales, 2007).
19. Liam McIlvanney, *Burns the Radical* (East Linton: Tuckwell Press, 2002), p. 228.
20. McIlvanney, *Burns*, pp. 235–39; see also John Gray, 'Burns and his Visitors from Ulster: From Adulation to Discord', *SSL* xxxiii–xxxiv (2004), pp. 320–34.
21. Owen Dudley Edwards, 'Burns and Ireland', in Johnny Rodger and Gerard Carruthers (eds), *Fickle Man* (Dingwall: Sandstone Press, 2009), p. 274.
22. Ibid., pp. 274–5. In 1809, Francis Jeffrey patronisingly remarked that 'Burns is certainly by far the greatest of our poetical prodigies – from Stephen Duck to Thomas Dermody. They are forgotten already; or only remembered for derision. But the name of Burns, if we are not mistaken, has not yet 'gathered all its fame' (Low, *Burns*, p. 178).
23. See Ronan Kelly, *Bard of Erin* (London: Penguin, 2008), pp. 74–5 and generally.
24. For modern rehabilitation, see Matthew Campbell, 'Thomas Moore's Wild Song: The 1821 *Irish Melodies*', *Bullan: An Irish Studies Journal* 4.2 (1999), pp. 83–103; Terry Eagleton, *Heathcliff and the Great Hunger* (London: 1995), p. 231; Leith Davis, *Music, Postcolonialism and Gender* (Notre Dame, IN: University of Notre Dame Press, 2005), p. 161.
25. *Letters of Thomas Moore*, ed. Wilfred S. Dowden, 2 vols (London: Clarendon, 1964), I: p. 143.
26. Owen Dudley Edwards discusses Burns' influence on other nineteenth-century writers like William Carleton, the 'Young Ireland' journalists Thomas Davis and Charles Duffy; and in a different political context, Samuel Ferguson (1810–1865), drawing attention to the last's important essay on

Burns in the *Dublin University Magazine*, Jan/March 1845. ('Burns and
Ireland', pp. 294–9). The two traditions of Irish Burns appreciation converged in the poetry of W. B. Yeats.

27. Low, *Burns*, pp. 99–107, 117–30.
28. *Liverpool Testimonials to the Departed Genius of Robert Burns*, *The Scottish Bard*
    (Liverpool: Merritt and Wright, 1800).
29. *Coleridge: Poetical Works*, ed. J. C. C. Mays, 6 vols (Princeton: Princeton
    University Press, 2001), I: p. 271, ll. 37–24.
30. Information on sales from the Currie/Burns Correspondence, Mitchell
    Library, Glasgow MS 10/C -196 C. Envelope 2, letters from Cadell and Davis
    to Currie. The first edition evidently sold out by August 1800. See also James
    Mackay, *Burns* (Edinburgh: Mainstream, 1992), p. 661.
31. William St Clair, *The Reading Nation in the Romantic Period* (Cambridge:
    Cambridge University Press, 2004), pp. 661, 633.
32. Low, *Burns*, p. 197.
33. But see my ' "The Shadow Line": James Currie's "Life of Burns" and British
    Romanticism', in Claire Lamont and Michael Rossington (eds), *Romanticism's
    Debatable Lands* (Basingstoke: Palgrave Macmillan, 2007), pp. 64–79.
34. James Currie, *The Works of Robert Burns*, 4 vols (Liverpool, London and
    Edinburgh, 1800), 1: pp. 1–2.
35. *Liverpool Testimonials*, p. 15.
36. Currie, *Burns* I: p. 281.
37. Low, *Burns*, p. 112.
38. Ibid., p. 108. On the medical theory underlying Currie's diagnosis, see my
    'Robert Burns and the Stimulant Regime', in Rodger and Carruthers (eds),
    Fickle Man, pp. 135–62.
39. *Letters of Robert Bloomfield and his Circle*, ed. Tim Fulford and Lynda Pratt;
    assoc. editor John Goodridge, http://romantics.arhu.umd.edu/editions/
    Bloomfield Letters/HTML. Letter 35, to William Vaughan, 22 July 1800;
    Letter 75, to Earl of Buchan, 19 January 1802.
40. Wordsworth, *Letter to a Friend of Robert Burns* (1816), in *Wordsworth's Selected
    Prose*, ed. John Hayden (Harmondsworth: Penguin 1988), p. 119.
41. Jane Austen, *Northanger Abbey, Lady Susan, The Watsons, and Sanditon*, ed.
    John Davie, with intro. by Terry Castle (Oxford: Oxford University Press,
    1990), p. 352.
42. Stafford, 'Burns and Romantic Writing', in Carruthers (ed.), *Edinburgh
    Companion to Burns*, p. 97.
43. Currie, *Burns*, I: p. 2.
44. Tom Nairn, *The Break-Up of Britain* (London: New Left Books, 1981), p. 145.
45. Echoed by Jeffrey in his 1809 complaint about 'that perpetual boast of his
    independence, which is obtruded upon the reader of Burns in almost every
    page of his writings' (Low, *Burns*, p. 184).
46. Currie, *Burns*, I: p. 31.

47. *Wordsworth: The Poems*, ed. John O. Hayden, 3 vols (Harmondsworth: Penguin, 1977), I: p. 588, ll. 33–6.

48. Daniel Sanjiv Roberts, 'Literature, Medical Science and Politics, 1795–1800: *Lyrical Ballads* and Currie's *Works of Robert Burns*', in C. C.Barfoot, 'A *Natural Delineation of the Human Passions*' (Amsterdam: Rodopi, 2003), pp. 115–28.

49. Wordsworth and Coleridge, *Lyrical Ballads*, ed. R. L. Brett and A. R. Jones, 2nd edn (London and New York: Routledge, 1991), pp. 7, 245, 241.

50. Davis, *Acts of Union* (Stanford: Stanford University Press, 1998), p. 129.

51. Low, *Burns*, p. 182.

52. Ibid., pp. 186, 195.

53. Davis, *Acts of Union*, pp. 135–41.

54. Alexander Peterkin, *A Review of the Life of Robert Burns* (Edinburgh, 1815). Scott's criticism of Burns appeared in an anonymous review in the *Quarterly* in February 1809 (Low, *Burns*, pp. 196–209).

55. Low, *Burns*, p. 284.

56. Mackay, *Burns*, p. 669.

57. Low, *Burns*, pp. 296–7.

58. On the Alloway cottage as a Romantic pilgrimage site, see Nicola Watson, *The Literary Tourist* (Basingstoke: Palgrave Macmillan, 2006), pp. 68–86.

59. The 'flat sonnet' was 'This mortal body of a thousand days'. Keats' allusion in this 11–13 July 1818 journal letter to Reynolds is to *King Lear*, Act V. scene iii, l. 17. See *Keats: The Complete Poems*, ed. Miriam Allott (London and New York: Longman, 1970), pp. 365–6.

60. 'The Study of Poetry', in *Matthew Arnold: Selected Poems and Prose*, ed. Miriam Allott (London: Everyman, 1991), pp. 262–3.

61. See my 'His Hero's Story': *Currie's Burns, Moore's Byron, and the Problem of Romantic Biography*', The Byron Foundation Lecture 2006 (Nottingham: Centre for the Study of Byron and Romanticism, 2007).

62. Pittock, *Scottish and Irish Romanticism*, p. 255.

63. Thomas Moore, *The Life, Letters and Journals of Lord Byron* (1830–1), New and Complete Edition, in 1 vol. (London: John, 1892), p. 8.

64. Moore, *Life*, pp. 214–15.

65. Richard Cronin, *Romantic Victorians* (Basingstoke: Palgrave, 2002), p. 26.

66. Moore, *Life*, p. 645.

67. *Life*, p. 386.

Chapter 11 – McCracken-Flesher

1. Coleridge recalled of the jointly produced *Lyrical Ballads*, 'the excellence aimed at was to consist in the interesting of the affections by the dramatic truth of such emotions as would naturally accomplish such situations, supposing them real' (*Biographia Literaria* (London: J. M. Dent, [1817] 1982), p. 168).

2. William Wordsworth, 'Preface [to *Lyrical Ballads* (1802)]', in *Lyrical Ballads and Related Writings*, ed. William Richey and Daniel Robinson (Boston: Houghton Mifflin, 2002), p. 392.

3. Edgar Johnson, *Sir Walter Scott*, 2 vols (New York: Macmillan, 1970), I: pp. 96, 113–14, 118.

4. Johnson, *Scott*, I: p. 213.

5. Pittock, *Scottish and Irish Romanticism* (Oxford: Oxford University Press, 2008), p. 28.

6. Letter to Lady Louisa Stuart, 31 January 1817, quoted in M. H. Abrams, *The Mirror and the Lamp* (Oxford: Oxford University Press, [1953] 1971), p. 214.

7. Scott, 'Essay on the Drama' (1819), quoted in Abrams, *Mirror*, p. 49.

8. Johnson, *Scott*, I: pp. 391–3, 461.

9. *The Letters of Sir Walter Scott*, ed. H. J. C. Grierson, 12 vols (London: Constable, 1932–7), XI: p. 476, fn. 1.

10. John Gibson Lockhart, *Memoirs of the Life of Sir Walter Scott, Bart.*, 7 vols (Edinburgh: Robert Cadell, 1837–8), I: pp. 61–79; VII: p. 393.

11. Thomas Carlyle, 'Review of *Memoirs of the Life of Sir Walter Scott, Baronet*', *London and Westminster Review* 6 (1838): pp. 306–7.

12. Georg Lukács, *The Historical Novel* (New York: Humanities Press, 1965), p. 2.

13. F. R. Leavis, *The Great Tradition* (Harmondsworth: Penguin, [1948] 1980), p. 14.

14. Nancy Goslee, *Scott the Rhymer* (Lexington: University Press of Kentucky, 1988); Trumpener, *Bardic Nationalism* (Princeton: Princeton University Press, 1997).

15. Pittock, *Scottish and Irish Romanticism*, p. 5.

16. Fiona Robertson, *Legitimate Histories* (Oxford: Clarendon, 1994); Ian Duncan, *Modern Romance and Transformations of the Novel* (Cambridge: Cambridge University Press, 1992); Ina Ferris, *The Achievement of Literary Authority* (Ithaca: Cornell University Press, 1991); Pittock, *Scottish and Irish Romanticism*.

17. William Wordsworth, *The Excursion* (London: Edward Moxon, 1841), p. xii.

18. Robert Miles, *Romantic Misfits* (Houndsmills: Palgrave Macmillan, 2008), p. 1.

19. Michel Foucault, 'The Discourse on Language', in Hazard Adama and Leroy Searle (eds), *Critical Theory since 1965* (Tallahassee: Florida State University Press, [1971] 1986), p. 158.

20. Walter Scott, *The Prefaces to the Waverley Novels*, ed. Mark A. Weinstein (Lincoln: University of Nebraska Press, 1978), p. 230.

21. Walter Scott, *Waverley*, ed. P. D. Garside (Edinburgh: Edinburgh University Press, [1814] 2007), pp. 3–4.

22. Johnson, *Scott*, I: pp. 440–54.

23. Walter Scott, 'Introduction to *The Pirate*', Waverley Novels vol. 24 (Edinburgh: Robert Cadell, 1831), pp. iii–xi. Hereafter referred to as Magnum.

24. Johnson, *Scott*, II: p. 821.
25. Jane Austen, 'Love and Friendship', in Margaret Anne Doody (ed.), *Catharine and Other Writings* (Oxford: Oxford University Press, 1993), p. 99. Northrop Frye recognises here Austen's own claim to Romantic sensibility (*A Study of English Romanticism* (New York: Random House, 1968), p. 29).
26. Henry Adelbert White, *Sir Walter Scott's Novels on the Stage* (Hamden, CT: Archon Press, [1927] 1973), p. 163.
27. Walter Scott, *The Pirate*, ed. Mark Weinstein and Alison Lumsden (Edinburgh: Edinburgh University Press, 2001), p. 318.
28. Walter Scott, *The Heart of Mid-Lothian*, ed. David Hewitt and Alison Lumsden (Edinburgh: Edinburgh University Press, 2004), p. 151.
29. Walter Scott, *The Fortunes of Nigel*, ed. Frank Jordan (Edinburgh: Edinburgh University Press, 2004), pp. 3–17.
30. Jerome McGann, 'Walter Scott's Romantic Postmodernity', in Davis, Duncan and Sorensen (eds), *Scotland and the Borders of Romanticism* (Cambridge: Cambridge University Press, 2004), pp. 128–9.
31. Thomas Carlyle, 'Chartism' (1839).

Chapter 12 – Hammond

1. All references to Byron's poetry are to *Lord Byron: The Complete Poetical Works*, ed. Jerome J. McGann, 7 vols (Oxford: Clarendon, 1986), except where explicitly stated otherwise.
2. Jerome McGann, 'Byron, George Gordon Noel, Sixth Baron Byron (1788–1824)', *Oxford Dictionary of National Biography*, ed. H. C. G. Matthew and Brian Harrison (Oxford: Oxford University Press, 2004); online edn http://www.oxforddnb.com/view/article/4279
3. *ER*, January 1808.
4. Pittock, *Scottish and Irish Romanticism* (Oxford: Oxford University Press, 2008), p. 7.
5. Byron to Mrs Catherine Gordon Byron, 12 November 1809, quoted from *Lord Byron: Selected Letters and Journals*, ed. Leslie A. Marchand (London: Pimlico, 1982), p. 30.
6. Quoted by Andrew Nicholson, 'Byron and the "Ariosto of the North"', in Gerard Carruthers and Alan Rawes (eds), *English Romanticism in the Celtic World* (Cambridge: Cambridge University Press, 2003), p. 135. See further McGann, *Complete Poetical Works*, II: pp. 192–3.
7. T. S. Eliot, 'Byron', in *From Anne to Victoria* [1937] and reprinted in his *On Poetry and Poets* (London: Faber, [1957] 1969), p. 202.
8. Bernard Beatty, 'The Force of "Celtic Memories" in Byron's Thought', in Carruthers and Rawes, *English Romanticism*, p. 108.
9. Ernest J. Lovell, jr (ed.), *Medwin's Conversations of Lord Byron* (Princeton: Princeton University Press, 1966), p. 59.

10. Quoted from *Byron: Poetical Works*, ed. Frederick Page and John Jump (Oxford: Oxford University Press, 1970).

11. Leask, *British Romantic Writers and the East* (Cambridge: Cambridge University Press, 1992), pp. 54–67.

12. Leask cites a passage in *A Letter to John on William Bowles' Strictures on the Life and Writings of Pope* (London, 1821), pp. 49, 45–6 as the clearest 'statement of literary orientalism in the period' (*Romantic Writers and the East*, pp. 62–3). The passage relates degenerate modern poetry to that of Pope through the homologising metaphor of mosque to Grecian temple. It reads: 'They have raised a mosque by the side of a Grecian temple of the purest architecture; and more barbarous than the barbarians from whose practice I have borrowed the figure, they are not contented with their own grotesque edifice, unless they destroy the prior and purely beautiful fabric which preceded, and which shames them and theirs for ever and ever.'

13. The lines alluded to in Scott's *Lay of the Last Minstrel* are to Canto 6 stanza 2 ll. 1–4, beginning: 'O Caledonia! stern and wild [. . .]

14. Sir Walter Scott, *Quentin Durward*, ed. Susan Manning (Harmondsworth: Penguin, 1992), pp. 3–4.

15. Robert Burns to William Nicol, 18 June 1787. See *The Letters of Robert Burns*, ed. J. de Lancey Ferguson and G. Ross Roy, 2 vols (Oxford: Clarendon, 1985), I: p. 123.

16. See *The Letters of John Murray to Lord Byron*, ed. Andrew Nicholson (Liverpool: Liverpool University Press, 2007), letter 68 (9 April 1815). Lockhart's *Life of Scott* maintains that Byron was immensely affected by Scott's reading aloud (p. 137).

17. At around the same time as Byron was composing the third canto of *Don Juan*, he was writing *Some Observations upon an Article in Blackwood's Edinburgh Magazine*, first drafted in 1820 though not published in Byron's lifetime. Written in response to an article by J. G. Lockhart in *Blackwood's Edinburgh Magazine* entitled *Remarks on Don Juan*, it incorporates muscular attacks on the Lake Poets (Wordsworth, Coleridge and Southey) and on the Cockney School of poets (including Keats and Leigh Hunt). Byron wrongly believed its author was John Wilson ('Christopher North'). What particularly incensed Byron was the rumour that he and the Shelley ménage (Shelley's wife Mary and her stepsister Claire Clairmont) had formed a league of incest while together in Geneva. Again falsely, he believed that this had been spread by the poet Southey.

18. M. H.Abrams, *Natural Supernaturalism* (New York: Norton, 1971), p. 13.

19. Bowles' reason for not putting Pope in the first rank of English poets was that his subject matter in poems such as *Rape of the Lock* was not intrinsically 'poetical', as for example, nature poetry would be. To Bowles, the closer a poet's subject came to the natural world and the further from the world of

human affairs, the better. It is not difficult to see why Byron would find this uncongenial.

20. Claude Rawson, 'Thoughts on Adventures', in Dennis Todd and Cynthia Wall (eds), *Eighteenth-Century Genre and Culture* (Newark and London: Associated University Press, 2001), pp. 138, 141. Rawson's views are anticipated in T. S. Eliot's essay 'Byron', p. 203.

21. Pittock, *Scottish and Irish Romanticism*, p. 7.

22. Ernest J. Lovell jr (ed.), *Lady Blessington's Conversations of Lord Byron* (Princeton: Princeton University Press, 1969), p. 220.

23. G. Gregory Smith, *Scottish Literature: Character and Influence* (London: Macmillan, 1919).

24. Hugh MacDiarmid, 'The Caledonian Antisyzygy', in Alan Riach (ed.), *Scottish Eccentrics* (Manchester: Carcanet Press, [1936] 1993), p. 285. The *OED* definition of the word 'antisyzygy' as 'union of opposites' based on an example of 1863 is absolutely not what MacDiarmid means by it. In his account of Scottish eccentrics, their distinguishing feature is a 'lightning-like zig-zag of temper' (p. 284) that is not synthesised into any state of union. Cut off from this distinctive way of inhabiting Scottishness, modern Scots are cut off from their national history and culture, substituting an excessive and sentimental love of their country for the creation of a genuine nationalism.

25. On sincerity in Romantic writing, see further Jerome J. McGann, *Towards a Literature of Knowledge* (Oxford: Clarendon, 1989), pp. 1–64. 'The poetry of sincerity – Romantic poetry, in its paradigm mode [. . .] typically avoids the procedures of satirical and polemical verse. Those latter forms – by their protocols – develop through publicly installed dialogical operations. When Romantic poetry opens itself to those genres it opens itself to the horizon of its antithesis, to the horizon of hypocrisy' (quoted from Stabler below, p. 29).

26. Susan Manning used the term in an unpublished lecture entitled ' "Ae Spark o' Nature's Fire": Was Robert Burns a Transcendental Philosopher?' at the Glasgow Burns Conference, January 2009 (I am grateful to her for providing me with a copy of the text); Peter J. Manning, *Reading Romantics* (Oxford: Oxford University Press, 1990), quoted from Jane Stabler ed. and intro., *Byron* (London and New York: Longman, 1998), p. 191.

27. *ER*, March 1809.

28. Richard Cardwell (ed.), *The Reception of Byron in Europe*, 2 vols (London and New York: Continuum, 2004), I: p. 9.

29. Pittock, 'Byron's Networks and Scottish Romanticism', *The Byron Journal* 37.2 (2009), pp. 5–14.

30. See 'Byron's Networks', and *Scottish and Irish Romanticism*, pp. 252–5.

31. Byron, *Letter to John , Esqre*, in *Lord Byron: The Complete Miscellaneous Prose*, ed. Andrew Nicholson (Oxford: Clarendon, 1991), pp. 126–7.

32. The term 'Byromania' was coined by Byron's wife Annabella Milbanke in a poem of 1812 entitled 'The Byromania', giving a name to the brand of

celebrity that Byron attracted and cultivated after the appearance of the first two cantos of *Childe Harold*: see Frances Wilson (ed.), *Byromania* (Basingstoke and New York: Macmillan, 1999), pp. 1–23. Prior to that, in 1811, an enemy to Burns' reputation, the Reverend William Peebles, invented a term called 'Burnomania' to describe *The Celebrity of Robert Burns Considered in a Discourse Addressed to all Real Christians of every Denomination*. Both 'manias' possibly derive from Edmond Malone's coinage 'Shakespearomania'.

33. Susan Manning, '"Ae Spark"'.

34. In popular cultural representation, Byron is more often exalted for being, in Lady Caroline Lamb's phrase 'mad, bad and dangerous to know' than for being a great poet. In July-August 2009, for example, Channel 4 screened two programmes in which the actor Rupert Everett went 'In Search of Byron'. The impression given the viewer was that Byron was important because he was (or, we should qualify, probably was) a bisexual sodomite rather than because he was a poet!

35. Caroline Franklin, *Byron* (London: Macmillan; New York: St Martin's Press, 2000), p. 81.

36. Quotations from *Marino Faliero* are from Page and Jump's edition cited above.

37. Beatty in *English Romanticism and the Celtic World*, p. 107.

Chapter 13 – Esterhammer

1. See, for example, Ferris, *The Achievement of Literary Authority* (Ithaca: Cornell University Press, 1991); Trumpener, *Bardic Nationalism* (Princeton: Princeton University Press, 1997); and Duncan, *Scott's Shadow* (Princeton: Princeton University Press, 2007).

2. Ruth I. Aldrich, *John Galt* (Boston: G. K. Hall, 1978), p. 90.

3. John Galt, *The Earthquake*, 3 vols (Edinburgh: Blackwood and London: Cadell, 1820), I: p. 297.

4. John Galt, *The Entail*, ed. Ian A. Gordon (London: Oxford University Press, 1970), p. 164.

5. John Galt, *The Ayrshire Legatees* (Edinburgh: Blackwood and London: Cadell, 1821), p. 16.

6. H. B. de Groot, 'The Narrative Perspective of *The Last of the Lairds*', in *John Galt: Reappraisals*, ed. Elizabeth Waterston (Guelph: University of Guelph, 1985), p. 103; see also Clare A. Simmons, 'Periodical Intrusions in Galt's *The Last of the Lairds*', *SLJ* 24.1 (1997), pp. 54–9.

7. John Galt, *The Last of the Lairds*, ed. Ian A. Gordon (Edinburgh: Scottish Academic Press, 1976), p. 144.

8. John Galt, *The Literary Life and Miscellanies of John Galt*, 3 vols (Edinburgh: Blackwood and London: Cadell, 1834), I: pp. 235–40.

9. For a fuller discussion of *Andrew of Padua* and its context in print culture, see Angela Esterhammer, 'London Periodicals, Scottish Novels and Italian

Fabrications: *Andrew of Padua, the Improvisatore* Re-membered', *Studies in Romanticism* 48 (2009), pp. 469–90.

10. John Galt, *Lawrie Todd*, 3 vols (London: Colburn and Bentley, 1830), I: p. iv.

11. John Galt, *The Provost*, ed. Ian A. Gordon (London: Oxford University Press, 1973), p. 1.

12. John Galt, *Sir Andrew Wylie, of that Ilk*, 3 vols (Edinburgh: Blackwood and London: Cadell, 1822), III: p. 120.

13. John Galt, *Annals of the Parish*, ed. James Kinsley (London: Oxford University Press, 1967), p. 10.

14. For a fuller exploration of the relation between *Annals of the Parish* and 'theoretical history', see Keith M. Costain, 'Theoretical History and the Novel: The Scottish Fiction of John Galt', *ELH* 43 (1976), pp. 342–65 and 'The Scottish Fiction of John Galt', in Douglas Gifford (ed.), *The History of Scottish Literature: Volume III* (Aberdeen: Aberdeen University Press, 1988), pp. 107–23.

15. Trumpener provides a compelling reading of the character Bogle Corbet as 'a product of empire on every level' and shows how he unconsciously manifests 'repetition compulsions' by transferring the colonial structures that have shaped him to the settlement he founds in Upper Canada (*Bardic Nationalism*, pp. 279, 288).

16. John Galt, *Bogle Corbet*, 3 vols (London: Colburn and Bentley, 1831), II: pp. 180–1.

17. Duncan, *Scott's Shadow*, p. 239.

18. Aldrich, *John Galt*, p. 154.

Chapter 14 – Garside

1. P. D. Garside (ed.), James Hogg, *The Private Memoirs and Confessions of a Justified Sinner* (Edinburgh: Edinburgh University Press, 2001), with an afterword by Ian Campbell.

2. Willy Maley (ed.), *100 Best Scottish Books of All Time* (Edinburgh: [Unesco], 2005); updated online 2007. A poll of readers conducted by Waterstone's bookshops in 1998 placed *Confessions* as the third favourite Scottish book.

3. *Memoirs*, pp. lxxiv–lxxix. For a fuller account of Blackie & Son's operations, and the effect on Hogg's work, see also Peter Garside and Gillian Hughes, 'James Hogg's "Tales and Sketches" and the Glasgow Number Trade', *Cardiff Corvey: Reading the Romantic Text* 14 (Summer 2005), at http://www.cf.ac.uk/encap/romtext/articles/cc14_n02.html

4. See Andrew Nash, 'Hogg's *Confessions*, S. R. Crockett and the House of Macmillan', *SHW* 19 (2008), pp. 117–21.

5. In *The Modern Scottish Novel* (Edinburgh: Edinburgh University Press, 1999), p. 39.

6. L. L. Lee, 'The Devil's Figure: James Hogg's *Justified Sinner*', *SSL* 3.4 (1966),

pp. 230–9. See also Walter Allen, *The English Novel* (London: Phoenix House, 1954), p. 124; and Kurt Wittig, *The Scottish Tradition in Literature* (Edinburgh and London: Oliver & Boyd, 1958), pp. 249–50 (where the 'Caledonian Antisyzygy' is cited in relation to *Confessions*).

7. David Eggenschwiler, 'James Hogg's *Confessions* and the Fall into Division', *SSL* 9.1 (1971), p. 26.

8. Douglas Gifford, *James Hogg* (Edinburgh: Ramsay Head Press, 1976); David Groves, 'Parallel Narratives in Hogg's *Justified Sinner*', *SLJ* 9.2 (1982), pp. 37–44.

9. Magdalene Redekop, 'Beyond Closure: Buried Alive with Hogg's *Justified Sinner*', *ELH* 52.1 (1985), p. 182; Douglas Jones, 'Double Jeopardy and the Chameleon Art in James Hogg's *Justified Sinner*', *SSL* 23 (1988), p. 180.

10. See Rosemary Jackson, *Fantasy* (London and New York: Methuen, 1981), p. 29.

11. See, for example, John Herdman, *The Double in Nineteenth-Century Fiction* (London: Macmillan, 1990), pp. 69–87; and Reinhard Heinritz and Silvia Mergenthal, 'Hogg, Hoffmann and their Diabolical Elixirs', *SHW* 7 (1996), pp. 47–58.

12. Barbara Bloedé, '*The Confessions of a Justified Sinner*: The Paranoiac Nucleus', *Papers given at the First Conference of the James Hogg Society* (Stirling, 1983), p. 15.

13. David Groves, *James Hogg* (Edinburgh: Scottish Academic Press, 1988), p. 117.

14. For a fuller account of these connections, see Garside, 'Printing *Confessions*', *SHW* 9 (1998), pp. 16–31.

15. Hogg's review letter is found in *Blackwood's Magazine* 2 (December 1817), pp. 305–9. Later critics drawing parallels between the structure of *Confessions* and the Kirkton edition include Ina Ferris, 'Scholarly Revivals: Gothic Fiction, Secret History, and Hogg's *Private Memoirs and Confessions of a Justified Sinner*', in Jillian Heydt-Stevenson and Charlotte Sussman (eds), *Recognizing the Romantic Novel* (Liverpool: Liverpool University Press, 2008), pp. 267–84.

16. The relevance of the event was discussed by Groves in his 'James Hogg's *Confessions* and *The Three Perils of Woman* and the Edinburgh Prostitution Scandal of 1823', *Wordsworth Circle* 18 (Summer 1987), pp. 127–31; followed, with greater emphasis on *Confessions*, by Barbara Bloedé in 'Hogg and the Edinburgh Prostitution Scandal', *Newsletter of the James Hogg Society* 8 (May 1989), pp. 15–18.

17. See Ian Campbell, 'James Hogg and the Bible', *SLJ* 10.1 (1983), pp. 14–29.

18. Gary Kelly, *English Fiction of the Romantic Period 1789–1830* (London and New York: Longman, 1989), pp. 260–73; Cairns Craig, *Out of History* (Edinburgh: Polygon, 1996), pp. 73–6.

19. See, for example, Douglas S. Mack, 'Responses to Hogg in Two Waverley Novels: *Redgauntlet* and *The Fair Maid of Perth*', *SHW* 19 (2008), pp. 90–115.

20. Murray Pittock, 'Hogg's Gothic and the Transformation of Genre: Towards a Scottish Romanticism', *SHW* 15 (2004), pp. 67–75. Pittock's views are more broadly contextualised in his *Scottish and Irish Romanticism* (Oxford: Oxford University Press, 2008).

21. See Barbara Bloedé, 'A Nineteenth-Century Case of Double Personality: A Possible Source of *The Confessions*', *Papers given at the Second James Hogg Society Conference* (Edinburgh, 1985), (Aberdeen: Association for Scottish Literary Studies, 1988), pp. 117–27; and Allan Beveridge, 'James Hogg and Abnormal Psychology: Some Background Notes', *SHW* 2 (1991), pp. 91–4.

22. Notably in 'The Upright Corpse: Hogg, National Literature and the Uncanny', *SHW* 5 (1994), pp. 29–49; and 'Hogg's Body', *SHW* 9 (1998), pp. 1–15.

23. Penny Fielding, *Writing and Orality* (Oxford: Clarendon, 1996), p. 129.

24. Karen Fang, 'A Printing Devil, A Scottish Mummy and an Edinburgh Book of the Dead: James Hogg's Napoleonic Complex', *Studies in Romanticism* 43.2 (2004), p. 175. See also Mark L. Schoenfield, 'Butchering James Hogg: Romantic Identity in the Magazine Market', in Mary A. Favret and Nicola J. Watson (eds), *At the Limits of Romanticism* (Bloomington and Indianapolis: Indiana University Press, 1994), pp. 207–24.

25. In *Blackwood's Magazine* 10 (August 1821), pp. 43–52. The 'Memoir' was prefixed to the 1821 edition of Hogg's *The Mountain Bard*.

26. See Garside, 'Hogg and the Blackwoodian Novel', *SHW* 15 (2004), pp. 5–20.

27. Among more recent examples are Scott Mackenzie, 'Confessions of a Gentrified Sinner: Secrets in Scott and Hogg', *Studies in Romanticism* 41.1 (2002), pp. 3–32; and Susan Manning, 'That Exhumation Scene Again: Transatlantic Hogg', *SHW* 16 (2005), pp. 86–111.

28. As discussed in Douglas S. Mack, 'The Body in the Opened Grave: Robert Burns and Robert Wringhim', *SHW* 7 (1996), pp. 70–9.

Chapter 15 – Toda

1. Julian M. D'Arcy, *Subversive Scott* (Reykjavik: The Vigdis Finbogadóttir Institute of Foreign Languages and University of Iceland Press, 2005), p. 51.

2. J. D. McClure, 'Scots: Its Range of Uses', in A. J. Aitken and T. McCarthy (eds), *Languages of Scotland* (Edinburgh: Chambers, 1979), p. 30.

3. D'Arcy, *Subversive Scott*, pp. 9–10.

4. Toda, 'A Scots-Speaking Heroine: Jeanie Deans Meets the Queen in Walter Scott's *The Heart of Mid-Lothian*', in P. Shaw (ed.), *Héroe y antihéroe en la literatura inglesa* (Madrid: Alhambra, 1983), p. 350.

5. Norman Blake, *Non-Standard Language in English Literature* (London: A. Deutsch, 1981), p. 141.

6. Toda, 'Archaisms and Scotticisms: Language and Historical Point of View in *Rob Roy*', *Anglo-American Studies* 5.1 (1985), pp. 23–33.

7. Graham Tulloch, *The Language of Walter Scott* (London: André Deutsch, 1980).
8. Norman Page, *Speech in the English Novel* (London: Longman, 1973).
9. Janet Sorensen, '"Strange Orthography and Singular Diction": Scott's Use of Scots in *The Heart of Midlothian*', in Ton Hoenselaars and M. Buning (eds), *English Literature and the Other Languages* (Amsterdam: Rodopi, 1999), pp. 63–74.
10. Walter Scott, *The Heart of Mid-Lothian*, ed. David Hewitt and Alison Lumsden (Edinburgh: Edinburgh University Press, 2004), p. 172.
11. David Murison, *The Guid Scots Tongue* (Edinburgh: William Blackwood and Sons, 1978), p. 5.
12. William J. Hyde, 'Jeanie Deans and the Queen: Appearance and Reality', *Nineteenth-Century Fiction* 28.1 (1973), pp. 86–92.
13. James A. H. Murray, *The Dialect of the Southern Counties of Scotland* (London: Asher, 1873), p. 189.
14. David Murison, 'The Two Languages in Scott', in A. N. Jeffares (ed.), *Scott's Mind and Art* (Edinburgh: Oliver and Boyd, 1969), pp. 224–5.
15. Pittock, *Scottish and Irish Romanticism* (Oxford: Oxford University Press, 2008), p. 202.
16. Tulloch, *Language*, pp. 255–6.
17. D'Arcy, *Subversive Scott*, p. 162.
18. Ibid.
19. Walter Scott, *The Letters of Malachi Malagrowther*, ed. P. H. Scott (Edinburgh: William Blackwood, [1826] 1981).

Further Reading

Alexander, J. H. and David Hewitt (eds), *Scott and his Influence* (Aberdeen: ASLS, 1982).

Alexander, J. H. and David Hewitt (eds), *Scott in Carnival* (Aberdeen: ASLS, 1993).

Alker, Sharon and Holly Faith Nelson (eds), *James Hogg and the Literary Marketplace* (Burlington, VT; Aldershot: Ashgate, 2009).

Andrews, Malcolm, *The Search for the Picturesque* (Aldershot: Scolar, 1989).

Black, Ronald, *An Lasair. Anthology of Eighteenth Century Scottish Gaelic Verse* (Edinburgh: Birlinn, 2001).

Black, Ronald, 'Alexander MacDonald's *Ais-Eiridh*, 1751', *Journal of the Edinburgh Bibliographical Society* (forthcoming).

Broadie, Alexander, *The Scottish Enlightenment* (Edinburgh: Birlinn, 2001).

Broadie, Alexander (ed.), *The Cambridge Companion to the Scottish Enlightenment*, (Cambridge: Cambridge University Press, 2003).

Brown, Terence (ed.), *Celticism* (Amsterdam: Rodopi, 1996).

Byrne, Michel, 'Mairearad Ghriogarach: Súil Thòiseachail air Bana-bhàrd air Dìchuimhne', *SGS* 23 (2007), pp. 85–122.

Cardwell, Richard (ed.), *The Reception of Byron in Europe*, 2 vols (London; New York: Continuum, 2004).

Carruthers, Gerard (ed.), *The Edinburgh Companion to Robert Burns* (Edinburgh: Edinburgh University Press, 2009).

Carruthers, Gerard and Alan Rawes (eds), *English Romanticism in the Celtic World* (Cambridge: Cambridge University Press, 2003).

Carruthers, Gerard and Johnny Rodger (eds), *Fickle Man: Robert Burns in the 21st Century* (Dingwall: Sandstone Press, 2009).

Chandler, James and Kevin Gilmartin (eds), *Romantic Metropolis: The Urban Scene of British Culture, 1780–1840* (Cambridge: Cambridge University Press, 2004).

Chitnis, Anand, *The Scottish Enlightenment: A Social History* (London: Croom Helm, 1976).

Chitnis, Anand, *The Scottish Enlightenment and Early Victorian English Society* (London: Croom Helm, 1986).

Connell, Philip and Nigel Leask (eds), *Romanticism and Popular Culture in Britain and Ireland* (Cambridge: Cambridge University Press, 2009).

Craig, Cairns, *Associationism and the Literary Imagination* (Edinburgh: Edinburgh Univeristy Press, 2007).

Crawford, Robert, *Devolving English Literature*, 2nd edn (Edinburgh: Edinburgh University Press, 2000).

D'Arcy, Julian, *Subversive Scott: The Waverley Novels and Scottish Nationalism* (Reykjavik: The Vigdis Finbogadóttir Institute of Foreign Languages and University of Iceland Press, 2005).

Davis, Leith, *Acts of Union; Scotland and the Literary Negotiation of the British Nation* (Stanford: Stanford University Press, 1998).

Davis, Leith, Ian Duncan and Janet Sorensen (eds), *Scotland and the Borders of Romanticism* (Cambridge: Cambridge University Press, 2004).

Drummond, A. L. and James Bulloch, *The Scottish Church 1688–1843* (Edinburgh: St Andrew Press, 1973).

Duff, David and Catherine Jones (eds), *Scotland, Ireland and the Romantic Aesthetic* (Oxford: Oxford University Press, 2007).

Duncan, Ian, *Modern Romance and Transformations of the Novel: The Gothic, Scott, Dickens* (Cambridge: Cambridge University Press, 1992).

Duncan, Ian, *Scott's Shadow: The Novel in Romantic Edinburgh* (Princeton: Princeton University Press, 2007).

Dwyer, John, and Richard Sher (eds), *Sociability and Society in Eighteenth-Century Scotland* (Edinburgh: Mercat, 1993).

Ferris, Ina, *The Achievement of Literary Authority* (Ithaca: Cornell University Press, 1991).

Fielding, Penny, *Writing and Orality* (Oxford: Clarendon, 1996).

Flegg, Columba Graham, *Gathered under Apostles: A Study of the Catholic Apostolic Church* (Oxford: Clarendon, 1992).

Freidman, A. B., *The Ballad Revival* (Chicago: University of Chicago Press, 1961).

Gaskill, Howard (ed.), *Ossian Revisited* (Edinburgh: Edinburgh University Press, 1991).

Gaskill, Howard (ed.), *The Reception of Ossian in Europe* (London/New York: Continuum, 2004).

Gelbart, Matthew, *The Invention of 'Folk Music' and 'Art Music'* (Cambridge: Cambridge University Press, 2007).

Glendening, John, *The High Road: Romantic Tourism, Scotland, and Literature, 1720–1820* (New York: St Martin's Press, 1997).

Gordon, Ian A., *John Galt* (Edinburgh: Oliver and Boyd, 1972).

Groves, David, *James Hogg* (Edinburgh: Scottish Academic Press, 1988).

Hughes, Gillian, *James Hogg: A Life* (Edinburgh: Edinburgh University Press, 2007).

Johnson, David, *Music and Society in Lowland Scotland in the Eighteenth Century* (Oxford: Oxford University Press, 1972).

Johnson, Edgar, *Sir Walter Scott: The Great Unknown*, 2 vols (New York: Macmillan, 1970).

Kidd, Colin, *Subverting Scotland's Past* (Cambridge: Cambridge University Press, 1993).

Lamont, Claire and Michael Rossington (eds), *Romanticism's Debatable Lands* (Basingstoke: Palgrave Macmillan, 2007).

Leask, Nigel, *British Romantic Writers and the East* (Cambridge: Cambridge University Press, 1992).

Leask, Nigel, 'His Hero's Story': Currie's Burns, Moore's Byron, and the Problem of Romantic Biography* (Nottingham: Centre for the Study of Byron and Romanticism, 2007).

Leerssen, Joep, *National Thought in Europe* (Amsterdam: Amsterdam University Press, 2006).

Low, Donald (ed.), *Robert Burns, the Critical Heritage* (London: Routledge, 1974).

McGinty, J. Walter, *Robert Burns and Religion* (Aldershot: Ashgate, 2003).

McGuirk, Carol, *Robert Burns and the Sentimental Era* (Athens: University of Georgia Press, 1985).

McGuirk, Carol (ed.), *Critical Essays on Robert Burns* (New York: G. K. Hall, 1998).

McIlvanney, Liam, *Burns the Radical* (East Linton: Tuckwell Press, 2002).

Mack, Douglas S., *Scottish Fiction and the British Empire* (Edinburgh: Edinburgh University Press, 2006).

Mackenzie, John, *Sar-Obair nam Bard Gaelach. The Beauties of Gaelic Poetry and the Lives of the Highland Bards* (Edinburgh: John Grant, [1841] 1907).

MacLachlan, Christopher (ed.), *Crossing the Highland Line: Cross-Currents in Eighteenth-Century Scottish Literature* (Glasgow: ASLS, 2009).

McLane, Maureen N., *Balladeering, Minstrelsy, and the Making of Romantic Poetry* (Cambridge: Cambridge University Press, 2008).

MacLeod, A., *Òrain Dhonnchaidh Bhàin/Poems of Duncan Ban Macintyre* (Edinburgh: Scottish Gaelic Texts Society, 1952).

Macpherson, James, *The Poems of Ossian and Related Works*, ed. Howard Gaskill (Edinburgh: Edinburgh University Press, 1996).

MacQueen, John, *The Rise of the Historical Novel* (Edinburgh: Scottish Academic Press, 1989).

Meek, Donald E., 'The Pulpit and the Pen: Clergy, Orality and Print in the Scottish Gaelic World', in A. Fox and D. Woolf (eds), *The Spoken Word: Oral Culture in Britain 1550–1850* (Manchester: Manchester Univerisuty Press, 2002), pp. 84–118.

Meek, Donald E., *Caran an t-Saoghail. Wiles of the World. Anthology of 19th Century Scottish Gaelic Verse* (Edinburgh: Birlinn, 2003).

Millgate, Jane, *Walter Scott* (Chicago: Chicago University Press, 1987).

Moore, Dafydd, *Enlightenment and Romance in James Macpherson's The Poems of Ossian* (Aldershot: Ashgate, 2003).

Moore, Dafydd (ed.), *Ossian and Ossianism*, 4 vols (London: Routledge, 2004).

Newman, Steve, *Ballad Collection, Lyric, and the Canon* (Philadelphia: University of Pennsylvania Press, 2007).

O'Brien, Karen, *Narratives of Enlightenment* (Cambridge: Cambridge University Press, 1997).

Perry, Ruth (ed.), *Ballads and Songs in the Eighteenth Century*, spec. issue of *The Eighteenth Century* 47 2/3 (2006).

Phillips, Mark Salber, *Society and Sentiment: Genres of Historical Writing in Britain, 1740–1820* (Princeton: Princeton University Press, 2000),

Pittock, Murray, *Scottish and Irish Romanticism* (Oxford: Oxford University Press, 2008).

Pittock, Murray (ed.), *The Reception of Sir Walter Scott in Europe* (London/New York: Continuum, 2007).

Reardon, Bernard M. G., *Religion in the Age of Romanticism* (Cambridge: Cambridge University Press, 1985).

Robertson, Fiona, *Legitimate Histories: Scott, Gothic, and the Authorities of Fiction* (Oxford: Clarendon, 1994).

St Clair, William, *The Reading Nation in the Romantic Period* (Cambridge: Cambridge University Press, 2004).

Sher, Richard B., *Church and University in the Scottish Enlightenment* (Princeton: Princeton University Press, 1985).

Sher, Richard B., *The Enlightenment and the Book* (Chicago: University of Chicago Press, 2006).

Simpson, Louis, *James Hogg: A Critical Study* (Edinburgh and London: Oliver and Boyd, 1962).

Skoblow, Jeffrey, *Dooble Tongue: Scots, Burns, Contradiction* (Newark: University of Delaware Press, 2001).

Sorensen, Janet, *The Grammar of Empire in Eighteenth-Century British Writing* (Cambridge: Cambridge University Press, 2000).

Stafford, Fiona, *The Sublime Savage: A Study of James Macpherson and the Poems of Ossian* (Edinburgh: Edinburgh University Press, 1988).

Stafford, Fiona, 'The *Edinburgh Review* and the Representation of Scotland', in Massimiliano Demata and Duncan Wu (eds), *British Romanticism and the Edinburgh Review* (Basingstoke: Palgrave-Macmillan, 2002), pp. 33–57.

Stafford, Fiona, Scottish Romanticism and Scotland in Romanticism', in Michael Ferber (ed.), *A Companion to European Romanticism* (Oxford: Blackwell, 2005), pp. 49–66.

Stafford, Fiona and Howard Gaskill (eds), *From Gaelic to Romantic: Ossianic Translations* (Amsterdam: Rodopi, 1998).

Stewart, Susan, *Crimes of Writing: Problems in the Containment of Representation* (Oxford: Oxford University Press, 1991).

Thomson, D. S., *The Gaelic Sources of Macpherson's Ossian* (Edinburgh: Oliver and Boyd, 1952).

Thomson, Derick S., 'Gaelic Poetry in the Eighteenth Century: The Breaking of the Mould', in A. Hook (ed.), *The History of Scottish Literature*, 1600–1800 (Aberdeen: Aberdeen University Press, 1987), II: pp. 175–89.

Thomson, Derick S., 'James Macpherson: The Gaelic Dimension', in F. Stafford and H. Gaskill (eds), *From Gaelic to Romantic: Ossianic Translations* (Amsterdam: Rodopi, 1998), pp. 17–26.

Trumpener, Katie, *Bardic Nationalism* (Princeton: Princeton University Press, 1997).

Tulloch, Graham, *The Language of Walter Scott* (London: André Deutsch, 1980).

Tulloch, Graham, 'The Search for a Scots Narrative Voice', in M. Görlach (ed.), *Focus on Scotland* (Amsterdam: John Benjamins, 1985), pp. 159–80.

Wallace, Miriam L., 'Nationalism and the Scottish Subject: The Uneasy Marriage of London and Edinburgh in Sir Walter Scott's *The Heart of Midlothian*', *History of European Ideas* 16 (1993), pp. 41–7.

Watson, Nicola, *The Literary Tourist* (Basingstoke: Palgrave Macmillan, 2006).

Wheale, Nigel (ed.), *The Postmodern Arts* (London: Routledge, 1995).

Wickman, Matthew, *The Ruins of Experience: Scotland's 'Romantick' Highlands and the Birth of the Modern Witness* (Philadelphia: University of Pennsylvania Press, 2007).

Womack, Peter, *Improvement and Romance* (Houndmills, Basingstoke: Macmillan, 1989).

Notes on Contributors

Alex Benchimol is a lecturer in English Literature in the School of Critical Studies at the University of Glasgow. His monograph, *Intellectual Politics and Cultural Conflict in the Romantic Period: Scottish Whigs, English Radicals and the Making of the British Public Sphere*, was published in 2010.

Thomas Owen Clancy is Professor of Celtic at the University of Glasgow. He has written extensively on both historical and literary aspects of medieval Scotland and Ireland, and is author with Gilbert Márkus of *Iona: The Earliest Poetry of a Celtic Monastery* (1995) and editor of *The Triumph Tree: Scotland's Earliest Poetry, AD 550–1350* (2008). He is also editor of *The Innes Review*.

Ian Duncan is Professor of English at the University of California, Berkeley. He is the author of *Scott's Shadow* (2007) and *Modern Romance and Transformations of the Novel* (1992). He has edited Hogg's *Private Memoirs and Confessions of a Justified Sinner* (2010) and *Winter Evening Tales* (2002); and Scott's *Rob Roy* (1998) and *Ivanhoe* (1996).

Angela Esterhammer is Professor of English Literature at the University of Zurich. Her publications include *The Romantic Performative: Language and Action in British and German Romanticism* (2000) and *Romanticism and Improvisation, 1750–1850* (2008). Her current research examines interrelations among performative media, print culture, periodicals and fiction during the early nineteenth century.

Peter Garside is Honorary Professorial Fellow at the University of Edinburgh. He has helped provide a number of bibliographical resources relating to early nineteenth-century British fiction, including *The English Novel, 1770–1829* (2000) and the online database, *British Fiction, 1800–1829* (2004). He has also edited a number of novels of this period, including Walter Scott's *Waverley* (2007) and published widely on Romantic literature, Scottish poetry and prose, and the history of the book.

Crawford Gribben is Long Room Hub Senior Lecturer in Early Modern Print Culture in the School of English, Trinity College, Dublin. He is author of several studies of religious cultures in Scottish writing, as well as *The Puritan Millennium* (2000), *God's Irishmen* (2007), *Writing the Rapture* (2009) and *Evangelical Millennialism in the Trans-Atlantic World* (2010).

Brean Hammond is Professor of Modern English Literature at the University of Nottingham. His most recent publications include a critical biography of Jonathan Swift for the Irish Academic Press and an edition of the 'lost' Shakespeare play *Double Falsehood* for the Arden Shakespeare series.

Nigel Leask is Regius Professor of English Language and Literature at the University of Glasgow, head of the School of Critical Studies and a Fellow of the Royal Society of Edinburgh. His most recent book is *Robert Burns and Pastoral: Poetry and Improvement in Late Eighteenth-Century Scotland* (2010).

Caroline McCracken-Flesher is Professor of English at the University of Wyoming. Her books include *Possible Scotlands: Walter Scott and the Story of Tomorrow* (2005) and the edited volume *Culture, Nation, and the New Scottish Parliament* (2007). A book on retellings of the Burke and Hare story is forthcoming from Oxford.

Kirsteen McCue is Senior Lecturer in Scottish Literature at the University of Glasgow and associate director of the Centre for Robert Burns Studies there. She has published widely on Scottish song in the eighteenth and nineteenth centuries and is currently editing two volumes of songs for the Edinburgh University Press *Collected Works of James Hogg*. She is on the key editorial team for the new Oxford University Press edition of the Collected Works of Robert Burns.

Andrew Monnickendam is Professor of English Literature at the Universitat Autònoma de Barcelona. He has written widely on the romance, and particularly on Christian Isobel Johnstone, whose epic *Clan-Albin* he edited for the Association of Scottish Literary Studies in 2003. *Back to Peace: Reconciliation and Retribution in the Postwar Period*, which he co-edited with his colleague Aránzazu Usandizaga was selected as a *Choice* 'Outstanding Academic Title' for 2008.

Steve Newman is Associate Professor of English at Temple University in Philadelphia. He is author of *Ballad Collection, Lyric, and the Canon: The Call of the Popular from the Restoration to the New Criticism* (2007). He is currently working on a manuscript, *Time for the Humanities: Competing Narratives of Value from the Scottish Enlightenment to the 21st Century Academy*.

Murray Pittock is Bradley Professor of English Literature at the University of Glasgow, head of college and vice-principal (Arts). His recent work includes *Scottish and Irish Romanticism* (2008), *The Reception of Sir Walter Scott in Europe* (2007) and *James Boswell* (2007). He is currently principal investigator of the AHRC Beyond Text project, 'Robert Burns, 1796–1909: Inventing Tradition and Securing Memory'.

Fiona Stafford's first book, *The Sublime Savage* (1988), was a study of James Macpherson and the Poems of Ossian, and she has since published further work in the field. Her most recent book is *Local Attachments: The Province of Poetry* (2010). She is a Professor of English Language and Literature at the University of Oxford and a Fellow of the Royal Society of Edinburgh.

Fernando Toda is Professor of Translation and Interpretation at the University of Salamanca and an expert on translation. He has produced highly regarded Castilian translations of Scott's *Heart of Mid-Lothian* (1988), *Highland Widow* (1991), *Two Drovers* (1991) and the *Malagrowther* letters (2004) under the title *Defensa de la nación escocesa*.

Matthew Wickman is Senior Lecturer of Scottish Literature at the University of Aberdeen and Associate Professor of English at Brigham Young University, Utah. He is the author of *The Ruins of Experience: Scotland's 'Romantick' Highlands and the Birth of the Modern Witness* (2007) and currently completing a project on the intersection (and intellectual legacy) of literature and mathematics in the Scottish Enlightenment.

Index